Murder myself,

Murder

I am.

By Jon Keehner

Corvus Latrans Publishing

Cover photo concept: Chris Peltier
Blood Diamond Ink

ISBN-10: 1492885479
ISBN-13: 978-1492885474

First published February 25, 2014.

Available from Amazon.com and other retail outlets.
Printed by CreateSpace

Corvus Latrans Publishing
corvuslatrans@gmail.com

This book is dedicated to Mum-Z; for all of her love, courage and perseverance over the years, and for whom this story will never end.

And for Rich, your positive influence on my life, and so many others, will be cherished and never forgotten.

Preface

THIS BOOK IS BASED UPON MORE THAN NINE YEARS OF FACTUAL RESEARCH WHICH INCLUDES EXTENSIVE REVIEW OF PUBLIC RECORDS AND COURT FILES AND DETAILED INTERVIEWS WITH PERSONS KNOWLEDGEABLE ABOUT THE SUBJECT OF THIS BOOK – THE MURDER OF RICHARD DUNCAN BY PHILLIP V. HILLMAN. PHILLIP AND SHARON HILLMAN WERE NOT INTERVIEWED FOR THIS BOOK. WHILE THIS BOOK IS BASED UPON TRUE EVENTS, THE NARRATIVE INCLUDES FICTIONALIZED ACCOUNTS OF THE THOUGHTS, DISCUSSION, STATEMENTS AND MOTIVATIONS OF SHARON AND PHILLIP HILLMAN, AS WELL AS OTHER PERSONS INTERVIEWED FOR THIS BOOK. THESE ACCOUNTS FLOW FROM MY RESEARCH AND REFLECT MY BEST OPINION AS TO WHAT TRANSPIRED BASED UPON FACTS OF RECORD. IN TWO INSTANCES NAMES HAVE BEEN CHANGED AT THE REQUEST OF THE WITNESSES BEING INTERVIEWED.

1

Saturday   July 20, 1974

Rays of morning sun slowly crept up over the granite peaks of the North Cascades. The spring run-off was all but over and the only sound serenading the morning blue sky was the lapping and boiling of the Sauk River as it ran gently through the Mt. Baker National Forest.

A raven pranced high overhead between the sunlight of an emerald Douglas fir branch and the darker, draping branches of a low hanging cedar. Occasionally, the raven would scream out, filling the mountain air as it tried to locate its unseen mate. In the tiny logging town of Darrington, Washington nine miles to the northwest; many believed that ravens held the spirits of dead loggers and were not to be harmed.

Ever.

The North Cascades were littered with small, three or four spot camp areas. Camping was becoming very popular amongst city dwellers and on summer weekends, most of the campgrounds would be full. Unwritten courtesies emerged between campers as more and more people shared the woods. "Campground etiquette" — it was called.

President Eisenhower's dream of a modern highway system in America had finally come to fruition and increased access to the outdoors for a lot of urban people. Residents of major cities no longer had to pack a truck full of canvas tents, woodstoves and provisions traversing treacherous and roadless wilds in order to enjoy the outdoors. The advent

1

of an ever growing National Park and National Forest system continued to bring the outdoors closer and closer to the urban areas they surrounded. Conversely, it also brought the urban way of life, and death, closer to the outdoors.

Twenty year old Phillip Hillman and his friend, 21 year old Nicholas Hansen were completely alone in the forested campground along the river. Phil liked it this way.

A year earlier, Phil had been discharged from the U.S. Army after serving just over seven months in Vietnam, three of them as a member of the 1st Division of the 7th Air Cavalry. But by the time he arrived in Vietnam in March of 1972, much to his disappointment, combat operations were all but over. Returning to the United States in November of that year he was eventually dropped from the roles for desertion; a few months later in March of 1973. After checking himself in to Madigan Army Hospital, the Army discharged him. Camping was a great escape from having to figure out what to do with his life after washing out of the military.

Phil had convinced Nick to quit his job at a brake shoe manufacturing plant and come camping for a few days. Nick and Phil had gone to school together, and Phil certainly was the leader of the two. But after Phil enlisted in the Army, Nick started down his own path; and war was to be no part of it. When he heard that Phil enlisted, he wasn't the least bit surprised. He remembered how, during high school football games, fights would sometimes break out and Phil could be a hundred feet away when it started but would always be right in the middle of it at the bottom of the pile before it ended. He was surprised when Phil invited him up to go camping a few days earlier.

As the shadow of Whitehorse Mountain abandoned its protection of the forested campground the young men finally began to stir.

"Fuck man. What time is it?" Nick began, fighting with the zipper to his bag.

Nick wrestled his worn blue jeans on to his small, thin frame and stood, stretching. He breathed a giant sigh of relief once comfortably out of his sleeping bag and in the cooler mountain air. After pulling the bunched up flannel he used as a pillow the night before up off the dirt, he slid his skinny arms in to the sleeves and buttoned it up. His fingers ran through his wiry brown hair as he surveyed the camp.

Still no one.

They had the whole place to themselves. Phil was right he thought; *this was the life.*

"Are you alive in there, man?" he said looking over toward Phil's sleeping bag.

Nothing.

He looked around the campfire.

What a fucking mess.

He fished through the pile of supplies sitting on the top of Phil's '63 Lancer for some paper plates. Somehow the front passenger door had been left open all night. Vaguely he remembered Phil digging under the front seat for a joint he swore had fallen out of his pocket. Instead he found more shotgun shells and proceeded to blast round after round in to the night sky.

Nick stretched and kept looking. Underneath a bag with a loaf of bread and some clam chowder in it he found the paper plates. He pulled a few out and turned toward the campfire. He knelt down and delicately set the edge of the paper plate next to a smoldering log and gently blew.

Above him the sky was a brilliant blue. It was going to be another gorgeous day.

"God my fucking head hurts!" Phil finally groaned from his bag.

He unzipped and pulled himself out, never really standing fully upright. He was only a little taller than Nick, but his physique was much more muscular. Nick watched as Phil rubbed his eyes and stretched his back.

"Gonna be another beauty of a day!" Phil said raising his voice.

"Yeah, and no other campers yet. It's like we own the fucking place," Nick added.

Phil walked over to the cooler and inventoried the beers. They still had more than a dozen. The ice in the cooler had begun to melt. He thrust his hand into the icy water, pulled one out and tossed it to Nick. He reached in again and pulled one out for himself. In one swift motion he popped the top and drained the entire beer into his throat. He let out a huge belch and tossed the bottle toward the fire. Phil cupped his hands into the cooler and splashed his short cropped hair with water, shaking his head vigorously from side to side.

Nick just watched.

As the water ran down his thick neck and broad shoulders, Phil reached in and grabbed another, closed the cooler lid and joined Nick near the fire.

"We should go up beyond the bridge maybe, and try some fishin'," Nick suggested.

Phil just stood staring in to the tiny fire. Each time he took a position around the circle, the gentle breeze shifted, filling his eyes with smoke. Branches snapped across his knee as he fed the fire and circled about.

"I bet its real good up there. Maybe catch breakfast, you know?" Nick continued.

Nick reached down and started tossing the bottles littered around the camp in to the fire just as he had seen Phil do moments earlier.

"What the fuck are you doing?" Phil asked. "I saved those for a reason!"

Nick stopped almost immediately. He knew very well that even though Phil was always a loyal friend, he also liked to have things his way. He wouldn't think twice about punching a guy out. To Phil, it was just normal, it's what *men* did.

Phil went in to the car and pulled a brown paper bag from the back seat.

"Here, put them in there and don't break any of them."

He tossed the bag toward Nick.

Nick opened the brown grocery bag and began placing the empty bottles inside as carefully as he could.

Phil chugged his beer and went back to his sleeping bag and grabbed his shotgun. He opened the trunk to the Lancer and pulled out a few handfuls of shells and put them in to the pocket of his olive fatigue jacket. He then grabbed a few more beers from the cooler and motioned for Nick to follow him.

A few hundred feet from their camp they came to a stop on a flat sandy spit. The river ran slowly and still, the only sound was an occasional gurgle of slow churning water and every once in awhile a rush of wind through the evergreen branches behind them.

"You know man, the first few months of basic training; it's all we did," Phil nodded down toward his shotgun, "shooting and handling a weapon. Saved my life over there, more times than I could count."

Phil looked at Nick expecting he would want to know more about handling firearms and shooting. Nick just took a swig off his beer and stared out over the river. He wanted no part of Vietnam and was thankful that by the time he was 18, it was mostly over.

"Cool. When I say 'pull' just toss the bottle out over the river as high as you can," Phil said.

He cradled the shotgun at his waist and turned toward the river. Nick reached in to the bag and fished one of the brown bottles out. He stepped to the side of Phil and cocked his arm.

"Pull!" Phil yelled.

BOOM!

With the report of the shotgun the high arcing bottle instantly turned to golden mist. Chards of brown glass fell to the river flickering in the sunlight.

Phil laughed.

"Fuck yeah!"

Nick grabbed another bottle.

"Pull!"

BOOM!

"Did you see what happened to that bottle? Fuck *YEAH!* It blew to bits! That's got to be 40 yards out there!" Phil exclaimed.

"Sure...man. That's cool. Let's head up to the bridge and do some fishin'," Nick suggested.

"Fuck NO! Here, you try it," Phil said as he handed Nick the shotgun.

"All right, but I don't know if I can hit anything with it," Nick argued apprehensively.

Nick took the shotgun from Phil's hands. It was warm; and lighter than he imagined. He was as nervous about the gun now, as he was the night before when Phil darted around camp shooting branches and reloading as fast as he could and then shooting more. It was kind of fun at first, but eventually he just thought it was weird. He was worried someone was going to call the cops about all the shooting, but Phil promised him it was different out here, no one was around for miles.

"This ain't Seattle, man. Jesus," Phil admonished him with a sly grin.

Phil grabbed a brown bottle.

"So, just say 'pull' and I'll throw it, when it's out over the water. *Shoot it.* It's easy, man. Just like killing someone," Phil laughed.

Nick looked at him nervously.

Killing someone?

Nick awkwardly lifted the shotgun to his shoulder.

"Uh....pull?" Nick said quietly.

Phil cocked his arm back and threw it forward as hard as he could but did not let go of the bottle.

Nick squinted his eyes and jerked backwards nearly tripping over a lone rock in the sand. He realized that Phil hadn't thrown the bottle.

Phil began laughing. He was already getting drunk.

"Got ya!" he laughed.

Nick appeared uncomfortable.

"You should see the look on your face right now man! You look scared to death. It's just a shotgun, relax!" Phil laughed some more.

"Ok...for real this time. Just say 'pull' and I'll throw it," Phil said as calmly as he could muster.

Nervously, Nick again put the shotgun up to his shoulder.

"Pull."

Phil cocked his arm way back and flung it forward with a deliberate grunt.

BOOM!

Nick opened his eyes. Phil was on the ground to his right with the bottle still in his hand laughing and rolling in the sand.

"You fucking idiot! What are you shootin' at?" Phil laughed again.

"Fuck you, man. *Real fucking funny!*" Nick nodded.

"You got to keep you eyes open when you shoot, you never really know! *You know?*" Phil joked. "Guys in my unit would shoot at *anything,* noises, movement—you got to be ready man, and not waste your ammo!"

Nick wondered why everything went back to Vietnam.

"Ok, I won't fuck with you this time, but wait to shoot until you at least see the fucking bottle, all right?" Phil stated.

Phil reached in to his pocket and pulled a beer out. He was feeling pretty buzzed already.

"Fuck... *Pull,*" Nick said for a third time.

Phil tossed the bottle high in the air out over the river. Nick saw it out of the corner of his eye and pointed the shotgun out over the river and pulled the trigger.

BOOM!

The bottle continued its arc toward the other side and splashed in to the cool river water disappearing under the surface for just a second and then popped up like a buoy in a stormy sea. The steady current of the river carried it away out of sight within a few seconds.

"Nice shot!" Phil laughed.

Phil took the shotgun from Nick and grabbed his shell belt. He finished his beer and grabbed another from his pocket and quickly downed that one as well.

"You see, you just got to get used to it," Phil said and he took off running toward the trees.

BOOM!...BOOM!

Phil reached in to his shell belt and dove to the ground; he rolled over on to his side and reloaded the shotgun as quick as he could. Nick grabbed his beer and ducked behind a rock. Phil jumped up and kept running through the ferns disappearing behind some maple trees.

BOOM!

A robin squealed and fluttered out of the trees and disappeared toward the dark tree line across the river. Phil turned and ran back in the direction of the river with the shotgun in front of him, pointed directly at Nick.

What the fuck is he doing?

BOOM!

A few feet to Nick's right, sand and gravel exploded in to the air.

"*WHAT THE FUCK! PHIL!*" Nick yelled as loud as he could while being careful not to spill his beer.

Nick peered out cautiously from behind the boulder into the labyrinth of vine maples and cedar saplings that Phil had disappeared into.

Nothing.

His heart raced even more.

What the fuck is he doing?

Nick took a swig from his beer. He sat frozen to the rock and waited.

"PHIL!?" he finally yelled.

Still nothing.

He strained to peek around the corner of the boulder to see any sign of Phil.

He was scared.

"PHIL! What the FUCK man!" he yelled again.

"You're DEAD!" Phil yelled from right behind him.

Nick turned suddenly to his left and behind him. Phil had belly crawled down the sand and flanked him along the tree line. He had the shotgun leveled at him as he lay prone in the sand from about fifteen yards away.

"*AAAAHHHH!!*" Nick screamed, crossing his forearms in front of his face to shield him from the blast.

Click!

The shotgun clicked and Phil rolled over into the sand laughing.

"Got you again, you fucker!" Phil laughed.

"FUCK Phil! *What the fuck?* That ain't fucking funny, man! Jesus!" Nick yelled as he fell back on to the rocks in relief.

Nick got up and finished the last of his beer. Phil just laid in the sand on his back laughing.

"Fuck you, man. I'm going to town for more beer. *Fuck this,*" Nick stated as he climbed up from the sand, wiped himself off and walked to the camp.

He didn't dare raise too much of a stink about it, he knew Phil liked to tease a little; but it wasn't wise to tease him back. Nick strode toward the campsite attempting to stay as far ahead of Phil as he could.

He's fucking crazy.

"Hey man, wait up!" Phil hollered from behind him.

"Fuck, I wasn't going to really shoot you. It was ten feet away from you; I know how to lay cover fire, man. Fuck. Don't be a fucking baby about it, all right?" Phil yelled trying to catch up to him.

Arguing with Phil about it wasn't going to do Nick any good. He knew it would probably just piss him off even more. He had let Phil know that it wasn't cool. He should just let it go and maybe some beers could just put it behind them.

"Sorry man. Didn't mean to piss you off. Just havin' a little fun with ya'," Phil said as apologetically as he could.

"Don't worry about it, let's just go to town and get some brewski's, eh?" Nick replied.

Phil reached in to the cooler and filled his pockets with as many of the remaining beers as he could carry.

When Nick heard that Phil had gone to Vietnam he wasn't sure if would be good for Phil or just make him worse. He was really curious but just didn't quite know how to bring it up. One thing hadn't changed however.

Phil was still an asshole.

* * *

Save for a couple of taverns, grocery stores, and the timber mill on the east end of town; Darrington consisted of mostly small, single floor dwellings surrounded by short chain link fences. Run down cars and stray pets dotted the gravel alleys between the homes.

Here it was, Saturday afternoon and not a soul could be seen walking the streets. It appeared as though everyone had gone home and went to bed. In the center of town, an orange 'open' sign in the lone grocery store stood as the only testament that the town was not completely abandoned.

Nick parked the car and looked at Phil. A lone logging truck full of fresh timber lurched up to the stop sign diagonally from where he was parked. The brake reservoir of the truck shrieked as it came to a brief stop; smoke and thunder rose as it crept forward, jerking and stuttering through the intersection as it turned left out of town toward the mill. Filleted chunks of bark and small branches fell from the neatly piled logs saddled into the trailer as it pulled away.

The sound of the diesel engine faded into the twang of country music coming from an antiquated building across the street. A glass door swung open and out stumbled two middle-aged men, visibly drunk and laughing their way up the street. They disappeared from view and all was quiet again.

Summer in the North Cascades.

Down the block, Officer Holley Ross sat in her patrol car reading the Saturday newspaper. The summer so far had been comparatively mild. A few hot days here and there, but the mountain air felt fresh and clean. Riddled with stories about Richard Nixon, the end of the Vietnam War and how Seattle was getting an NFL franchise, the paper was an interesting distraction from the boredom of Darrington. Nothing ever seemed to happen here.

Eighteen miles north of Darrington, the newly christened Highway 20, also known as the North Cascades Highway, had all but removed Darrington from the map five years earlier, when it opened in 1969. Travelers heading from Seattle to the tourist town of Winthrop; 100 miles to the east, could now take a much quicker route via Interstate 5, north to the city of Burlington and then drive east across the North Cascades on the new modern highway; completely bypassing Darrington.

When the highway opened, most folks in the town didn't even notice the town had been circumvented. Although Darrington was a fantastic 'jumping off point' for the area's campgrounds and beautiful mountain scenery; it was never really known as a tourist town.

For many, the town's biggest claim to fame was that Bob Barker, the host of the television game show 'The Price is Right' was born there in 1923. To most Darrington residents, the new highway happily removed the burden of having to be polite to rude outsiders. Drivers looking to fill up their cars with cheap gasoline before heading across the pass asked residents repeatedly if they had known Bob Barker. Folks grew tired of telling, over and over, how Bob Barker may have been born there, but he moved away after the death of his father in 1931 at the ripe old age of eight.

Officer Ross loved the day shift. The real action, she knew, wouldn't come until later that night; settling domestic disputes and the occasional bar fight between friends. Periodically she would get someone speeding through the town, and once pulled over, she would have to let them know that Highway 20 was about 18 miles up the road, north, out of town; and that no, *she did not know Bob Barker.*

She reached down and felt for her sandwich on the seat next to her. Once she let go of the newspaper with her right hand the corner fell down onto the steering wheel. She looked up and scanned the streets. No one had come through town in almost an hour. Across the street at the Red Top Tavern however, she noticed a young man walking out the door with what appeared to be a case of beer.

She had been briefed in her duties over the past year about the change in the law which rose the legal drinking age in Washington to 21 and, as the lunch she had packed was nearly finished, this would be a good time to relieve the early afternoon boredom and check out the young man.

She unbuckled the seatbelt of the patrol car and hopped out crossing the street where the young man was now walking briskly away from her.

"YOU!" she yelled after the man, "STOP right there!"

She picked up her pace to a vigorous walk and the man stopped, tossing his head back toward the sky.

Phil remained standing, facing away from her and did not move. She carefully observed him and placed her hand on to her service revolver as she approached him. Once she was about 20 feet away from the subject he quickly turned and faced her.

"Hey? What's up? How's it going today, officer?" Phil said with a huge smile across his face.

Happy and respectful, his voice was like he was meeting his girlfriend's parents for the first time. He lowered the case of beer to waist level and took a few steps toward her. She noted he was wearing camo pants and a dark green t-shirt. His crew-cut sandy brown hair barely moved in the mild breeze.

Officer Ross stopped right in front him.

"May I see your driver's license, sir?" Officer Ross demanded.

"Why? I haven't done anything wrong, have I?" he asked in the politest voice he could muster.

His wide smile bemused her. He was used to charming people to get what he wanted, especially women.

"The legal age to buy alcohol in Washington is 21, sir. You do not look to be 21 years of age. May I see your driver's license please?" she repeated.

The back of his neck began to itch, just for a second. He tilted his head to the right and shrugged his right shoulder to try and stop it without setting the beer down.

He had to think quickly.

He wasn't sure if he had any warrants and he certainly didn't want to find out. But this was a bitch cop; this should be easy he figured.

Officer Ross stood motionless staring at the subject. She recognized the itch as a 'tell'; a sign that this subject may not be telling the truth, but he looked harmless enough.

She waited.

"Fuck...I didn't buy this," he admitted as he knelt down, the case of beer clanking on the sidewalk in front of him.

He knew if he had to take off running that it would be quicker without the beer. The gravel alleyways and short chain link fences would make for an effortless getaway. Ditching this cop would be much easier than he was used to in Seattle.

What was her problem anyway?

"I watched you walk right out of the Red Top Tavern—with that case of beer in your hands as you walked out the door. Perhaps we should just go inside and ask the person working: 'who just bought that case of beer?' Are you sure you want to lie to me right now?" she said sternly.

"Ok—Ok. I don't have my license on me, my buddy and I just went swimming up at the Sauk and I took my wallet out so it wouldn't get wet.

10

You swim in the Sauk much? What's the big deal anyway? Its just beer?" he asked.

Office Ross didn't budge.

"Yeah, I just got back; back from Vietnam," he offered.

Phil expected that once she knew he had served, that all would be forgiven. He had served his country for crying out loud. And now he's going to get hassled for a little beer? Up here? In *Bum fucked Egypt?*

She continued to stare at Phil, unmoved.

"Look, I don't care if you're the President of the United States. No ID, no alcohol. I am going to ask that you either surrender the beer or come with me to the station until you can provide proof of identification. If you just give up the beer, I'll take your name down for my report and let you go about your business. Have you already been drinking?" she asked.

"Yeah, a little bit," he grinned, already knowing that he was going to walk away from this disrespectful bitch.

He may have to go get more beer somewhere else, and be a little more careful, but it beat going to jail or receiving a ticket.

Cops were fucked.

She reached into the breast pocket of her uniform and pulled out a small tablet and a pen.

"Ok—what's your name—start with the last name first, first name and then middle."

"Fornia, Charles Mark," he smiled.

What a dumb bitch.

He tilted his head again and shrugged his right shoulder to itch his neck.

She wrote down the name, address and date of birth on the small tablet and dropped it back into the breast pocket of her uniform.

"Listen, *Mark*," she began to lecture, "I know you have had a few beers, I do not want to see you driving, alright. What kind of car do you have?"

"Uh—it's a '63 Lancer. Blue," he answered.

She scribbled on her notepad.

"My friend walked over to the grocery store to get dinner, I'll have him drive since I forgot my license—up at the campsite," he enthusiastically agreed.

Officer Ross picked up the case of beer and crossed the street back to her patrol car and placed it into the back seat. She turned toward the Red Top Tavern and strode in the direction of the door to remind Annie and the other bartenders that the legal drinking age was now 21. She looked down the street to her right and then to her left.

The young man had disappeared.

Murder myself, Murder I am.

Around the corner and through the alley Phil anxiously searched for the thoroughfare leading to the grocery store where Nick was waiting. He spotted the Dodge Lancer in the parking lot ahead of him and to his right.

"I almost got fucking busted!" he laughed as he strode up to the car where his friend Nick sat in the passenger seat.

"What happened?" Nick asked.

"That dumb bitch cop caught me—I got a case of beer at the tavern—and she fucking took it because I didn't have no ID," he answered.

Nick sighed and started the car.

"Once I told her I was in 'Nam though she decided to let me go. She said she wished there were more men who served like I did," Phil proudly proclaimed.

Nick rolled his eyes subtly so that Phil would not notice.

"Fuck. I'll just go get it. The liquor store is right next to that- 'Jake's five and dime'- or whatever," Nick pointed out, puzzled.

"Eh, fuck them. *Cops are stupid.* I told her my name was Mark. Mark Fornia!" he laughed, "And she believed me! No one… no cop…no fucking campers-- no one is going to tell me what I can and can't do out here! You know, you just got to tell people what they want to hear. *Idiots.* Let's get some booze and get back up to camp and get wasted! It's Saturday night!"

*   *   *

Darkness filtered through the trees and in to the campground as the remaining splash of sun disappeared to the west. Nick heated up the last of their clam chowder over the fire. After they finished eating, Phil gathered up the empty cans and trash that had collected around the camp over the last day and a half. He sauntered away in to the blackness surrounding them and tossed the garbage from their dinner toward one of the garbage cans over in the camp spot next to theirs. A minute later he stumbled back in to camp.

"I am fucking *wasted,*" Phil said as he joined Nick next to the fire.

"Fuck yes," Nick agreed.

He swayed right to left on the log as he held his beer in the air toward Phil.

"Isn't it fucking great to…" Phil paused and took a drink, "to have the whole fucking place to ourselves?"

He reached down to pet his dog.

"We can hunt, shoot…. *fucking hunt*…shit, fish and drink all we want. When we want," Phil continued, slurring somewhat.

"It's fucking nice, man," Nick agreed.

"And that cop, in town. She knows, man. She knows what it means to go to war and come back," Phil continued slurring. "It's like my old man, and how he—and how he... came back from World War II, they were fucking heroes, just like us."

Innocently, Nick started to laugh.

"I don't think people think... you guys are *heroes,* man," Nick pointed out.

Phil's fist violently clenched around the beer can he was holding and his jaw clenched tightly.

"What the *fuck* do you...what the fuck do *you mean* by that, man?" Phil asked in a dark, stern tone.

Nick squirmed a little and shifted his feet in the dirt.

"Nothin' man, I'm just sayin', most people think 'Nam was just a-- a fucking waste of time and shit—not you, I mean--- No, not you. *You pretty much missed it*—I'm not talkin' about you; but the guys who *fucking* saw combat and shit—those guys are messed up, man."

Phil swayed side to side and as he turned to stare Nick down he stumbled and nearly fell in to the fire. Catching himself he stood upright, right next to his friend. He lifted the now crushed can in his fist toward Nick.

"What do you mean—*I pretty much missed it?* What the fuck do—what the fuck do you know?" Phil yelled at Nick, "*the guys who saw combat?*"

Adrenaline shot through Nick's body. He sat upright and shook his head.

"No...No...No...I'm not sayin' *you.* I mean—I mean the guys who—you know—the guys who killed people and shit," Nick corrected himself, trying to undo what he said.

"What? You don't think—you don't think I *killed anybody?* Is that what—what you fucking think?"

"NO! I just mean—*fuck.* I don't know what I-"

"*Fuck you.*"

Phil stared in to the fire as it popped and cracked shooting a blazing ember right over Nick's shoulder. Nick jumped back as though he had been shot.

Phil didn't even flinch.

"You want to go into the fucking woods? I'll give you five minutes. *Five fucking minutes*—and I could hunt you down...I could hunt you down... and *kill you.* Like a *fucking gook.*"

"That's not what-"

"We fucking served man... *you fucking watched*.....on the news....no fucking respect."

"No...that's not-" Nick tried to say again.

"*Five minutes....*" Phil belched.

"Man I'm just sayin'...I just mean that...the guys who were killin' people and shit. You know?....*man?*"

"Oh, so that *is it!* You don't think...you don't think I *fuckin' killed anyone?*"

Phil was furious.

"No, man, that's not what I...that's not what I said. *Shit,*" Nick answered again.

But it was no use. Somehow Phil decided that Nick didn't believe him. He couldn't believe that Nick was so stupid.

It wasn't enough that he could outshoot Nick with the shotgun.

It wasn't enough that he could circle him along the river and *could have* killed Nick if he wanted.

It wasn't enough.

How dare he.

Phil continued to pace around the fire, "I went in to the jungle man... and we...and we hunted them down. There aren't many people who can do what we did."

Phil lit up another cigarette and stared at the fire, ignoring Nick. As the fire burned down they just sat, drinking and smoking weed. He couldn't believe Nick thought that the war was over before he got there. Nick should be thanking him for what he had done over there, not arguing with him.

But no one seemed to give a shit about Vietnam.

"I'll fuckin' show you. *Just wait until tomorrow.* You'll see. You'll fucking see. I'll stalk and kill a fucking deer and hang it in camp like we used to do over there. We'd kill a fuckin' bushbuck and hang it along the camp- to ward off the enemy. *You'll fucking see.*"

Nick glanced over at Phil. He knew Phil was probably serious but he was in no condition to argue any more. It was late and he was fucking tired. Without a word Nick rose up from the fire and fell onto his damp sleeping bag. His feet hung over the edge in the dirt.

Phil spit into the fire once more and grabbed a smoke.

Fifteen minutes later, surrounded by empty beer bottles, Phil, too, was passed out in his bag.

2

Sunday morning, the camp along the Sauk remained quiet and motionless. Outside the ring of rock where the fire had burned the night before the ground was once again littered with brown beer bottles and cigarette butts. For awhile they tried to get them in the fire. But eventually the beer and weed took over. It was a surprise that neither of them had fallen in to the fire and ended up with serious burns.

"Aah.….fuck. Hey, man. You awake?" Nick's voice slurred from one of the two sleeping bags cast on the dirt.

"Yeah…what time is it? My fucking head hurts. I need a beer," Phil painfully answered from the other bag.

Both of them were somewhat hung-over. They awoke half expecting to see other campers in the area that may had come in after they passed out in their bags the night before. Phil's black dog jumped and whined where it was tied to the rear bumper of the car.

The campground was still empty.

Phil and Nick crawled, slowly, out of their bags. Cast in a sea of dark green and black, the towering cedars and fir trees kept the campground enveloped in shade for most of the morning.

Phil shivered.

"*Fuck.* I wanted to be up at sunrise. Better hunting," Phil complained.

He was anxious to prove to Nick that he could stalk and kill *anything*.

He rubbed his head vigorously and watched as Nick struggled with the zipper once again on his bag like an inch worm in the throes of death.

Phil laughed.

"Not a big fuckin' deal—let's just drink breakfast and get after it," Phil continued and turned his back toward Nick.

Nick was relieved that Phil was not pissed from the argument the night before but he could tell it was still a little awkward.

Stiff and sore from sleeping on the uneven ground, Phil hobbled over to the car. Squeaking and grinding, Phil flung the door open. He grabbed a couple of beers from behind the seat and tossed one at Nick, nearly hitting him in the head.

Phil remained uncharacteristically silent.

Striding over to the makeshift fire-pit he had constructed from river rock two nights before, Phil tossed a couple of paper plates on to the smoldering embers. Within seconds they burst into flames; the smell and smoke of burning cedar swirled toward the Sauk.

The fern covered floors of the evergreen forests reminded Phil of the jungles of Vietnam. He pulled out a small bag of dog food and tossed some on a paper plate for his little black dog.

Twisting and tugging, Nick finally wrestled the zipper of his bag open and joined Phil around the small fire. Together, they shotgunned two beers each. It was going to be a great Sunday. No people, no distractions; just a couple of good friends in the scenic wilderness of the North Cascades.

"Hey man- last night…I wasn't sayin'."

"*Don't worry about.* You'll see…soon enough," Phil cut him off.

When the veterans from World War II returned home, they were heroes. They didn't have to put up with this bullshit. They got respect. He expected the bullshit from the long-haired, pot smokin', hippie faggots; but not his friend. Now Nick was acting like a two-bit punk. But Phil would show him and he would see. He would see that he deserved the respect and admiration the World War II vets had gotten.

They tossed the empty beer cans aside and Nick belched. Phil pulled a cigarette from his green fatigue jacket and lit it. He clenched the cigarette tightly in his mouth and put his foot up on to the pile of dead logs Nick labored in to the camp the night before; and tightened the laces on his boots.

Nick was beginning to realize that Phil hadn't changed much since high school and it was still best to just go with Phil's crazy notions—it was simply better that way. And besides; Nick thought, no one was getting hurt; *except for maybe a deer.*

Phil pointed up the road.

"I think if we head up, that way, along the river, there are a couple of open clear-cuts; as long as no fuckin' cars come they should be in there. But you *have to be quiet*," Phil explained.

With a purpose he strode over to the trunk of the car and whipped out his shotgun. The sight of that 12 gauge Winchester once again made Nick a little nervous.

On the first night camping, he watched as Phil fired round after round into the darkness. Nick jumped every time sparks flew from the muzzle and the weapon barked its authority.

Phil just laughed and hollered all night.

"All right, man. Let's get to it," Phil commanded.

Nick stood up and tucked in his flannel shirt. The morning air was still cool, but by noon it would feel like summer again. He was a little apprehensive about deer hunting in the spring. Nick was not an avid hunter or an outdoorsman by any stretch of the imagination.

And that shotgun?

Nick just stood at the fire and stared out toward the river.

"Fuck, man. It's really not even deer season. Do we really have to fuckin' kill a deer and shit? Why don't we just go fishin' and fuckin' pound some brews?" Nick asked nervously.

"I nee...t...ill...a uffin...ear," Phil said inaudibly.

He reached up with his powerful hand and pulled the cigarette from his mouth.

"*I need to kill a fuckin' deer,*" he repeated.

Phil flicked the cigarette into the fire, somewhat annoyed.

"Now let's go, and just be *fucking quiet.*"

Nick realized it was no use. Phil was going to do what he wanted, despite any of his objections.

Phil tied up his dog and placed two shells into the shotgun and tossed it up on to his shoulder. He and Nick slowly made their way down the gravel road along the river.

Nick trudged along behind him trying to be as quiet as he could. A half hour later the gravel road faded into an old logging trail. The damp soil was much quieter to walk on and Nick's apprehension about hunting out of season began to ease up a bit. Every few minutes Phil stopped and scrunched down on one knee as though he had seen something.

Eerily silent he sat there, staring at nothing.

Nick listened intently, all he could hear was the constant low hush of the river as he searched the dark green surroundings for a deer. Every once in awhile he gazed upwards at the brilliant azure blue sky above.

Phil stopped.

"Let's smoke one real quick," Phil whispered back to Nick.

He motioned him forward along side him.

Nick pulled a joint from the breast pocket of his flannel shirt and lit it.

As he began to inhale the first drag, Phil dropped quickly to the dirt and motioned Nick to do the same.

"Deer," Phil whispered.

He pointed up the trail looking back at Nick.

"We need to get closer. Stay right behind me *and be quiet!"*

The swirling of rushing water from the river made a great covering backdrop for his stalk toward the deer.

Quietly, they continued down the path through the trees. Phil led the way carrying his double barreled shotgun in his arms. From Phil's viewpoint to the left of Nick, he could see the deer drawing closer. Slowly, the Winchester shotgun came up to his shoulder. Phil wasn't sure how well #6 sized shot would kill a deer, but he didn't really care.

"Back in 'Nam, one slip or cracking twig and I would have been dead," Phil whispered louder; looking back over his shoulder at Nick.

His pulse raced as he knew how impressed Nick must have been.

"We'd set up ambushes, and drag their bodies off the trail and bury them," he explained.

Nick took another hit from the joint.

Whoa.

Nick froze; the deer was only about 25 yards in front of him now. The scene in front of him was still as a picture; the only motion was the deer's thin white and black tail flicking in the morning air.

Why wasn't he shooting?

Nick's eyes strained toward the deer. Every muscle stiffened in his back. He couldn't even let a breath out.

Shoot…..shoot!

Crack!

A twig snapped beneath Phil's foot and the deer exploded away from them and to their right. Phil sprung up and planted the shotgun to his shoulder. In one fluid motion his finger found the trigger as his thumb clicked off the safety. His eye focused straight down the barrel as he swung the weapon, bringing the deer into his sight picture.

BOOM!

Nick uncontrollably flinched with the roar of the gun; he looked;

BOOM!

-and then flinched again as the second barrel let loose. His ears quietly began to ring.

"Fuck!" Phil exclaimed as he lowered the shotgun and cracked it open to eject the spent shells.

Unharmed, the deer loped away into the morning shadows of the forest. Thin, dark smoke swirled out of the empty chambers of the shotgun.

Nick began to laugh, "What would have happened if that had been in Vietnam?"

Phil turned beat red and began to rage. He wanted to load that shotgun and blow Nick's fucking guts across the river.

Not so funny now.

His blood boiled.

He tipped his beer back and slammed it toward his mouth, his fist crushing the can, spraying beer and foam down his throat. He reached into his fatigue jacket for another one, staring at Nick with the eyes of death; he wiped the foam from his mouth and shotgunned this one down, too.

Phil was starting to catch a buzz.

He continued to glare at Nick.

Not yet fully aware of the anger flushing within Phil, Nick led the way back toward the dilapidated blue Lancer. What took them an hour to hike while trying carefully to be silent, only took 15 minutes at a brisk pace.

Phil just shook his head. He would have killed that fucking deer, and showed Nick, *had it not been for a damn twig.*

*   *   *

The afternoon was dragging on and the buzz was more like a long hangover than the fun Nick hoped for when he let Phil talk him into quitting his job and going camping for a few days. It was obvious Phil was a little miffed that Nick dared to poke a little fun at him. Nick hoped he could ease the tension little bit as they just stood around the fire ring.

"Let's just go to town and get some more beer, fuck. So much for hunting, eh, man?" Nick joked.

Phil wasn't amused.

Nick grabbed a couple of the empties from the car and tossed them out onto the gravel. Phil came up to the car and grabbed some more shells out from under the front seat and looked over at Nick.

Empty beer cans littered the front seats.

Phil drew in a long sigh and tossed the shotgun in to the back seat and draped his duffel bag over it to conceal the weapon. Not yet ready to give up on the idea of showing Nick his stalking and killing skills, Phil reluctantly agreed; for now.

"Yeah, sure, let's go to Darrington. We can hunt some more when we get back," Phil said as he climbed into the passenger seat.

His dog jumped across his lap and in to the back seat.

It was Phil's car but he liked having Nick drive, which meant he could drink more and relax. Cops were getting testy about being drunk behind the wheel.

Nick breathed a sigh of relief as he removed the heavy flannel he was wearing and pulled another joint from the glove box. Phil tossed Nick a lighter and told him to fire it up. Just as Nick shifted the car in to reverse a quick movement caught his eye.

"*Deer!*" Nick shouted as he pointed toward a small doe trotting across the gravel road in front of them.

Nick's hand smacked the steering wheel and he winced in pain. He shook his hand violently back and forth to relieve the throbbing in his fingers. He slipped the transmission back in to park. Phil piled out of the car and loaded the shells he pulled from under the seat in to the shotgun and stepped in front of the car.

This was his chance.

Nick's heart began to race—*it wasn't deer season.*

It just wasn't cool. He took a drag off the joint.

Through the light skim of dirt and dust clouding the windshield of the car he could see Phil standing ten feet in front of the car with the shotgun once again raised to his shoulder. About 25 yards further out, the doe stopped along the edge and cautiously stared at Phil.

Gravel shifted beneath Phil's feet as he took aim--

BOOM!

The deer jumped straight up like a bucking bronco and bounded back across the road on Phil's right. Phil took off at a dead run toward where the deer had disappeared into the ferns and moss covered cedar deadfall.

Nick sat in stunned silence, massaging his sore hand and puffing on the joint. Overhead, a small airplane tracked across the sky. Nick wondered if they were being watched.

Was it the police?

Fish and Game?

The plane continued its straight path across the sky toward the west and disappeared. He shook his head and realized the weed he was smoking was taking effect. And considering his paranoia—it was good.

Minutes passed.

He popped open another beer from behind the seat and took a swig.

Phil had not come back and he couldn't hear or see any sign of him. If he went into the woods looking for him, Nick wondered, would Phil think he was a deer, *or worse,* and shoot him by accident?

Shit.

He tipped the beer back into his throat again and sat in the front seat waiting. Finishing the beer, he tossed the empty into the bushes out the window.

Giggling to himself, he half expected Phil to come stumbling out of the shrubs and get hit by the empty beer can. He reached behind the seat into the tattered brown paper bag for another one. His hand swirled about the empty bag.

He was high as fuck.

Damn. No more beer.

Where the fuck was Phil?

As he sat in the front seat daydreaming, he was sure Phil was stalking him now as a joke and was going to come leaping out of the dense vegetation along the gravel road at any time in an attempt to scare him. Nearly 10 more minutes passed and *still* no sign of Phil. He really wished Phil would get back. They needed more beer and he didn't dare drive off and leave Phil alone.

He was way too stoned for this.

Couldn't they just hang out around camp or go fishing or something?

No running through the woods.

No hunting.

It would be so much less stressful if Phil just put the fucking gun away. The stories were cool and all, and Phil was cool, *but man he seemed to have such a short fucking fuse.*

Nick got out of the Lancer and slammed the door shut.

"Stay here!" he commanded the dog.

He methodically walked toward where he had last seen Phil.

"Hey!—I'm coming in—don't shoot me you fucker...," he hollered.

The only sound he could hear was the steady swirl of the Sauk and the soft breeze dancing in the trees. In the distant darkness of the forest a chipmunk chattered and abruptly stopped.

"Phil?!—Hey man—where are you—this ain't funny!— Come on... man...fuck."

Nick searched along the edge of the gravel road and then stepped down into the fern crusted forest. The chipmunk chattered again, much closer.

"PHIL?!!—*what the fuck man?!*—Hello?!"

Nick nearly tripped over a rotting log and stumbled forward. Despite the sunny day—the sword fern and vine maple understory was still somewhat damp. He felt the moisture seeping in to his shoes.

A few yards into the maze of green plants and shrubs he glanced back toward the logging road. For a moment he felt disoriented amongst all the maple and fir trees; he could no longer look make out the shape of the blue

Lancer parked on the gravel road behind him. His surroundings shifted from warm, blue sky and bright green forest to drab shades of brown and gray.

It was menacing.

The Lancer blocked the road and he worried someone would come down the road and not be able to pass the car. This would only give Phil reason to be pissed at someone again — he didn't need that.

But Phil had been gone awhile.

It seemed every time he hung out with Phil, Phil would just go looking for a reason to fuck with someone.

Off to his right in a rare patch of sun filled earth a slight shimmer caught his eye.

He froze.

Squinting, he leaned forward, focusing on what caught his glance. He reached down to the prickly green leaf of an Oregon grape bush and pulled it closer to his eyes.

Blood.

It was just a bright red droplet and although he had never seen blood out in the woods — it was unmistakable. He took a few steps forward. His pant leg caught on a fallen branch and he twisted, nearly falling over.

Fishing was so much fucking easier.

Ahead of him a few more feet he saw another glimmer of crimson; a swath of blood smeared along the side of a log. Bubbles permeated from the viscous liquid. Along the edges of the stain it had started to turn darker maroon, almost brown as it started to dry.

He took a few more steps and peered between the maple saplings.

"Phil!" he yelled again; half hoping to get an answer, half hoping to alert Phil of his presence so he wouldn't get shot.

Following the blood trail he came up over a slight rise and could now see down in to a shallow, mossy draw. To his right Phil's olive green fatigue jacket hung from a low bent branch.

"Hey man — did you get it?" he hollered in to the small hemlock grove.

Cautiously he walked toward it making as much noise as he could.

"Phil! — Hey, we're outta' beer, man. What the fuck?"

At the foot of the hemlock he found Phil straddled over the dead deer, his sleeves rolled up; gripping his knife.

A freshly killed deer can be a grizzly sight. Phil's movements with the knife were deliberate and calculating. The tip of the knife parted the red tissue below the diaphragm and the pungent smell of death creeping out from beneath the hemlock tree nearly made Nick vomit. Phil's arms were covered in blood up to his elbows. Phil wiped his forehead with the knife still in his hand. Once he finally noticed Nick was standing there he looked up and smiled.

"I fuckin' got it!" Phil exclaimed.

Phil turned back toward the deer and pulled the entrails out as air rushed out of the dead deer's lungs. Nick gagged again.

"Jesus."

Nick groaned looking away.

"Look at where I hit it!"

Phil turned the deer sideways and lifted the front left leg exposing bloody, torn tissue beneath the fur.

His grin went from ear to ear.

"That's…uh…awesome, man," Nick muttered under his breath.

"No!—*look at that fucking entrance wound*—no way she could have survived that! Look at that shit! FUCK *yeah*!" Phil's tone changed from one of excitement and jubilation to demanding and expectant.

Nick didn't want to look at the eviscerated animal but he didn't want to make it obvious to Phil that he didn't want to look at it, either.

"*Fucking look at it*! Did I not fuck that deer up—or what?"

Phil again lifted the dangling front leg of the dead deer.

"What? Are you scared?" Phil joked. "Are you scared of a little shotgun blast?"

Nick wasn't sure what to say. He was *really* stoned.

"We need more beer, man--- *fuck*. Phil—what did you shoot this for?" he finally asked.

He peeked at the bloody mess again and quickly glanced away.

"Then we'll go get some! Fuck. It's only 15 minutes. I got to get this thing drug back to our camp and skinned out first."

Nick recognized the tone of voice. He knew he better just wait.

"I shot it so we could eat it, man. Haven't you ever lived off the 'fat of the land' before? This is what you do—this is how you *survive*."

Nick just stood, trying not to breath in any more of the putrid smell than he had to.

"WOOHOOO!!" Phil threw his head back and hollered in delight.

Phil finished gutting the dead animal in record time. He was good with his knife and hunting trips with his family friends in eastern Washington as a boy had taught him well.

Fondly, he remembered packing his warm clothes, piling in to the truck and traveling across the Snoqualmie pass to a remote deer camp. Here they would set up tents, cook on propane stoves and tell stories about hunts' past. He could take a few hits off the McNaughtons bottle as it traveled around the camp fire each night. The men would tell stories about World War II and Korea. If they were lucky, his friends' father would kill a nice buck and strap it to the front of the truck, proudly showing off the trophy all the way home until they dropped it off at the butcher.

Around the campfire, Phil would tell tales and keep them entertained with his quick wit and charm. For a 10 year old, he was pretty fun to have around they would tell him. The more they would try and teach him about the outdoors, the more interested he became. He studied and learned and found that by the time he was 15 or 16 when he could demonstrate his superior knowledge of the outdoors; these men would shower him with adoration. To many of these men, he was their pride and joy—at least during hunting camp.

During the rest of the year, he would have to sit and listen to his alcoholic father belittle and admonish him for not being smarter in things that mattered; math, science and accounting.

These were the things that would serve him later in life.

Not hunting—as far as Phil's father was concerned, in a civilized world one could simply go to the grocery store and buy food. Outdoor skills and hunting were for a dying generation.

Phil hated that he could never please his father.

He wanted to—very much. He hoped he would be a great financial success and have a family and be a war hero like his dad. He wanted it so bad that he could taste it. Partly because he genuinely wanted to please him and partly because he wanted to prove to his father that his father was wrong about him. But Phil would dream of the outdoors—knowing that when he grew up—he could go fishing, hunting and camping whenever he liked.

Fuck that old man.

Once he finished gutting the deer, he reached down and grabbed the deer by the ears. The doe was heavier than he thought, as he drug it across the deadfall and detritus of the forest out to the road. Behind him a pair of magpies had already begun tearing at the steaming pile left behind. He propped the shotgun up on a stump next to the deer. His shell belt hung down across his torso and he tapped it with affection.

Suddenly he stopped, let go of the deer's ears and looked to his left. The deer's lifeless head dropped to the ground with a dull thud. Blood droplets from the deer's mouth splattered red across Phil's boots. Keenly, he searched for the sound of a grouse he believed he had flushed out earlier. He knew how impressed Nick would be if he also had a couple of birds to toss onto a spit and turn over the fire for dinner. Grouse—those would be delicious.

For a minute he stared intently, listening.

Nothing.

24

Peaking high above the tree line, the July sun beamed down. Skinning the deer became a top priority. Phil remembered how the men at his deer camp always told him that nothing spoils a deer faster than not skinning it fast enough. No, he would not let that happen to this fine creature; he had 'too much respect for nature.'

He cradled the shotgun across his chest with his right arm and reached behind him to again grab the deer by the ears. Blood and hair streamed into the gravel as he drug the deer back to the car perched in the middle of the road.

He laughed. *Maybe now Nick would shut the fuck up.*

In one of the empty campsites next to theirs he remembered a great tree from which to hang the deer and skin it.

Once at the car, Phil reached down and grabbed the two rear legs of the deer and with his other hand grabbed the front two legs. With a grunt, he hoisted the deer up on to the hood of the car.

THWACK!

The deer landed on the hood and blood continued to run out of the deer's mouth down the hood and onto the chrome headlight bezels. Phil wiped his hands on a grass bush next to the road and hopped in the passenger side of the car.

"Just back this thing up the road and we'll hang it from that big tree at the campsite next to ours, shouldn't take long," Phil said.

Nick backed the car into the other campsite and sat on the hood of the Lancer watching while Phil carefully cut through the hide of the deer around its back legs. With the precision of a surgeon, he quickly began tugging the summer thinned hide off the animal. With efficient strokes, Phil quickly exposed the muscle and fat tissue beneath the hide. A few minutes later the hide and head of the black-tailed deer lay on the ground under the hanging carcass in what appeared to be a melted clump of what had, an hour earlier, been wandering the forest.

Much to Nick's relief, the campground was still empty.

Phil reached into his pack and pulled a few paper towels to wipe the blood off his knife. Nick jumped up and felt moist warmth seeping in to his pants where he sat in the blood which had pooled on the hood from the trip up the road. He swiped his hand across the back of his thigh and Phil laughed when he noticed what was bothering Nick.

"Don't let a little blood scare you, man," Phil laughed.

Nick ignored him.

"Cool, let's go to town and get some beer, I am fucking thirsty," Phil continued.

"Are you sure we should leave that hanging here?" Nick asked as he opened the car door.

"Fuck. Who cares?" Phil answered.

"No one is going to tell me I can't live off the fat of the land!" Phil repeated. "See? *I told you!* Just like killin' gooks. *Easy.* Now, let's go drink some fuckin' beer!"

Phil and Nick hiked up the river beyond the bridge to a spot where a pool had formed behind a fast rushing part of the Sauk. The forest fronted the river and provided some cool relief from the afternoon sun. After fishing and drinking beers all afternoon they slowly wandered back to their camp to make dinner. Nick watched as Phil carefully heated a can of clam chowder they had found under the seat of the car.

The afternoon of drinking had left both of them pretty inebriated. Nick was glad that the shotgun had remained in the car for most of the afternoon. Phil could tell that Nick was irritated about the whole thing, but he could really have cared less. At least now Nick had seen it firsthand, *now he knew.*

Phil sat in front of the campfire with a renewed spirit. Even in the way he brought the beers upwards to his mouth he could barely contain his smile.

Life was good.

"I bet you're glad to be back home...eh, man? *Outta that shit hole, I mean,*" Nick slurred as he tried to light a cigarette.

Puzzled, he stared as the filter began to melt. He had placed it into his mouth backwards.

"It was fucking nuts...fucking...over there man," Phil answered.

Struggling with the cigarette, Nick pulled it from his lips and turned his head to the side in a confused manner, blinking and trying to focus on what the fuck wasn't working.

"*Fuck.*"

He tossed the wasted smoke in to the fire and giggled as he wrestled another from the mangled pack in his breast pocket.

"I don't talk about it. I don't talk...I ain't no *fucking whiner.* You know. It's like my father and his...my father and his buddies- they didn't come back—they didn't whine about *shit!* What happened- *happened. You know—happened!* What I mean?" Phil's upper body swirled and tossed around like the arm of a mixing bowl.

Nick finally got his cigarette lit and he pulled it out of his mouth to stare at the cherry on the end one more time just to be sure.

"Yeah, I know man; hopefully you can...hopefully you can just...you know, put it behind you- forget and shit," Nick agreed.

"Forget?...why the fuck would I want to forget?....I am fucking ....*forget?* I am fucking proud of what we did—*forget? Forget shit,*" Phil answered him, somewhat irritated, "killing is fucking easy, man. Easy."

Nick looked up at him and laughed, "Especially, when they... when they fucking...especially when they jump out in front of the *car*. Like that deer. That was fucking easy!"

Phil, who was in the process of raising his beer to his mouth stopped mid-motion and glared at Nick.

He still didn't get it.

"It wasn't like that...like that in the *shit, man*. What the fuck do- what the fuck do you know?" Phil demanded.

Innocently, Nick just kept drinking.

"I know man—those guys that were in the shit—they *are fucked up!* They are—in the shit!" Nick agreed.

Phil cocked his head to one side and stared across the fire at Nick.

"What do you mean—those *guys?* I was fucking there man. I told you—*what? You still* don't think I fucking...I was - you still don't think I was in the shit? I fucking told you," Phil stood up and began yelling at Nick.

Nick leaned back as far as he could without falling backwards on to his head.

"*I fucking told you*—I'd stalk a fucking deer down and fucking—and fucking kill it. *WHAT HAPPENED?*" Phil pointed in the direction of the dead carcass hanging in the tree, "Dead *fucking deer*- hanging in the *fucking tree!* You little fucking pussy!"

Phil was standing right over top of Nick now and screaming.

"Whoa! Man—*easy! It's cool....it's cool. Calm dowm. I'm not sayin'...I'm not sayin' that, man.* Fuck." Nick squealed, his arms above his head in a defensive posture.

Phil cocked his arm back like he was going to deck him and then pulled back and stared at him.

"You're fucking... fucking lucky, man," Phil said as he turned and jerked his beer up off the ground and threw it back toward his throat.

"Fuck, man. Sorry—*I wasn't sayin'* anything about you. Fuck," Nick said, lowering his arms to his side and turning to find his beer.

"It's cool, man. It's cool. I get what you're sayin'," Phil remarked as he plopped back down on to the log across the fire from Nick.

Phil got exactly what he was saying; *Nick didn't believe a word of Phil's stories about combat.*

Nick didn't dare say another word.

Nick didn't understand why *Phil was so fucking pissed.*

3

The old man grunted, wiped his nose and started his car. The ferry lane at Friday Harbor on San Juan Island wasn't too crowded for a Monday morning and it shouldn't take too long to load up. About 75 miles north of Seattle, San Juan Island had grown in popularity over the years.

Most people who populated San Juan Island during the summer ventured up on Friday, spent the weekend in their summer cabins and headed back to Seattle or wherever they were from on Sunday. A few would take in the sights along the scattered beaches or venture to the northwestern corner of the island and visit Roche Harbor or Hotel de Haro.

Some of the crazies even came up just to hike a few minutes north of Roche Harbor to the 'Mausoleum'; a collection of marble pillars and a granite table where John McMillin placed the ashes of his family in concrete urns shaped like chairs. This way, they could all sit together at the table for all eternity.

He maneuvered the car on to the ferry and shut the engine down. The ride in to Anacortes took about 90 minutes. But the older he got, the more impatient he seemed to become. At 83 years old, Newton Thomas had experienced and seen firsthand the changes the 20th century brought to the world. At age ten he watched as the horse gave way to the motor car. He was 23 when World War I broke out in Europe, at 36 he followed as Lindbergh flew an 'aeroplane' across the Atlantic. Newt was 48 when

Hitler invaded Poland and 72 when an assassin's bullet took the life of John F. Kennedy. He marveled most recently at how a man could possibly travel to the moon and return safely to Earth. He truly was blessed to see one of the most rapidly changing times the world had ever seen.

His first love however, and fondest memory of his generations contribution to the world was that of Teddy Roosevelt's legacy of conserving the outdoors for future generations.

Living on the island was nice and he very much loved 'island life'; but it was nice to get off the 'rock' and go exploring once in awhile. Retired and with no close family nearby, he liked to go camping during the weekdays—less 'weekenders' he called them. This way, the folks he did run into during the weekdays were probably on a vacation or more serious about their camping than the 'weekenders'. He believed these people enjoyed the outdoor experience more, and thus, were better company to sit and reminisce about the changes in the world.

He planned on getting over to the mainland tonight, and Tuesday or Wednesday he would go find a nice quiet campground up in the North Cascades somewhere. It had been awhile since he had ventured into the area. Logging activities were changing the landscape and although he knew there would be no stopping the clear-cutting that was destroying the forest; he figured he would get a last look in before it was all gone.

Newt, as he was called by most everybody, loved camping and everything it meant. Too quickly, he remembered, generations began to forget about our westward expansion and the rugged sacrifices which were made to stretch our nation between the oceans. Camping, hiking, hunting, fishing—all of it served as a reminder of the struggle and sacrifices from which this great nation ascended.

He believed in honor, duty and the law of the land. Be good to people and they will be good to you. Stand your ground and be righteous; and you will be free and prosperous. Despite his age, he still liked to pack up his Ford Galaxy and head in to the hills to remember, relive and rejoice in nature.

The North Cascades area was one of his favorite places. He was worried however, about this latest generation. Fighting a war that many did not agree with in a land and against a country that was half the size of the State of Washington. To compound matters, these kids were coming back and coming to the woods and parks not to rejoice in nature but to *escape from the demons* which haunted them.

He just hoped and prayed they'd learn some respect and watch how those before them had done it. Learn the lessons of the past and get right with themselves and the rest of the world. Before they did that, he figured, he'd be long gone from this planet and back up with the Lord.

So be it.

Anacortes was a welcome sight to Newt. The ferry ride was long even though the salty smell of Puget Sound always put a smile on his face. Children and their parents scrambled in and around the cars packed on to the ferry deck. Doors slammed, engines roared to life and crewmen shuffled in front of the commotion. Exhaust fumes began to drown out the warm seaside breeze and he was ready to get moving.

One by one, the deckhand signaled each row of cars to gently move forward. The metal decks slammed along the pier where the vessel docked and gave way to the off loading ramp each time a car would motion across. Some drivers would try and sneak out into the other line, hurried to get moving. He was in no hurry — but he found it downright rude that others would break the rules.

There is a system, he thought to himself.

Why can't anyone follow the system anymore?

Patiently as he could he waited until it was his turn to disembark the ferry.

Cars lumbered up the hill away from the dock and jockeyed for position as the multiple exit lanes merged in to one single lane. Pine trees and summer homes dotted the bluff extending up from the shoreline. In the distance across the water now disappearing behind him, the forested islands melted in to the last remnants of white morning fog. As he drove up the steep hill away from the shoreline, Newt rolled his window down to draw in one last, deep breath of the sweet seaside air.

He fumbled under the map in the seat next to him to grab his gold rimmed spectacles.

They were down there somewhere.

He knew he was not supposed to drive without them but keeping track of them was no small chore. Glancing in the rear view mirror he double checked the contents of the backseat to make sure he hadn't forgotten any of the essentials. Spare clothes, his blue and gold tent and of course, a plethora of air cushions and a green air mattress.

Air, he thought to himself, *who would have ever thought sleeping on air could be so comfortable?*

Whenever a ferry would discharge in to the town, traffic bottle necked for a bit at the first stoplight in Anacortes. As he sat waiting behind dozens of cars he caught a glimpse of the Cascade Mountains ahead of him to the east.

He could see them from the living room window at his modest shack on the Island; in fact the view of the mountains was why he had chosen the meager abode. But crossing Puget Sound brought them into much closer view. From this side of the water he could now make out every stone gray rocky outcropping of the snowcapped peaks that he just couldn't see from the island.

Even without those *damned* spectacles.

Glacier Peak, Pilchuk, Mt. Baker—he loved them all and had hiked on and around most of them. His chest drew tightly upwards as he sighed; his hiking days were long behind him.

As the light turned from red to green, he stared in disbelief as the cars barely began to move. Ahead of him he could see a mother leaning over the backseat of a wood paneled station wagon reaching for drinks and candy bars to pacify the screaming children dwelling behind them.

"Let's go!" he said under his breath.

Newt didn't have a mean bone in his body, but he was always frustrated at the lack of 'get with it-ness' displayed by today's youth. The light was green—that meant go.

He always managed to be polite, however. He was not a bitter man. To be rude would, in a sense, lower him to their level he thought. One could express his dismay at any given situation but still remain civilized.

The long line of cars finally began to meander through town dissipating a little at every junction until finally he was out on the open road and headed east through a mixture of tulip and alfalfa fields.

Scattered across the landscape, brown, weathered barns reminded him of simpler days. Wind rushed in to the little Ford and tossed his map onto the floor sounding like tearing sheets of paper. Startled, he glanced down at the speedometer and realized he was now traveling at over 60 miles per hour. He quickly eased off the accelerator. It had been almost a year that the new 55 mph speed limit had been in effect. He thought the idea was stupid when they first brought it up and he thought it was stupid now.

But it was the law.

Back at home, island radio had little to offer Newt. He could tune his portable AM in and get some stations from British Columbia to the north and at night he could sometimes get KIRO or KOMO out of Seattle. But whenever he hit the mainland, he liked to catch up on world events without having to strain his ears through static and constantly adjust the dial on the radio perched on his kitchen table at home. He had extended the antenna outdoors, but it did little to improve anything.

Turning the dial on his dash, the radio sprung to life. He had saved his favorite station on the push button deck. When he bought the car new, a few years back, he made sure that it was equipped with both an AM and an FM radio. He marveled at how technologically advanced radios had become.

A button to mark favorite stations.

Genius.

31

'How was Nixon fairing?' he wondered. 'Are we ever going to get a baseball team again?' He was annoyed at how the Seattle Pilots played for a season in Seattle and then quickly exited.

Baseball wasn't his favorite thing in the world, but the small group of Boy Scouts he adored so much certainly loved catching a game. 'It was good to get boys involved with positive activities', he nodded.

This was why Newt spent so much time mentoring young boys. It seemed life had gotten so fast for families today with commuting to work, telephones, record players and color television that nobody wanted or had the time to take boys out to do good things. There seemed to be less of teaching them right and wrong. For him it was simple, follow the rules, be courteous and stay active.

He turned off the highway and headed toward the town of Burlington to the northeast. The shortcut into Burlington dumped Newt right on to Interstate 5 and shaved 15 or 20 minutes off of his overall travel time. He was in no hurry, but why not be efficient? From here he crossed Interstate 5 and continued on into the town of Sedro-Wooley, 15 or 20 minutes further and turned back east again along Highway 20.

Sedro-Wooley was a fair sized town and he figured he would stop there for groceries and take a short look at the map. Traveling on Monday meant a shorter ferry line, and it also meant that many of the good campsites which would already have already been occupied the day before would now be vacant.

No worries.

There are tons of little spots to pull over, pitch his tent and listen to the sounds of nature over a good stew for dinner and a warm pot of coffee in the morning.

He didn't plan on being gone for too long. His weary frame precluded the one or two week outings of his youth. But he figured he would check out some familiar haunts for a few days and get back to Friday Harbor by Thursday or Friday.

He pulled off the highway into the grocery store. In front of him a woman with a small child held hands as they crossed the parking lot in front of the store. The mother admonished the small child for failing to look both ways before crossing the car lane. The little lesson made him feel good—there might be hope for these kids yet.

He parked the car and made his way in. He caught up to the woman and her child when she suddenly stopped and yanked the little girl out away from Newt's path into the automatic swinging doors.

"Please, go ahead, sir," She awkwardly motioned—

Newt declined—

"I am just old, honey—not decrepit. You were here first, -Please."

He wandered about the store and pulled his handwritten menu from the pocket of his worn blue jeans. Slowly and deliberately he grabbed his meals, some soda and some coffee and made his way to the check-out line. The clerk asked for his driver's license so he could write it down on his check. Quietly and without issue, Newt made his way out of the store and back to his Galaxy waiting in the parking lot.

Newt climbed in to the car and peered over at the plethora of maps tattered and sun faded. He always had them with him but rarely used them. He knew the area very well; he had been camping around the northwest for nearly 75 years. Maps were for people who didn't want to get lost; he fell into the category of people who *liked* to get lost once in awhile. To him, that was what the spirit of adventure and exploration was all about.

A few years earlier, he had taken a young friend of the family, John Sundstrom, to Australia and New Zealand and although Newt was always cautious and well prepared for an emergency, part of the fun was not having a set itinerary or place to be at any certain time.

What if you found a spot you wanted to stay at for a few extra days?

What if the spot you found wasn't what you had hoped?

What if you met interesting people and wanted to stay?

Newt always believed life would take care of itself. He turned his car out of the parking lot and on to the highway toward Darrington. There were a lot of interesting campgrounds up that way and because the weekenders would have all headed back to Seattle, he should have free reign to pick his camping spot.

One of his favorite parts of camping was choosing where to camp—a good view, protection from the sun or rain shower that could come across the northwest at anytime—and flat, soft ground good for pitching a tent. Some of the campgrounds had such hard, well-packed ground that one couldn't even drive in a tent stake unless one wanted to use railroad spikes and a 30 pound sledgehammer. Other spots were so soft and powdery that the spikes wouldn't even stay.

Over use.

That was the problem these days. Too many people were using too few camp spots and not being good stewards.

An hour later he pulled in to Darrington and stared affectionately toward Whitehorse Mountain. He liked the feel of the small town. In some ways it reminded him a lot of the small southeastern Alaska towns he had visited and lived in while running a cannery for his family during the forties and fifties.

Newt drove slowly through town. He loved the old buildings and the old saw mill. He pulled over to the side of the road and grabbed his map again. He wasn't lost, by any means. But the map was a great reference to try and determine which camp area he wanted to check out first.

He unfolded the map and quickly found Darrington, to the north he could hit the North Cascades Highway and go closer to the North Cascades National Park; but that would probably be really crowded even on a Monday. To the south he could head down the Mountain Loop Highway toward Granite Falls. He remembered he had camped at a fairly large camp area near Verlot a few years earlier with a small youth group. The campground was probably big enough and had enough campsites that it wasn't full yet. It was getting late in the afternoon and it was only a few miles. The map showed a few new campgrounds along the way which might be empty as well; Sauk, Red Bridge and White-Chuck. It seemed as good a plan as any so he pulled the Galaxy back on to the road and took a right heading south.

The North Cascades National Park can wait until Tuesday.

Within minutes he was off the pavement and the sound of the gravel road indicated he was getting further away from civilization. He traveled about 40 minutes up the road and passed the Verlot Ranger station and dropped back down toward Granite Falls. The gravel road meandered around the foothills of the Cascades and once the terrain leveled out it met the Stillaguamish River.

He passed the Red Bridge Campground and saw a trailer and a couple of other vehicles so Newt kept going. A few miles down the road he found the Wiley Creek Camp Ground where he had been before. The memories of camping there with the youth group warmed him somewhat so he pulled off the gravel to his right.

To his surprise, he found only a couple of vehicles and a few tents. Three or four campsites were open and he felt he picked one that seemed fairly private but close enough that he felt he could socialize with some of the other campers. He carefully backed the car into the spot and slowly made his way to the trunk to set up camp.

Immediately he noticed the group camping next to the spot he had chosen was quite loud and appeared to be drinking alcohol among other things. He respected people's privacy but at the same time, he felt he may not enjoy himself as much with the carrying on that looked like would be going on.

Newt decided he would head back toward Darrington; the White-Chuck Campground seemed almost empty when he passed it earlier in the day. He jumped back in to his Ford and headed east and then north along the Mountain Loop Highway back in the direction of Darrington.

*   *   *

At around 1:30 PM, Nick and Phil drove in to town and picked up a half gallon of McNaughtons and some more beer. Both of them were sick of cooking and they decided to grab lunch at the Burger Barn. After lunch they grabbed some more supplies, anxious to get back to their campground.

"Where's that fucking bottle?" Phil asked as he sat down in the seat of the Lancer.

He was in no mood for Nick's anti-Vietnam, anti-war bullshit today. He just wanted to get fucked up and forget about it.

Phil reached behind the seat as Nick closed the door to the car. He pulled the half gallon bottle out and split the tape seal on the bottle. He unscrewed the cap and took a huge drink off the bottle.

"Fuck, be careful, man. I don't want a run in with that cop again. Alright?" Nick cautioned.

He pulled the Lancer out on to the highway and turned right back toward their camp a few miles up the road. After eating lunch Nick felt kind of home sick. Having quit his job on somewhat of a whim, it was now Monday; the weekend camping trip was going on its fourth day and it seemed Phil had no designs on ending it any time soon. He could still tell that Phil was pissed, but he didn't exactly know what he had done wrong.

"When do you want to head back?" Nick finally asked just as the highway turned from asphalt to gravel.

"Head back?!" Phil laughed.

"Yeah, I mean, I have to look for work and shit; you know? How much longer do you want to stay?" Nick asked again.

Phil sat in the seat somewhat silent. He gazed out the window at the forest as he pulled a cigarette out and lit it.

"I don't know," Phil said softly.

Nick now felt uncomfortable. He didn't mean to upset Phil but he really had to start thinking about what he was going to do now that he quit his job. Phil's parents were rich; he didn't have much to worry about.

A few minutes later they pulled in to the campground. Phil had been hitting the bottle every few minutes and it seemed almost a third of the bottle was already gone. Under the bridge past the campground they could see a blue Toyota Landcruiser parked near the river. Two men were now fishing just past the bridge.

"*What the fuck!*" Phil exclaimed when he noticed the vehicle and the two men.

"What? What's wrong?" Nick asked as he steered the car next to their camp spot and parked.

"Fucking people here. *Fuck!*" Phil said disappointingly.

Who cares man? They are just fishing, it doesn't look like they are camping or nothin'," Nick observed.

"Yeah but I kind of wanted to see if…see if them grouse would come back in to camp so I could shoot 'em. But if there's a bunch of people around. *Fuck,*" Phil continued.

He took another hit off the bottle.

"*Fucking assholes,*" Phil stated.

Phil was getting pretty drunk Nick thought.

"Fuck it. Let's just go fishing up beyond them. We can fish here just as much as they can. Fuck 'em!" Phil yelled in the car and pointed toward the bridge.

The two of them grabbed their fishing gear and hiked up the road beyond the bridge where the two men were fishing. About 100 yards past the bridge they settled in along the pool they had fished in before.

Every fifteen minutes or so they set their poles down and returned to the half gallon of McNaughtons. Within a couple of hours Phil, who had taken nearly three or four shots to each one of Nick's, was severely intoxicated. Nick decided they should cut back a little and suggested they return to the camp and have a couple of beers and just relax. They gathered up their poles and hiked back down toward the bridge.

The two men who were fishing stood quietly under the bridge.

"Hey, how's it goin'….you fuckers," Phil said to one of the two men.

Both of them just glanced at each other and continued fishing.

"You guys wanna' a…you guys want a *fuckin'* drink?" Phil asked again and extended the bottle toward the man closest to him. His arm swayed gently.

"Come on Phil; let's just go to the camp," Nick argued.

Nick reached out to grab Phil by the arm but Phil jerked his arm away.

"*Fuck that!*" he said, "Have a drink with me, *you fuckers!* Have a drink with a *fucking soldier!*"

The two men looked at each other again and realized Phil was very intoxicated. They were about ready to leave anyway and reeled in their lines.

"Come on Phil; just don't worry about it, man," Nick demanded gain.

"Your friend's had a little too much, maybe?" one of the men said to Nick.

"Yeah, maybe. He just got back from 'Nam. Well, a year ago I mean," Nick answered.

"That's too bad," one of them replied sympathetically.

"*Fuck you!*" Phil said as Nick began pulling him toward the camp, "Too bad? *Fuck you…pussies.*"

Phil looked back at the two men as they packed up their Landcruiser. He gave them an evil stare.

"Fuck you," Phil said again mostly under his breath.

Nick and Phil sat down near the camp site and set the bottle of McNaughtons down on the table. Phil stared toward the other end of the campground where he hoped to go shoot the grouse. He saw a Ford Galaxy nosed in to the parking lot and an older gentleman unpacking his camping gear.

"What the... what the *fuck*?" Phil said out loud.

He stared down toward the old man.

"Take it easy man, it's a fucking campground. What did you expect?" Nick asked him nervously.

"Some fucking respect. Some...I fucking served my country....I fucking served...and these fucking...and these assholes."

Phil grabbed his shotgun and cracked it open. Nick jumped up and stepped between Phil's line of sight with the other campground and Phil.

"What the fuck man, calm down! It's a public place. Jesus, Phil!" Nick exclaimed.

Phil placed a round in the shotgun and took a deep breath.

"It's fucking hot out man, let's just go check out those other campgrounds and then go back up to the bridge and go swimming or something, we can take the bottle," Nick said looking for anything to divert Phil's attention away from the old man.

"Fine," Phil said almost falling over, "But we're bringin' the fuckin' gun. No one is swimmin' in our spot."

Phil took a few steps back toward the car.

"And I'm *shootin'* a fuckin' *grouse*," he continued, slurring his words.

He pointed up at the sky.

"If I fuckin' see one."

Nick really didn't want Phil to bring the shotgun with him, but it seemed the only way he was going to get Phil to just walk away. Phil was really drunk. A little swimming in the Sauk would hopefully sober him up enough for him to come to his senses and not be so angry.

Nick pulled the car out of the lot and turned up the highway. Hopefully, Phil would calm down a little.

"Fuck!" Phil yelled, "I forgot the...I forgot the *fucking bottle!* Turn around!"

As they pulled back in to the campground Phil just stared at the old man and a family who had also shown up and was now unpacking their camp gear. Nick left the car running and hopped out to grab the bottle.

"Fuckers," Phil muttered.

Nick jumped back in the car as quick as he could and headed back out to the highway. A few miles up the road they realized the river was no longer along the highway and if they wanted to swim they were going to have to go back so they turned around and returned.

Against Nick's better judgment.

"Stop! I want to ask this old….ask this old geezer if he…" Phil yelled as he jumped out the door and walked over to the old man's camp.

Nick just sat in the car wondering what in the hell Phil wanted with that old man. A minute later Phil returned to the car and plopped in to the front seat.

"Fuck him," Phil said looking in the back seat.

After parking the car, they walked up to the bridge and sat down on the rocks next to the river. The bridge was far enough around the corner that Phil and Nick could no longer see the camp area.

For an hour or so they sat on the shore drinking the McNaughtons and stepping in to the cool river water. Both of them slowed down on the drinking a little and began to collect themselves. Phil still seemed mad. Mad at something.

A few minutes later Phil took off running with the shotgun.

"Let's jump off the bridge!" Phil remarked as he jumped up and climbed on to the edge. He clutched the shotgun and continued out toward the middle of the river.

Nick followed him, cautiously.

Phil unclipped his shell belt and set the shotgun down next to the edge of the overhang. He stumbled and nearly tripped. His foot hit the shotgun and it jumped toward the edge. He reached and grabbed it while his other foot hit the shell belt. One half of the shell belt dangled over the water below. Phil glanced down to see what he had just stepped on; as he shuffled his feet he knocked the belt completely in the water.

All of the ammo was gone.

"FUCK!" Phil yelled. *"FUCK!"*

He looked at Nick with fire in his eyes.

"What happened? What is it?" Nick asked from about 15 feet away.

"I dropped the fucking shells in the water. Goddamit!" Phil yelled.

"No biggie, man. We can't hunt here anymore anyway. That old man is here. Let's just drink, man and chill you know?" Nick suggested.

Nick was relieved the shells had fallen in the water. But he didn't dare show it.

"NO… *wait*," Phil said picking up the shotgun.

A huge grin crept across his face.

"I got one in the...I got one in the chamber still. I'm gonna' kill a fucking... a fuckin' grouse... and no one... is going to stop me! *GARRYOWEN!*"

4

Newt unpacked his supplies and slid in to the weathered picnic table.

All of the camp spots were empty except the last one. He shook his head in disdain when he noticed the camp table at the only other occupied site was littered with empty food wrappers and beer bottles. Next to the fire pit he could see more beer bottles and trash in the bushes where the breeze had distributed them. He figured if they left it that way he would go clean it up once they left.

His stomach growled.

It was time for an early supper and then he wanted to sit back at the table and enjoy his book. The weather was so nice he decided he might just stay a few extra days and start exploring the North Cascades National Park a little tomorrow or Wednesday. The park had been created only five years earlier and he was excited to see what it had in store.

At the other end of the campground he heard a couple of voices and noticed Phil and Nick returning from their swim at the bridge. One of them appeared to be carrying a shotgun.

What in the world is he doing with a gun?

Newt looked back at the family who was now settling in. Something was definitely wrong with the trailer. Two men were unpacking tools and a jack from the back of an International.

As Phil and Nick approached, Phil suddenly stopped and stood fully upright. As drunk as he was his momentum nearly carried him over backwards.

"*Bullshit,*" Phil said.

Nick looked up at what had gotten Phil's attention and noticed the trailer and large family that had moved in beyond the old man's camp.

"Fuck this... I got one more ... I got one more shell. *Grouse.* I'm gonna' shoot a... fuckin' grouse. If they all don't like it...*fuck...* maybe they should just *fucking leave,*" Phil said sounding very irritated.

"Jesus, man. Just let it go. We don't need a grouse," Nick argued.

"No one is going to tell me," Phil fired back, "I *fucking served-*"

Phil jumped right up in to Nick's face and violently shoved him in the chest, his sledgehammer like forearms sent Nick tumbling backwards nearly eight feet. Nick caught his balance just before he nearly tripped and went on to his face.

That was it. Nick had had enough. He didn't know why Phil was so pissed or why he thought everyone wasn't giving him the respect he deserved. He no longer cared. He'd hitchhike to Darrington and call someone if he had to. This was bullshit.

"You no what? *Fuck you man.* I am not going to have anything to do with it. You are just going to piss a bunch of people off, you know what I mean. But go ahead, you go...there ain't gonna' be any grouse over there any way. I'm gonna' go fishing," Nick yelled back.

Phil opened the door to his car and the dog jumped in to the backseat.

"*Fuck you*....you'll fucking see. *Fuck you,*" Phil hollered after him.

Phil turned and looked at the dog.

"Stay!" he yelled and slammed the car door shut.

Phil cradled the shotgun in his arms and slowly approached where the two men were working on the broken trailer. As Phil approached he could make out the two men whispering to each other and he knew they must have been talking about him and didn't want him to hear. He knew the gun made them nervous.

Fuck 'em.

When people got a little nervous he tried to come across as overly friendly so as to throw their fears right back in to their faces.

Or so he figured.

"Hey, how is it... *how's it* going?" Phil asked with a big smile on his face.

"Oh, eh—yeah," one of the men muttered under his breath, hoping Phil would pick up on the idea that they did not want to interact with him at all and if they appeared uninterested enough that he would keep on going.

The man with the gun smelled drunk.

"I said—Hi! How's it *fuckin'*.....How's it going?" Phil repeated, this time a little louder and closer.

"Flat tire, eh?" Phil continued, obnoxiously leaning in right where the men were working.

Both men stared up at Phil and stopped working. They exchanged glances and one of the men walked off toward the other trailer. The older of the two wiped his hands with the rag resting on the jack and stood upright, directly facing Phil.

"Hi there, I am Bob," he extended his arm to shake Phil's hand.

Phil just stared at him and peered down at the axle.

"That sucks, man," Phil replied.

"Eh...," he said, turning back toward the trailer, uninterested in the young man with the shotgun.

The day before, Bob and his family had been camping at the Red Bridge Campground about nine miles up the road. Red Bridge Campground seemed a fantastic place to unwind from the stresses of modern life. Time with friends and family was a treasure, and as a shift supervisor for Fluke Manufacturing, Bob knew this well.

The campground at Red Bridge was set along the Stillaguamish River in a rain forest like setting. Levitating between the mossy green branches of cedar and pine across the waterborne stones of the riverbed, the bridge crossing the river served as a scenic backdrop to this forested hideaway. They decided to move over to this camp spot on the Sauk River after seeing it on their way in to Darrington for propane.

Inside, Bob's three year old daughter Kara chirped and giggled as she pushed toys around the floor of the Traveleze trailer. Outside in the warmth of the late afternoon sunshine, his wife Tamia shuffled sleeping bags around the back of the fully packed International Travel-All and made small talk with Bob's 15 year old sister, Kathy.

Across the parking lot, his parents unpacked groceries from their Pontiac sedan. His parents had driven from Klamath Falls, Oregon and were ready for a calm, low stress vacation. He just needed to get this trailer straightened out.

"Seen any....seen any grouse?" Phil asked.

"No—but I don't even think its grouse season is it?" the man asked.

"We eat everything we kill—it's no biggie. Did you see that deer I got?" Phil pointed toward the camp spot where the old man had moved in next to.

Bob continued to appear as disinterested as he could.

"Do you guys hunt?" Phil continued.

"Nope."

Not wanting to engage anymore with the kid with the gun, Bob stated he did not. Hoping the conversation would just end and that Phil would move on.

"That's too bad. Grouse are good eatin'. *Don't you think?...* I've already killed one... and cooked and eatin' it. There were some over there, yesterday," Phil again pointed toward the old man's camp, "but he moved in and probably chased them all out. *Fucker.*"

"This isn't a real good place to hunt," Bob said as he bent back down to work on the axle.

Phil continued to stand behind Bob, somewhat off balance he slowly swayed back and forth.

"Eh...it's cool. I just got back... back from 'Nam. *I stalked that deer like a fucking-*" Phil pointed toward the tree again.

"There's a lot of kids around and people camping, maybe you should head up the road and hunt," Bob continued as the young man who had gone off to the trailer returned, not saying anything to Phil.

"Yeah, that's what...what the old man said. *Fuck him,*" Phil replied in a more direct tone.

The two men continued to try and ignore Phil.

"Yeah," Phil teetered and nearly fell over, "my old man was in dubya dubya...*two.*"

The two men working on the trailer shared a nervous glance with each other and kept on working.

"Good luck," one of them said.

Phil stood there, towering over the two kneeling men. He gripped the shotgun tighter and took a deep breath.

He knew what they wanted.

They wanted him to leave. They had no intentions of being friendly. A couple of assholes who think they own the campground.

I was here first Phil thought to himself.

The men continued working deliberately not looking up at Phil. Phil began to get madder and madder. He turned away from the two men and took a few steps toward the other camp spot.

He stopped and stood motionless for a minute. He looked down at the safety on the shotgun. He closed his eyes and took another deep breath. He opened his eyes and turned back toward the two men.

"Have a good night," he said in the most polite voice he could muster and began to walk away in the direction of the old man's camp.

*   *   *

Under the bridge near the creek Nick just sat throwing rocks into the churning water. He reached down and grabbed his beer and took a swig.

Fuck.

He couldn't believe Phil was going to go shoot grouse in the campground with all those people there.

What a stupid idea.

Who cares if the old man took the spot next to us? It was a free country, couldn't he camp there also? And those other people, with the broken trailer, there were kids running around.

How drunk was Phil anyway?

He took another swig of beer. The deer hanging in the tree was just too much. Surely someone would call the police, it wasn't even deer season.

This was a bad idea.

Fuck.

Up at the old man's camp, Newt wrestled through his pack looking for the mini can opener he always carried with him. It was nearly time for dinner and it was easier to cook in the last light of the day then to fumble for matches, utensils and other things under the light of a flashlight.

In days past Newt had always brought a gas lantern and a full complement of cooking and eating ware. But, as he got older, he realized he needed less and less to get the job done and proper planning and execution was more effective than carrying 200 extra pounds of equipment with him.

He had cut the deer down out of the tree a while ago so the little kids in the trailer next door didn't have to stare at it. He had nothing against hunting, but he figured a little discretion should be used when displaying game animals, but the fact that the season wasn't even open bothered him more. And in the heat of the summer, the deer had already begun to putrefy. It was completely wasted. It seemed the younger generation of campers and outdoors people had no regard for the rules. Sure, when he was a boy the rules weren't really needed, there were tons of game, tons of space and a lot fewer people. But after World War II the population began to explode, and now all these kids were old enough to head out and flood the outdoors. Everything would be fine, he thought, if they would just use *some common sense.*

Newt found the can opener and moved back to his table to open the can of pork and beans. He peeled the lid back and poured them into the small pan sitting on the Coleman stove next to him. He pulled off his wire rimmed glasses and tore off a small paper towel to wipe them clean.

Across the camp he saw the young man with the shotgun standing with his back to the two men working on the trailer. He looked toward the other trailer to see if the kids were playing about, it made him nervous that someone was going to hunt right here in the campground. There were thousands of acres to hunt up road, why the hell would he do it here?

And with kids around.

He glanced over to his Galaxy and got up from the table, he noticed the windows were down and he didn't want the front seats to get wet should an unexpected rain squall come through the area.

The two men working on the trailer stopped what they were doing for just a moment and watched Phil, who was now about halfway over to the old man's camp.

"Did you put my .38 where I told you?" Bob asked.

"Yeah—it's right inside the door on the floor. I told them all to just stay inside. They're kind of scared, but I told 'em it was just a good idea. No need to get involved with that guy anymore than we have to," the younger man replied.

"Well we should be able to get this wrapped up and then just move to another spot. I know its going to be dark soon, but I would rather just move, there are too many camp spots up here to deal with this guy," Bob said as he reached for the ratchet lying under the axle.

"What about the old guy, you think he'll be alright?" the younger one asked.

"I am sure he has seen his fair share of this sort of thing. Maybe the kid will just decide to go drink the night away and put the gun away for the night. I talked to him a little while ago, I am sure he'll be fine," Bob replied.

Phil reached down into his pants pocket and pulled out another beer. He nearly dropped the shotgun as he opened it. He was going to kill a grouse for dinner whether these assholes liked it or not.

Fuck them.

He only had one shell left anyway.

Where the fuck did Nick go? Asshole.

He shotgunned the beer.

And how dare that old man cut my deer down?

He stumbled forward.

I'll fucking hunt wherever I want to.

He headed toward the old man's campsite.

I'll kill wherever I want. I served my fucking country.

Fuck that old man.

The younger man peeked up from the trailer and saw Phil making a straight path for the old man's campsite. It looked as though he was almost running.

"Hey. Hey," he tapped Bob's knee and pointed toward the old man's campsite, "look at this—what's he doing?" he asked.

Phil strode right up to the old man sitting cross legged at his camp table. The beans were nearly coming to a boil as the propane stove sizzled. Newt put down the book he was reading and peered up at Phil.

"You know hunting season is closed!" Newt said sternly to the young man standing at his table, "and can't you put your deer somewhere where we don't have to look at it? It's bad enough that you poached it. I don't care about that; but use some common sense young man."

Phil could barely stand without tipping.

"Hey man, just wanted to see… to see if you wanted a drink or somethin'. You know where the good fishin' is?" Phil asked.

"NO. I don't want a drink. Maybe *you* should drink somewhere else. And keep it down," Newt responded.

"Fuck you. Man." Phil said with a deadly tone. "*Fuck you.* We were camped here earlier and you just…we were *fucking*…moved in. You saw the deer hangin' why didn't you…fuck you…. just pick another spot? *FUCK YOU!*"

The men working on the trailer dropped what they were doing and stood up looking toward the old man's campground, one of them darted for the trailer and threw the door open.

"Stay inside!" he shouted, "DO NOT COME OUT HERE UNTIL I SAY!" and he slammed the trailer door shut.

"What he is he pointing that gun at?!" the woman in the trailer screamed as the trailer door slammed shut.

"Fuck you! Old man. Fuck YOU!" Phil shouted.

He raised the shotgun up toward Newt.

Newt's eyes opened wide up.

His jaw dropped open; he could not believe the young man in the camo pants was pointing the shotgun at him. He knew he meant it and he dove off to the side of the camp table he was sitting on and screamed out. His hands hit the pine needle covered forest floor as the shotgun blast deafened his ears and everything slowed down to a mesmerizing crawl.

BOOM!

It seemed time had stopped as the momentum from the dive off the table carried him away from the kid with the gun. In the next second he saw the glow from the lantern swirling in and out of the green branches above, he remembered Alaska and fishing, he remembered climbing up Ayers rock in Australia, he thought about the children he never had and the friends he had made and the things he had witnessed in this most amazing century of mans existence on this planet.

He wished he hadn't gone camping.

His ears rang and went suddenly silent as the pellets from the shotgun blast tore through his torso. Like a really bad cramp, he winced and cried out; and then it was quiet. He saw the clouds above him and heard the river rushing in the distance.

He couldn't move.

He couldn't breathe.

He couldn't talk.

He just laid there. His ears ringing. He tried to raise his arms to crawl into the brush, like a wounded animal trying to escape what he knew was coming.

His arms didn't move.

Light headed and dizzy, he struggled again to get his chest to move up and down, he was suffocating, it felt like warm water was stuck in his throat and he wanted to cough it out but couldn't. His intestines hung out of his ripped up torso and his right elbow stung like a thousand bees had gotten him all at once. His vision was blurry without his horn rimmed glasses but he saw a figure standing over him and looking down at him.

The kid's jaw was clenched tightly.

It was the young man in the camo pants with the shotgun.

What was he doing here?

Newt drew in a breath and could barely muster enough energy to force it out.

Down by the river Nick jerked his head up when he heard the shot.

What the fuck?

He labored to stand up, he was still pretty drunk. A shot of adrenaline raced through his body.

Did Phil really go grouse hunting with all those people around?

Phil bent down and grabbed the old man by the collar and turned him on to his back. He could feel the old man's warm skin and bristled hairs between his neck and wool shirt. Air rushed from Newt's lungs and he tried to groan. Phil began dragging him; his mangled and shattered arm trailed along like a limp dish rag. Pain encompassed his entire body. He squinted and tried to grasp what was happening, but Newt was confused and disoriented. A few feet behind the tent, Phil released his grip on the old man's collar; Newt's head and shoulders fell to the earth and bounced into a disfigured slump. In the brush a few yards further, Phil pitched the shotgun.

One of the men from the trailer came toward Phil with something in his hand.

"Where's the old man?" he yelled.

Phil looked over at the man and cupped his hand to his ear, "What sir? I can't...I can't hear you."

"You better get those hands in the air!" Bob yelled at Phil.

"He's right here…, he's ok," Phil answered as he raised his hands into the air and took a step toward the man approaching him.

The man stopped and asked again, "Where's the old man. Let me see him. Have him step out."

"Sir, I don't know what your…*what your fucking* problem is," he took another step toward the man from the trailer, "let's just talk."

"What was that gunshot?" Bob asked.

"I shot a grouse," Phil answered.

His voice was quickly becoming more coherent.

The woman in the trailer and a young girl poured out of the door and ran for the car parked on the other side. She labored with the keys and the car roared to life.

"Let me see the old man," he demanded a third time and fired the pistol into the air.

"Whoa!" Phil yelled, "What's the problem here, man?"

The car backed up quickly, jerked to a skidding stop and then roared off toward the exit of the campground and turned up the gravel highway. The engine roared in the distance and faded.

Newt lay on his side in the brush. Blood filled his throat and he could barely breathe. He gently coughed and pain shot through his insides like razors in a blender. Blood ran down the side of his cheek and pooled gently in the pine needles his face had come to rest in. His chest gently twitched uncontrollably.

The fingers in his left hand opened and closed attempting to grip something that wasn't there. The sky was a beautiful blue above him.

He closed his eyes again, *someone help me. I need help.*

"What did you shoot?!" Bob demanded, leveling the pistol at Phil.

"I didn't shoot anything," Phil said, "I don't know what you're talking about?"

"I heard a shot, now you know what I'm talking about. WHERE IS THE OLD MAN?" he demanded again, "You just lie down, right there in the road. AND DO NOT MOVE."

Near the river, Nick called the dog into the car and fumbled for the keys.

What the fuck were those shots?

He tossed the half empty beer toward the creek and turned the car around to head up the gravel path where he heard the shots. As Nick came around the corner he could see Phil lying chest down in the road and one of the men from the trailer standing about 25 feet away.

It looked like he had a gun pointed at Phil.

Nick jammed the car into reverse and backed down the gravel path away from the scene and out of sight.

Holy shit.

The man stared down the road at the blue Lancer and wondered what the fuck is he doing?

He gripped the pistol tightly and looked around for cover.

Did the other kid have a gun, too?

Was he parking the car and sneaking this way?

This wasn't good. His family was huddled in the trailer and if this guy showed up with another shotgun he'd be outgunned and his family were sitting ducks in the trailer.

My god.

Nick sat silent in the car. What the fuck is going on?

Nick was confused. *Did that guy shoot Phil?*

His hands gripped the steering wheel and started to sweat. He smacked his forehead down on to the steering wheel. There was no other way out of the campground.

Shit.

He wondered what to do. He looked at the dog who just stared back.

Nick threw the car into drive, it was time to see what was going on, he could drive up right behind Phil and just ask; if anything went down he could dive back in to the car.

He slowly crept up the gravel path, Phil came into view lying in the middle of the road, it looked as though he was holding his head up and talking to the other man. He stopped right before he got to Phil and opened the door slowly.

"Hey, what's going on?" he hollered toward Phil and the man holding the pistol.

"Ask your partner!" the man yelled back.

"No, seriously! What's going on?" Nick cried back.

"Ask your partner," the man replied again, sounding more irritated than before.

"And get out of that car where I can see you!" he yelled at Nick.

Nick peered down at Phil and then glanced over at the dog; he looked down at the ground and figured he should probably do what the guy said before he got even madder. He moved away from the car door and began walking toward the man, he searched to his right at the old man's camp and saw no sign of the old man.

"Get down!" the man with the gun yelled.

Bob's hand trembled a little bit, just for a second. He took a deep breath and steadied his arm with his other hand.

"Hey, you shoot me, you're in trouble. I'm clean," Nick said to the man and pulled his coat away showing he wasn't carrying any sort of weapon.

Nick stepped at an angle toward the old man's camp to see if he could see the old man anywhere.

"Hey man, I just want to talk to you for a minute, what happened?" Nick asked again.

"Stop right there!" Bob yelled at Nick.

Nick looked over at the man and changed the direction of his walk from the old man's camp toward the man. He glanced over at Phil for some sign of what to do. Phil had now laid his head down sideways in the gravel.

The man cocked the pistol.

Nick immediately froze and sat down on a log.

"Where's the gun?" the man asked.

"What gun, man? I was just fishing. Down there," Nick pointed in the direction of the river.

"The police will have to look for the gun," Phil said as he lifted his head from the gravel and looked menacingly toward the man.

Nick asked the man for a smoke. The man ignored him and kept his eyes fixed on Phil and then on him; and then back to Phil. Nick sensed the man was getting very nervous.

"Hey man, can I have a cigarette, please? *Fuck,*" Nick pleaded again.

Bob tossed him a lighter and his pack of smokes. Nick took one from the pack and lit it.

"Can I have a smoke too, sir?" Phil asked.

"Sure, but you--" the man pointed toward Nick, "You take them over to him."

Nick stood up from the log and stared at the man, slowly he moved over next to Phil, Phil smiled at him and Nick again looked at the man.

Bob extended the pistol directly at them and a somber look came across his face. This made Nick nervous. He focused again at Phil and offered out a cigarette from the pack and lit it for Phil. Nick sat next to Phil in the road.

"Can I sit up, too? Sir?" Phil asked.

"Go ahead, but slow. I'm just scared enough to shoot somebody. This pistol is trained right on you—one of you moves fast and I'll shoot you!"

Bob wanted to go over to the old man's camp and see if he was badly injured. The way Newt yelled when the shotgun went off didn't sound good. But he could be over there, lying down and dying. But he feared the two young guys would try and run off, and if they had more guns in the car or back at their camp they could come back and kill everyone who saw what was going on.

Hang on old man, hang on.

Newt struggled to breathe; he tried to turn his head but couldn't move anything. His chest was twitching less and less. The sky darkened as he drifted in and out.

It was cold.

Incredibly cold.

He wanted a blanket. He tried to cough and became more and more light headed. He was scared and very, very tired.

In the distance, the waters of the Sauk turned dark. The branches of the cedar and hemlock trees hung low, and the lone raven which pranced and soared along the treetops all afternoon looking for its mate let out a chilling scream and flew east toward the mountains, alone.

An hour or so later a Snohomish County sheriff patrol car pulled into the campground. Bob stepped away from the two young men and they got up and moved toward the officer and the forest Ranger that was with him.

It was nearly dark.

"There's a man dead or close to it over there," Bob said as he lowered his pistol, "and that one over there shot him."

He pointed at Phil.

The sheriff's deputy brought Phil over to the patrol car, handcuffed him and placed him in the rear seat. He then took Nick off to the side and began asking him what was going on? Bob turned his pistol over to the sheriff deputy and went over to Newt to check his pulse.

Nothing.

Newt had died.

5

Homicide detectives Lee Trunkhill and Doug Engelbretson showed up on the scene about 45 minutes later and found Phil asleep in the back of a Snohomish County patrol car. The sun was dropping below the horizon as darkness was beginning to settle in between the trees along the Sauk.

At some point Phil vomited in the back of the car.

It was 9:27 PM.

They awoke him and Detective Trunkhill identified himself and introduced the other detectives.

"I am Detective Trunkhill, this is Detective Bemis and this is Detective Engelbretson."

Detective Trunkhill removed the handcuffs from Phil and sat in the backseat with him. Phil rubbed his wrists and stretched. Detective Bemis sat in the front seat and Detective Engelbretson squatted outside the rear door of the patrol car to dictate Phil's answers to the questions Detective Trunkhill was about to ask him.

"You are under arrest for first degree murder. OK? Let me repeat so I know you understand; you are under arrest for first degree murder. Do you understand?" Trunkhill asked Phil.

"Yes," he answered with a startled look on his face.

"What is your name, son?"

"Phillip Van Hillman."

"How old are you?"

"20."

"I want you to pay close attention. I am going to advise you of your constitutional rights."

Detective Trunkhill read Phil his rights from the standard form and asked Phil if he understood. Phil indicated that he did.

"What did I just advise you?" Trunkhill asked.

"You said I could remain silent; I could have an attorney and that if I couldn't get one that you would provide me one," Phil answered somewhat unamused by the situation.

Trunkhill handed him the form outlining his constitutional rights and asked Phil to sign it if he understood. Phil signed the form.

On the other side of the campground, sheriff deputies began setting up battery powered floodlights around Newt's camp. Near the entrance to the campground a patrol car blocked the entrance; it's red and blue lights danced and reflected off the trees.

"Ok, so do you know what day it is and what time it is?"

"It's July 22, 1974 and it's about 9:30 PM," Phil answered.

Detective Engelbretson peeked at his wristwatch and noted that it was 9:32 PM. Phil was only two minutes off.

"We'd like to ask you some questions, is that ok?"

"Sure," Phil answered.

"You understand you are being charged with murder in the first degree, right? Do you still want to talk with us?"

"Sure—no problem," Phil answered. He did his best to act as though nothing was wrong.

"What's your name? Can you spell it for us?" the detective asked.

Phil spelled out his first, last and middle name.

"What's you're address and phone number?"

Phil looked at the detectives and slowly dictated the information for detectives. His head was pounding and he felt somewhat disoriented. He was starting to sober up and really needed a beer.

"And your date of birth?"

"March 8, 1954," he answered.

This was going to be easy, he thought. They don't even care that old man's dead.

"So how old are you?" Detective Trunkhill continued.

"20," Phil answered.

He looked out of the back window of the patrol to see if he could see Nick. Over near the old man's camp a number of deputies and a couple of other men wearing green windbreakers stood around in a circle where he had drug Newt off in to the bushes behind his tent.

Nick was nowhere to be seen.

"Where do you work?" Trunkhill asked.

"I don't right now. I was working at the Food Giant on 45th, in Seattle, right by my house."

"Any arrests in the past? Any trouble with the law before?"

"No sir."

Trunkhill wanted to establish that Phil was coherent and understood what was happening. He paused for a second.

"Do you know what day it is?" Trunkhill asked.

"Yeah, it's July 22, 1974. And it's about 9:30 or ten," Phil smiled.

Trunkhill made a note on the edge of his pad.

"Are you in the armed services?"

"No, I've been out over a year now," Phil answered.

That was the question he had been waiting for. He sat back in the seat and relaxed.

"So when did you last have the shotgun?" Trunkhill questioned. He looked away from Phil so as not to alert him as to the importance of the question.

"I had it earlier in the day," Phil remembered.

"And where is it now?"

"I don't remember where it is now," Phil answered.

Detective Trunkhill was not amused.

"Ok. I would think if you had a shotgun earlier, you might keep a little better track of it. But that's ok. I am sure it will turn up," Trunkhill said.

Phil shifted in the seat and itched his neck.

"Is the car yours? Is it in the trunk of the car, maybe?" Trunkhill pressed.

"Yeah, it's my car. But I don't think it's in the trunk," Phil answered.

Detective Trunkhill reached in to his briefcase and pulled out a form.

"Well, I have a form here that if you are willing to give us permission to search the car you can just sign it. Of course, anything we find in the car can and will be used against you in court," Trunkhill informed him as he handed him the form.

"I don't care. I'll sign that- you can search the car," Phil said.

Trunkhill wanted to make sure Phil was in a sound enough mental state to sign the form so he asked him his age again. Phil again said he was 20.

"Ok, what's the year and model of your car?"

"It's a '63 Lancer."

"And the license number?"

"I don't honestly know it," Phil grinned.

54

"And again, you understand that anything found in the car can be used against you in a court of law?"

"Yes. I know," Phil answered.

"What kind of gun is it? A pistol... a rifle...?"

"It's a shotgun."

"What kind of shotgun is it?" Trunkhill asked.

"It's a 12 gauge but I don't remember the brand name."

Trunkhill continued to scribble across his pad. Phil looked around again for Nick. The lights were on in the trailer where the man with the gun had come from.

"Is it a pump or a double barrel or?"

"It's a single shot."

"Oh yeah? So let me ask you, what kind of rounds are you using in it? Buckshot? Slugs?" Trunkhill quizzed.

"I use #6 shot. But I'm out of them."

"So you haven't even shot the gun today?"

"No."

Trunkhill flipped the page he was writing on to the back and continued.

"So have you guys smoked any dope or had anything to drink today?"

"No, we didn't smoke any dope but we did have a few beers. I think...maybe...four?" Phil answered.

"Where are you guys camped?"

"We're camped down by the bridge. You might not have seen it because we don't have a tent or anything just our sleeping bags," Phil pointed out.

"How long have you guys been camping here?"

"Since Friday."

"Have you been smoking any pot or using any other drugs?" Trunkhill continued.

"No we haven't been smoking grass or anything. Just beer. And yesterday we had some McNaughtons," Phil responded.

He was getting irritated that this was taking so long.

Trunkhill made a few more notes on his pad and turned in the seat to face Phil.

"So. Why don't you tell me what happened tonight?" Trunkhill asked.

"I don't know. That guy back there pointed his gun at me and told me to 'freeze'," Phil stated pointing out the front of the patrol car toward the trailer.

"Well, did you shoot your shotgun?"

"Oh no. We did not shoot at all today. I mean...we shot some branches off of the trees. But that was yesterday," Phil assured him.

"So, what are you guys doing up here, what have you been doing?"

Phil grinned, "Just livin' off the fat o' the land."

Phil sat back in the seat and began shaking his head.

"You know; I don't even understand what I'm being charged with," Phil claimed.

"Well, as I stated before, and I'll inform you again; you are being charged with first degree murder," Trunkhill responded in a very clear and concise tone of voice.

"Jesus Christ! That's pretty serious!" Phil exclaimed.

His mannerisms and movements accelerated. He shifted in the seat and seemed visibly stressed. This wasn't going to be as easy to get out of as getting caught with a case of beer.

"Have you done any speed or anything like that today?" Trunkhill continued.

"No," Phil said emphatically.

"Had any 'blackouts' or anything like that?"

"*No!*"

"Can you tell me about the argument you had with the old man?" Trunkhill quizzed.

"What? I didn't have an argument with the old man!" Phil stated.

His armpits were beginning to become noticeably perspired. He continued to move and shift side to side in the back. His neck really itched.

"I wouldn't murder anybody; that's wicked!" he decried.

"You wouldn't *kill anything?*"

"Well, I might kill an animal or something like that."

Phil looked down into the blackness where his feet were. He sat there silently as Trunkhill paused.

"So, what's your friend's name?"

"His name is Nick. Nick Hansen."

Trunkhill continued to question Phil about where Nick lived and where Phil's mother lived. He asked Detective Engelbretson to notate that Phil had alcohol on his breath.

"Did you fire the shotgun toward anyone today?"

"No. Absolutely not."

"Did Nick maybe, fire it toward anyone today?"

"I don't *think* he has," Phil answered.

Detective Bemis shook his head and made eye contact with Trunkhill.

"Did Nick fire the gun *at all* today?" Trunkhill continued.

"No, I don't think he did," Phil answered again.

On of the deputies appeared at the patrol car and asked Detective Trunkhill if he could speak with him. Detective Trunkhill climbed out of the backseat and handed the questioning off to Detective Engelbretson.

"Ok, so how many beers did you have today?" Detective Engelbretson began.

"I had about six or seven beers."

"Did you have them all at once or …about how often?"

"They were pretty much evenly spaced throughout the day," Phil answered.

"Where did you get the beer?"

"We went to town earlier today and got it," Phil replied.

"How did you get beer? You aren't 21?"

"Nick bought it, he's 21," Phil answered.

"So what were you doing down by the old man's camp?" Engelbretson asked.

"I was walking down into here and this guy in a yellow shirt said 'freeze'. I laid down in the road and I didn't argue. He didn't ask me nothin'. He just said 'lay down in the road'."

"And then what happened?"

"Nick came up from the river and that guy told him to lie down in the road also," Phil continued sounding as surprised as he could.

"So where is your car at now?" Engelbretson continued.

"It's still up the road unless someone moved it."

"So tell me about Nick. What's his story?"

"Well, he was working up until a couple days ago; he worked at a place where they made brake shoes," Phil answered.

After sidetracking Phil with questions about Nick he quickly jumped right to the heart of the matter.

"What do you know about the old man getting shot?"

I don't know *anything* about *anyone* getting shot. Except a couple of branches we shot yesterday," Phil answered, again as convincingly as he could.

Detective Trunkhill reappeared and sat back down in the front of the patrol car.

"Well, looks like we found a shotgun, a few feet from the victim, in the bushes," Trunkhill informed them.

Engelbretson jumped on the opportunity.

"Phil, I think you shot that old man. I think you killed him and now that we are going to be able to prove it, why don't you just tell us?!" Engelbretson turned directly at Phil.

"I didn't shoot anyone! I wouldn't shoot an old man like that!" Phil argued.

"Oh yeah? Ready to take a polygraph? Ready to see if you're telling the truth or not? You shot that old man and drug him off into the bushes.

We have two witnesses who *watched you do it*. It's time to come clean about this. It'll be a whole lot easier if you do!" Engelbretson raised his voice.

"Sure! I'll take a polymorph or whatever it's called! I didn't shoot anyone and neither did Nick as far as I know! I didn't drag no old man back into the bushes and sure as hell didn't toss my shotgun back there!"

Phil was now pissed again.

Didn't these guys know he was in Vietnam?

Engelbretson shook his head.

"I'll take a lie detector. *Fuck you!*" Phil yelled back.

"Do you understand you are under arrest for *first degree murder?*" Engelbretson continued trying to put the pressure on Phil.

"Yes. Yes I get that!"

Phil shifted in the seat even more. He looked around outside the car. The lights from the patrol cars illuminated the campground. He could see the family from the trailer standing outside of it with deputies.

"You know what? You got *the wrong guy!*" Phil argued. "And I can hardly wait to go to court and prove it. *Fuck you.*"

Phil was getting madder and madder.

"And I don't know who the right guy is! I didn't hear no shot and I didn't see anybody get shot. This is bullshit."

Detective Engelbretson stood up out of the back of the car. He and Deputy Phil Duggins took nitric acid swabs from Phil's hands and placed him back in the patrol car.

Engelbretson interviewed the family who witnessed the murder and took their statements. He asked them to leave the trailer just as it was so he could process it tomorrow during the daylight.

At 11:25 PM Detective Engelbretson rode the Snohomish County Sheriff helicopter back to Everett to await the arrival of Nick and Phil.

In an interview with Detective Trunkhill in 2013, Trunkhill claimed that before Nick and Phil were transported to the Snohomish County Jail, Detective Trunkhill asked Phil 'Why he did it?' According to Detective Trunkhill, "The young man stated rather coldly, *he wanted to see what it was like to kill someone.*"

After arriving at the Snohomish County Jail, Phil was given a breath analysis to determine his blood-alcohol level. The test was performed at 1:00 AM- more than five hours after Bob Duggan began holding Phil at gunpoint.

Phil's blood-alcohol reading at the time of the test was *.16*.

*   *   *

At 8:00 AM the next morning, Detectives Engelbretson and Trunkhill had Nick brought in to an interview room. He was not being charged with any crime but was being held as a material witness. Engelbretson wanted to question him as quickly as possible and lead Nick back and forth through different parts of the story to see if he could trip him up in any way. It was possible Nick was an accessory to murder but they didn't quite know yet.

"You are not being charged with a crime at this time. We are holding you as a material witness. Would you talk with me without an attorney present?" Detective Engelbretson began.

"Yeah, sure, I have nothing to hide," Nick answered.

Detective Engelbretson was tired but used to the long hours.

"Ok, so why don't you just tell me what happened."

"Well, the other day we drove in to the camp and Phil got out and talked to the old man," Nick began.

"What was said?"

"I don't know; I just waited in the car," Nick answered.

"So we left and then we turned back around and went back and Phil said he wanted to talk to him again, I think he was going to grouse hunt but I don't know for sure," Nick explained.

Nick shifted in his seat.

"I went down to the river and then I heard a shot and a noise like an old man screaming or something," Nick continued.

Engelbretson continued to jot notes on his tablet.

"So I came back up to the camp and Phil was standing there with his hands in the air," he stated sounding somewhat surprised.

"Ok, let's stop right there for a minute. Let me get some background on you, ok?" Engelbretson asked.

Nick wiped his hand over his face and put his elbows on the table in front of him.

"Any criminal history I need to know of? I mean we're going to run your name so don't start lying to me right now. Be straight with me and I'll help you out of this jam as much as I can, but you have to tell me the truth and you have to tell me everything, ok?" Engelbretson began.

"Well I have a case pending for marijuana possession in Seattle and I had a burglary charge but it was dropped. I mean, Phil is the crazy one. Not me!" Nick sort of laughed as he said it.

"What do you mean?"

"Well, *fuck*. Phil is fucking wild, you know? He's been through Vietnam and shit. I mean, killing would be nothing to him. Sometimes that mother fucker *scares me*...especially with that shotgun," Nick continued.

Nick paused and stared at Detective Engelbretson. The severity of the situation was hitting him. He wanted to believe that Detective Engelbretson was really going to help him, but he knew cops were always trained to be your friend, and then they turn on you. But he had few options. He didn't want to go down for this, this was serious business. Shaking his head, he wondered how in the hell it had gone from some partying in the woods to a fucking dead man so damn fast. He let out a long sigh.

"You know, Phil doesn't know what he's doing some times. I mean, he got high on something out there in the bush…in Vietnam. He *fucking killed people* over there, man; *fuck,*" Nick said as he shook his head and bowed forward into his arms crossed on the table in front of him.

He was exhausted.

"Did you hear what he said to the old man?" Detective Engelbretson asked Nick again to see if he could trip him up.

"No! Like I said. I didn't hear anything, it seemed like the old man was nice, you know? Phil wasn't going back to rob him or anything like that," Nick stated, frustrated.

"So how far were you camped away from the old man?" Engelbretson continued.

"I don't know…maybe a block and a half," Nick answered as he raised his head up from the table and sat backwards in the chair nearly falling.

"Did you ever think Phil was going to harm the old man?"

"NO! Not at all. I mean, he only had one shell," Nick yelled, becoming even more frustrated that this whole situation had elevated so fast.

"How do you know he only had one shell?"

"Because we went swimming a couple hours before and Phil accidentally kicked his shell belt in the water- off the bridge," Nick answered.

"Was that old man alone in his camp?" Nick asked the detectives.

"Yes," Engelbretson answered and quickly moved on to more questions.

"Did you have any idea at all what Phil was going to do when he went to the old man's camp?"

"Again…No! *I thought he was going to shoot a rabbit or grouse or something!*" Nick remarked very adamantly.

"Do you think Phil knew what he was going to do?" Engelbretson asked.

Nick again leaned back in his chair and drew in a deep sigh. He paused and looked toward the ceiling of the interview room.

"Uuehhh….*he must have.* You don't go up and shoot an old man and not know why you do it. Right?" Nick admitted.

60

Detective Engelbretson stood up and walked around the conference table toward Nick.

"What did him and the old man talk about!" Engelbretson asked loudly.

Nick put his hands up out in front of his face and shrunk back away from Engelbretson as though he were going to be beaten like a misbehaving dog.

"*I DON'T KNOW!......Fishing!* Phil said something when he got back about fishing, that's all I remember," Nick cried.

"Did he have the shotgun the first time?"

"Yes! But it wasn't loaded!"

"And the second time?"

"Yes, it was loaded then, I saw him load it!"

Nick was scared.

"I told him I was going fishing and he mumbled something but I couldn't understand it, I didn't really even care what he had said enough to ask him to clarify, I just went down to the river!....I mean, I think he may have said something like he was going to go hunt over by where those people were. *I think?*" Nick shrieked.

"And after you heard the shot? Then *what happened?*"

Nick sat upright again, realizing Detective Engelbretson wasn't going to strike him.

"I saw Phil on the ground with his hands over his head. So I drove the car up and then there was this man with a gun. I mean, he scared the shit out of me. I asked him, 'What's going on?' and I told him not to shoot me, so I started to walk over and the man told me not to come any closer so I asked him again 'what happened?'"

Nick paused. He was nearly out of breath but his words were flowing out of his mouth as fast as he could.

"The guy with the gun wanted to see the old man come out and I just said, 'so where's he at?' And the guy with the gun didn't say anything. I went over by Phil and I asked him, 'what the hell did you do?' and Phil told me 'the old man told me to get fucked.' Or something like that. That's when I figured that Phil must have shot the old man or something," Nick finished.

He paused again and sat shaking his head as he clenched his lips.

"I was really *scared then.* I just stayed on the ground until the cops got there. The guy with the gun just held us there," Nick sated softly.

"Did Phil say anything while you were on the ground?"

"I just asked Phil, 'why in the hell did you have to do something like that?' and Phil just said 'the old man just told me to get fucked.' I mean, I asked that a couple times, I was stunned, but Phil never said nothin' else," Nick answered.

Nick put his elbows back on the table and looked at Trunkhill who was just taking notes.

"Phil has had trouble before, you know? He's got way more serious problems than me. He was in the hospital for trying to kill himself and shit. They kicked him out of the Army for medical reasons- for being on junk. It sucks man. He hasn't got a dad and they just kicked him out of the house so he went in to the Army," Nick continued.

"Where does he live now?"

"He's been with his sister. But, I want you to know- I don't think like he does. Phil...he don't give a shit what he does," Nick stated.

"What do you mean?" Trunkhill asked him as he leaned forward.

"Phil, he goes out and picks fights when he's been drinking. I mean, look at the guy, he knows how strong he is; and when someone gives him attitude he gets mad *real quick*. Like I asked him, and he said 'the old man just told me to get fucked.' He got mad," Nick finished.

"And the lid of marijuana we found in the patrol car?" Engelbretson asked.

"Not mine. I think Phil had a joint or somethin'," Nick suggested.

"How many shots did you hear?" Trunkhill asked.

"I heard two, the shotgun first and then a second one, a minute or so later," Nick stated.

Engelbretson and Trunkhill both stood up and told Nick they believed his account. But he had better remain truthful throughout this whole incident.

*　　　*　　　*

A few minutes later Detectives Engelbretson and Trunkhill were back on their way to Darrington to follow up with the witnesses in the campground. They had arrested Phil for first degree murder and they needed to make sure they had premeditation so the charge wouldn't be dropped to second degree murder. No matter how hard they tried to grill Nick, it appeared that he would not be able to testify or swear that he knew Phil was going to kill the old man; just that the old man and Phil had argued. So far, that wasn't going to be enough to establish premeditation.

At around 11:10 AM detectives returned to the White Chuck Campground. Detective Trunkhill along with another detective began taking and documenting measurements of the crime scene and Captain Fisher along with Sgt. Nelson videotaped the area. Near Newton Thomas' camp they found a dead deer carcass, perfectly skinned.

Detective Engelbretson joined Ione Duggan in her trailer to take a follow-up statement. After writing down her personal and contact information, Detective Engelbretson asked her to begin describing the events of the day before.

"Well, at about 2 o'clock Bob hauled the trailer down here from another campground that we were staying at. He was in the back leveling it or something and I saw this boy come down with a shotgun and went to the back of the trailer and start talking to Bob," Ione began.

"Did you hear what they talked about, ma'am?" Engelbretson asked.

"No, I couldn't hear them that well, but he did say something about 'grouse', that much I am certain," she continued.

"And he wasn't there too long, but when he left I could just tell something wasn't right; that shotgun. It made us a little leery," she stated.

"Do you remember what he was wearing?"

"I just know they were old; *his clothes.* But nothing really stands out. Maybe he had a hat on? I don't really remember," she answered.

"Ok, did you see where he went when he walked away from the trailer?"

"Yes, he went toward the old man's camp," she said as she pointed out the window of the trailer.

She sat back down at the small table in the trailer.

"We have a .38 in the cupboard, it's my husband's. Well, Bob was sitting in the doorway of the trailer and I was standing next to him; Bob had told me to fetch the pistol and I slid it under the couch where he was sitting. Anyway, I saw the young man standing there looking at the old man's camp," she continued.

"Did he have the gun?"

"Yes, it was in his hands just about waist level and it was *pointed toward the old man's camp*," she gasped.

"Could you see the old man?"

"No, in fact, I never did see the old man. The only reason I knew something was going on was because I asked Bob 'what's he pointing that gun at?' And that's when the shot went off!" she stated emphatically.

"What happened next?" Engelbretson asked her.

"Well, Bob grabbed that pistol from underneath the couch and told that kid to 'hold it!'" she continued.

"Bob jumped out of the door way and ran toward that tree. I was just shocked! Bob hollered at him again and went for another tree a little closer. Right before that he told me that as soon as it was clear to get to the car and race up to the Ranger Station to get some help. *Good Lord!*" Ione shook her head and continued.

"So, little Kathy was so scared that she wanted to come with me. As we were running for the truck we heard another shot and I saw it was Bob firing in the air. Kathy jumped in the back seat and we went about 15 miles up the road to the Ranger Station and I told them, 'for God's sake get some help. There has been a shooting at the campground!'" she stated.

"Did you tell them the old man had been shot?" Engelbretson asked.

"No, at that time I didn't know what was happening. So the Ranger called the Sheriff and they told me to stay at the Ranger Station," Ione said.

Engelbretson flipped through his notes.

"Deputies noted that you were here when they arrived?" he asked.

"Well, I couldn't stand it anymore so I drove back down. I mean Kara, the kids. When I got here Bob had them both lying down in the road. I was so scared," Ione finished.

"Alright, thank you," Engelbretson said.

A few minutes later Ione exited the trailer and went to help pack up the International.

Detective Engelbretson stood outside the trailer and admired the beautiful scenery. As he stretched his arms and paced about for a minute, a white tow truck rumbled in to the campground. A heavy set man pulled the wrecker up near where Engelbretson stood and rolled his window down.

"I'm John Fox, Pine Tree Towing—I guess you got a couple of impounds out here for me?" he hollered over the loud exhaust of the truck.

Detective Engelbretson directed him down to the old man's camp to contact Detective Trunkhill. Both the suspect's and the victim's cars had already been processed.

A few minutes later, Bob Duggan entered the trailer and Engelbretson hoped he would find some evidence of premeditation.

Detective Engelbretson took Bob's contact and personal information just as he had done with Ione.

"So tell me what happened, and I'm just going to take some notes, ok?" Engelbretson began.

"Saturday night we camped up at Red Bridge, a few miles up. We drove up from Mountlake Terrace. That's where I live. And we were going to Darrington to get some propane and other supplies and we saw this campground; we thought it was empty so we decided to move over here for the night," Bob began.

Ione brought Detective Engelbretson and Bob each a cup of coffee from outside of the trailer.

"So I dropped off my wife and my dad and Kathy to kind of 'hold the spot' while we went to get water for the trailer. Well, it tipped on us and we had to get a wrecker to come and upright it" Bob kind of laughed.

"When did you first run in to the two young men?" Engelbretson interrupted.

"Ok. Yeah, well when we got the trailer here, Tamia and Dad said they had seen this blue car," Bob pointed toward the Lancer, "pulling in and out of the campground and acting kind of weird. They just kept pulling in and stopping and staring. I didn't really think anything of it at the time. So, I started to level the trailer out and this young kid, I don't know how old, but this young kid wearing camo comes over," Bob continued.

"Did he have the shotgun?"

"Well, it was kind of funny, he had this stick stuck down his pants, I don't know, about two feet long and he was carrying the shotgun," Bob began.

"Could you describe it?" Engelbretson asked.

"I think it was a 12 gauge, I'm not sure. I don't really duck hunt. I hunt deer, but not birds. But I knew it well enough to know it *was* a shotgun."

"Ok, go on."

"And he comes up to me and says, 'hey man you seen any grouse?' So I told him 'no, but I ain't looking for any either.' And so he says, 'I've already shot one and cooked and eaten it.' He then tells me that he and his partner are grouse hunting. I wished him good luck and he left," Bob finished as he sipped the coffee.

"So I walked over to the old man's camp. He had come in while my wife and Dad were waiting here earlier that day. I asked him if he was alright; he was just sitting at his table eating, and he said he was fine. I told him I was worried about those two younger fellas and he said he had spoken with them; they had said something about grouse hunting. He told me he scoffed at them and sent them on their way after telling them it wasn't even grouse season," Bob continued.

Bob shook his head and stared out toward the old man's camp and his belongings still sitting on the table behind the yellow crime scene tape.

"So then, just after I got back to the trailer the two young guys came back. That's when I asked Mom where Dad's gun was. She put it under the couch and I just had an uneasy feeling about it so I told everyone to just come inside the trailer. When I looked out I could see that kid, the one I talked to earlier, I could see him backing away from the old man's camp with his gun leveled toward the camp, Mom even asked me what he was pointing his gun at; he backed in behind that tree over there and out of sight for just a second and that's when I saw the old man come running around the corner of his camp and just as he was about to get to a full run I heard the shot- I couldn't see the kid with the gun- he was behind the tree, the old man- he…"

Murder myself, Murder I am.

Bob paused and took a sip from his coffee cup and looked outside again.

"...he screamed just as I heard the shot and tumbled head over heels in like a somersault and landed right by the garbage can. I grabbed the .38 and told everyone to just lie down on the floor. I gave my mom the keys and told her to go to the Ranger Station for help as soon as she thought it was safe to get out. I jumped outside and hid by that big tree, right there by the corner of the trailer. I mean, I had no idea what he was about to do or what," Bob continued.

"That was probably smart," Engelbretson agreed.

"So I could see that one guy, the one who shot him, I could see him grab the old man by the shirt collar and he drug him back in to his camp. I could see his head over the bushes as he was dragging him. He still even had that stick in his pants," Bob stated.

"OK, good. What happened next?"

"Well, I was really scared, I fired a shot over his head and about a minute later he came out of the camp. He didn't have the shotgun or that club with him anymore. He walked right out in to the middle of the road. I yelled at him to put his hands up and he *looked back at me* and said 'What, sir? I can't hear you.' So I leveled that .38 at him and told him he better get his hands in the air. He did, and then he asked me 'What's going on? What's happening?' I couldn't believe what I was hearing," Bob said.

"So did you talk with him much? Can you tell me exactly what you remember him saying? And I mean, during the entire time you held him here, it could be very important," Engelbretson asked.

"Yeah, at this point my mother and my sister took off for the Ranger Station, but the kid said 'can I show you that I'm clean?' and I said 'sure' so he slowly opened up his fatigue jacket and he wasn't even wearing a shirt. So I asked him 'where's the gun?' and he said 'what gun' I just stood there looking at him, then he said 'sir, I know of no gun.' *Unbelievable* I thought," Bob continued.

"Did that kid ever admit to doing it?" Bob asked.

"I can't comment yet on an ongoing investigation," Engelbretson smiled.

Bob knew what he meant and shook his head.

"So I told him he was lying. *I heard a shot!* That's when he looked right at me and said 'hey man, I just shot a grouse.' And I said 'let me see the old man' and he said 'what old man?' I was just stunned at what he was saying, you know?" Bob said.

"I see it all the time," Engelbretson stated.

"Then he says 'I didn't see no old man' and I tell him a couple of times, 'have the old man come out', like three or four times and finally he says,

66

'the old man is sitting on the bench' I just couldn't believe it. So I ask him 'where's the gun' and he says 'What gun?' right after he had just told me he shot a grouse. I saw the old man tumble to the ground; I knew he was up to something. So I ask him where his partner is and says 'hey man I'm alone,'" Bob stated.

Ione knocked on the door to the trailer and poked her head inside. She noticed Bob was not yet done and quickly closed the trailer door again.

"Well of course, then the other kid drives up from the river in the car. And the first one asks me if 'we can talk about this' and his buddy comes walking in and he tells me 'If you shoot me you're in trouble, I'm clean' and he kept walking toward me and I cocked the revolver back, I mean I was scared at this point, I didn't know if they were going to try and rush me or what. So the other kid asked me 'what's going on?' and I tell him to ask his partner. So I held them there for awhile and they each wanted a cigarette so I gave them one. I told them that I was just scared enough to shoot somebody if they tried anything. An hour or an hour and a half later the Ranger and the Sheriff showed up. When they got up and went to the patrol car, they acted like nothing had even happened," Bob finished.

"When did you know the old man was dead?" Engelbretson asked.

"After the Ranger got here I ran over to the old man's camp and found him behind his tent, he was dead," Bob answered.

Engelbretson paused and went over his notes.

"Well, that should do it. Thank you, if you remember anything else, call me," Detective Engelbretson said as he handed Bob his card.

Detective Engelbretson stepped out of the trailer and met Detective Trunkhill near the old man's camp while they were videotaping the crime scene.

"I don't have anything that suggests premeditation. Our best bet it is to try and re-interview the suspect or his buddy, Nick and see if one of them might say something that shows he was going after him, but I think it's a long shot," Engelbretson said.

Detectives spent the afternoon finishing up measuring and videotaping the crime scene. Near Phil and Nick's campground they found two ears from a deer nailed to a fir tree. A few feet beyond the large Douglas fir they found a pile of black feathers and what appeared to be, *a dead raven.*

When they returned to Everett to interview the suspect again, his family had already contacted a very high profile attorney from Seattle, Anthony Savage. He advised Phil very strongly to not speak with police or investigators again, under any circumstances.

Phil's trial was set for October.

Once his attorney's reviewed the evidence and the statements it became very clear to the defense as well that no 'premeditation' existed in this case. They informed the prosecution they would plead not guilty to murder in the first degree but would plead guilty if the charge was dropped to murder in the second degree.

Most likely, it would carry a standard 20 year maximum sentence. However, in the State of Washington at the time, sentences handed out by judges were a *maximum* sentence and not a minimum. Exactly how long Phil would have to serve before he was released was up to a state agency known as the Board of Prison Terms and Paroles. Once an inmate was incarcerated, the inmate could petition the board to be released on parole.

In October of 1974 Phil pleaded guilty to second degree murder and Judge Daniel J. Kershner sentenced him to incarceration in Washington State Prison for a term not to exceed 20 years. No members of Newton Thomas' family or any of his friends or associates attended the sentencing; nor does any record exist suggesting they were notified of the proceedings.

Jon Keehner

6

On November 7, 1974; Phil was transported to the Washington

Corrections Center in Shelton, Washington. The prison in Shelton opened in 1964 and was affectionately called 'The Boys Club.' Most inmates in Washington are processed through Shelton and many are re-assigned to a different facility within weeks. Phil's 20 year sentence meant that unless he was convicted of another crime, *the maximum* amount of time he would be incarcerated was 20 years; or until 1994. However, the Board of Prison Terms and Paroles would ultimately decide when he should be released. Depending upon how well Phil followed the rules and regulations, he could earn 'good time' and petition the Board to release him earlier.

Although there was no 'minimum sentence' at the time, the Board typically followed precedent in determining how long to remand offenders. Participating in work training programs, seeking counseling and other behavior modification therapies while avoiding written citations for rules violations were obvious markers toward measuring how long an offender should serve.

Early in 1975, Phil met with the Board of Prison Terms and Paroles regarding how long his minimum sentence should be. Members Eugene Carr and Bruce Johnson interviewed Phil and took into account that Judge Kershner made no recommendation toward a minimum sentence and Snohomish County Deputy Prosecutor David Metcalf recommended a minimum sentence of *five years.*

Five years.
For Second Degree Murder.

Eugene Carr was well known in law enforcement circles after a fairly notorious stint with Seattle Police Department in the late 1960's where he went about cleaning up a number of different corruption issues with the Seattle Police.

On July 24, 1975 the Board set Phil's minimum sentence at 20 years, noting that Phil was armed with a deadly weapon. The report also indicated the reasons for the decision:

Mr. Hillman was involved in a rather senseless, brutal, direct shot-gun slaying of an elderly man up in the mountains for no apparent reason, with no apparent rationale. The question of motivation is still quite unclear. The action itself was most brutal and senseless. He was apprehended almost immediately thereafter by a camper who was nearby who saw most, if not all, of the incident. There are also indications in Mr. Hillman's social history of serious emotional disturbance, resulting in (redacted), *a variety of aggressive acting out toward others. I think the Board that interviewed him recognized that this was a cold-blooded, unprovoked murder. With his background he is obviously a disturbed individual who needs, in our opinion, long term controls.*

Bruce Johnson
Eugene Carr

The report also set Phil's next progress hearing for November of 1976. The decision to set his minimum at 20 years was not a surprise given the history of the Washington Parole Board during the time period. Only 14 years earlier, the Board had set a minimum sentence of 15 years for a man named Gordon Heinz, convicted in 1962 of second degree burglary. He was paroled in 1974 after serving twelve years of his sentence.

Less then five months later on December 23, 1975 Phil received a violation for possession of drugs and in June of 1976 was caught smoking marijuana.

In November of 1976 Phil interviewed with Board members Helen Ratcliff and Jack Berry. Although both members agreed that cutting Phil's minimum time down from 20 years was not appropriate due to his two drug violations, they appeared to disagree on whether or not to review Phil's progress in a year or wait two years before holding his next review. The first report dated November 9, 1976 shows a marked change in the Board's outlook for Phil:

BOARD OF PRISON TERMS AND PAROLES

Jon Keehner

Olympia, Washington

Name: HILLMAN, Phillip
Number: 242731
Institution: WCC-1
Type of Meeting: Progress
Date: November 9, 1976
Members: HRB & JMB

Board Decision:
The panel has met with him today to review his progress, we are (redacted) *denying four and a half (4 1/2) months. The panel is in disagreement over the rescheduling of the next in progress review, therefore, the Full Board will vote on the next action.*

Reasons for Decision:
This young man has really worked in the Barbering course, where he has completed the course with straight A's in a year. He also paid his own way to take the state exam and passed that exam. He's carrying through with more schooling in the Barber trade. Further, he has had an introduction to the owner of "Rag's" Barber Shop in Olympia where he can get work, if and when he is placed on Work Release.

However, his behavior in the institution has been such that he has lost four and a half months good time credits, this is because of smoking marijuana and alleged "strong arming." He makes no effort to state that he was not smoking marijuana, but he does state that he has not "strong armed" anybody.

The above information above can go to the resident.

The D.D. for the Board to vote on is whether or not he should have a November '77 in person progress or a November '78.

Mrs. Ratcliff is recommending an in person in '77. I feel that this is merited in view of his effort in schooling and what appears to be a rather long minimum term. Because of the denial of good time, of course, a cut is not appropriate at this time, but I think we should keep close watch on this man to see if we can't reduce that minimum term.

Helen Ratcliff

After violating prison rules twice in the previous 12 months and less than two and a half years after killing Newton Thomas, the Board now had

71

a very different take on the minimum sentence of 20 years for Phil. However, Jack Berry disagreed with Mrs. Ratcliff and issued his own report dated November 9, 1976:

BOARD OF PRISON TERMS AND PAROLES
Olympia, Washington

Name: HILLMAN, Phillip
Number: 242731
Institution: WCC-I
Type of Meeting: Progress
Date: November 9, 1976
Members: HRB & JMB

Board Decision:
This is BERRY dictating on Hillman. As Mrs. Ratcliff stated we agree on the denial of good time and no cut.

I recommend the rescheduling of November '78 for progress.

Reason for Decision:
He has a mandatory that won't be up 'til February of '78. I've re-read the offense that occurred and it is pretty clear from the statements made by a witness that this was a cold blooded, senseless murder that was committed by this individual. Apparently the old gentleman that was shot had done absolutely nothing to desire being killed. He has lost his good time, I see absolutely no reason for scheduling him earlier, other than his own request, there isn't any other reason for it and there for I see no purpose in seeing him a year from now, thus my recommendation of 11-78 progress.

Jack Berry

Because Mrs. Ratcliff and Mr. Berry disagreed on whether or not to grant Phil the privilege of a progress hearing in a year (1977) or make him wait two years (1978) the full Board would vote on the decision in January of 1977.

In Phil's interview with the board, Mrs. Ratcliff noted that Phil denied any "strong arming"; however on December 21, 1976, less than six weeks later, Phil and another inmate had a disagreement resulting in Phil receiving a violation for assault. Three weeks later, he was transferred out of the Washington Correction Center at Shelton to the Washington State Reformatory in Monroe on January 17, 1977. His Board vote took place two days later and five of the seven Board members voted to delay his next progress hearing until November of 1978.

Although Phil was not granted a progress hearing in November of 1977, an administrative hearing was held to determine how much good time credit Phil had earned in the previous year. Despite the fact that he assaulted another inmate in December of the previous year and had been transferred to Monroe, on November 16, 1977 the Board granted him five months of good time credit.

Six months later, on May 5, 1978 Phil again had another drug violation added to his record. The details of which were outlined when he finally did receive another progress review in November of 1978 in front of Board members Eugene Carr and George Johnson:

BOARD OF PRISON TERMS AND PAROLES
Olympia, Washington

Name: HILLMAN, Phillip
Number: 242731
Institution: WSR
Type of Meeting: Progress
Date: November 11-6-78
Members: EMC & GWJ

Board Decision:
Granted 4 months good time, denied 2 months and rescheduled 11-79 progress.

Reason for Decision:
He seemed to have turned things around since April, when he had his last infraction. He was intoxicated under the influence of some drug, he told us it was valium, but nevertheless, the syringe and needle were found and he was unable to walk without staggering and he could not speak right. Otherwise, he's programmed well, he's completed basic barber course, has a license, he's now in an advanced course and we were informed that he is one of the most advanced students in the barbering vocation in the institution. We were also concerned with the fact, that with the infraction involved, due to the seriousness of the crime, we tried to consider all factors. Instead of scheduling an 11-80 progress we decided to move him up and schedule a year progress.

Eugene Carr
George Johnson

Yet again, even after another drug violation and being caught with a needle and syringe, Phil was rewarded with only having to wait a year for his next progress review, rather than two years. It is during this time period that he meets his future wife, Sharon Dunn when she decided to join a friend at a dance held at the prison in Monroe.

On November 26, 1979, Board members Eugene Carr and George Johnson recommend that the full Board grant Phil a parole hearing in two years time. However, they now appeared to be additionally concerned with Phil's mental state of mind as noted in their report:

BOARD OF PRISON TERMS AND PAROLES
Olympia, Washington

Name: HILLMAN, Phillip
Number: 242731
Institution: WSR
Type of Meeting: Progress
Date: 11-26-79
Members: EC and GJ

Board Decision:
THIS IS A DEFERRED DECISION AND NOT TO GO TO THE RESIDENT. We are adopting the cert and the panel members of George Johnson/Gene Carr are voting to schedule a parole meeting November 1981. We are also requesting of the institution a psychiatric report with clearance for that parole meeting and we would also expect that he would be on work release successfully for six months prior to that parole meeting. If the vote fails, a November 1980 progress.

Reason for Decision:
This is a murder two. He got 20 from the panel with five of it mandatory. The judge made no recommendation and the prosecutor made five. He has a clear conduct record now for 18 months. Since he has been at the reformatory, he has been in the hair styling/barbering program receiving B+ grades. He is the first student to graduate in the advanced program. He also has completed several programs in alcohol education and denies any drug involvement in the institution. His family is still supportive as are other members of the community. Our one and primary concern at this point is <u>psychiatric reports for clearance.</u>

Eugene Carr
George Johnson

On January 11, 1980 the full Board voted on this deferred decision and unanimously granted Phil a parole hearing in November of 1981. Although Phil denied 'any drug involvement in the institution', it was very clear from the previous report and from his record of violations that he had been involved in some sort of drug use while in Monroe. However, as noted in nearly every other report; obtaining skills as a barber despite failing to follow the rules while locked in prison seemed to be the path of redemption for a murderer. It would appear that the ability to keep a man's coiffeur in order was a sorely needed skill in the community.

Only four and a half years earlier the Board was demanding a 20 year minimum and 'long term controls.'

Phil was now eligible to work at the "Honor Farm" at the Monroe Corrections Center. The Farm was set up as a minimum security facility to help transition soon to be released inmates back into society. Here, inmates work and live with literally nothing between them and the community as far as fences, gates or other controls. In fact, in the late seventies and early eighties, a road between rural Snohomish County and State Highway 203 actually cut right across the center of the farm. There were no signs or any other warnings to drivers that they were about to, essentially, drive through the middle of the dormitories and administrative buildings of the farm. There were no fences and inmates could literally stand on the road if they so desired.

The State of Washington felt it was safe and that no such protective measures were required. The idea was that, in order for an inmate to be eligible to work on the farm, they must be near the end of their sentence and 'to risk walking away' would simply not make sense to the inmate. Why risk adding escape charges to your sentence when you are about to be released anyway?

On May 24, 1980, Phil escaped from the Monroe Honor Farm.

It appeared as though his family was having some difficulties and although he did return to the Farm at the convincing of a family member a day and a half later, he and the family member did stop at a local bar near the prison and had a drink before he turned himself back in.

The full dangers of this type of "Honor Farm" would not become evident to the State of Washington until nearly two and a half years later, when another of its inmates, Charles Campbell, walked off the Honor Farm and killed three people. Fourteen years later, Charles Campbell was famously strapped to a 2 X 12 plank while resisting his impending execution and subsequently met his end minutes later, with a noose wrapped around his neck compliments of the State of Washington.

On July 30, 1980, two months after escaping from the work farm; the Department of Social and Health Services petitioned the Board to increase Phil's minimum term as a penalty for escape. On December 29, 1980 the Board concluded that Phil had, admittedly escaped from the work farm and sanctioned him as follows:

Murder myself, Murder I am.

Conclusions:

2) That it would be in the best interest of the public and for the best welfare of said resident that the minimum time of confinement be redetermined by order of the Board as follows:

#1 Add escape time
#2 Add 6 months to minimum term
#3 Deny 6 months good time
#4 Schedule 11-81 progress, however, would consider parole after 12 months successful and clear conduct record at work/release and positive psychological report.

A year earlier, Phil had been granted a parole hearing for November of 1981; now, after escaping prison, he was being penalized by having to wait *until November of 1981* for his parole hearing.

The sanctions for escaping meant *essentially nothing.* He had a parole hearing scheduled for November of 1981 *before* the escape; and he had a parole hearing scheduled for November 1981 *after* the escape.

Additionally, in the same hearing, the Board acknowledged that they had previously ordered him to a twenty year minimum term and *confirmed* that his release date was tentatively set for February 14, 1993. With the additional six months added and the *one* additional day for the escape, his new release date was set as August 15, 1993. However, if he earned the maximum amount of good time allowed by law, his release date could be as early as October 30, 1989.

Less than a year later on November 16, 1981 the board agreed to grant him parole if he served three more months on work release.

Nearly eight years earlier than his earliest possible release date; and 12 years earlier than the full term of his sentence.

Interestingly, the official report from the Board of Prison Terms and Paroles which is required to list or disclose in some written fashion the reasons for the Board's Decision, *was left blank:*

BOARD OF PRISON TERMS AND PAROLES
Olympia, Washington

Name: HILLMAN, Phillip
Number: 242731
Institution: WSR
Type of Meeting: Progress
Date: 11-16-81
Members: WH and JT
76

Jon Keehner

Board Decision:
Adopt cert. and recommend parole to BAP after three months of work release.

Reason for Decision:

On February 26, 1982, Phil walked out of prison.

Despite having killed Newton Thomas seven and a half years earlier, the Board had decided that serving seven and a half years of the 20 year minimum was enough. They decided that barbering, group therapy and anger management was enough evidence of rehabilitation to turn him loose on the citizens of the State of Washington. Despite multiple drug violations while in prison, despite assaulting another inmate and being transferred thereafter to another facility and despite escaping from the work farm. He simply needed to stay out of trouble, maintain close relationships with his family support network and *not drink*.

Phil's sister, Jody, had married while he was in prison and now owned and operated a tavern in Fall City, Washington. Phil moved to north Seattle and acquired employment at a Barber shop in the Northgate area of north Seattle. He was required to check in with his parole officer every couple of weeks and as he progressed, the restrictions would be loosened if he continued to meet the conditions of his release.

Phil turned 28 in March and it wasn't long before he began drinking again. His 'support network' was well aware of his parole conditions however his parole officer was never notified as to the fact that he was now drinking. As the summer progressed, the drinking and drugging spiraled out of control.

On Friday, the 13th of August, Phil went to a local tavern and got into a fight with another patron.

No arrests were made.

Since his release from prison, he now carried a hunting knife in his car, and after the fight, fearing for his safety, he procured the knife from his glove box and carried it in his pocket. A few hours later the tavern closed and not yet ready to head home, he decided to stop by the house of a guy he had met a couple of times and see if he was still up and wanted to drink some beers or smoke some dope. He had taken the guy's sister out on a date a few weeks before and the guy seemed pretty cool. It was after 2:00 AM and most everything was closed.

7

Saturday   August 14, 1982

*T*ap...*Tap*...*Tap*.

Half asleep, he thought he heard something. He rolled over. Maybe it was just one of his sisters or his mother awake upstairs.

*TAP...TAP...**TAP!***

Startled, James sat up in bed and looked around the basement where he lived. On the corner of 55th Street and Roosevelt Avenue in Seattle, his mother's house was right across the street from a local tavern and noises outside were not that uncommon.

He glanced over at his digital clock. It was 2:25AM.

Friday the 13th was over.

He took a deep breath and turned onto his side. In the corner of his bedroom the box fan whined. The August heat lingered throughout the night.

BANG!...BANG!...BANG...

What the fuck?

James jumped up from his bed. Someone was definitely knocking on the tiny window to the basement. It wasn't that unusual for one of his friends to stop by that late on a Friday night, but he did have to get up for work tomorrow.

He slid the thin cotton sheet down toward his feet and slowly rose to see what was going on. He stepped delicately toward his desk across from the foot of his bed and flipped the switch on the desk lamp.

Tap…tap….tap…

He went over to the window. Outside the window he could only make out a shadowy figure. Someone was there but his eyes had not yet adjusted to the light and he could not make out who it was.

"Who is it?" he asked as he reached for the lock on the window and slid it open.

"Hey man, it's me… Phil," the voice answered.

"Who?" James asked again rubbing his eyes.

"It's me, Phil. I took your sister out that one time. A few weeks ago," Phil answered.

James rubbed his forehead as his eyes adjusted.

Phil?

"What do you want? I got to work tomorrow," James said.

Phil crouched down and peered into the window. He lost his balance for a second but quickly recovered. James could clearly see his face now.

"Sorry man. I just need to talk. I need to talk to someone, is that cool?" Phil asked as he looked behind him toward the street.

James met a lot of people working as a bartender and often lent an ear to anyone who needed to talk. It was late, but he could give him a few minutes he thought.

"Sure. I guess. But I have to work tomorrow. Early," James answered as Phil pulled the window open.

Phil lowered himself into the window. His large frame barely made it between as he dropped down on to the floor of the basement room. Now that he was out of the darkness outside, James recognized the man in his basement. He had barely spoken with him before any more than just 'in passing' but he did remember how his sister Penny had gone on a date with him.

What does he want?

"Got anything to drink?" Phil asked as he sat down on James desk.

"No man. I have to work tomorrow," James answered, "I mean- I have water?"

"Sure that would be cool," Phil answered.

He muttered something under his breath. Obviously, he was somewhat drunk.

James went through the door and upstairs to get a glass of water. He still wasn't quite sure what Phil was doing there and wasn't quite sure how to get rid of him either. He figured Phil was probably looking for some after hours partying or maybe hoped that James and his sister Penny were up and once he figured out the situation; James figured Phil would probably just leave.

Quietly he went upstairs and grabbed a glass out of the cupboard. The floor of the old house creaked and groaned as he made his way across the kitchen floor. A minute later he returned downstairs to find Phil still leaning back on the desk across from his bed. He set the glass next to Phil on the desk and turned to sit on his bed. What in the world Phil wanted to possibly talk about he had no idea.

He sat on to the bed and looked toward the floor.

Wham!

Without any warning, just as he glanced to the floor his chest erupted in pain. For an instant he thought Phil had hit him in the chest.

What did I do to make you mad?

His hands went up to his chest. The pain seared through his body. He couldn't even think. His blood soaked t-shirt turned crimson.

What's going on?

Phil grabbed him and violently swung him in a full circle around the room and on to the bed. James landed on his back on the bed and Phil dove on top of him. James saw for the first time what was happening. Phil had a large hunting knife in his hand.

James felt the warm, wet liquid on his chest and grimaced in pain again. It was hard to even breathe. Although he saw the knife, it still didn't fully register what was happening to him.

In a flash, Phil jammed the knife downward toward James again. Phil had the knife clenched in his left hand and the knife missed James in between his right arm and the right side of his rib cage almost in the pit of his arm.

Phil never said a word and hardly made a sound.

James reacted by tucking his right arm in toward his rib cage to try and clasp Phil's arm before he could pull the knife upwards to strike again.

He really thought he was going to die.

James screamed as much as he could. His lungs wrenched in pain as he screamed.

He screamed as loud as he could. Adrenaline cancelled out the pain in his chest.

He could see his blood splattering all over Phil and out of the corner of his eye on his arm.

Phil pulled upwards with huge force to free his hand and the knife from where James tried to pinch it between his biceps and rib cage. Phil, who was in top physical shape, easily powered his hand out from the clutches of James' arm. As he pulled upwards the razor sharp steel sliced deeply into James' biceps and lacerated the muscle tissue and arteries with ease. Blood slopped into James' face. The salty liquid stung in his eyes.

Still, Phil said not a word.

James screamed with all of his might.

"HE"S TRYING TO KILL ME!!"

"AAAAHHH!!"

"LOCK THE DOOORS!!!!"

James was horrified. He was much smaller than Phil but he had to fight him off somehow or *he was going to die.*

He screamed again.

As loud as he could.

He knew if he stopped screaming no one would come to his aid.

He tried to raise his right arm to ward off Phil's attack but the laceration left his arm lifeless and limp. Every movement shot pain into his chest. His right arm hung like jelly.

His left hand thrust upwards toward Phil's mouth to fight him off.

Phil tried to bite his fingers.

The only thing James could think to do was to try and shove his fingers in his throat. He twisted and writhed to get the 200 plus pound man off of him.

His chest burned like it was on fire.

Phil fought his arm away from his face.

He screamed again; the screams were getting weaker no matter how hard he tried.

He saw Phil's left arm come up again to thrust the knife in to him again. His hand came up and the knife thrust into the tissue and tendons of his wrist.

Blood droplets rained down into his face again.

His fingers felt like a shock of electricity went through them and then quickly they went cold and numb.

He had to stop that razor like dagger from striking him again. He had to get that knife to stop bloodletting his body. His numb fingers wrapped around the blade and Phil jerked it out of his hand.

He thought his fingers were going to fall to the floor.

Phil had him fully pinned and squeezed him with his knees.

The only sound Phil was making was the depth of his breathing.

The door to the basement burst open and James' sister Penny screamed and wildly swung at Phil. The iron fire poker hit him solidly across the side of his back as he turned to ward off the blow.

James rolled off the bed and scampered toward the door.

"The police are on their way!" Penny screamed as she continued to wildly fling the wrought iron instrument around the room.

Phil turned toward the window and jumped up in to the small opening. His arms flexed as he pulled himself through and disappeared in to the Seattle night.

Penny turned toward the door and ran upstairs following the bloody footprints and red smears on the walls.

"Oh my god! Who was that?!" she screamed as she reached down to feel James forehead.

He collapsed at the top of the stairs and was lying on his back. He stared blankly at the swirling room above him.

"Are you OK? What happened?" she asked.

"James!" she screamed.

She looked at all the blood. It scared her.

So much blood.

"Get me a towel or something!" she screamed to her mother.

James' fingers were dangling by the bone and tendon left behind. His right biceps was nearly split in half. His wrist looked like it had fallen in to a lawn mower.

And his chest.

Clotted blood gurgled with his breathing. It became shallower and shallower. His mother called next door to a neighbor; anyone who could come and help save James' life. He was weak and barely breathing.

"I think that was the Phil that I went to lunch with that one time. Oh my God! What in the hell?" she cried.

"James? Can you hear me? Stay awake. Don't go to sleep. Please. Stay awake!"

*   *   *

James woke up in the Intensive Care Unit at Harborview Hospital in downtown Seattle. His right biceps had nearly been cut in half and throbbed intently under the gauze bandage. His left hand was wrapped delicately and he struggled to move his fingers. He tried to sit up and as the muscles in his diaphragm tightened the pain tore through his chest.

He coughed.

That hurt even more.

He could barely remember anything after his sister had come in and ran off his attacker with the fire poker.

"Good morning," the nurse smiled, "how are you feeling?"

"What…What happened?" he asked looking around.

"Well, you lost a lot of blood. That's for sure. I was here the night they brought you in. Oh, yeah. You lost A LOT OF BLOOD," she said.

He took a drink from the cup of water next to him. It was warm.

"But you're strong. You did good and came through. We all knew you would," she said as she opened the closet and pulled the blankets out.

He could tell she was lying.

He looked around the hospital room. He could hear the beeping of machines on the other side of the curtain. A respirator whirred up and then out. Whoever was on the other end of the room was not doing well.

He lifted his arm and the tubes of the IV restricted his motion.

It hurt.

Everywhere.

He gazed toward the television but both his arms were bandaged so tightly he could barely move them.

A few minutes later his sister quietly entered the room.

"How you feeling?" she asked.

"It hurts all over," he answered.

"We thought we lost you," she said and quietly began crying.

She put his bandaged hand softly in to hers.

"Do you remember anything?" she asked.

"Phil. That guy that you- he just…..he just went fucking berserk. I don't know why. Do you know why?" he asked.

She shook her head.

"We already filled out a police report. A detective, a *homicide* detective took a statement. They didn't know if you were going to make it. My god. What did he want?" she asked, tears still rolling down her face.

"I don't know. He just wanted to talk or something and then- I remember I got him some water and then he," James paused and closed his eyes.

"He wanted to kill me," he finally finished.

His sister looked at him and adjusted his pillow.

"Did they catch him? Is he in jail?" he asked.

She just sat there staring at the television that wasn't on. She sighed.

"*Did they get HIM?*" he asked again.

"They put out a warrant," she said quietly.

"A *warrant*?" he demanded.

His blood pressure shot up and his heart rate increased.

"Calm down, calm down. You can't get excited; you have too many holes in your body. You have to heal up, just try and relax," she answered.

"So he's still out there. He wants to fucking kill me and he is still out there?" he wondered.

He was frightened.

Would he come here?

Did something happen to Phil that somehow he mistakenly blames me for?

"You have to stay here with me, please!" he asked his sister.

"Of course, but I have to go to work-"

"NO! Please. If he wants me dead he's going to come back, they leave me alone in here all the time," he pleaded.

"Calm down, calm down. I'll make sure someone is here. I'll tell the police, they will do something," she assured him.

"No Penny! I think this guy wants- I think he wants to kill me for some reason, and I don't know why!" James argued.

His injuries were severe but he had stabilized. Mostly he needed to avoid irritating the injuries and watch for infection. He felt like a sitting duck in the hospital. James checked out of the hospital and went to stay at some friends' house across Lake Washington in Bellevue. At least until he knew the police had arrested Phil.

*   *   *

Within a few days of the stabbing word got back to Phil that James believed he was trying to kill him. On Wednesday, Phil went to the front of James' house and knocked on the front door.

The trauma of the incident had James' mother and his two sisters understandably on edge. James told and retold the story over and over and it just seemed to make no sense. After hearing the knock his mother went to the window overlooking the entryway stairs to the front door and gasped at what she saw. Here was Phil standing at the front door knocking and looking around. She immediately went to the phone and dialed 911. The police operator explained they would send a patrol over immediately. She hung up the phone and went back to the window.

Phil was gone.

James called police detectives working the case and was stunned when they told him that a warrant had been issued for Phil, but that the police couldn't come running every time Phil showed up at his mother's door.

A few days later the same scenario played out again.

Frustrated with how the police were dealing with this incident, James finally went to stay at home rather than with his friends in Bellevue. He had heard through his network of friends who knew people who knew Phil that Phil wanted to apologize to him and explain what had happened.

Frustrated that the police did not seem to be taking the incident seriously, James figured he would try and get Phil somewhere that he knew where he was and then call the police to go and arrest him. It was the only way he was going to get any sleep at all.

On Saturday August 28, 1982, James received a phone call from Phil wanting to meet at the Hungry-U Pizza across from James' house. He agreed and called detectives to let them know what was going on. He was unable to get a hold of them and left a message with the front desk person at the detective squad. Not wanting to confront Phil alone, he contacted a number of friends to join him at the restaurant in the unlikely event Phil attacked him.

James was extremely nervous.

At around 1:00 PM James met a couple of friends at the Hungry-U and ordered a pizza, waiting for Phil to arrive.

The plan was to have one of James' friends immediately call 911 as soon as Phil showed up and James would try and delay him until the police showed up. The small group enjoyed a pizza and waited.

Nearly 40 minutes later it seemed Phil was not going to show. James worried he may have seen the large contingent of friends he had with him and decided it wasn't to his benefit to meet James in this fashion. A few minutes later one of the employees from the restaurant asked if a 'James' was in the restaurant.

"I'm James....why?" he asked.

"You have a phone call."

James took the receiver as a couple came to the front counter to pay their bill.

"Hello," James said.

"Hey man, it's me. Phil."

"What's going on?" James asked.

"Hey man, why don't you just meet me out front of the tavern down on the corner? If your mom sees me she is going to call the cops again, you know?" Phil asked.

James remained silent. He wasn't sure what to do.

"Look, I am sorry about the whole thing, I'm not trying to kill you or nothin' like that man. I just- sometimes I......I don't know. I'll explain it when I see you," Phil continued.

The couple standing next to James paid their bill and remained next to James. The man reached into his jacket and showed James a badge while motioning for James not to alert Phil that the police were there in any way.

James was very surprised.

"Uh, sure man. I'll be down there in a few," James answered and hung up the phone.

"Who are you?" James asked as he stared at the couple.

"I am Detective Billy Baughman, Seattle police. We got word that the man who assaulted you was going to meet you here?" he asked.

"Yeah, but he's kind of paranoid. That was him; I'm going to meet him down the road on the corner. He's there right now. You can go get him," James said.

"Well, it's better if you meet with him and confirm his identity to us, we'll have the area surrounded. He isn't going to harm you. We'll be right there, watching everything," Detective Baughman assured him.

James told his friends to just wait in the restaurant. He stepped outside and walked a block down to where he saw Phil waiting for him on the corner. He thought it would be easy but he began trembling. This man nearly killed him only 14 days ago and now he was just supposed to walk up to him? He wondered how long it would take for police to grab him once it was clear who he was.

What if they don't?

James could barely force himself to keep walking toward Phil. Once he was about 15 feet from Phil, Phil started talking.

"Hey man. I am so sorry about-"

Just as Phil started to talk two officers rushed from around the corner and tackled Phil to the sidewalk. James turned right around and walked as fast as he could back to the pizza joint.

He hoped it was over.

James was scared. It seemed to him that the police didn't take this very seriously, but he really didn't know. If they let Phil out on bail or something was he going to come after him then? He didn't know.

He was just scared.

*　　　*　　　*

After his arrest, Detective Baughman asked Phil if he would talk to them. This time however, Phil knew better. He invoked his right to remain silent. Nearly a month and a half later, on October 13, 1982 Phil was ordered by King County Superior Court Judge Jerome Johnson to Western State Hospital's Mentally Ill Offender Program for a period of up to 15 days to be observed, evaluated and treated. On October 21, 1982 Dr. Brett Trowbridge and Dr. Donald Allison reported their findings to the court:

Dear Judge Johnson:

Mr. Phillip V. Hillman was admitted to Western State Hospital's Mentally Ill Offender Program on October 13, 1982 pursuant to your order number 82-1-02654-5 for a period of observation, evaluation and treatment lasting up to 15 days. He is charged with second degree assault. Mr. Hillman had been drinking in a tavern until closing time, after which he went to the nearby home of a person of whom he had only met once or twice before. He pounded on the door, waking this person up, and asked him if he wanted to drink some beer. They consumed some beer, after which Mr. Hillman said that he was still thirsty, so this person brought him some ice water. As he was giving Mr. Hillman the ice water, Mr. Hillman allegedly attacked him in an unprovoked fashion with a knife, stabbing him three times, after which he attempted to choke him. The victim allegedly called for help, and his sister allegedly ran in to the room saying she was calling the police, after which Mr. Hillman allegedly fled through the window and ran off down the street. Following his admission to the hospital, Mr. Hillman was placed in the Mentally Ill Offender Program's evaluation unit to undergo psychiatric, psychological, social and physical examinations, including clinical observation.

During his admission Mr. Hillman has been alert, cooperative and oriented. No delusions, hallucinations or other symptoms of major mental illness have been noted and his mood and affect have been appropriate. He appears to be of average intelligence and has produced a good flow of goal directed speech. Mr. Hillman spent eight years at the Monroe Reformatory after being convicted of second degree murder in 1973. He got into a fight with a 77 year old man at a State Park. The argument was about who would remain in a given campsite; during the argument Mr. Hillman killed the man. He was released recently and has been doing part-time jobs to support himself. Mr. Hillman was in the psychiatric ward at Madigan at one time after returning from a tour of duty in Vietnam. At the time he was apparently depressed and suicidal. Mr. Hillman is unable to explain the alleged assault, except to state that he had gotten into a fight in the tavern and had gotten cut on the left arm. This was the reason he had taken his knife out of the glove box of his car and carried it with him into the house. Concerning the alleged stabbing incident, Mr. Hillman can only say "I just got a weird feeling and stabbed him." He admits that he was intoxicated at the time. Our diagnostic impression is antisocial personality with drug and alcohol abuse, mixed.

It is our opinion that Mr. Hillman is competent to stand trial. He fully understands the nature of the proceedings against him and is able to assist his attorney in preparing a defense. It is further our opinion that at the time of the alleged assault, he could distinguish right from wrong and could appreciate the nature and quality of his conduct, despite his intoxication at the time. It appears to us that Mr. Hillman is dangerous and requires institutional control.

Since our evaluation is complete and Mr. Hillman is competent, we request that he be returned to court for further proceedings. He requires no psychotropic medications. Please feel free to contact us at any time if there are any questions concerning this case.

Sincerely,

Brett C. Trowbridge, Ph.D., J.D.
Clinical Psychologist

Donald F. Allison M.D.
Staff Psychiatrist

This letter verified Phil's competency to stand trial for assaulting James Sylte. Besides the simple typographical errors such as listing Phil's birth date as August 3 instead of March 8, significant errors in describing both the events of the assault and also the previous murder showcase a number of challenges psychological, psychosocial and psychiatric reports have in accurately describing events.

For example, the police report and James Sylte's statement specifically state that Phil pounded on the window- not the door. This seems trivial at first, but when a man has been attacked and brutally stabbed and most likely would have been killed had it not been for his sister coming to his aid, the inaccuracies contained in psychological reports such as these begin to mitigate the severity of the crimes.

Additionally, the report erroneously states that Mr. Hillman spent eight years in Monroe Reformatory where actually he only spent six years (after spending a year and a half at Shelton); it erroneously reports that the murder occurred in 1973 (it occurred in 1974); it erroneously reports that Newton Thomas was 77 (he was 83). It also states that Mr. Hillman *got into a fight with a 77 year old man at a State Park.'*

None of the statements made in 1974, even with the most liberal of definitions characterizing what occurred between Phil and Newton Thomas, describes what took place as a 'fight'.

These factual inaccuracies do not appear to have ever become relevant, but they are worth noting in the sense that if psychiatrists and psychologists are being relied upon to recommend to a court of law whether a person is competent to stand trial, suffers from a mental illness or other diagnosis which can severely affect the outcome of a murder or assault case, *shouldn't they at least be able to get the details correct?*

Interestingly, the report contains a very profound statement as well. Just as the original Parole Board hearing had found seven years earlier; Dr. Trowbridge and Dr. Allison conclude the letter by stating:

"It appears to us that Mr. Hillman is dangerous and requires institutional control."

On October 29, 1982 Phil plead guilty to second degree assault. In order for the court to accept a plea, he was required to write down, in his own words what he did that resulted in the charge:

"On or about August 13, 1982 in King County Wash. I did assault James A Sylte, a human being, with a knife, thereby inflicting wounds on said James A. Sylte. The blade exceeded 3" in length. That I willfully assaulted James A. Sylte.

Jon Keehner

That I was at the time armed with a knife. That the knife in question was a deadly weapon.

Phillip V. Hillman

And that was it.

On November 29, 1982 Phil was sentenced to not more than 10 years in prison. On December 15, 1982 Phil was admitted to the Washington State Penitentiary in Walla Walla.

He would have to face a parole board hearing whereby the State of Washington would determine what amount of his remaining sentence for murdering Newton Thomas he would have to complete. This hearing would determine whether the two sentences should run concurrently which meant that he could serve both sentences out at the same time or if they would run consecutively; where one sentence is served before the next one commences. For example, a person could be sentenced to five years for one crime and ten year for the next. If they run concurrently, then the offender would essentially serve 10 years because both sentences were being served at the *same time*. If the sentences are to run consecutively, then the person would serve the 10 year sentence and then the 5 year sentence for a total of 15 years. However, once again, time off for 'good behavior' can reduce both sentences substantially.

On April 25, 1983, the Board ordered a minimum sentence of 87 months, or a little more than seven years. The Board could have ordered him to complete his sentence of 20 years before even beginning to serve the sentence for nearly killing James Sylte, but instead, they simply termed him at 87 months. A month later, an audit revealed that Phil's minimum sentence had been 'miscalculated' and they increased it to 108 months, *nine years*. This would essentially mean that his expected release date would now be November 10, 1992.

His release date before walking away from the Monroe Honor Farm two and a half years earlier was February 14, 1993. Thus, his punishment for walking away from the Farm and later on attempting to kill James Sylte was that *his release date was now three months earlier than it was before.*

Essentially, he was now to complete less than his original minimum sentence for killing Newton Thomas and serve *nothing* for trying to kill James Sylte.

Barbering and hair styling truly must have been the *path to redemption.*

8

While serving time in Walla Walla, Phil married Sharon Dunn who he had met in 1978 while serving time at Monroe. A few days before the hearing which set his new sentence at seven and a half years, Phil was busted for illegal possession of alcohol and narcotics in Walla Walla. A year and a half later, in order to be closer to her and to his family he requested and was granted a transfer in October of 1984 to McNeil Island Corrections Center outside of Tacoma, Washington.

In April of 1986 the Board once again conducted a progress review. They had previously asked for a psychological evaluation to be made available for the reviews but never received one. The Board did note that Dr. Gerald A. Rapp had conducted a psycho-social evaluation on February 7, 1986 while at McNeil Island and added it to their review:

February 7, 1986

Criminal history:

Mr. Hillman was committed after a conviction for assault II with a weapon (knife) in November, 1982. He was a resident of Washington State Penitentiary for almost two years until his transfer to McNeil Island in October, 1984. This is Mr. Hillman's second incarceration; the first occurring in October, 1974 through February, 1982 after a conviction for murder II.

Jon Keehner

Personal and Medical History:

The file contains sufficient background history on Mr. Hillman as he has been incarcerated almost continuously since 1974 with the exception of a six month period on parole status during 1982. I did review with him his background history and found him to be quite open in describing his early family problems, particularly the difficulty in dealing with an alcoholic father, his early attempts at suicide as an adolescent, his continuing emotional problems in the Army, particularly when he was in Vietnam and the development of his alcoholism and violent behavior when intoxicated. After his last commitment, he appears to have settled down and matured a great deal, particularly since his marriage to Sharon in 1983 while he was at the Washington State Penitentiary. At thirty-two, she is a year older and works in an accounting department of a tug and barge company in Seattle. He says they share a lot of common interests and that she is one of the main reasons he has calmed down so much. His early years at Washington Corrections Center were quite stormy with numerous infractions and behavior problems; however, he has not had an infraction since April, 1983. He was programmed positively by working as a barber and for the recreation crew and he has also participated in individual and group therapy. When eligible, he would like to parole to his wife and live in a rural area outside of Seattle. He prefers physical labor work, such as working in a warehouse, though he can always fall back on his skills as a hair stylist.

Diagnostic impressions:

Mr. Hillman appears to have been significantly remorseful and upset over his last commitment to the point he has made a strong effort to participate in programs that would help him understand himself and his problems and how to prevent future acts of aggression and violence. Basically, he sees himself as a person who, due to early family experiences of neglect and rejection, developed a great deal of fear and defensiveness, particularly fearing that he would be a failure and would amount to nothing. As his alcohol abuse became worse, so did his problems with his anger and temper so that as he was a likeable, easygoing person when sober, he became, by his own description, a "monster" when drunk. He became overly sensitive and personalized things other people would say, then start fights over relatively insignificant things. Since his recommitment, he has experienced a number of positive developments in addition to his marriage. He has re-established relationships with all of his family and is particularly pleased that he has a good relationship with his father, who stopped drinking several years ago and is doing well as a semi-retired engineer. Also he upgraded his barber license while at Washington State Penitentiary and feels that his participation in Alcoholics Anonymous and in group therapy has helped him develop a good deal of insight

91

into his problems. He has concluded that he cannot drink because he cannot control himself when under the influence. He has also learned that there are better ways of handling his feelings and problems than by drinking.

Test interpretation:

Mr. Hillman was re-administered an MMPI test and the resulting profile was compared with the one obtained in November, 1982 at the Reception Center. The highest score on the test continues to be on the scale measuring psychopathic deviancy which is frequently seen in prison populations and often described as passive aggressive personality. However, as noted by Felix Messaia in his report of November, 1982, there continues to be an improvement in Mr. Hillman in terms of gaining overall maturity, the calming of his tendency toward impulsive acting out behavior, an increased self confidence and ability to manage his life and a reduction to more normal levels of activity and energy. Overall he appears to be a person who is learning to be more comfortable with himself and life as it comes. As the anger and the bitterness of the past has subsided, he no longer needs to fight with those around him and can concentrate his energies into constructive activities that will benefit him when he is released.

Conclusions and recommendations:

There is a significant improvement in Mr. Hillman, even from his last evaluation done by Dr. Page at Washington State Penitentiary in September, 1984, I agree with Dr. Page, however, that Mr. Hillman's future adjustment is entirely dependent on his ability to stay free of alcohol dependence. His suggested conditions for release appear to be appropriate for his problems, including full-time employment, abstinence from alcohol and drugs and ongoing mental health supervision, possibly through group therapy. I also would agree with his suggestion for marital counseling since his wife's participation in helping him adjust will be critical. Her ability to supportively nurture him through re-adjustment into the community and help him maintain his parole conditions will be quite important to his eventual success. Quite wisely, they have decided to defer having a family until they have had time to spend together and he gets himself squared away. In the meantime, I encourage him to remain in group which he indicates has helped a great deal in maintaining himself while incarcerated.

Gerald A. Rapp, PSW IV

Once again it appeared that barbering, group therapy and A.A. were going to lead Phil down the path to rehabilitation. The Board was equally impressed:

Jon Keehner

BOARD OF PRISON TERMS AND PAROLES
Olympia, Washington

Hillman, Phillip	*:Name*
242731	*:Number*
McNeil Island Correction Center	*:Institution*
Progress	*:Type of Meeting*
March 17-21, 1986	*:Date*
Mena & Kenney	*:Panel Members*
30	*:Docket*

Board Decision: The action of this panel is to adopt the good time cert and schedule an in-person parole meeting 90 days prior to his earliest eligibility date.

Reasons:
Mr. Hillman has been doing great. He remains infraction free since the last time that he was seen by the board. His counselor Mr. McCain indicated to us that he is a good worker. Mr. Hillman indicated to us that he is now a state licensed hair stylist which he feels is a very good skill to have. He was moved from Walla Walla to McNeil where he can have more visits from his family. His father is in Oregon and he visits him on occasion however his mother and wife and sister are all here in the Seattle area and visit him quite regularly. He has had twenty trailer visits and they have been positive. He says that he has completed a small business management which he says will benefit him when he gets out into the community since he wants to start his own business. He attends a group therapy with the assistance of Mr. Rapp, the institutions sociologist and he says that that has been very beneficial to him. He does however, have a one to one counseling with Mr. Rapp on a monthly basis. He indicated that he is very excited about being considered for national weight lifting recognition and he is very short of becoming eligible for that. He appears to have a real positive attitude and is ready to be paroled whenever the time comes.

In 1986, the Washington Legislature passed Substitute House Bill 1400 which directed the newly formed Indeterminate Sentence Review Board (formerly the Board of Prison Terms and Paroles) to review all sentences handed out prior to the Sentencing Reform Act of 1981 in order to adjust the minimum terms so that the old sentences were now more like what was intended by the Sentencing Reform Act. These reviews were called '1400 Reviews'.

Between April and June of 1987, the Indeterminate Sentence Review Board re-evaluated Phil's sentence. When he was convicted in 1982, his original charge was Assault in the First Degree, however in a plea deal, the prosecution agreed to plea it down to Assault in the Second Degree. This fact now became very important because the Sentencing Reform Act considered Assault *Second* Degree to be a substantially less serious crime. The standard sentence for this was now 24-26 months versus the 90-108 months that an Assault in the First Degree carried. Had the prosecution known in 1982 that the Legislature were going to change the law in this fashion, it is likely they would never had plead the crime down to Assault Second Degree.

On June 12, 1987, Phil had once again been disciplined for an infraction. This time he refused to provide a urinalysis. Three weeks later, on July 6, 1987, the Board released it's decision regarding the 1400 Review:

State of Washington
Indeterminate Sentence Review Board
1400 Review

Inmate name   *HILLMAN, Phillip Van*
Doc Number   *242731*

Aggravating and mitigating circumstances:
(Phil) went into home late at night & attacked the victim w/o provocation. Stabbing him in the chest with a 6" knife. He then choked the victim. Victim knew (Phil) and had let him in.

Criminal history:
Murder 2nd degree- shot 83 year old man at campground at close range- one bullet to chest. Victim was well known for helping young boys- 1000's over the years in Seattle. 5 year mandatory.

Institution behavior:
Infraction 4-12-83 poss. alc/narc.

Community resources:
Relationships with family members re-established

Community concerns and public safety issues:
(Phil) has history of (redacted) see original psych 11-14-74- many (redacted) problem- parents severe alcoholics. Needs strong substance abuse program or is high risk to re-offend.

Victim concerns and comments:
———

Hearing officer summary and recommendations:

94

Very dangerous under alcohol/ has killed once already. Plan would have to be very specific for monitoring. Reset at mandatory.

Decision:
Reduce minimum term to 90 months from 108 months.

Phil's sentence had been reduced from nine years to seven and a half years for the assault on James Sylte; who was never given the opportunity to make comments on the review. The victim concerns and comments section was left blank.

It was becoming very clear to Phil however, that barbering and business classes weren't what the Board wanted to hear any longer. More and more the Board was becoming concerned with Phil's alcohol and drug use and the consequences therein. If he were going to get paroled any time soon, he had to start making it known that he was aware of his drug and alcohol problem and start taking steps to address it. *Tell them what they want to hear.* His next progress review was in November of 1987.

Indeterminate Sentence Review Board
Olympia, Washington

Hillman, Phillip	*:Name*
242731	*:Number*
McNeil Island Correction Center	*:Institution*
.100 Parolability	*:Type of Meeting*
11-12-87	*:Date*
GL & DC	*:Panel Members*
MICC1187	*:Docket*

Board Decision:
The panel finds Mr. Hillman conditionally parolable, and we are going to reschedule a 4/88 in person parole meeting. We would request headquarters screening committee to favorably consider placing him in a work release setting in order that he may be observed in a less restricted setting prior to parole. Mr. Hillman comes to us toady with an extensive violent history coupled with extensive alcohol abuse and substance abuse. He was paroled in 1982 from a murder second after serving 85 months (we are not aware at this time of what the Sentencing Reform Act range for that crime would have been). He has now served 60 months for an assault second committed approximately six months after having been paroled for the murder conviction. We conducted this hearing at the request of HQSC, and in the light of their concerns in a letter dated 6-30-87 we have taken the above action. His institutional adjustment has been favorable, his work record is outstanding, he is reliable and relates well with staff and inmates. He presented

himself very favorably to the panel today. He seems to have an excellent grasp of his problems and how he is going to deal with those in the future. However, given his track record, he was not able to successfully do this when he was last paroled in 1982. Mr. Jerry Rapp made a presentation to the Board. In his opinion, Mr. Hillman is as parolable as he ever will be, citing that he has grown up and matured, but yet that he has a Dr. Jekyl and Mr. Hyde personality whenever he is drinking. Any parole plan must be highly structured to avoid any use of alcohol or illegal drugs through close monitoring over an extended period of time, and his length of parole supervision should minimally be very lengthy — possibly minimally 36 months or longer. Mr. Hillman was in Vietnam. We would have recommended that he also participate in a veterans program specifically designed for Vietnam era veterans.

The reasons for the decision were not disclosed as was usually the case for this type of hearing. However, on February 16, 1988, Phil was transferred to Reynolds Work Release facility pending his final parole hearing scheduled for May of 1988. A few weeks later, on March 7, 1988, Phil once again violated prison rules. The final parole decision would be made based on a .100 Review Sheet prepared on April 25, 1988.

Indeterminate Sentence Review Board
.100 Review Sheet

Hearing officer: BANKS
Date prepared: 4-25-88
Date of last review:11-16-87
Type of last review: .100

Inmate name: Phillip Hillman   Doc# 242731

Time adjustment since last review

3/25/88 Board decision changed in person parole to .100 hearing.

Institution adjustment since last review/board action

4 infractions from 4/83 – 3/88. The behavior included poss. Nar/alcohol, refuse test, w/r plan modify which was the last one. It involved him driving a vehicle. He is employed at a car dealership. He has participated in (redacted) with Mr. Rapp. Participated in academic programming. No STOP participation noted but did go to (redacted).

Community Support

Plans to parole to his wife.

<u>*Hearing officers summary and recommendations*</u>

The file material indicates the most important issue for Hillman is to remain Subst. FREE. HE MUST NOT DRINK OR TAKE DRUG. (Psy report 86-87). Is institutional behavior is satisfactory and he has adequate support through his wife and his employer. Plan must include substance abuse monitoring and must include treatment if assessment indicates such. We should consider revocation if he violates in the area of subst. abuse. Mental health treatment is also indicated.

<u>*Parolability issues/checklist:*</u>

Substance abuse: X alcohol/subst.   *Mental health: X Suicide att.*
Sexual deviancy: *Assaultive behavior:X Especially*
       when drinking.
Other:
Comments: Psy of 8/26/87 describes Hillman as an individual who is self-centered, impulsive. The psy report indicates his chances of re-offense are high given his antisocial patterns.

This report shows the Board how severe Phil's alcohol and drug abuse has become while in prison. Most notably, this report refers to a psych report produced less than a year earlier which indicates that *'his chances of re-offense are high given his antisocial patterns.'* No reference is made indicating that treatment is available, or that this outcome is likely if his substance abuse continues.

It simply states that he is likely to re-offend.

Based on this preliminary review the panel made its recommendations to the Board on May 3, 1988.

Indeterminate Sentence Review Board
Olympia, Washington

Hillman, Phillip   *:Name*
242731   *:Number*
Reynolds Work Release   *:Institution*
.100 Parole   *:Type of Meeting*
5-3-88   *:Date*
DW & GJ   *:Panel Members*
1   *:Docket*

Murder myself, Murder I am.

Board Decision:
The decision of the panel is to take a deferred decision. This is a full board vote due to loss of life. We are recommending in favor of parole to the plan dated 3-16-88 as modified. The panel is recommending an extraordinary period of parole supervision of 30 months. We recommend adopting the good time certification at the time of parole.

Reasons:
The panel finds that Mr. Hillman's rehabilitation is complete and he is a fit subject for release and his parole release is consistent with the purposes, standards and ranges of the SRA (Sentence Reform Act), having served a very aggravated, exceptional sentence under the SRA guideline ranges as well as a substantial portion of the prosecuting attorney's recommendation.
Mr. Hillman has met the pre-conditions to parolability identified by the November 1987 .100 panel; I.E., he is successfully matriculating through work release, having found employment. In fact he has progressed to the point where on the 16th of this month he will be in step five, which is the highest phase of work release. His parole plan as modified appears to meet his needs. Successful reintegration in to the community depends to a significant degree on Mr. Hillman's absolute abstinence from the use of drugs or alcohol. His assaultive history is intimately related to the use of alcohol and to a lesser extent, drugs. He would also benefit tremendously from successful completion of the Harborview anger/ stress management program, and this should be a mandatory requirement before any consideration for reduced supervision or conditional discharge from supervision.
Mr. Hillman presented himself in an extremely favorable manner at the hearing, fully acknowledging his need to maintain abstinence in the community. It his perception that if he gets as much as one dirty UA (urinalysis) or BA (breathalyzer) then he should be removed from the streets since he recognizes that that would lead to criminal activity resulting in incapacitation.
Mr. Hillman has spent 13 of the last 14 years behind bars. It is hoped hat the parole conditions and available community resources will assist Mr. Hillman in maintaining his sobriety and a pro-social lifestyle. The alternative is to be returned to the institution to finish out the unserved portion of the prosecuting attorney's recommendations, and perhaps, if he re-engages himself in substance abuse and assaultive behavior, service of the remainder of his maximum sentence. The 30 months of supervision is strongly recommended given the fact that Mr. Hillman, since his return from Vietnam, has demonstrated an inability to avoid assaultive, serious, violent behavior when under the influence of drugs or alcohol. It is essential that he be monitored for an extended period of time to insure fidelity to his dry parole conditions for the protection of the community. While the panel believes that once he has completed anger/stress management he is a good candidate for reduced supervision levels, he nonetheless should be subject to substance abuse monitoring for the entire period of supervision.

Less than a week later the full Board voted unanimously to parole Phil. No longer was barbering or business school supposed to keep Phil stable in the community. Repeatedly, the Board, psychologists and other Department of Corrections staff recognize that Phil must stay alcohol and drug free. He was drunk when he killed Newton Thomas and he was drunk when he nearly killed James Sylte. However, after repeated violations of substance abuse, alcohol and narcotics infractions; the consequence he most often received amounted to *nothing*. He had escaped from the work farm and nearly killed a man but was sentenced to less time than he was doing for the murder before.

He now knew how to say what they wanted to hear.
On June 2, 1988 Phil Hillman walked free from prison.
Again.

*   *   *

Phil and his wife Sharon, now living together for the first time since being married, moved in to a low rent apartment in Seattle's Rainier Valley. The area was known for extensive drug dealing and drug use. To offset some of the rent, Phil agreed to become the apartment manager and routinely had to evict tenants engaged in nefarious behavior. He was in top physical shape and his time in prison made it nearly impossible for anyone to intimidate him.

As a felon, he was barred by State and Federal law from possessing a firearm, yet the stress and danger of evicting the types of tenants he was dealing with, justified, in his mind, purchasing and possessing a shotgun.

Less than four months after being paroled; paroled under the condition that he *absolutely abstain* from alcohol or drugs, he went on a 13 day bender drinking and smoking cocaine. In December of 1988 he was arrested and charged with violating his parole.

After fully investigating the incident, the Board issued its decision regarding revoking his parole on February 6, 1989:

V. Evidence relied upon:

Parolee pleaded guilty to the violation specified. He stated that for some unexplainable reason. He was offered cocaine and for the next 13 days he secluded himself and drank and smoked cocaine. He stated that other than being under a lot of pressure as manager of an apartment complex with several apartments being used as dope apartments, he evicted those known to be selling/ using dope. He cooperated with local police in eradicating drug sales, which caused he and his wife to receive threats. (He did receive a letter of appreciation from Chief of Police, Seattle, WA for his cooperation.)

Based upon the foregoing findings of fact, the Indeterminate Sentence Review Board makes the following:

<u>Conclusions:</u>

I.   *That said parolee has violated the conditions of his parole as stated above.*

II. *That it would be in the best interest of the public and for the best interest of the parole that an Order of Continuation of Parole be issued and that said parolee be placed back under the supervision of the Department of Community Services.*

III. *Reasons for Decision:*

Parolee volunteered and entered a drug treatment program which he paid for. He continues out-patient follow-up treatment through AA and NA. He is gainfully employed as a car salesman. He has informed his employer of his problem and his supervisor and the auto dealer owner are supportive of him and have written letters acknowledging his potential value as an employee.

Parolee has a very serious criminal background as evidenced by his two commitment crimes. His conduct and behavior are unforgivable as he presents an unacceptable risk when intoxicated or loaded. In spite of a strong recommendation by the CCO to continue on parole, serious consideration was given to revoke. Parolee's wife is supportive and appears sensitive to her husband's problems but will not tolerate any relapses. She is willing to cooperate with the CCO and report any abuses. If any relapses with either alcohol or drugs within the next 24 months parole will be revoked.

He would remain free.

Despite all of the warnings about his dangers when using drugs or drinking, his Community Corrections Officer, Marsha Meadows, recommended keeping him in the community.

It now appeared that car salesmen were of greater need in the community than barbers.

A few years earlier, Marsha Meadows had revoked the parole of a man named Franklin Noheart. Mr. Noheart contended that the Department of Corrections had violated his constitutional rights by placing him immediately back in prison before his parole revocation hearing and he named Mrs. Meadows in his lawsuit. This lawsuit, although probably common in the profession, may have left Mrs. Meadows a little hesitant to revoke another parole.

Fortunately, Phil's wife, Sharon was willing to cooperate, and would not tolerate *any relapses.*

9

Wednesday   June 21, 1989

Starbuck, Washington.

Railroad tracks, dust and tumbleweeds.

Through the window of the blue pop-top Volkswagen camper bus buzzing along the highway, the small towns of eastern Washington looked mostly the same to me. My face pressed against the glass and I stared, trying to empty my stressed out mind in to the ditches along the two lane highway.

There wasn't much to look at.

Rolling hill after rolling hill covered in wheat or barley. Occasionally a farmhouse would come into view, a small rambler, a detached shop garage and a white fence. They all looked the same to me. Why did they all have fences?

I had been drug and alcohol free for about three months now and somehow, I was hoping my step-father, Rich, would notice through his gold rimmed Aviators and console my self-pitying ass. With his arm casually resting out the window of the bus, his head remained cocked to one side and he just kept on driving, waiting for me to say something.

The game was on.

We were traveling along Highway 261, somewhere in the middle of southeastern Washington. As we came around every new bend in the road, I prayed for a convenience store or a gas station, something.

Starbuck did not have a new gas station or well-lit convenience store. The main road going into town was lined with galvanized sheds and agricultural equipment. Bright green John Deere's and glowing red New Holland combines contrasted the tan, brown and pale wheat fields.

I hadn't seen another car in almost 45 minutes.

The mid-morning sun was starting to become an annoyance to my 20 year old persona. I grabbed the cheap black sunglasses off the dash that I had stolen from some poor sucker at an A.A. meeting in Bellevue earlier that week and threw them on my face with as much disgust as I could.

Rich was a pretty big guy at 6'2" and probably weighed more than 275 pounds, but he was one of those 'big dudes' (I always called him) that never raised his voice or lost his temper. He had medium length straight brown hair that he always sort of parted to one side. For the most part he was a teddy bear. I liked that about him.

Rich married my mother three years earlier when I was 16. He always wore plain pocket blue jeans with a brown belt, and any number of the freshly pressed button up dress shirts my mother regularly labored to provide.

I didn't live with him and my mother as I had moved to my father's house when I was nine years old but I regularly visited my mother and Rich, first at their new home in Woodinville, and then at the house he built my mother on Lake Margaret, a few miles east of Duvall.

I had attended high school in Bothell, Washington and Rich had an office a few miles from the school where I would often visit him during lunch. Rich could tell that I already had a pretty good (and patient) father and saw no need to try and fill some father or step-father type role. He was much like that friend who was old enough to know better, but still young enough to understand why I did the stupid things I did.

Like many teens, high school was filled with a plethora of 'less than perfect' choices regarding drugs, alcohol and the type of people I chose to hang out with. It seemed at every turn my parents were barraging me with questions as to who I had been hanging out with or where I was at. But when I would go with Rich somewhere for hours, usually off-roading east of Duvall in his Subaru, I merely had to mention that I was with him, and the questions from my parents would cease. They both knew if I was with Rich, I wasn't getting into trouble. Whenever I needed some time away from the constant disappointment my choices had become, I could just go hang with him.

Rich grunted under his breath as his big arms pulled on the steering wheel of the bus. We pulled off the highway into the little farming town and came to a stop in front of what looked like a four bedroom rambler with a daycare built off of one end and a small convenience store off the other.

It would have to do.

A gentle warm breeze carried the heat off the pavement toward the dirt parking lot. There was something about early summer that I always loved. The VW bus grumbled and vibrated as Rich turned the key shutting off the engine.

Save for a couple of heavily oiled gravel cross roads, this was a one street town. I stretched and yawned as I reached for the door handle. Maybe we'd get a Coke or something-or some smokes. I was almost out of smokes.

One often has to rely on the charity of others when you're 20, broke and without a job. And that's exactly what I was. Hopefully, I thought, Rich will offer to get me a couple of packs of my own smokes. I did not want to be saddled bumming his Kent III's off of him the whole time.

Those were Barbie tampons.

And smokes were too hard to shoplift unless we went into a grocery store. The clerks in these small town variety stores always lurked around the counter, waiting, watching; like they didn't have enough problems of their own.

As I hopped down from the seat I reached back into the pocket of my ripped up 501's and rubbed my ass. It was sore from being on the road for the last four hours. Rich was not really a morning person but it seemed he loved to start these adventures at 7:00 AM or as close to that as he could get. At the time, I rarely *got to bed* by 7:00 AM. Most of my days over the past few months were spent sleeping and most of my nights were spent in A.A. halls and meetings around the greater Seattle area smoking way too many cigarettes and choking down black coffee hoping to find the answers as to how I went from a prospective Air Force Academy cadet to a complete drugged out teen-age fuck up in the less than three years.

In a couple of days I was supposed to report to Chelan County jail to serve the remainder of my sentence for selling weed to an undercover cop a couple of years earlier. It was the 'remainder of my sentence' because I had most of it suspended in lieu of doing community service. However, after getting caught 'joy-riding' the YMCA van I was supposed to be working on for my 'community service', the judge was less than pleased. A week ago, during my status hearing, he saw fit to revoke my suspended sentence. How I had convinced him to let me go to get 'my affairs in order' and report back to jail in a few days is still a mystery to me.

I wasn't convinced yet that I would report as required, but things were leaning that way. What the fuck else did I have going on? Jail sounded like a great place to get some sleep and not have to listen to anyone bitch about getting my life in order.

Rich loved taking spur of the moment road trips and believing that I was somewhat dissatisfied with my current situation of having to go spend a few weeks in jail, he offered to have me along. I had no money, no job and certainly no prospects.

But 7:00 AM?

Somehow, I was convinced, getting up and heading out at that early was some sort of punitive conspiracy between Rich and the judge. To get revenge, I slept most of the way over from Duvall, but Rich could have cared less. The way he always figured it, I'd change when I was ready, not before.

My black leather biker jacket was almost too hot to touch as I peeled it off and left it on the front seat of the bus. It was nearly 80 degrees. My curled hair hung down past the collar; and nothing said to the world 'I don't care' like a mullet, stolen sunglasses and a biker jacket.

Rich slammed the door to the bus and asked if I needed smokes or wanted anything to drink.

"I'll get 'em," he said softly, "I'm sure you're probably saving your money for "soap on a rope" or something like that," he laughed.

It was always in his nature to make light of the most fucked up situations.

Soap on a rope? Oh, I get it. Jail. Ha ha.

Rich loved to start conversations as he was walking away. He'd drop some crazy notion and before you could even respond, he'd be gone.

"You know, you ought to buy a house over here and open up a drug treatment center," he said half joking and half serious as he strode off into the convenience store.

Buy a house? *Here?*

Was he nuts? I don't have a job, don't have any employable skills except for a few months installing car stereos and I'm headed to jail in a couple of days.

A treatment center?

Although I was certainly not on a winning streak, even for a 20 year old, getting sober was the best thing I had ever done. My shit world attitude still remained, but underneath the bullshit lies and generally annoyed attitude, things were going to get better. Rich knew it better than I did.

I lit my last smoke and leaned on the front nose of the bus. The breeze occasionally kicked up dust in front of the bus and sent it right in to my face.

How irritating.

Murder myself, Murder I am.

A couple of minutes later Rich's head poked out the front door of the convenience store, "What kind of smokes do you want?" he hollered.

"Winston Lights," I answered, relieved.

I pulled my newly acquired shades down from eyes and onto my nose to peer out at my surroundings. I hoped someone was watching, but no one was.

As Rich turned back inside the door he bumped into a lady coming out and nearly knocked her bag from her arms. In the process of trying to clear out of her way he nearly knocked himself out cold as his head hit the metal edge of the door. He disappeared back into the store rubbing his forehead and laughing at himself.

Ouch.

When he returned, he was carrying two white plastic sacks full of Coke, Sprite, Dr. Pepper, various candy bars, packs of smokes and three or four different types of beef jerky. He threw them in between the front seats. I tossed my smoke down into the dirt and reached in to throw my leather jacket into the back of the bus.

"This should get us through until tonight," he exclaimed with a huge smile on his face.

"I tell you what — you keep your money you have — I'll buy everything and you just cook and drive if I decide to have a Foster's or two. You'd be doing me a favor."

I had prepared myself for the 'tough love' outing; one of those shameful trips with a friend where you don't want to ask. I was too proud — and too ashamed at the same time. Without even bringing up the subject of my despondency, Rich let me know that we were going to have a good time on this trip. Whether I was broke or not; and he never said a word about it.

I was always fascinated how a guy who, six months earlier had traveled with my mother to Australia and Fiji and came home to sit and show pictures to his banking, contracting and real estate friends who all made six figures could also pile into a 1979 Volkswagen bus camper van and take a cruise around northeastern Oregon with no particular itinerary in mind with his wife's broke ass 20 year old son.

Rich noticed the weathered phone booth across the parking lot and unclipped his pager from his belt loop. He glanced down at the display.

"I have to go call your mom real quick," he stated as he strode off across the dirt nearly tripping on a small tumbleweed that whipped across the lot.

I sat in the front seat and watched him through the bug encrusted front windshield of the bus. He nearly dwarfed the payphone and stood laughing with the receiver to his ear.

It must be nice, I thought, to have a successful real estate business and a blossoming construction company. It was easy to be envious of what people had, but Rich was so easy going, it couldn't be happening to a nicer guy. Success for him was merely a vehicle to help out others and treat my mother to nice things. He was certainly not a philanthropist; Rich enjoyed nice cars; my mother's house was only a year or two old and was situated on lakefront property northeast of Duvall; but Rich never rubbed his success in anyone's face. He dressed modestly, acted modestly and truly believed if he could do what he had done in the real estate business, anyone could; provided they made good choices and decisions.

He certainly didn't encourage the poor choices I made that landed me in trouble with the law, but he understood that no matter what someone had done, all they had to do was choose to do something different.

Me included.

Rich hung up the receiver and clipped the pager back on to his belt loop. The early summer heat was rising and he rolled up the sleeves of his button down shirt as he headed back toward the bus and worked his big frame into the front seat.

"Well, have you ever been to Hell's Canyon?" he asked as he turned his head to look behind the bus as we backed out of the parking lot.

"It's very different from the Oregon side than on the Idaho side," he explained; as though I knew what the Idaho side of Hell's Canyon looked like.

He reached into one of the white plastic bags and pulled out a package of beef jerky.

"Which one do you want? We've got peppered, Teriyaki, spicy…" his hand rattled around the bag.

"And there are a couple of packs in there for you. Now that you are a member of the 'junior felon club' I feel it's my duty to see you off to the pokey with a good couple of days," he laughed.

"And since you're cooking and driving—as needed," he added.

The bus slowly began to accelerate back up the highway toward Walla Walla. I grabbed one of the packs in the bag and smacked it into my hand repeatedly.

"Your mother says hi, by the way. She says to keep you out of trouble," he joked.

"Trouble?" I asked, "What kind of trouble can I get in out here, with you?"

"I know, I know."

"So what happened in Wenatchee? I mean, you have to go back to jail-what happened? I thought you were done with that?" Rich asked.

"Hand me my smokes would you?" he pointed to the pack of Kent III's on the dash that had slid across to my side when he turned left on to the highway. The bus had finally gotten up to cruising speed and with both windows down, it seemed we almost had to yell to hear each other.

"Aaa…fuck," I began.

"Remember when I had to work on that YMCA van at Dad's shop so I could get credit for my community service? I kind of fucked up," I said.

Rich laughed as he clicked and clicked and clicked his lighter trying to light his smoke. Vigorously, he shook it trying to get one last light.

My father owned a body shop in Bothell and it afforded me the opportunity to work on cars and other fabrication projects. He opened it in 1971 and I can't remember a time when I wasn't in or around cars. That shop was like an asylum from the world for me. I had access to welders, grinders, power tools, spray painting booth—and from the time I was old enough to hold them my father had patiently showed me how to use each one.

"I was supposed to put a back-up alert in it and do a couple other things after they dropped it off at Dad's shop on Friday afternoon," I continued.

"Troy showed up Friday night and he had the weekend off and we decide we could go to Houghton beach and pick up some girls and some beer and shit."

Troy was one of my best friends in high school. A few summers earlier we had painted his '69 Firebird in my dad's shop. We were nearly inseparable during high school and for the couple of years after, at least until I got sober. He was a dear friend, and by far one of the most responsible friend's I had. But I knew continuing to hang out with him after I decided to quit drinking and drugging would be akin to asking him to amputate his leg simply because my leg had been amputated also. I was the one with the problem, not him.

Rich was really smiling now, barely able to keep the cigarette in his mouth.

"So we ended up at the 7-11 in Bellevue—at Factoria; and we'd had a couple of beers—and we went in to get some more. When we were leaving I didn't realize how long the van was and I backed into a lady's LeBaron and cracked the front bumper of her car."

"You backed in to someone's car? Jesus!" Rich was laughing hysterically now.

"Go on," he begged.

"Well, I opened the door and a Corona bottle fell out and you know how the parking lot is kind of steep right in front of the Factoria 7-11?"

Rich nodded exhaling a drag, "Yeah," he said.

"It rolled all the way down and hit her in the feet where she was standing looking at her cracked bumper. She looked up at me and then at the van with 'YMCA' painted across the side and asked me what we were doing in a 'YMCA' van at ten o'clock at night and I didn't know what to say—so the first thing that came to my mind was that were picking some kids up that had been at the movies."

"YOU SAID WHAT?" Rich howled and slapped the steering wheel, continuing to laugh out loud.

"I know, it was a dumb thing to say because she immediately asked why I had been drinking before picking up kids. I just said we were killing time and she went right to the payphone and called the cops. Luckily, when the cops showed up and because I had only had one beer, they said it was private property and they couldn't do anything but that I should go straight back to the YMCA."

"Oh yeah, I see now why the judge wasn't happy," Rich said trying to be serious as he nodded his head in agreement with the judge's decision.

"That wasn't really what did it," I said.

"Oh shit!" Rich laughed. "There's more? Of course there is, *there always is*. This is great."

"On the way back to Bothell I figured we might as well have a beer or two because *who would pull over a YMCA van?* So we pounded two or three more beers and stopped at Burgermaster in Kirkland."

Oh Shit…Oh shit," Rich continued to laugh. "This is FAN-tastic!"

"So we had a couple more beers at Burgermaster and decided to cruise down Lake Washington Boulevard, along Houghton Beach to see if we could find some girls. Well, traffic was really backed up and we decided we should just fuck Houghton Beach and go to lake Chelan instead—so I jumped into the left hand turn lane and gunned it—we were doing about 60 down Lake Washington Boulevard in the left hand turn lane."

Rich nearly sprayed the windshield with his Diet-Pepsi. He began shaking his head and kept laughing.

"So, we ended up not going to Lake Chelan but went cruising around Redmond, Woodinville and Bothell and then went back to Troy's house in Issaquah at like two or three. We thought it would be great because we knew no cop would pull over a YMCA van."

"So, what—let me guess the lady you backed into turned you in?" Rich asked.

"Well it kind of got fucked up when Dad got into the shop on Monday. He got a call from the guy at the YMCA who wanted Dad to listen to all the messages that were left on the answering machine at the YMCA. I forgot that it had the phone number painted on the side of it in fucking 12 inch letters. Apparently, like six or seven people called complaining about the YMCA van speeding through Kirkland, and the YMCA van that had beer bottles falling out of it and the YMCA van that backed in to the ladies car."

Rich was nearly in tears at this point. He removed his Ray-Bans and had to wipe his eyes from laughing so hard.

"Oh shit—Oh shit," he kept laughing as his huge frame rocked back and forth in the driver's seat of the bus.

"So how did your Dad react?" he quizzed.

"How do you think?" I laughed back, "He wasn't too excited about the whole deal. The bigger problem was when I went back to court last week and the prosecutor read the transcripts of the phone calls out loud in open court. The judge asked me if this was true—to which I could only say yes. He told me I had abused the opportunity they gave me and ordered me back to jail to serve the remainder of my sentence."

"Well," Rich said, his tone had finally grown more serious—"at least we'll have a good time before you go— that story is worth the price in my book. Wow!"

I settled back in to the seat and continued to stare out at the rolling wheat and barley covered hills.

"Now, I have to ask," Rich continued, "You know why that wasn't the best decision in the world—right?"

"Yeah," I answered.

"Good, I won't say anymore—I have done the 'obligatory' step-father objection to your poor choice-- but that's a great story, though. Unbelievable "

Rich grabbed the map off the dash and handed it to me.

"We need to go to highway 12 and head south through Walla Walla. From there we'll take Highway 204 and cut over to 82 into La Grande. It's a really nice drive. I think there is a forest service road shortcut we can take, but we'll see," he said.

He rattled off the directions and highway numbers like I had any idea where or what we were doing. All I knew was that we were probably somewhere near Oregon and Idaho

Or Washington?

Actually, I had no clue.

And Rich was *looking for a shortcut?*

During those times in high school when I would often stop by his office; whether I was skipping class or just bored, Rich always had something going on and needed to take the Subaru out into the woods. I often joined him as he looked at prospective building lots or land or something. On the spur of the moment he would invite me and my friend Scott to go with him and within hours we would be on some obscure forest service road in the Cascade foothills looking for a secret shortcut that probably didn't exist, but Rich had heard about from a friend of a friend.

After ten or 12 beers we didn't care if we ever found it. Rich would simply yell, 'Beer me!' and from the back seat Scott would toss forward a couple of beers. On most occasions we would end up at the Berry Bowl Pizza outside of Snohomish before they closed at ten and then head home.

Most of the drive into northeastern Oregon was uneventful. Occasionally he would jerk the bus over to the side of the road at any given number of random gravel turnouts with such unexpected quickness that I felt I might fall out the door at any time. Rich would turn off the engine, untangle himself from the driver's seat, clip the keys to his belt ring and suggest we have a smoke and take pictures with the new digital camera he purchased for the trip.

Rich motioned me over to every possible landmark along the highway and snapped photo after photo. He explained how he was going to use the camera to take pictures of the homes he was building while they were in progress and then give them to the buyers as an extra little 'gift.' Something extra that he didn't have to do, but thought it would be cool.

"People like seeing their house in the different stages of the build—ten or 20 years from now, whoever owns the house will really appreciate them," he explained.

"You know," Rich started, "One of these days you should fly to New York for me."

"What the fuck for?" I asked.

"Airline miles—every once in awhile United or American offers roundtrip tickets to New York where its worth it to me to buy the ticket just for the airline miles. But the airlines mileage rules require that you actually fly. But you can just fly under my name, they don't even check for ID. Why would they care?" Rich laughed.

"Airline miles?" I quizzed.

"Yeah—they will offer triple or quadruple miles for certain trips and then discount the ticket so much that I can earn half of a trip to anywhere in the world United flies. For a $250 ticket I can get enough miles to take your mom to Hawaii or Europe or wherever," Rich explained.

He loved to travel. Whether it was to some far off five star exotic destination or renting a Subaru and driving across Denali National Park with a friend; traveling and driving was his thing. Rich and my mother had traveled to Hawaii, Fiji and Australia; and even gone to New England to see the fall color changes.

"I think I want to take your mom to Germany—I know she lived there for a bit and wanted to go back. Don't tell her—its going to be a surprise," he chuckled. "I can't wait to see the look on her face. You know—one of these times if you want—go do your jail thing and go to work somewhere doing car stereo or whatever—and if you just set aside a little bit here and there we should go to like Brazil or Peru or something and rent a car and drive around."

Peru? Brazil? Actually the thought seemed really cool. Probably not going to happen—but I played along.

"Yeah—I might try and get a job at Car-Fi in Bellevue—the dude that owns it is sober and a couple of sober friends I have all work there. That would be cool," I replied.

Before I could follow up with so much as a word we came around a near hairpin corner in the highway and Rich swerved over to the right and jammed on the brakes sliding into the gravel turn-out.

"Oh shit!" Rich yelled.

"FUCK!" I yelped throwing my arms up in front of my face and bracing for some sort of impact.

Dust and gravel kicked up in front of us and the bus stalled, lurched and came to a sudden stop. We were now up in the lower foothills of the Blue Mountains and the breeze had kicked up somewhat; the dust cloud caused by nearly flipping the VW bus carried over the hill and away from us. We both sat in silence for a moment.

And then Rich started laughing.

"Remember that time outside of Cathcart—what, you were 16 or 17, and the road flooded out but I decided to try and take the Volvo through it anyway?" he reminisced.

We had come across a flooded out road in rural Snohomish County and Rich was convinced the water was only six or eight inches deep at the most. He backed the car up the road a little and then shifted it into first gear and punched it. As we hit the water it kept getting deeper and deeper and we were going slower and slower until the water started to come up over the hood and the diesel station wagon came to a grinding halt. A tow truck ride and $1000 later it was fixed.

"Yeah—that was funny!" I replied.

Rich owned a couple of different older Subaru station wagons that we would take out into the forest service roads east of Duvall. But that was the first—and last time he ever tried to do anything like that in his new Volvo again.

Rich threw open the door and motioned me over in front of the Wallowa-Whitman National Forest sign and snapped a few more photos. I was still shaking from nearly crashing the bus, but Rich was still just chuckling to himself.

"I need a beer after that!" he exclaimed. "We'll stop in Enterprise or Joseph and see if they have any Foster's. You can get a root beer or something."

Rich was mindful of the fact that I was not drinking. He even asked if hanging out with him was going to make me want to drink. Every time we stopped for him to grab some beer or something he made sure to get me something special that was non-alcoholic. Even if it was a bottled Coke or obscure weird local soda — he always offered. By the time we found a campspot somewhere in the hills outside of Joseph, Oregon; I had enough Jolt Cola in me to power a small city.

We stopped at a small store along the highway and Rich picked up a couple of Foster's Lager in the big cans and handed me something called 'Rat Soda' and smirked away. He unclipped his pager again and headed to the back of the store to call my mother one more time because we were headed up into the hills where a payphone was unlikely to be had.

I waited outside for a few minutes until Rich appeared, smiling, "Ok, your mom is all taken care of. We just have to call her tomorrow morning when we get to a payphone," he said.

I was amazed at how quickly Rich returned his pages. I had a pager when I was dealing drugs, but I was never as responsive as he was. 'Do what you say' he would always counsel, 'And do it when you say you will. That's very important in the real estate business.'

Rich spent the next hour and a half as we drove toward some unknown campsite explaining to me how to be successful in business — no matter what kind it was. He suggested I open a pressure washing business or new construction cleanup or anything. He had contacts and referrals that he would provide. We both knew that, given my current situation and outlook on life that it probably wasn't going to happen.

But it didn't matter.

Rich knew that if he offered up a positive opportunity enough times, that eventually one might take hold. And that was good enough for him, there were enough people in the world saying what couldn't be done. He focused on what could.

We pulled into a small campsite nearly at dark. I gathered some wood for a fire and Rich shifted things around the cooler. He popped open another Fosters lager and watched as I crafted a small fire from the newspaper we picked up in Enterprise and some dried out kindling.

We were camped along a huge open meadow high up in the mountains just to the west of Hell's Canyon. Rich was never afraid to head out into the woods in one of his cars to rally around but an outdoorsman, he was not. He very much preferred to have someone with him who could assist with things like campfires, outdoor cooking and the like.

It cooled off somewhat so I grabbed my leather jacket from behind the seat and threw it on.

Rich unstrapped the pop-top and raised the camper top on the bus. He carefully grabbed our bags and laid them out in the opposing beds. I grabbed the hibachi from the back, poured in the remaining Matchlight briquettes and set them ablaze. We stood around the campfire, smoking, laughing, him drinking Fosters and me getting wired on Jolt Cola and whatever other weird soft drink Rich found in the little stores we came across. By the time we passed out in the VW bus I probably had ten different ideas for small construction related businesses.

The next day we drove to Hell's Canyon and a number of other scenic lookouts in the Wallowa-Whitman National Forest and headed back toward Duvall. On the drive home Rich mentioned that he had spoken with my mother about maybe coming to stay with him and Mom once I got done with my jail time.

Two days after we got home, I piled in to his brand new Mustang GT he bought a few months earlier and Mom took me to Chelan County jail in Wenatchee.

When I got out, I moved my stuff in to the basement of her house in Duvall and got a job installing car stereo at Car-Fi in Burien. It was about 90 miles round trip between Duvall and Burien, but it left little time to get myself in trouble. I settled in to a comfortable routine; getting up at 7:30, driving to Burien, working until six or seven and then going to A.A. meetings after work and driving back to Duvall to arrive in time to hang out with Rich for an hour or so while he worked in his office in the basement and go to bed and do it again.

On my 21st birthday a few weeks later, Rich called me at work and asked what I was going to do for my 21st. He never said, but I think he was a little worried I might decide to drink for my 21st and he asked if I wanted to take him Subaruing outside of Duvall. He would do the drinking, he said; if I did the driving and stayed sober.

For a few months the routine of driving to Burien and then back again was great, until I started seeing a girl I met attending A.A., Dawn. As I started to spend more of my off time with her, I began staying at her apartment in Lynnwood, as Mother would never allow her to stay at her house since we were not married.

In January, I began working at a car stereo shop in Redmond, which was less than half the drive to Burien. During this time I started staying at my friend Tom's apartment in Woodinville. I saw Mom and Rich less and less the first few months of 1990 and one of the last times I ever saw Rich he mentioned how he was thinking of buying property over in northeastern Oregon where we had gone camping the summer before.

114

After seeing how much he loved the area, I was not at all surprised. I knew if he and Mom ended up moving there, they would be very happy.

On April 30, 1990 Rich decided to take a road trip to northeastern Oregon to look at property in the area. He packed an overnight bag and his briefcase into his Mustang GT and headed east.

He was only to be gone two days.

10

Tuesday   May 1, 1990

Rich pulled into the Motel 6 parking lot and parked underneath the front entrance cover. The drive from La Grande, Oregon to Moses Lake, Washington took about four hours and he was ready to sleep. Duvall was still five or six hours away to the west on the opposite side of the Cascade Mountains and although he was not afraid to drive straight through, he was in no hurry and depending on how he felt in the morning, he may take a more northerly route over the North Cascades Highway. It had been a long time since he last traveled the highway, and it would be a great excuse to spend a few extra hours behind the wheel of his Mustang.

None of the properties in northeastern Oregon seemed to stand out but he certainly had a few worth discussing with mom. His route across the North Cascades would allow him to take a look at some recreation property near Monte Cristo, Washington. He wasn't overly excited about buying recreation property in that area, but since the prospects in northeastern Oregon were not yet what he was after, he figured he should at least take a look. Maybe he could buy it now and turn it as summer rolled in.

He climbed laboriously out from behind the steering wheel and stood looking around the motel into the darkness stretched out behind it. Moses Lake was about 65 miles west of Spokane along Interstate 90. In the fall and winter months the flooded wetlands surrounding the town would be filled with duck and goose hunters. During the summer, recreational

116

boaters and campers would line the immense shoreline. But it was May, save for the occasional travelers along the Interstate, it was mostly empty.

It was fully dark now and he turned away from the back of the motel. Looking toward town he could see an endless maze of lights dotting the towns landscape. Mini-industrial parks, agricultural storage buildings and streetlights stretched out for miles. Moses Lake had grown significantly in the last few years.

The front office of the Motel 6 was well lit and the woman behind the counter smiled as she peeked up from the black and white television in the corner.

"Need a room?" she quickly asked and plopped a pen and a sign in card on the counter in front of him.

"Yes, just one, and for one ni--" he started.

She quickly cut him off and focused back toward her television, "29.99 plus tax—need a credit card—sign, print and date at the bottom."

Rich laughed, "You've done this before I take it?"

She was not amused and stared in silence at the television.

"Actually, I have 16 children. I know, hard to believe, but really, I have sixteeeeeen.....chiiiiildren," he mused slowly, staring to see if the woman was even paying attention.

"And they really want to have a pillow fight tonight---badly!" he continued, "So I'll need some extra pillows."

The woman blankly stared at the television, patiently waiting for Rich to finish filling out the card.

"And can all three of my wives stay in the room with me also?" he said with as straight of a face as he could.

Without even taking her eyes from the television she plopped a stack of registration cards back up on the counter, "You'll need to fill a card out for each room, four kids per room that's four rooms, and I don't care how many wives you have in the room as long it ain't more than four people to a double queen room."

Rich laughed, amazed that the woman had heard every word he said and had no reaction. What must go on at these places?

"I'm just kidding," he laughed, "Sixteen kids? Really?"

She tossed a key up on the counter and gave him directions to the room.

"Do you want the card on file to cover calls from the room, sir?" she asked as he headed toward the door.

"Yeah, I have to call my wife, so that's fine," he answered.

"Which one?" she winked as he headed out the door.

Rich parked the Mustang right out front of the door and settled in to the modest room. He unclipped his car keys and his pager from his belt.

He picked up the phone and dialed my mother.

"Hi, it's me," he said affectionately.

"How is the trip so far? Anything good?" Mom asked and set her book down into her lap.

She was nearly asleep and the house was quiet except for the barely audible whir of the furnace vent.

"No…not really. I mean one guy has this really nice 200 acre piece but he wants WAY TOO MUCH for it, and power is still 12 miles away and it's just a ways out further than I thought, but we'll see," Rich answered.

He paused.

"How was your day?" he asked.

"Fine, just moving the stuff out of the downstairs but some of it is too heavy, you'll need to help me tomorrow night. Remember they are coming to put carpet in downstairs," she replied.

"Yes. I should be there by four; I also promised Diana I would help her paint her basement as a 'condition of sale,'" Rich laughed.

Rich had sold mom's friends Denny and Diana a house just across the lake. He often spotted great deals on homes where just a little clean up or paint would raise the value of the house immensely. Finding these great deals and passing them along to friends and family was one of his favorite parts of what he did for a living.

"Well, just come home—we'll find something, it might take a little time," Mom said as she leaned across the bed and turned off the lamp on Rich's side of the bed.

"Colleen and I are going shopping at Bellevue Square for some more baby stuff," Mom continued, "We'll be back before four and then we can move that stuff out of the basement."

"Oh, that's right. The 'joyous occasion' is about to descend upon us," Rich started to laugh, "Maybe I'll send Colleen and Tim some black balloons to mark the 'joyous occasion'."

"You're horrible!" Mom laughed back.

"Or how about this, how about this," Rich continued laughing, "I'll get some infant sized sweats with 'Hawthorne Homes' embroidered on the chest, that way we could write them off."

Rich was laughing, "And we could get logoed blankets and logoed toys- and write them all off," he finished.

"I don't think so," Mom laughed.

She loved Rich's sense of humor.

"Yeah, well, I think I am going to drive over the North Cascades Highway, I haven't been over that in a long time, should be a nice drive. If the weather is clear I may go over the Monte Cristo Highway and drop in to Granite Falls and then home—either way I should be back late afternoon if not sooner. If it's going to be any later I will call you or page you. I love you," Rich said.

"I love you, too. Drive carefully," Mom said as she hung up the phone.

*   *   *

A few miles south of Darrington, smoke from the smoldering logs 12 feet away from the tent wafted in and out. It was thick and dank. Damp cedar and wet pine never really burned that good.

But it was camping.

And for Phil and Sharon, it was a much needed escape from their meager apartment in Pine Lake. They had moved out of the Rainier Valley and Phil now worked as a team leader at Evergreen Ford in Issaquah, a few miles east of Seattle. Two months earlier he purchased a brand new Ford Ranger pick-up and the couple was anxious to get out in the woods and start using their new truck. They traveled to the forested foothills of the North Cascades the day before to camp somewhere along the Sauk River.

At night, absent the moon, a canopy of cedar and fir trees intermittently darkened the star filled sky above the highway into blackness. Under the shadow of Glacier Peak, one of five active volcanoes in Washington, just 10 miles to the east, the road was dotted with trailhead parking lots and Forest Service campgrounds.

During the peak of summer the graveled trailhead lots would be full of late model SUV's and hikers. During winter the scene would repeat itself - cross country skis or snow shoes would replace the latest REI hiking fashion footwear. But during the autumnal and spring transitional periods, few souls braved the sporadic, almost spasmodic weather patterns of the western slopes of the North Cascades.

The lots were empty. The roads were silent, and the Sauk River run-off had not yet peaked into its constant and droning roar.

An unusually long winter, even by western Washington standards, made the camping a little on the soggy side; but they were determined to make the best of it. She hoped the trip would just be the two of them and their dog, and no alcohol. But on the way up he somehow convinced her that they could just get a little, and 'keep it under control'.

So far, it wasn't working.

Sharon had agreed a little over a year earlier to report any relapses in Phil's drinking to his parole officer. But she knew that if she told his parole officer, she would essentially send him back to prison.

She could ill afford for that to happen.

As soon as they arrived he started shotgunning beers. They were in the woods, he told her, and no one was going to get hurt.

"*What?*" he pointed out.

Was he going to get too drunk and hurt a tree?

At first she played along, thinking it might be different. They had a new apartment, a good paying job; he was finally fitting in to the real world. But soon he moved on from the beer to the half gallons of Jack Daniels he had surprisingly stashed in the truck before they left. All day they drank and laughed and talked about how great things were going.

But early in the afternoon he really started to get mean and paranoid. This was a side she seldom saw, but knew was dangerous when she did. Once he hit a certain point it was just best for her to let it play itself out.

Finally, he passed out around midnight; tomorrow they were going to explore some of the Forest Service roads around the area. He'll probably stay sober enough to drive, she figured. And besides, it *was* kind of a 'vacation' of sorts.

She turned her head and buried her face into the jacket she wadded up as a makeshift pillow. It too, smelled like smoldering wood. Outside, her dog Rusty slept motionless not more than a few feet from the coals. Inside, Phil was sleeping. She was afraid to move for fear of waking him. She could smell the whiskey permeating from his pores as he snored; tossing and turning in the sleeping bag next to her.

Camping in May?

It had been sunny all week at home, but at night it was freezing cold up here in the mountains.

"Sharon?" he groaned, half asleep.

"I'm right here," she quietly answered.

He muttered something inaudible and fell back asleep. She shivered. Trying to cross over him and unzip the screen of the tent without waking him might be worthless.

She was sick of his drinking but camping seemed like a good idea at the time. Now the smoke was making her sick. Or maybe it was the cherry wine coolers she had put down last night.

She gazed upon his tired face while he slept. He had been working at the dealership so much lately.

And drinking.

She laid there, for hours it seemed, until light from the early morning sun slowly transformed the black and gray globs of the dampened night into beautiful emerald green trees. She wanted to get out of the tent and stretch and walk and not have to smell the whiskey or feel the touch of a man who was choosing booze over her. The constant run off of the snow melting in the creek to the right of the tent could provide some cover noise.

Maybe he wouldn't wake up?

Moving around would probably warm her up a bit. Her shoulder blade ached as the rock beneath the tent that he refused to dig out the day before when they pitched the tent had taken its toll.

But then he started drinking.

She begged him to give up the hard stuff and stick with beer. It had only been six months since he finished up outpatient treatment and certainly drinking was better than the ounces of cocaine he had been putting up his nose. Just beer she pleaded — just beer.

But she knew he was misunderstood. She knew he meant well and wanted to do good. But he just couldn't get there yet. It was all too much. You go to college you get a good job. You make money-- have 2.5 kids-- a cat and a dog-- and if you're lucky maybe even a three car garage.

But he couldn't shake the booze.

He couldn't shake the cocaine and the pot.

And when he got mad---.

It wasn't good.

She knew he would never hurt her. But when he drank--- she drew a deep sigh — but when he drank.

In the distance, the roar of tires on the gravel highway down below the small shelf they were camped on began to drown out the creek, her chest tightened hoping the car would keep right on going and wasn't coming up to the campsite they were in.

He didn't like to share the campsites with others.

That was well documented.

She shivered again and he rolled over muttering something. The car continued down the gravel highway and faded into the distance.

She prayed he wouldn't wake up yet. It was just easier if he slept in. It was easier if he just slept it off. It was just easier when he didn't drink. On rare occasions he would take a few days off from the drinking. Go to a couple A.A. meetings and then the promises would start coming. They were gonna' get out. They were gonna' get to somewhere better. He wanted to do good things. Start a business — something. Together they could do it.

But then he would slip. First it would just be a little pot to take the edge off. Then it would be just a beer after work or a beer before bed. He would still go to A.A. meetings but he worked and he earned his booze. He remembered how his father would have a cocktail before dinner after a productive days work. Within days the 'reward' would morph into *his right*. The A.A. meetings got further and further apart and then the vodka or whiskey would start to show up. Pints first, then fifths and soon it would make 'economic sense' to just pile up the half gallons. He would ramble about high school fights and Vietnam and worse.

Times were tough after Vietnam.

And it was hard. It was no wonder he drank and sometimes, sometimes he got angry and when he got angry, well, he just lost control. It wasn't his fault. They made him like he was, they did this.

She cuddled up next to him and wrapped her arm gently over his torso. Soon she no longer cared about the frigid weather or the rock beneath her shoulder. She was wanted, and soon she was back to sleep.

11

Wednesday May 2, 1990

The blue skies of eastern Washington stretched far above the tan, shrub covered hills. Knifing into the early morning sun, Highway 17, between Moses Lake and Ephrata, Washington stretched out before him.

It was 5:00 AM.

Reaching for the near empty pack of Kent III smokes in the seat to his right, Rich propped his knee up into the steering wheel so that he could depress the switch on his left and lower the window. He lifted his hand up under his chin and spat the Nicorette gum out into his palm casting it out onto the highway. He peeled the foil flap away from the torn opening of the pack and shook one of the long white smokes into his mouth. The smell of yard fires and sagebrush swirled in and out of the car.

CLICK.

He reached for the cars built in cigarette lighter. It warmed his freshly shaven chin as he pressed the glowing coils into the cigarette. Arching his back, he kicked his torso a little sideways in the seat. The over-used mattress at the Motel 6 had left Rich's large frame a little stiff and sore. Although he loved road trips, car rallies and even the occasional jaunt to New York just as a way to increase his air miles; the Motel 6's of the world always reminded him why he worked the long hours, seven days a week to provide himself the lifestyle he enjoyed. The wary respite of these low budget highway inns also kept him close to where he came from. He was anxious to return home and show Mom the pictures of the beautifully forested properties that were for sale. Even if they were more money than he wanted to spend on them.

Twelve years earlier, like thousands of teens, Rich supported his love of cars and photography by working at a McDonald's fast food restaurant. Shortly after graduating from Edmonds High School in 1978 he moved to La Grande, Oregon to manage a newly opened McDonald's franchise.

Straws and napkins, he thought to himself. The key to running a good drive-through was making sure every car received *straws and napkins.*

The beautiful and scenic landscape coupled with the 'small town on the rise' sense of community captured him early. From the first snowfall in LaGrande to the warm summers of the Wallowa-Whitman—Rich knew this was where he wanted to be. He had returned to the Seattle area after only a couple of years to learn the real estate trade. Sometimes he wished he had never gone back to Seattle.

Ahead of him smoke bellowed from the exhaust stacks of a large semi-truck struggling along the highway in central Washington. He depressed the clutch of the small sports car, shifted in to third and flew past the semi like it was standing still.

He smiled.

He reached in to the glove box and pulled out a tattered, well used map. It had been awhile since he had traveled the curving and winding North Cascades Highway. The fire engine red Mustang always had a way of waking him up in the morning and rejuvenating his energy. Rich had mentioned to Mom the night before that he might take the route through Twisp.

On track to get home early anyway, the diversion north would only add four or five hours to his trip. Glancing down at the gas gauge he quickly calculated that with a little less than half of a tank remaining, he should easily be able to make it into the town of Twisp only 135 miles away.

His route from Moses Lake took him north across the desert scablands of eastern Washington to Sun Lakes. From here he turned north and drove along a stretch of Highway 17 which, for nearly 12 miles was as straight as an arrow; and in to Bridgeport, Washington. A few miles after crossing the Columbia River he turned left on to Highway 97, passed through Brewster, Washington and then made a right on to Highway 153 where the eastern slopes of the North Cascades settled in to the Okanogan River valley.

Rich had been making pretty good time but he was ready for a Pepsi. He loved soft-drinks- the bigger the better. Smoking was bad—soft-drinks were bad, hell, it seemed everything good, *was bad.*

He glanced down at the gas gauge. It was nearly six-thirty.

The morning sun illuminated the snow clad crests of the North Cascades. He opened the sun roof an hour earlier and despite the early morning chill, he loved the sun beaming down on him and the car-- it just felt like life was good.

The Texaco station in Twisp was perched on a small outcropping on the east end of town along Highway 20 which stretched over the mountains to the west. Small buildings of varying architectural themes and generations lined the few small blocks that made up the town. The streets were empty save for a few scattered early 80's cars parked along the sidewalks.

He pulled into the pump island and turned back the key. Eerie silence amplified the sound of the door opening and closing as he made his way to the trunk of the car. He clipped the keys to his belt, as was his habit. It was nearly 60 degrees now and Rich removed the light jacket which made having the sun roof open bearable and placed it in the back seat. Rich pulled the gas nozzle from the pump and began filling it with premium. He grabbed the roadmap off the passenger seat and casually sat back on the front fender of the car.

Darrington…Monte Cristo…Granite Falls.

He folded the map up and tossed it through the open roof into the car and headed in to pay for his gas. He glanced down the hillside into the open field behind the station and saw a few deer grazing in the overgrown alfalfa. He took off his sunglasses and pulled gently on the heavy glass doors to the storefront.

"Just gas?" the young lady asked at the front counter.

"No, I need a pack of Kent III's and an extra large Pepsi, also," he answered walking over to the fountain drinks.

He jerked the largest cup they offered from the stack on the counter and tossed it under the ice dispenser.

"I like your car," she said as the ice dropped into his cup.

He looked toward her.

"What does 'Duvall' mean?" she asked in reference to the personalized plates on his car.

He peeked into the cup and pressed it further into the lever dispensing more ice.

"Oh, I am from a town called Duvall. Ever heard of it?"

"Isn't that by Seattle? --I love your car."

He slid the cup to the left and pressed the button splashing cold Pepsi into the ice.

"But they are more to get people to ask. I am in the real estate and construction business, in Duvall."

He snapped a lid onto the beverage and whipped a straw out from the bundle to the side of the fountain before he sauntered over to the counter. His keys jingled from the clasp on his belt. He fingered through his wallet and tossed his Texaco card on to the counter.

She casually swiped the card, grabbed a pen from the dark coffee cup resting on the front counter and slid the credit card slip toward him.

"16.02."

"Have a good one," Rich nodded as he picked up his copy of the receipt and strode out the door.

Rich climbed in and headed west through town and up the North Cascades highway. The long winter had left the shaded north facing slopes of the hills and valleys along the narrow two lane highway covered in snow. An unusually warm day seemed to be melting it off quickly and a number of the twists and curves were covered in running water. As Rich approached the summit of the pass he reached down and ejected the motivational seminar cassette tape that he had been listening to for nearly a week as he drove around.

He looked up into his pager he had clipped to the visor.

Zero messages.

It was far too early for anyone to be looking for him yet. He did not have to be back in Duvall until 4:00 PM and as early of a start as he got he would have plenty of time to stop and see the sights along the highway as well as check out the recreation property outside of Monte Cristo. Darrington was still an hour or so away if he didn't stop and from there it would only be a couple hours if he took the Mountain Loop Highway through Monte Cristo and in to Granite Falls.

He had all day to explore the area.

*   *   *

Drip...Drip...Drip...

Slithering down the branches above, droplets of water from an early morning squall snapped and popped on the fabric of Phil and Sharon's tent. Morning mist hung in between the trees obscuring the high mountain view. The only motion was the drooping and swaying of a clump of cedar branches where a squirrel danced from limb to limb. Most of the forest floor was sopped brown and snow free. When the spring breeze was just right, taking a deep breath, you could almost get a faint whiff of sea air from Puget Sound, 40 miles to the west.

It was almost 9:30.

She was amazed that he could drink so much and still get out of bed. Next to the fire pit, Rusty laid curled in a tiny ball. Sharon's head was pounding; the morning rain left the camp air so humid, it made her sweats and hoodie feel damp as she pulled them on. She stepped out of the tent and walked over to their Ford Ranger. Inside the center console she found an empty pack of cigarettes, a baggie full of shotgun shells and a bottle of Nuprin.

Relief.

She poured a couple of the small pills in to the palm of her hand and shot them to the back of her throat. She grabbed a bottle of orange juice out of the cooler and swallowed the pills. Rusty stood up, stretched and trotted over to her near the truck wagging his tail as he crossed the small campground.

It was going to be a great day.

Phil opened his eyes and stared at the inside of the tent. His head felt like he had been hit with a rock.

Rolling over, his elbow smacked in to the wood stock of the double barrel shotgun. The woods were a dangerous place, especially up here. He knew that first hand.

He sat up and pulled his sweats back on as he slid out of his sleeping bag.

"Bring me a beer, would ya'?" he hollered out of the tent toward Sharon.

She walked over to the cooler and fished one of the three remaining beers out and walked it over to him.

"We're just about out," she said quietly and lit up a smoke.

"Eh, I got another case behind the seat. Besides, it's a special occasion. That's why I brought another one of THESE!" he exclaimed and produced a half-gallon bottle of Jack Daniels.

His grin went from ear to ear. Opening the beer he took a drink.

She gave him a cold stare. It was only a few weeks earlier that he had put a dent in their brand new truck. It wasn't much, but the damn thing was brand new. Once, he even ran it across the lawn at their apartment.

"C'mon! Look, I know you're still mad about the truck. YOU DRIVE! Ok?" he smiled and grinned at her.

She was still unmoved.

"We're camping; this is supposed to be fun. We'll just go cruise around today, maybe go up to the lake or something. It'll be fine," he said convincingly.

His grin widened even further.

She smiled and gave in.

"Ok, but I'm driving!" she laughed.

On rare occasions she actually had a good time drinking with him. She hoped today would be one of those days.

She milled around the table at the campsite and made breakfast while he played with Rusty and focused on the Forest Service map to find the way up to a lake he remembered going to once before.

The light fog was beginning to dissipate as the sky above became brighter and brighter. She poured him a cup of coffee and he poured a couple shots from the Jack Daniels bottle in to it.

"Here!" he finally exclaimed happily as he pointed to a spot on the map.

She put a paper plate in front of him and looked over his shoulder.

"The lake is up this road, I remember there was a shortcut, a logging road that cut right up from the Mountain Loop Highway to the Forest Service Road that goes up to the lake. Otherwise we have to go all the way up to the North Cascades Highway and cut back. That will take hours. We can just find the shortcut. *Easy*," he explained as he started breakfast.

An hour later they climbed in the Ranger and headed out to explore the logging roads in hopes of finding the shortcut to Mt. Pugh. Rushing white-water creeks cascaded along the highway and the occasional run in with a black bear, a deer or even a mountain lion make the drive one of the more scenic in the entire region. Phil was already getting pretty drunk. But with Sharon driving, it did not matter much.

They headed north out of their camp toward Darrington, the gravel road was still pretty soft. Occasionally as she let her attention drift, the truck would get pulled in to a rut on the soft shoulder and nearly pull them off the road. He continued to drink and scolded her for not paying attention as she drove. She laughed and brushed it off. Eventually they came to the intersection of Forest Service Road 23 and the Mountain Loop Highway.

"Dammit! We missed the…the road somewhere back there!" Phil scolded his wife.

"Fuck, Phil! I didn't see any road that we could take- I mean there was a trail or something, but no road," she argued back.

He took a swig from the bottle and leaned out the door and vomited.

They both laughed.

"Well….*fuck*….Let's go back *that way!*" he laughed as he pointed to where they had just come from.

It was early in the day and this was what they had come for. Spending time together and cruising the logging roads. They had not seen another car since they arrived the day before.

Sharon turned the truck around and headed back up the highway. About a mile and a half up the road a small skid path took off up the hill to the left. The road had obviously not been traveled much over the winter and the water clinging to the lower branches weighed them down, severely restricting the path.

"Take this one....I ...*think*... this is.....the one," Phil slowly instructed her.

He tossed back another beer and flipped the can out on to the road.

"Are you sure? I don't want to scratch up the sides of this brand new fucking truck. Jesus. You already put a dent in it, remember?" she reminded him.

The truck just idled in the road as she stared at Phil. He didn't look at her; he just fished for another beer behind the seat. Rusty stood up in the back seat, stretched and stared at him.

"*I said...TAKE.....THIS ONE!!...FUCK!*" Phil yelled as his fist smacked the dash.

"Alright...alright...don't have a fucking cow, Jesus."

Sharon put the truck in to four wheel drive and turned up the narrow path. The engine whined and purred as they slowly climbed upwards looking for the cut-off to Mt. Pugh. Branches slid and cracked along the side of the truck. Her face winced every time it sounded like the truck was getting scratched or dented. The further they went up the path the narrower and steeper it got; eventually the road came to sudden end.

"*Fuck*. This ain't it," Sharon said, frustrated.

The path had narrowed so much they couldn't even turn around.

"It has to....It has...to *be here.....somewhere. Shit,*" Phil mumbled somewhat incoherently.

He reached for his map from the dash and stared at it while he took a couple of hits off the Jack Daniels bottle.

"*I think.....we...turned to ....we turned to fuckin' soon,*" he offered and looked over at Sharon.

He was so drunk he was swaying gently in the seat.

"We can't even turn around! Fuck!" Sharon yelled as she searched behind her out the window of the truck.

"Just fucking back down!" Phil yelled.

"Jesus! What a fucking mess!" Sharon yelled back.

She put the truck into reverse and slowly they began moving backwards off the mountain. The branches hung so low at some points she swerved off the path because she could not even make out the skid road. She stopped and pulled forward, re-centering the truck on the trail and slowly rolled backwards again. An hour after turning up the path they found themselves safely back on the Mountain Loop Highway.

Phil again peeled the map off the dash and gazed at it. His body gently swayed as the Jack Daniels and beer had fully taken effect.

"*Up.....there,*" he slurred and pointed up the road.

Sharon let out the clutch and continued up the road, she didn't even want to get out of the truck and see how badly scratched it was.

She grew irritated.

"Why don't we just go pack up and get back home early?" Sharon suggested as they drove up the highway.

"*What?....NO!...Mount Pugh....*" Phil slurred.

"You don't have to work tomorrow. We can just hang out at home. It'll be nice," Sharon tried to convince him.

"FUCK NO!" Phil yelled.

It was no use. She had seen him this way before. At the rate he was drinking they were going to be out of booze soon anyway, and then he would be much more amenable to heading home.

"THERE IT IS!" Phil yelled as his arm pointed to the left and nearly knocked the cigarette out of her mouth.

Startled, Sharon slammed on the brakes and the truck skidded to a stop.

"That's...it!" Phil joyfully exclaimed.

"Are you sure? That doesn't look any different the other one," she argued.

"It has to....It has to be the right one," he muttered and pointed at the map, "and stop fucking naggin' at me!"

Sharon glanced over at him confused, "*What the fuck are you talking about?*"

"You know. You *fucking know,*" he slurred back at her.

The road looked a little more recently used than the last one. She turned up the road and headed in to the trees. About 150 feet up the trail the road turned to the right and steepened. Another 50 feet ahead the road dropped off into a 30 foot wide ditch. The winter runoff had been so severe that the road was completely washed out. She jammed on the brakes and stopped right before it.

"Well. Shit....Looks like we can't go this way," she stated as she looked out the rear of the truck to back down and turn around.

"Just *fucking hit it!*" he yelled at her.

"What? That's like 30 feet across. There's no way..."

"JUST FUCKING GO!" he yelled again, "It's four wheel drive. GO!...GO!....GOOO...!!"

She peered over at him in disbelief.

What an idiot.

"There is no fucking way, Phil. I am NOT wrecking this brand new fucking truck!" she argued.

"I said *fucking go! Now fucking go...God damn it!*" he yelled even more pissed off than before.

130

She let out a huge sigh and put the truck into first gear. Slowly she let the clutch out and the truck crept forward and down in to the washout. It was much steeper than it looked and the nose of the truck slid down the soft dirt and came to a halt.

"NO! You have...you have to go... *fast! FUCK!*" he yelled as the truck sat motionless.

She threw the truck in to reverse and let out the clutch.

Nothing.

She threw it back into first and again, *nothing.*

They were stuck. And stuck good.

He pumped his fist in to the dash. She just bowed her head in to her hands.

Why did I let him talk me into this?

"Goddamit!" she finally yelled.

"Well...if you wouldn't have.....fucking tried....to *crawl through it!*" he yelled back at her.

They sat in the truck for nearly five minutes in disbelief at their predicament. He opened the door and stumbled out into the washout. His foot nearly disappeared into the cold mud. The truck was nose in to the washout at nearly a 45 degree angle. As she attempted to back out the rear wheels simple dug into the soft soil to the point that the rear bumper was resting on the edge of the dirt.

"We need to...we need to get a fucking tow truck," he stated scratching his head.

"How the fuck do we do that?" she asked.

He grabbed a few beers and the bottle of Jack Daniels along with his shotgun and coat.

"*FUCK!*" he yelled.

The Mountain Loop Highway was about 350 feet back down the skid trail. She grabbed the dog out of the cab and they hiked back down to the road arguing about how to drive in off road conditions. The predicament sobered him up some, but now *he was pissed.*

The two of them sat near the edge of the highway and waited. The road wasn't too heavily traveled, especially during early May and it was even possible no one would come along the road at all. They were nearly 10 miles from Darrington and she figured it would take them three to four hours to hike out.

She tossed her jacket down on to a wet cedar log and sat.

This was fucking great.

He dropped right down on the dirt of the short logging road and tossed back a few beers. She looked around at the mixture of young maple trees and cedars. She was sick of the forest.

"Jesus, Phil! *Maybe you ought to put the beers down?* At least for awhile? Who is going to pick up a guy along the road that's fucking wasted?" Sharon argued.

Phil looked at her with a deadly stare.

"*Fuck you,*" he began, "this is you're fucking...you're fucking fault."

"*My fault?* What the fuck are you talking about?" she asked throwing herself backwards in to the dirt in disgust.

Phil just took another swig from the beer.

"Every time!....Every time Phil, you get drunk and something happens. Now were fucking stuck-"

"*Bullshit!*" he shot back, "you were the *stupid bitch* who got us....who got us stuck."

"That is such-"

"Don't *fucking blame this*...on my... don't blame... drinking!"

Sharon shot upwards.

"No!...No!...you shut the fuck up and listen. No one is going to pick up a *fucking* drunk and help us do *shit!*"

"Oh bullshit. Someone 'll be along...*bullshit,*" Phil slurred. He was getting angrier and angrier, "*I served my fucking country.*"

"Right after you got that fucking truck you *wrecked it!*" Sharon continued, "*drunk!*" Sharon looked away, "you have *to stop drinking!*"

"Fuck you."

"It's the truth, Phil! Look what happens- *every time!* And what the fuck does serving your country have to do with it? *Jesus!*"

Sharon was irritated, this was it; this was the last time. Even if they finally got to Darrington and got back here with a tow truck, it would probably be dark and she would have to make dinner back at their camp without a lantern. She just wanted to get out of this shitty wet forest and get home and take a shower.

Bullshit.

Above the treetops she could hear the thumping of a raven's wings. Alone, the enormous black bird cried out. It flew directly over them in a straight line and as it faded out of sight, it filled the forest with another scream.

"I'll *fucking get us...get us out of here*" he continued, "then you can't *fucking* bitch....you'll see.

"Oh, whatever."

"This has nothing...nothing...to do with *fucking DRINKING!*" he yelled, "Garryowen. *Bitch.*"

Just as she stood up to go grab one of the last beers she heard a car approaching. He was lying down on his back resting and quickly he jerked upright.

Jon Keehner

He heard it too.

They both peered down the highway and nearly a half mile down the gravel they could see a bright red car drawing closer. Phil squinted toward the approaching car.

It looked like a new Mustang GT?

"I'll fucking get your whiny ass home. *Just do exactly what the fuck I say.*"

*   *   *

My mother pulled her blue Volvo into the closest parking spot to the front entrance of the mall that she could find. Next to her, my sister, Colleen, who was 8 ½ months pregnant groaned and labored to get out the door. This was my mother's first grandchild and she loved to shower myself and my sister with spur of the moment shopping sprees.

They arrived at Bellevue Square Shopping Mall at about 1:00 PM. Mother was in somewhat of a hurry because she wanted to make sure she got home in time to fix dinner for Rich when he got back from his trip to Oregon and then head out to her church meeting.

Rich certainly never expected dinner to be prepared for him whenever he got home; he was fine grabbing a Big Mac and a Diet Coke; but my mother really enjoyed doing it. It was only 1:00 PM, but Mother liked to be punctual and did NOT like to be rushed and pressed for time. She knew wandering in and out of the department stores and baby boutiques at Bel-Square with her pregnant daughter would not be real fast, but a good solid plan of action to hit all of the necessary stores couldn't hurt.

"Hold on—I'm going to call Rich's car phone again. I just want to make sure he's not going to be home any earlier than four," she said as she picked up the receiver in her car and dialed.

The phone rang three times and dropped. She dialed his pager number and entered in her phone number when prompted.

"Ok—we can go—he must be out of service," she said.

Mother and Colleen wandered in and out of the shops for an hour or two and returned to the car parked outside. Colleen opened up the rear hatch to the station wagon and placed the bags full of baby blankets, toys and newborn outfits into the cargo area. Mother turned on the ignition and dialed Rich's car phone number again.

A voice recording came on the line after four rings, "The customer you have dialed is out of the service area. Please try again later."

She hung up the phone and redialed Rich's pager number. When prompted she entered in 911. That was her code that she used when she wanted Rich to stop whatever he was doing and call her, even if it meant stopping at a payphone. She knew that the cellular car phone coverage areas did not cover nearly as much area as the pager network did. But within a few minutes, she expected Rich would pull over and call her back.

It was nearly 3:00 PM and she needed to stop by a friend's house to pick up some Mary Kay products before making the 45 minute drive back out to Duvall to get dinner ready and prepare for her meeting. Colleen was understandably cranky as well; she was ready to have the baby, as soon as possible. Walking around the mall and driving for any extended length of time, was not fun.

Just as Mother shifted the car into reverse, the car phone rang and startled Mother so much she jammed on the brake and threw the car into park.

"Rich!" she said into the phone, slightly raising her voice, "Where are you?"

"Karen?" The woman's voice came across the phone, "This is Linda. What time are you coming over? I have some great products to show you. Are you bringing Colleen? I have some Vitamin E rub she might love. It prevents stretch marks!"

"Linda—Linda--" my mother interrupted "We'll be over in a bit, I have to hang up—I am waiting for Rich to call."

Linda tried to break into the conversation but Mother kept speaking.

"We'll be there in a few—Ok ---bye."

Mother deliberately hung up the phone as Linda was talking; she did not want to miss Rich's call.

Traffic in downtown Bellevue was typically heavy; especially for a Wednesday afternoon. The trip up I-405 to Linda's house would take about a half an hour and from there it was another 30 minutes to Duvall. Mother looked at her watch and called Linda back.

"Hi Linda, I have to get home, Rich is coming back today I just don't think I'll have time to stop by," Mom said.

"Oh…no problem, Karen. Why don't I just meet you at Colleen's? I'm going to be out that way anyway. Then you can just head home from there?" Linda suggested.

Mom didn't want to be rude but she was very adamant about being home in time to make dinner. If Linda was willing to meet at Colleen's, why not?

"OK, sure that will work. But I can't stay for very long. We'll just have to get what I need and then I have to go, ok?" Mom finished.

Mom hung up the car phone and sighed. She hated to be rushed and she had a very uneasy feeling. Something just wasn't right.

An hour later, after meeting with Linda and dropping Colleen off, she headed across Union Hill Road between Redmond and Carnation. From there she made her way north along the Snoqualmie River Valley in to Duvall. It was nearly 4:30 PM and Rich might even be home by now. He never *expected* Mom to have dinner ready for him, but it was something she really enjoyed doing. She had tried calling his car phone a couple of times as she planned on being home by four when he arrived but he must have been out of the service area as he didn't answer either time.

It took about fifteen minutes to get from Duvall up Cherry Valley to their home on Lake Margaret. As she drove by his office at Duvall Realty she could see that his Mustang was not in the lot. She didn't expect that he would stop by the office before going home but she was curious as to why he wouldn't answer his car phone.

She was anxious to help Rich get some of the downstairs furniture moved and dinner made before she went to her meeting at 7:00 PM. She called his car phone and then his office number at the house.

No answer.

She dialed the Duvall Realty office number and the receptionist said they had not seen him or heard from him since he left for northeastern Oregon.

She dialed his pager number again and entered her car phone number.

Where in the world are you?

Mom pulled in to the driveway at home. She hit the garage door opener and was surprised that Rich's Mustang wasn't yet in the garage. She pulled in to the garage and glanced down at her watch; it was nearly 5:00 PM.

This is really weird.

She brought her bags in from the trunk of the Volvo and set them down in the living room. Rather than unpack her purchases and promptly put them in the laundry, she made her way upstairs in to her office. The window of the office overlooked the gravel driveway and the street, about 100 feet through the trees. She had paged Rich nearly a dozen times today and he had not called back. She called his car phone, his home office phone and even the phone at Duvall Realty.

And still nothing.

Mom had a very uneasy feeling as she picked up the phone in her office and dialed Rich's pager number again. She entered in her office number and hung up and dialed his car phone again.

Nothing.

She dialed his office number at Duvall Realty and the receptionist said she would leave a note for Rich to call her if he should happen to stop by. Mom was really surprised that she hadn't received a message or something because he promised her he would be home by four. It was now five and Rich *never* failed to call if he was going to be late.

Mom went downstairs and disjointedly started dinner. Her meeting was in less than two hours and she would need to leave by 6:20 PM to make it to Monroe in time. Before she even pulled anything from the refrigerator she went back upstairs and called Rich's phone again.

She was irritated now. But she realized that he may have just gotten a flat tire or maybe he lost his pager or something.

Something.

He would not just wander in late without calling.

After paging him four or five more times over the next hour she began to really worry. She called her friend, Diana who lived across the lake from her and Rich and told her she was not going to be going to meeting tonight. Something had happened to Rich and he might call needing her to come and get him or something. She was really worried.

He was now more than two and a half hours late.

Mom tried to stay busy in the kitchen but every few minutes she would go upstairs and page Rich. After hanging up the phone she traced the phone cord to where it plugged in to the wall. She picked up the receiver and verified the phone was still working.

It was almost 10:00 PM.

Mom grabbed a mineral water from the refrigerator and went back up the stairs. She pulled out her phone book and began calling Rich's friends to see if any of them had heard from him. It wouldn't surprise her if maybe he had car trouble and he had instructed whoever he got a hold of to call her and they simply had not done so.

By 11:30 she had called nearly every friend of Rich's she could think of. None of them had heard from Rich either. She redialed his pager number and left her 911 code again.

She decided that perhaps he had gotten stuck out on one of those side roads he loved to adventure down and he was probably getting himself unstuck. She knew he would call as soon as he was able to but she was still very upset that he couldn't call. She turned down the comforter on her bed and climbed in to read for awhile. She would wait up until he got home and there had better be a good reason for not calling like this.

Something had to have happened to his phone and he might have lost his wallet and had no money.

It seemed far fetched, but *it had to be what had happened.*

Within minutes she climbed out of bed again. she couldn't sleep. Something was wrong and she knew it.

It was nearly midnight and he was supposed to be home by now.

He was supposed to be home eight hours ago.

12

Thursday   May 3, 1990

Mom sat in her office and dialed Rich's pager number every five minutes. From the faint glow of the porch light she could barely make out the trees and shrubs lining the gravel driveway. As she looked out the window she could see the headlights from the cars coming up the road to the stop sign out front of the house. Each time a glow appeared she would jump to her feet and lean out over her desk against the glass hoping to see the red Mustang pull into the driveway.

She never did.

Her night was filled with dialing the pager number over and over until her fingers cramped. Each time she would enter the number she would call out silently to some unknown force to please connect; she prayed the phone would ring, that he would call back.

Her legs and arms got so sore from changing positions in her office chair that she eventually laid down flat on the floor and stared at the ceiling while she dialed. The faint glow of headlights torturously crept in to the room through the window every time she was about to give up hope.

Rich?

As the headlights passed and the room faded to darkness again, her fingers found the number on the phone and dialed, soon it was by feel. The pattern of the numbers had been typed so many times she didn't even have to look at the phone.

The frustration steadily grew. She knew if Rich was late it was with good reason. And there was no point in preparing a long lecture — Rich was a responsible adult. He would call her the first moment he was able.

That was what started to scare her the most.

He would call. *And he hadn't.*

Maybe his car phone had a problem — but then he would surely use a payphone.

It didn't make any sense.

Where are you?

As the hours wore on she would make herself stop dialing and go through the house, checking the thermostat, making sure the doors were locked and then climbing back up the stairs to her office and re-examine her date book. She wanted to believe that she had her dates mixed up; that somehow she had forgotten that Rich was actually not supposed to be home until tomorrow. She strained her memory to the point of giving herself a headache.

But she knew Rich was not supposed to be home tomorrow.

He was already overdue.

The stress was becoming so overwhelming that she wondered if this was just a bad dream. She quickly realized why people used the term 'pinch yourself' to wake themselves from a lucid nightmare.

*   *   *

Darkness and near freezing temperatures had long since filled the western foothills of the North Cascades. It was nearly three in the morning. Sharon's hands trembled, struggling to keep a grip on the frozen handle of the shovel. She was in shock at what Phil had done hours before. She wanted to vomit every time her mind filled with that picture of Phil-.

She tried not to think about it. Phil had said he would get her home. That he would handle it.

He sure did.

Her mind couldn't string together a coherent thought. First she got the truck stuck- and now she had gotten this red Mustang stuck in the snow.

Why did this fucking red car have to show up?

Again she forced it out of her mind.

Furiously she threw snow back over her shoulder and she cut the spade of the shovel back in behind the rear wheel of the Mustang.

It was cold and she felt like screaming. Her knees were nearly frozen and despite the numbness overtaking her legs, they were beginning to swell and hurt. She had been shoveling for two hours and the car seemed no closer to being free than when she started. Cold air ripped and clawed at her lungs. For a minute the desperate shoveling stopped as she sat on her knees in the snow. Her frozen breath drifted around the car. It was he who demanded they try to get through to Granite Falls. It would be quicker he said.

It would have made for the perfect getaway.

From where they were at the Mountain Loop Highway turned to the southwest and steepened as it climbed upward along the south fork of the Sauk River finally peaking at Barlow pass. The road however, is not plowed; and in some years, the entire route may be rendered impassable by two or three hundred yards of drifted snow that simply refuses to yield the beauty of its passage until the required sunlight and daily temperature have paid their penance.

From here, the highway drops to the south and crosses the south fork of the Stillaguamish River and parallels it to the west eventually gliding under the northern shadow of Mt. Pilchuk and arriving in the bedroom community of Granite Falls.

Although snow was still blown deeply in the forest, the spring melt off was accelerating and only the shade provided by the dense evergreens had kept the drift in this portion of the road from melting away. When the car began to bog down in the snow, his derailing intolerance and screaming made her panic, and jump on the gas; thinking the drift was small enough to plow through.

He should be out here digging.

She knew better.

In the back seat he was nearly passed out from shooting Jack Daniels and chasing beer. Intolerant of her incessant groaning and whining he was becoming more and more agitated.

It was *her fault* they were stuck anyway.

He drifted back to sleep.

She tossed the shovel hurriedly aside and flung open the drivers door. The ignition chime echoed through the side road.

Ding… ding …ding…

The branches which hung over the road amplified the little dinging into an audible beacon; what little adrenaline was left shot through her body again as she dove into the seat to start the car again. Her paranoid delusions were starting to get to her.

The door chime?

After two days of drinking Jack Daniels coffee, cases of beer and two fifths of vodka, she just needed to get home, get out of here, and get out of this fucking snow.

A shower of red light shot out on to the snow piled to the rear of the car as her foot settled on to the brake pedal. The slivered crescent of the moon was creeping silently above the trees. Venus hung closely like an accomplice. She crossed the stick shift into reverse and the grinding clunk of gears drew a snarled groan from him.

The whiskey bottle had fallen from his right hand onto the floorboards. She slid her waterlogged foot off of the clutch and hoped, finally, that she had removed enough material to free the car. The shovel was still lying outside where she had tossed it, but if she got enough momentum to get back on the gravel and out of the snowdrift, she could hike back up and get it.

She let a little more of the clutch out...a little more... more....*shit*. The clutch was all the way out and still the car remained.

Motionless.

You asshole!

She screamed and pumped her wrists simultaneously into the steering wheel.

You fucking asshole!

The blast of the horn startled him awake and he jerked upward and smashed his elbow into her cheekbone. The neck of the Jack Daniels bottle drove into his ankle and completely awoke him; alarming him that they were still stuck and he was out of whiskey.

"*Fuck!*" he screamed.

He reached for the shotgun jammed between the passenger seat and the door; and looked around, startled. He had taken his worn out high-top sneakers off and thrown them in the front seat.

His feet smelled.

He grabbed the last Coors from under the piled camping gear in the back hatch and shoved the cardboard carton under the seat. Belching loudly, he shotgunned the beer. The little white dog just laid there in the front floor.

The light of early morning was turning the black outlines of the North Cascades in to snow capped cones of gray rock and granite. On the distant horizon, dark clouds broke away the purple-blue skyline. Back in the trees, small birds hurried about from cedar tree to cedar tree as winter was beginning to break. Their chirping was almost as annoying as the door chime.

Her hands were cramping from gripping the shovel for so long. She was sick and tired of digging.

Sick and tired of shoveling.

Sick and tired of *being sick and tired.*

Day was coming, someone would, no doubt come up the road just as they had; thinking it had melted clear and see them. He was passed out doing nothing.

What the fuck was she going to do?

She dropped down on to her knees and sobbed. Her emotions began to race. She saw it again in her head. She heard it again.

She grabbed the shovel and swung it at the back of the car. Black tempered glass exploded out of the side window onto the snow as she screamed in frustration.

The birds stopped chirping.

"THIS FUCKING CAR!!"

For a moment, her groaning harmonized with the dull drone of the Sauk River. For a moment she was away from all of it. The sound of the river was her only guide back to the real world. For a moment, it was quiet.

A few yards in to the trees to her right a motion caught her eye in the pale dusk. A coyote unabashedly trotted across the snow a few steps and turned to stare at her. Proudly clutched in his mouth was a pile of black feathers, he had somehow captured a raven. He dropped his head down and turned to the side. Apprehensively he stared at her. The raven, still alive, struggled to free its wing from the grip of the coyote's mouth.

In a flash, the coyote was gone.

She dug for another 45 minutes, methodically engineering a trail in the snow for the axle and body of the car to clear. Her hands were raw, her knees were burning and she needed cigarettes. He had smoked them all.

She opened the rear hatch and tossed the shovel in on top of the half packed tent and rain fly. As she closed the hatch his sleeping bag shifted and kept the hatch from closing. She trodded around the side and pulled the blue nylon bag out from the hatch jam. She reached back around and the hatch closed with a thud. Her leg nearly cramped as she depressed the clutch pedal and turned the key. The car roared to life and she crossed her fingers as she moved the shifter into reverse and slowly let out the clutch. The car shuddered gently and as the tires finally grabbed traction, the car jerked backwards, nearly throwing her face into the steering wheel. She was so tired, it was difficult to turn back around and put the car in first gear after backing gently on to the side of the road.

Clear gravel.

Finally.

* * *

At around 5:00 AM, Mom saw her friend Diana's husband, Denny drive by and she knew Diana was probably awake. For the first time in hours she dialed a number other than Rich's pager.

"Hi Diana, I'm sorry to call so early, but I still haven't heard from Rich," Mom began to softly cry, "I think something is definitely wrong."

"Oh Karen...I'll be right over. We'll get a hold of him, I am sure it's just car trouble or something," Diana said encouragingly.

"I don't know...this is just not like him," Mom replied.

"Give me two minutes, I'll be right there," Diana said and hung up the phone.

Diana lived just a few hundred yards around the lake from Mom and Rich. Her car pulled in to the driveway moments later.

Mom opened the door and Diana came inside. Together they made their way upstairs to mom's office. The daylight was now bright enough that headlights no longer reflected in to the room. Mom sat staring out the window and nervously stood up every time she saw any sign of motion or heard a car out on the street.

Diana suggested that they call King County Police and file a missing persons report and then start calling hospitals and police agencies along the route Rich was supposed to take back home.

"911 what are you reporting?" the voice on the phone began.

"Um, yes, I need to report my husband missing. He was-" Mom started.

"When was he supposed to return ma'am," the voice cut her off.

"Well, I was just coming to that, he was supposed to be home yesterday about 4:00 PM. He was driving-"

"Where was he last seen?" the voice cut her off again.

"What? Where was he- he was in Moses Lake when he-"

"I am sorry ma'am. Technically he was last seen in Moses Lake. You should start with them. That's all I can do," she retorted.

"Moses Lake?" Mom asked; stunned at the tone the 911 operator was taking with her.

"Yes, if that's the last place he was seen, they would be the agency to call," the woman answered.

"LISTEN! He would not just 'not come home' and not call- he IS missing," Mom cut back at her.

"I understand ma'am. You need to call Moses Lake police Department. OK? Thank you," and she hung up.

Mom looked at Diana, "We need to call Moses Lake apparently. What *a crock.*"

Mom dialed information and scribbled the number of Moses Lake Police Department across her yellow legal pad. For a minute she laughed to herself; imagining how she was going to tell Rich when he finally did show up about how King County wouldn't even take the report.

What a pain in the ass.

Rich would laugh, she imagined; and say, 'Well I guess I better not get lost in King County ever.'

The voice on the phone broke her out of her daydream, "Moses Lake Police is this an emergency?"

"Hi, well, no… well, yes; I need to report someone missing," Mom answered.

"Ok, what's going on?" the man asked.

"Well, my husband was supposed to return from a trip to northeastern Oregon yesterday afternoon and he hasn't called, hasn't shown up and no one has heard from him," Mom began.

"Where is he from?" the man asked.

"Well, we live in Duvall, near Seattle and he spent Tuesday night at the Motel 6 in Moses Lake and we haven't heard from him since. I called King County and they said we needed to start with you," Mom answered.

"What's his name?" the man asked and began typing into a computer.

"Rich Duncan," Mom answered.

For ten minutes Mom stayed on the phone and answered questions about Rich, where he was last seen, what he was wearing, driving and doing when she last had contact with him. The man informed her that he would enter an APB into the system and flag the car as a car being driven by a missing person. This way if the car were impounded or ticketed it would alert law enforcement.

Other than that he said there was little else they could do.

Mom asked what action she could take and the man let her know she could try calling hospitals and other law enforcement agencies in the small towns along the route Rich was expected to be driving because sometimes accident reports take a little time to make it in to the computerized network which exchanges information between law enforcement agencies.

"It sounds like they think he may have been in a car accident and we should start calling hospitals. He said 'sometimes the information just doesn't get out that quick,'" Mom said to Diana as she hung up the phone.

"See?" Diana reassured Mom, "maybe he is just in a hospital somewhere."

"*Great. And he can't call*? That doesn't sound good," Mom worried.

They looked at the tiny towns on the map and dialed information and asked for the number of the local hospitals.

*   *   *

Sharon drove with one hand on the wheel, for a second she gazed upwards toward the brightening morning sky; Venus and the moon danced quietly between the trees.

Of course now that the car was free, he was beginning to wake up.

She was scared.

This was not the time to vent on him again. The sun was nearly fully over the peaks of the mountains now. She reached for her sunglasses behind his seat. Her hand bumped into the wood of the butt stock on the shotgun. She felt the plastic frames and wrestled them on to her face. The whir of gravel quickly acquiesced as they came onto the comfort of asphalt again.

They needed to get the truck unstuck as soon as possible. The longer it sat there, the greater the chances someone else would see it and if they found the...- her lip quivered and she drew in a deep sigh again. Twenty minutes later they were in Darrington. She hit the turn signal and pulled off the highway and parked a block away from the Unocal 76 station.

She looked at the clock on the car radio and realized nothing was going to be open yet. The station looked closed and in some way she was relieved. She was not ready to see anyone.

Not yet.

She wondered if she ever would be.

"What do we do now? *PHIL!?*" Sharon gasped.

In the seat next to her he just sat, calmly looking about the town.

"We can't just sit here. Fuck!" Sharon continued.

"I know, I know! Let me think a second," Phil screamed.

Both of them stared out the front windshield. Whatever they did, they did not want to be seen driving this bright red Mustang.

"What have you done? Phil. What have you done?!" Sharon yelled.

"We need to just get out of here so I can think- *fuck!*" Phil yelled back.

In an instant he threw open the car door and turned down the sidewalk heading for the service station.

Toward the southwest, he couldn't help but stare at the beautiful Whitehorse Mountain illuminated in the early morning sunlight.

He plucked a business card from atop one of the pumps at the Unocal and dropped it into the breast pocket of his fishing vest. He took a look in to the window of the station and; realizing no one was anywhere to be seen, he briskly paced back to the car.

"Let's just get the fuck out of here. I'll take you home and I'll clean the car out for prints and shit and I'll come back up here and just park it somewhere—and walk to the tow company," Phil said as he dropped in to the bucket seat beside her.

Without a word she pulled back out onto Highway 530 and headed southwest away from the impending sunlight, people were going to be up and about soon. The sunlight and temperature of day was about to offer up its penance.

"What are we supposed to do if someone sees us in this fucking car? Jesus! This thing is bright *fucking* red!" she argued.

"Do you have a *better idea?*" he yelled back, "just keep driving."

They pulled into a BP station in Arlington, Washington about 45 minutes later. She strained looking in the mirror to see which side the gas door was on. Someone would surely know it was not her car if she parked with the pump handle on the wrong side.

Surely they would call the police.

And they needed to fill the car up.

She wanted to run.

She stopped next to the pump and shut the car down. It was 50/50.

This was it.

Her paranoia was rising.

A brown Pathfinder pulled in across from her. The man glanced their way and smiled.

She nearly got sick and vomited right in front of him.

The man threw open his door and made his way in to pay. She turned off the ignition and climbed out of the car. She turned and looked at the driver's quarter panel, no gas door. She let out a huge sigh and, for a second, almost smiled. She trudged around the back of the car and found the gas door.

Whew.

She stared at the hole in the glass where she had smashed the side of the car with the shovel. It seemed like eons ago. She opened up the gas door and turned the filler cap. The pump nozzle rattled along the filler opening and fell home. She lifted the handle and squeezed the trigger.

Nothing.

She dropped the handle and lifted it again. She squeezed.

Nothing.

Her entire body felt the burn of another shot of adrenaline.

This can't be happening.

The man in the brown Pathfinder quickly jumped through the swinging glass door of the service station, puzzlingly looking in her direction. He wore brown sandals, cut-off blue jeans which were too small and his salt and pepper curled pony tail hung from beneath his Peter Pan Seafood baseball cap like a lifeless siren. The sun bounced off his glasses with a flash. He was saying something as he approached her and suddenly it seemed like everything was moving in slow motion.

His lips moved, his hands and arms gestured like an octopus in the near frozen waters of an aquarium. Her stomach began to convulse, the taste of stomach acid and bile ranked through the back of her throat, her knees became weak and started to tremble ever so slightly. She stared out across the road into the flat and flowing green pastures. Dairy cows and rusting barbed wire fences. These would be the last things she would see as a free person.

And she wanted to remember them.

"Hey—it's pre-pay only.......HEY!" the man pointed to the sign on the top of the pump.

"It's pre-pay only—" he smiled half wittingly so as not to embarrass her.

Sharon turned white and felt flushed.

"Are you ok?—yeah—a lot of people don't see the sign," he pointed again, "but they have been ripped off a lot—see the cameras?"

It was pre-pay only? She read the red letters scattered across the top of the pump. How had she not seen it? The decal was on every pump.

She was not thinking clearly.

This was bad.

Swallowing the lump in her throat she went inside to pay with cash. The man moved around the side of his Pathfinder and began to pump his gas.

She just wanted to get out of the gas station, there was no convenience store inside and he was starting to get hungry. She knew how he would get. He rarely became hung over, he was a professional drinker. Convenience stores sometimes had cameras and no matter how remote the chance of anyone ever checking convenience store video footage seemed. It made sense to go to a mainstream grocer.

He pulled himself up from the passenger seat and out into the sunshine. The wind was coming in from the west and it made the 50 degree weather seem a little cooler. He put on his sun glasses and made his way across the parking lot. The dog tried to join him but she called him back and scolded him into the rear seat.

Minutes later he returned from the Safeway store with a jug of milk, a box of doughnuts and a newspaper.

She just wanted to get home.

13

⸾By nine in the morning Phil and Sharon had made their way back to Pine Lake, just north of Issaquah, and the confines of their apartment. She had driven down Highway 9 through Snohomish in to the small town of Woodinville. Rather then deal with the morning traffic from Interstate 405 south through Bellevue she turned up the Woodinville-Duvall Road until she came to Cottage Lake and Avondale Road. Here, she headed south toward Redmond, then east and south along the eastern shores of Lake Sammamish. He just sat there reading the sports section, mumbling to himself.

She was exhausted and worn out. She plopped down on the couch and nearly passed out from the emotionally draining experience of the last 14 hours. Her head hurt, her eyes hurt, her nose hurt. Her knees and her wrists were sore and aching. Her feet were soaked and she could barely pull the snow soaked sock from her rigid foot. The once white cotton hosiery was now a dingy gray sweat soaked rag. She tossed it toward Rusty thinking he might want to play fetch, but even he had had enough. He curled his tail in and around him as he lie on the linoleum under the kitchen table.

Closing her eyes to sleep was even painful. The arm of the couch seemed to be digging into her neck. She was too exhausted to even go into the bedroom to get a pillow.

She couldn't think. She needed sleep, but she knew there would be little of that. She stared at the white ceiling and gazed off, lifelessly staring beyond the drywall boards into the apartment above her. Wishing she could change places with whoever lived above them. She wanted to go back in time and do something different.

If only she hadn't gotten the fucking truck stuck.

Maybe if they had camped somewhere else. Why did she tolerate his drinking? Her mind was moving too fast and it was manifesting itself into a dull throbbing pain penetrating and flowing throughout her entire body.

She wanted to be sick.

How could he not be tired?

Immediately he began making phone calls. He needed to get their truck unstuck. In his hand he clutched the business card from the service station that was still closed early this morning.

She crossed her arms above her head so that he could not see her face. She did not want him to think she had gone to sleep but she also did not want him to know if she was awake. She needed her space. Beyond the light of the lamp on the desk across from her, she watched as he sat on the corner of the dining room table jotting notes on the back of business cards.

The phone receiver stuck to the side of his face as he nodded and she was amazed at how confident and reserved he could be. He hung up the phone the last time and pulled some white plastic grocery bags out from under the sink. Her eyes followed him up the hall toward the bedroom but she did not move a muscle. She looked back at Rusty still lying under the table. The dog didn't even move save for his eyelids as he peered around the room quizzically.

He returned from the bedroom wearing white sweat pants and a chartreuse and black tank top. In his left hand he still gripped a few wadded up, white plastic bags. In his other she could see the jeans and t-shirt he had been wearing stuffed into one of the white bags. She could not remember any obvious blood stains on them but trying to remember meant thinking back. Thinking back increased the dull thud of the throbbing headache she was futilely trying to push away.

He mumbled something to her but she couldn't fully make it out. He knew she was finished for the day. He could see how she laid on the couch and never moved. He would have to take care of this. Ditch the car, ditch the clothes and even if by some strange set of circumstances they could tie him to it, without any hard evidence he would walk.

He just had to get rid of the car without being seen.

He threw the bags into the back seat of the Mustang and returned to the bathroom closet for a washcloth. They lived toward the back entrance of the apartment complex and few residents interacted with each other, save for Marjorie who lived upstairs.

She seemed to always be asking about what they were doing or where they were going. Most of the people living in the complex were temporarily here waiting for a job to develop somewhere else.

He wiped down the interior glass and all the surfaces with Windex and followed them up with a light coat of Armor all. This, he believed, would keep any finger prints from being discovered once the car was eventually found.

He considered what to do with the car. On the one hand he considered taking it to a remote road and walking away would be the best bet. But he was tired, and how would he get back to Darrington to get his truck? Besides, when they eventually figured it out, it would be tougher for them to pin down where he was from if the car was found near where he got it.

They would probably think some local crazy from Darrington had done it.

*   *   *

Thursdays were always slow at the car audio shop. I had been working at Car-Fi in Burien since I got let out of jail the previous summer after traveling with Rich to northeastern Oregon. But the long drive between Duvall and Burien coupled with the long work days had finally taken a toll. After the Christmas season hit, I decided to make a change and quit working in Burien and began working at Sound Advice in Redmond.

Redmond sat on the north end of Lake Sammamish about 15 miles north of Issaquah, which cornered the south end of the lake.

I was lucky enough to bring some of my customers from my previous job at Car-Fi with me here, to Sound Advice. In the car stereo installation business it seemed to work that way. While working at Car-Fi in Burien, I had begun building a huge audio system in a 1989 Ford Escort Pony. The customer had brought the car to Redmond about two weeks earlier to change some of the rear cosmetics. Luckily, the owner of Sound Advice, Kevin Epps, gave us free rein to do whatever we wanted, within reason, with our time.

Myself and another installer, Dan, would often arrive around 9:00 AM when we opened and sat around watching his little black and white TV that sat on his bench; bullshitting about the state of the world and how if everyone saw things the way car stereo installers did, the world would be a better place.

I had just moved in with a friend in Woodinville, a small town about 15 minutes north of Redmond. He had a one bedroom apartment but we figured in a couple months we would get a two bedroom. In the meantime I just crashed on the couch.

I had been living with my mother and Rich out in Duvall, but my mother was not too keen on having my girlfriend, Dawn, spend the night at her house. In fact, it was absolutely never allowed. While I had been working in Burien, it was cool because Dawn had her own place; but after her social security checks she was receiving due to her father's death quit rolling in, living on her own became more difficult. Once she had to move out of her own place, I began staying at my friend's house more and more until he just asked me to start paying rent.

On this particular Thursday, Dan and I were going over some ideas on how to change the back end cosmetics of the car I was working on. Two other installers, Eric and Rick, were tossing in their two cents worth every chance they got. Very little work got done, but we all loved where we worked and it was fun being the new kid on the block so to speak. Because most of my co-workers were married and somewhat responsible adults, they seemed to love hearing about my sober adventures; wine, women and song; minus the wine of course.

"Jon!—Line one," the intercom to the shop crackled, "Jon—line one."

"It's probably this guy wondering if I figured out what the fuck we were going to change with how the amps look, yet," I laughed, pointing at the little black Escort nudged up into my corner of the shop.

"Should we go with the whole motorized, plexi-glass amp rack—the stairway to the gods?" I mused.

I picked up the receiver and hit the line one button, "This is Jon can I help you?"

"Jon? It's Mom," I recognized my mother's voice on the other end.

She rarely called me at work, especially since I had moved out. Her voice sounded particularly serious so I tried to lessen the lecture I was probably about to receive because she (I supposed) had probably just opened a ticket or some other bill of mine that had been sent to her house by teasing her a little bit.

"Sorry," I said in a high pitched squeal, trying to disguise my voice "Jon's in jail," I laughed and looked over at my co-workers; they too, were amused.

"Jon- this is serious," her voice started to crack and she began to cry and then stopped—and then started again.

"Mum-Z?" I said, "What's wrong?"

I expected her to tell me that my sister who was expecting her first child any day now had finally gone into labor, or that she was really upset that I was still a little on the irresponsible side *or something*. But she usually reserved those conversations for when she saw me in person.

150

"Have you heard from Rich at all since yesterday?" she asked.

I could tell she was upset.

"No, I haven't talked to him since Saturday. *Why?*" I asked.

"Rich hasn't come home!" she began crying, "He hasn't called me back," her voice rose to a near yell, "and I've been paging him and paging him all night," she began to sob.

"What?" I said.

"What do you mean, he hasn't come home? Where is he?" I asked, startled because Rich always stayed in constant contact with my mother.

Even when we would go 'Subaru-ing' in the middle of the night he would page her just to let her know we weren't lost or stuck somewhere.

"*I DON'T KNOW!*" she sobbed," I just know he hasn't called," she struggled for breath, "or answered my pages," she sniffled, "or anything. I have called the police but they aren't any help. I just don't know."

She called the police?

Her crying was getting deeper and longer.

"I think something terrible has happened! This just isn't like him. Oh, Diana is back. I have to go. I'll call you if we hear something, if you hear from him — you tell him I am a mess and to call me, right away!"

At that moment I wasn't sure how or why or what was happening. At first it seemed like a big misunderstanding. Surely Rich was just stuck or lost or something.

But my gut knew.

I dropped the receiver and it hit the concrete shop floor with a high pitched crack. The guys in the shop just stared at me. For a moment I thought my knees were going to give out. My hands trembled as I walked over to the car we had been discussing amp locations and motorized racks and lights and plexiglass. I turned away from the car and sat down on the floor behind it cross legged and drew my hands up to my face and began to quietly cry. I knew at that moment that if Rich had not called Mom in over 24 hours, *something horrible had to have occurred.*

Dan and the other installers, who had not said a word since I dropped the phone gathered around me and just stared. No one said a word as I struggled to keep from crying anymore than I already was. After about what must have been two or three minutes, Dan kneeled down next me and put his hand on my shoulder.

"What happened, man? You alright?"

"I think my step-dad is dead," I said, crying, "I think he's dead. My mom hasn't heard from him since Monday night."

I shook my head back and forth and tried to process some other explanation. As hard as I struggled, I simply couldn't find one.

Dan grabbed my head and pulled me into his chest as tears rolled down my face, "It'll be alright, man. I'm sure he's fine."

Eric and Rick stood there staring.

No one said a word.

*　　　*　　　*

Around 11:00 AM Phil left the apartment. Sharon was nearly passed out now and he had brought the telephone out of the bedroom and replaced the one in the kitchen. It had a longer cord and he wanted the phone right next to her head so she would hear it ring. He needed to keep her on an even keel throughout the day. Going to go back to prison wasn't in his plans and he wasn't sure how this was going to play out with her. If he took care of everything well enough, she might just be able to keep quiet. It would be tough, this he knew; but she loved him.

She had married him in prison, Phil thought, and in some secret way she must have thought this could happen. In some sick way, he thought, she probably hoped it would happen. The excitement of deep secrets and knowing what others don't was kind of a rush. They would always remember what had happened; it would be their secret.

It would bind them.

After a while she would become as guilty as he was because she had not come forward. He just needed to get through these first few days. Once this was further behind them he would get help and stop drinking; he would finally be the husband she wanted.

He just had to ditch the car and get the Ranger unstuck. They just had to go about their normal lives like this had never happened. Dozens of unsolved murders occur every day, he said.

He would leave the car and walk away.

She was so tired and exhausted he was sure she wasn't going to be a problem — at least for awhile.

He drove down the street about two blocks into the car wash. Washing the car seemed to help sober him up and clear his mind. The early spring sun in the morning above Lake Sammamish could warm any soul.

Even his.

He pulled out of the car wash and into the morning traffic.

He came into a construction zone; the smell of new asphalt filled the car through the open window and sunroof. Pine Lake, it seemed, was perpetually under construction.

The Seattle suburb of Issaquah had blossomed from the last truck-stop town west of Snoqualmie Pass as travelers headed east on Interstate 90 from Seattle, into an "upwardly mobile" community of manicured home developments, poorly designed strip malls and gridlocked roads. Pine Lake, a few miles to the northeast was a 'relief valve' of sorts to all of the expansion occurring in the area. It had literally exploded in population overnight during the late eighties and was struggling to define itself with respect to urban development and planning. At one point, a large water park and amusement center were constructed, only to be torn down less than three years later for a business park, which was subsequently altered to correct a poor off-ramp design from I-90.

He looked back down at the car.

Wow.

An '88 Mustang GT.

Gripping the wheel with one hand he romped on the accelerator a little bit. The Mustang lurched forward.

He smiled.

As a sales team leader at Evergreen Ford in Issaquah he was very familiar with this car. He tapped on the power window switch and the tinted window slid silently down into the door. His short hair danced across his forehead. He reached across and turned up the radio a bit.

Sports TALK 950. Perfect.

Fire engine red wasn't particularly his color he thought, but the personalized plates were cool- "DUVALL". People probably thought he was some sort of important business man.

His fingers tapped out a beat on the steering wheel.

A lawyer perhaps.

Or maybe a successful business owner.

His grin widened. He glanced down at the business card he pulled from the center console.

Duvall Realty? A real estate man.

Cool.

At the stop light, he looked over at a blonde girl in a convertible VW Rabbit and smiled.

She smiled back.

He was getting used to this now.

He really liked it.

His job at the dealership paid him better than he had ever made before. In 1989 he cleared almost 50 grand. He could never have made fifty grand in a year as a barber — probably not in two or three years. And yet, for some reason, success was hard for him to deal with.

Everyone went to the bar after a strong day of sales. Everyone drank Tanqueray and tonic or Martinis and went home to their wives or husbands or girlfriends and lived happy normal lives. Everyone got up in the morning and felt good and reveled in their accomplishments. Alcohol was a reward; a marker; a signal of a job well done.

Of satisfaction and advancement.

Alcohol was the way we celebrated and showed the world; and our friends; and our colleagues that we had done good. Alcohol was at the front of the grocery store when we walked in; alcohol was kept cool and fresh for our enjoyment in the back.

Alcohol was everywhere.

Alcohol was the devil.

He sighed and placed both hands on the wheel as the car dove into the tight corners of Eastlake Sammamish Parkway. He downshifted into third and stepped on the gas again, the seat tightened around his back. He dropped the clutch and threw it into fourth, *fuck yeah.* He knew this car could probably run at 130 or 140 all day long.

It was almost 12:45 now; he had to meet the tow truck driver at 3:00 PM. It was about an hour and a half back to Darrington so he was making good time. In this thing he could make it there in an hour if need be-

COP!

FUCK...

...he casually let off the gas and stepped on the brake- but not enough to cause the car to visibly shift forward. He prayed he hadn't been speeding. He glared into the rear view mirror and sweat formed on his brow.

The motorcycle cop definitely was pulling him over.

The shotgun was on the floor under his jacket.

Did he remember to load it? *Of course.*

He came around the bend as he slowed down and another motorcycle cop pulled another car over right in front of him.

There were two of them.

He's pulling over another car? *What!?*

Oh shit.

He knew he could get the cop before the cop even knew what happened. He knew what that double barreled Stevens lodged between the door and seat could do at close range. But that second cop?

Fuck.

King County Police Officer Jerry Hamilton was new on the force. Some people in life were meant to fight fires, some people in life were meant to sell jewelry and some people in life were meant to keep the sheep safe from the wolves.

This was Officer Hamilton.

He wanted to take down criminals in a big way and working traffic was his way into law enforcement. His dream was to eventually chase

154

down hard criminals — by working in the warrants division. It was dangerous work. Most cops don't want to have anything to do with it.

Officer Hamilton on the other hand, craved it.

Nine hundred and ninety nine out of a thousand stops were routine, but he knew that you could never predict when the one would come that wasn't routine. Whether that meant someone was having a baby in the back seat or if a cold blooded killer was cruising his victim's car with a loaded double barreled shotgun hiding between the passenger seat and door, and two plastic grocery bags full of a dead man's keep, he did not know.

Officer Hamilton however, did know procedure. And he followed it. If he was going to work in the warrants division he knew there would be no letting your guard down. If you did, you could end up dead. He approached the car cautiously from the driver's side. Phil had pulled over far enough onto the shoulder that hopefully the protruding maple branches would keep the cop from coming up on the passenger side.

According to Officer Hamilton, he had been traveling 51 MPH in a 40 MPH zone and the front plate of the Mustang was missing. He handed him his license and frantically searched for the registration while giving the cop his correct home address as the one on the license was not current. Officer Hamilton turned and walked back to his patrol motorcycle and raised the microphone to his mouth.

Had he placed the registration into one of the trash bags on the seat?

Shit.

Was the shotgun hidden?

What if the Officer wanted him to get out of the car?

Did they know?

They would have had their guns drawn.

License and registration? Proof of insurance?

He knew he didn't smell of booze anymore. He had changed clothes, scarfed down the milk and donuts and not had anything to drink for hours.

But he had drank a lot.

A lot.

He worried it might just be seeping out his pores. Cops were trained for this, but he was not drunk. He could pass a field sobriety test. He looked into the rear view to see what the cop was doing.

His forehead dampened.

The increasing breeze coming across the lake felt cool. He ran the palms of his hands along the tops of his thighs up and down from his knees to his hips.

Deliberately he stopped.

Murder myself, Murder I am.

He looked down at the clock on the radio; it was 12:52 PM. In the rear view he could see the cop look up and gaze toward his driver's mirror. The tinting in the back window was too dark for the cop to see him in the rear view but as their eyes locked in the driver's rear view mirror a lump formed in his throat. He wanted to look over at where the shotgun was lying, but he knew he was being watched. He smiled and ran his fingers through his short, matted hair.

Look natural.

He wanted a fuckin' drink, bad. Again he glanced into the drivers mirror, *the cop was gone.*

He could see the motorcycle still parked, but the cop was nowhere to be- the clipboard nearly hit him in the jaw as Officer Hamilton leaned through the open passenger window and thrust it toward him with a pen.

He was leaning too far into the car to notice the shotgun lying under the jacket and the trash bags probably did not seem out of place.

He was being given a verbal warning for speeding, for not having insurance and for not having registration. He was being cited for not having the front plate however.

Shit.

He had 15 days to respond or pay the $133 fine. Officer Hamilton told him to drive carefully and have a nice day.

Have a nice day?

He was now fucked and he knew it.

It would only be a matter of time before they tied him to the car. He was given a ticket in the man's car less than 24 hours after he went missing?

He was on parole for murder and an assault. Oh yeah, he was fucked and he knew it. She was there, she had seen it all.

Fuck.

She was back on the couch sleeping. When she finds out about this she will freak the fuck out. He couldn't keep driving this around. It was fire fucking engine red with personal plates that said DUVALL.

And the front one was obviously missing.

How long would it be before another cop pulled him over for it?

He drove north into Redmond, Washington and then retraced the 80 mile route from earlier in the morning back to Darrington. As he drove, the suburban landscape of Redmond and Woodinville faded in to the gently wooded farmlands of central Snohomish County. Before he realized how much time had passed, he had returned to the darker, more deeply forested foothills of the western slopes of the North Cascades.

At 2:45 PM he pulled into a payphone along Highway 530 just west of Darrington and called her collect. He explained how he dumped the trash bags along three different turnouts along Highway 9 and not to worry, he would take care of everything. She sounded different now that she had rested for a while.

He rewiped the car down and got rid of everything, he told her. No need to worry, this was all going to work out. He had a few minutes to kill before meeting the tow truck driver at 3:00 PM and he did not want to show up early as that might be something to make someone remember him or what he looked like. He went into the bushes behind the phone booth and ditched the shotgun so he could get it later.

Mid afternoon was really warming up and he was wearing gray shorts underneath his white cotton sweats. He took off his sweat pants and discarded them as well. He knew she would panic and do something stupid so he kept the fact that he got the ticket to himself. He had to tell her eventually *but not until he could keep a close eye on her.*

He had to come up with something. He wasn't going to go back to prison.

Not for this.

But the ticket complicated things.

A lot.

14

An hour and a half after getting the ticket, Phil made his way into Darrington and made a right turn off of Highway 530 onto Commercial Avenue. He searched for an inconspicuous place to ditch the car.

A couple blocks down Commercial, he turned left onto Darrington Street. He pulled into the northwest corner of the parking lot of the Serve-U grocery store at the corner of Darrington Street and Givens Avenue and with a napkin in his left hand he wiped down the gear shifter, the steering wheel and the window switches very quickly and discreetly. The grocery store had been closed for weeks, maybe even months.

He pulled on the door handle with the napkin and subtly pushed it into his pocket as he exited, making sure to close the door with his sleeve covering his palm. Not wanting to attract any attention as though he were leaving the car for any length of time, he purposefully left the window down and the door unlocked. Anyone who noticed the car would most likely think nothing of it; that the owner must be close by and returning shortly. Hopefully, passers by would pay it no heed.

"Hey Roy!" he heard.

"Nice car!" the girl's voice got closer and more direct. He pretended he was in a hurry and ducked away from her toward the Red Top Tavern a block down the road.

"Oops," she giggled covering her mouth and nearly tripping, "you're not Roy, sorry," she laughed as most embarrassed teen aged girls do.

At first she thought it was Roy Bryson, a friend who had recently moved out of Darrington. She followed him across the parking lot for a moment trying to catch up to him as she was wondering what Roy could have been up to which allowed him to drive a hot red car like that. But just as she called out to who she believed was her old friend, she realized this man was not quite as stocky as Roy and continued about her business.

He wandered about the outside of the closed grocery store for a minute. Quickly, he walked north on Givens Street toward Seeman Street. He turned east and walked just past Montague where he was supposed to meet Mr. Fox. The snow cap on Whitehorse Mountain was brilliantly illuminated in the springtime sunshine.

A white Ford F-350 wrecker with 'Pine Tree Services' sprawled across the door was parked nose in alongside the service bay doors. A man in his late twenties or early thirties wearing greasy blue coveralls and a dirty 76 ball cap looked out from the counter. His name patch had come mostly unstitched but the red letters 'Ed' could still be made out across the grease stained, white cotton background. He rose and moved around the counter to meet him before he came fully into the stations cramped service desk area.

"Is Mr. Fox around? I was supposed to meet him here," Phil asked.

"You must be from down below, eh?" Ed answered wiping his hands.

No one from Darrington called him 'Mr. Fox.'

Ed explained that John Fox Sr., the driver/owner of the towing service had been called to take his wife to Everett due to a dental emergency. John was certainly very sorry for the inconvenience and he did not know how long this trip would take, if he could not wait, John instructed, he was of course free to make other arrangements. Ed was not certain how long it would be. Phil did not want to come across as an impatient asshole. Certainly he'd be remembered then.

But the ticket; *was it really going to matter?*

He looked to his left and a Darrington Police cruiser immediately caught his attention. His gaze could not be peeled from it as it cruised slowly by and turned down Montague.

His jaw clenched.

Had they found the car already?

He needed a drink. It had been a few hours and this was turning into a clusterfuck. If he got another tow, then more people will have seen him in town.

Fuck.

He told Ed he would wait for a bit and check in later. He tried to be pleasant and natural; not hurried or desperate.

Heading west down Seeman Street a couple of blocks he found the Skyline restaurant. Just inside the first set of double glass doors he found a phone booth. He called her again and informed her of the delay and reassured her everything was going to be fine. He had it all worked out. There was nothing to worry about. Convinced she was no longer hysterical, he hung up.

He walked in through the second set of double glass doors and turned right into the lounge. It was dimly lit and he felt anyone who he interacted with him would most likely not be able to recognize him again. The bartender, Kathy Ford, stood behind the bar talking to a young woman in her early thirties, Roberta Howe. She was drinking coffee and by the conversation it became apparent she worked the later shift behind the bar.

He ordered a double Scotch and nearly shotgunned it down. He looked over his shoulder toward the door.

And ordered another.

Kathy stared at him a little strangely. He got up from his seat and walked out through the door to look back up Seeman Street toward the tow yard. He wasn't exactly aware what kind of vehicle John Fox Sr. drove, but if he saw one at the station he might know that he had returned.

Nothing but the white wrecker.

He pushed in through the double glass doors again and sat down in front of his second double tall on the rocks. He turned and looked back over his shoulder at the door again. Bert (Roberta) stopped talking and glanced nervously at Kathy. He noticed this and nodded toward them and smiled. The only sound emanating from the yellow light of the cocktail lounge was the clinking of ice cubes as he tipped the glass back and wispy conversation of two women not wanting to be overheard but not wanting to be known they did not want to be overheard.

The two women kept quietly talking. About thirty minutes later he went outside and took a long look up the street again. It was almost five o'clock.

Where the fuck was that old man?

At about 5:45 PM he paid for his drinks and went out to use the phone. He called Pine Tree Services to see if word had gotten back as to when Mr. Fox was going to return. Ed hadn't heard from him yet. He told Ed to pass it along that he was going to wait for Mr. Fox to return. He needed the tow and he was not mad that Mr. Fox had to go to Everett unannounced.

Things happen.

But, he liked the service he received from the tow yard in the past and wanted to do business again. He tried to remain pleasant and unhurried.

But he was really getting nervous. Surely somebody was starting to wonder where the man in the red Mustang was.

Just as he was about to hang up Ed told him to hold on, the other phone line was ringing, and it might be Mr. Fox. A few moments later, Ed came back on the line and told him that Mr. Fox was going to be in around seven o'clock if he was still in town and needed that tow. He hung up the phone and quickly called her back at the apartment.

He had finally gotten a hold of the tow truck guy and that everything was working out, he explained. She was getting nervous again, he could tell. Her tone was higher in pitch and she was almost crying. He was worried she had been talking to her mother.

That could be disastrous.

This was going to be tough enough without her interference. She could tell he was buzzed again. He had to keep the drinking somewhat under control, for if he were blasted again, the tow truck driver might report him.

The drinks were working however. For a moment he had a euphoric sense of purpose. Everything was going to work out. He just had to get his truck unstuck. He smiled warmly.

The ticket.

His heart sank again.

Fuck.

Along the bar, the lady who served him earlier was gone and the woman who had been chatting with her and drinking coffee when he arrived was now serving drinks. No one else had come in so he sat back in the same chair. She had removed his empty glass and wiped down the bar. It was still wet and he could see the streak marks left from the bar towel. It felt awkward.

Maybe he should wait outside?

But someone would notice him. A stranger; an out-of-towner aimlessly about the sidewalks of Darrington. He couldn't keep drinking, but he had to. He wanted to.

The tow driver was a goofy old man. Why would he care if he had a few drinks? His truck was stuck for fucks sake. Who wouldn't? He ordered a double brandy.

He just needed to relax.

Brandy was soothing, warming and comforting. Yes, he would enjoy a brandy, it was all good.

At about seven he paid for the brandy and left. He felt fabulous, his stride was long, his chin was high; he could do this. He liked this lounge. These people were cool. Darrington had always been good to him.

The brandy had served its purpose.

He swung the double doors open and moved out onto the walkway. The coolness of dusk was settling across the town. He wished he had kept the sweatpants now. It was a bit cool.

He turned and made his way toward Montague Street. It was almost seven o'clock and if Mr. Fox was ready to tow him out, he could leave this town for good, Mr. Fox was a fair man, a good man. His thoughts were becoming slurred.

Ed had long ago locked up the service station doors and gone home for the night. The white F-350 was still nosed along side the garage bay doors. To the west he could see the formation of clouds littering across the sky in front of the golden red sunset. It was a clear evening and he thought he could make out the northern Olympic Mountains on the Olympic Peninsula.

He loved the mountains.

At fifteen after seven he thought about going back to the Mustang and simply driving back home.

That would be stupid.

Maybe he should leave a note that he was at the Skyline and Mr. Fox should join him for a cocktail prior to extracting his truck.

That would have been even more stupid.

He went back to the phone booth.

At seven thirty his buzz was starting to taper off. As he lifted the receiver he heard the low, dull roar of a tow truck. John Fox Sr. finally pulled into the lot. He darted back in to the Skyline and threw two tens and a five down on to the bar and slid back outside.

He greeted Mr. Fox and piled into the wrecker for the trip up the hill. He wanted to get this over with and get back down to the bar. He needed another drink.

But not until after.

What a day. The ticket. The tavern. Now, the tow. What else could go wrong? It was time to relax and just get the truck unstuck and go.

The wrecker lumbered up the Mountain Loop Highway, it was about ten miles out of town. He had been trying to find the Mt. Pugh trailhead but it was darker out when he was last here and the monotonous and unchanging landscape made it difficult.

He was sweating and his bare legs uncomfortably stuck to the vinyl seat of the Ford tow truck. He rolled the window down but it seemed awful breezy so he rolled it back up.

Too hot.

He rolled it back down.

The driver peeked over at him out of the corner of his eye. An awkward silence ensued and he rolled it down just a crack and looked to

Mr. Fox for his approval. In silent agreement they nodded toward each other. The window was fine.

Where the fuck was the road?

Somehow yesterday, he had directed her to turn up the wrong road. He was wasted and she was not much better off. It's no wonder they ended up nose down in a washout.

They drove past the White Chuck Campground, a place he had camped before. A few minutes later he pointed on the left where the small logging road hit the Mountain Loop Highway. John Fox signaled left and turned up onto the road.

He signaled?

The road was a little steeper than he remembered but he was pretty wasted yesterday. The branches hung lower than he remembered also.

Was he that fucked up?

The wrecker slowly crawled up the road. The tires slipped and jerked catapulting jagged, baseball sized rocks down toward the highway. It was starting to get dark but they probably had an hour or so before it would become real difficult. He rolled down the window all the way and gripped the rain sill of the cab of the truck. They came up to the first water bar and he was surprised at how much larger it was without the lingering effect of a belly full of whiskey. The truck climbed up the dug out ditch slowly, the rear axles however could not clear. The truck came to a halt.

Phil hopped out and began tossing fallen branches and loose logs into the water bar to help get the tow truck traction. He was moving with a purpose. John Fox more or less shook his head. This guy was bound and determined he thought; almost panicked to get up that hill. He wasn't even thinking straight.

John backed the truck down the hill into a small turn around and turned 180 degrees to back up the hill. He decided to winch the wrecker beyond the water bar. As soon as Phil saw this, he grabbed the winch cable and started running up the hill toward the nearest tree of suitable size to hoist the truck up across the obstacles. He wrapped the cable around an old snag and gave the signal to start winching; as soon as the cable became taut, even before the truck began to move upwards, the old rotten snag to which he had secured the winch cable began to give way and tore in half with a soft, dull crack. Without even hesitating he grabbed the cable and ordered the driver to freewheel the spool.

He would find another tree. *He had to.*

John was impressed with the strength and determination with which Phil took the winch cable up the hill and re-secured it to a 20 inch cedar. With a whir the winch drug the wrecker up and over the water bar.

Phil breathed a sigh of relief and wiped his brow. He needed a drink and needed one soon. He climbed in the cab and leaned forward encouraging John to hurry up the hill.

Things were moving forward now. This was good. He could get the truck out, and get a drink. John got the truck turned around and headed up the road.

It was only one or two hundred feet further. The ruts in the path were much more difficult for an F-350 wrecker than his little Ford Ranger. The width of the full size truck caused the right front tire to fall continuously into the ruts left over from the wet spring.

He suggested they stay as far to the left as possible. Branches slid and drug along the drivers side of the cab. The rut grew into a ditch and John feared the wrecker was going to slide into it and require another winching just to get it back out of the hill. Just before John was about to turn the wrecker around, the tailgate of the 1990 Ford Ranger came into view. It pointed nearly straight upward toward the sky.

He thought it had nosed in at about a 30 degree angle but now he could see it was more than 45 degrees. Suddenly the wrecker jerked and jolted to a stop. John piled out of the drivers side and reached into the bed for something.

What the fuck was he doing? He was reaching for something.

Fuck.

John pulled out a mid size chain saw, flipped a small lever on its left side and jerked on the cord. Nothing, He jerked again. With a growl, blue smoke sang out the side of the saw as it growled to life. What the fuck was he doing? Had he seen something?

John stepped in front of the nose of the truck and began sawing a small Douglas fir. Clearing the tree out of the way would allow the wrecker to unabatedly continue to the Ranger. He was nervous now. The chainsaw was loud. He needed a drink.

He needed a fucking drink.

The tree fell away to the side and Mr. Fox placed the chainsaw quietly in the back. The wrecker pulled up alongside the washout and he turned the big truck around using a shallow turnout. In less than 15 minutes they had the truck righted and turned; nose facing downhill.

He checked the camping gear in the back and let John know he would follow him down to the road and then to town where he would pay the tow bill. John knew he wasn't going anywhere but back down to the main road so he jumped in the big Ford and slowly crawled it back down toward the Mountain Loop Highway.

At the bottom of the skid road John turned the wrecker on to the Mountain Loop Highway and waited. Nearly 20 minutes passed and the man in the Ranger was nowhere to be found.

What was taking him?

A few minutes later the Ranger banged and creaked down to the road. Phil followed Mr. Fox back into Darrington and parked around the side of the service station. Anything to lower the chance that someone would see the truck and recognize it again. Finally, he was done with this shit.

He walked with Mr. Fox to the glass door of the service station. Mr. Fox's keys clanked against the still night air. It was almost cold out.

That drink was coming ever closer.

He should call her to make sure she is still hanging on. The ticket would wait though.

What time was it?

He took the bill from Mr. Fox and looked at it.

86 bucks was cheap.

He handed him his Unocal card. Mr. Fox slid the card and picked up the phone.

What the fuck was he doing?

He depressed the phone again receiver and dialed the number again. Without an authorization number Pine Tree Services was out on the hook for the last hour and a half. Phil wrote his home number and address on the back of the card and John Fox noted the license number of the 1990 Ford Ranger on the credit card slip. He thanked Mr. Fox and turned into the night.

A block down the road the Skyline was still open. He had time for one more before he hit the road and was finally done with this town.

15

Friday   May 4, 1990

Phil pulled into the apartment parking lot just after midnight and drove through quickly and deliberately.

Nothing appeared out of the ordinary.

The parking lot lights were still on; it didn't look too suspicious. He turned around the block and pulled back into the complex. Still woozy from the drinks, it had been an hour since he finished the beer he picked up in Arlington. The drive back seemed to take forever and that bitch from the Skyline acted like she remembered him.

What a stupid bitch.

And that red-haired girl who had seen him get out of the car, she was probably too stupid to remember him also.

His exhausted frame swayed side to side as the truck crept across the speed bump into the parking space; his elbows bounced off the steering wheel. Slowly his body straightened up from the turn. It wasn't that sharp or quick of a turn; but 200 pounds of drunken attitude can be hard to keep straight; steering wheel or not.

His eyes were starting to glaze as he popped open the door to the truck. His left foot slid out and his right foot got caught up in the clutch pedal.

He looked toward the apartment stairwell entrance and noticed the porch light was off. It was never off. He had turned it on when he left.

He thought.

He dove into the bushes next to his truck and scurried behind the dumpster. Adrenaline can sober someone up real quick and he was sober now. Crouching around the side of the dumpster fence he reached down and wiped the beauty bark stuck to his knees off onto the asphalt. He scurried between the Ranger and the Chevrolet truck parked one space over. From the rear of the Chevrolet he could get a better look into the sliding glass door of the apartment.

She had turned him in?

That bitch.

He looked at the cars in the lot. None of them seemed obvious. But would they really be here and not outside waiting for him?

Maybe they were watching him now.

He ducked behind the Ranger again and stared up the hill into the darkness behind the apartment complex. The rockery was nearly straight up but he climbed it unnoticed to get a better look around.

Why was the fucking porch light off?

He could see in the rear sliding glass door. In the shadows under the kitchen table he could make out Rusty, lying motionless in the light spilling in from the hallway.

Nothing moved.

The bedroom window was closed, the light was off and the Levelor blinds were down and shut. In the apartment above, shades of blue and gray light flickered from the window. He heard what sounded like a man arguing in a courtroom. Back across the parking lot he focused, trying to pick out any car which he didn't recognize.

On the road behind him he could hear a car approaching in the distance. The glow from the headlights lit the tops of the trees. The evening breeze drew a silent song from the leaves. His cheeks were cold and tight. Crouching down even further he squinted back into his apartment. He half jumped and slid along the edge of the rockery back along the path he had scurried up. His hand felt the frosty grass along the edge. He crossed the parking lot past his truck trying to look normal in case he was seen. If they weren't there, he didn't need one of his neighbors thinking he was prowling for cars.

Once safely cloaked in the shadows of his apartment building, he quickly slipped around the corner onto the lawn and slid along the siding of the building up next to the patio attached to his apartment. Without looking around the corner he stopped and held his breath. Straining so that he could hear voices inside the apartment he froze. He could hear a man's voice again. A man's voice asking if the defendant always carried a gun.

Fuck.

"Objection your honor!"

What? *Objection?*

It was the fucking TV.

He jerked his head around the corner for just a second to see if any obvious figures could be made out in the kitchen.

No one.

Rusty, under the table.

He breathed. He stared again. The apartment looked empty.

He took another breath. He climbed up over the railing to the deck. He glanced around beforehand- if the neighbors were going to call the cops, breaking and entering into his own place was not how he wanted it to go down. One leg dropped quietly onto the concrete patio and then the other. He felt something give in his upper thigh. Physically, he was in excellent shape, but at 36, even regular trips to the gym can't stop every grain of the marching sands of time. A shallow pain had started to appear in his back the day before.

She was still asleep on the couch. He grabbed the handle to the sliding door and pulled.

Nothing. It was locked.

He tapped on the glass hoping to wake her up.

Not wanting to risk drawing any attention by climbing the railing to the deck again; he tapped on the door. He did not want to bang on the glass so loud that the neighbor upstairs might be alarmed.

A prisoner on his own patio.

He pulled his keys from the pocket of his windbreaker and tapped on the glass some more. She twitched and rolled over. He tapped again. Rusty wagged his tail and watched.

What a watch dog. This was not going to work.

He looked up and could now see her standing in the slider looking out at him. He made his way toward the door with the keys gripped tightly in his hand.

She unlocked the slider and let him in.

Their glances never met, she couldn't even look at him. He turned sideways not wanting to even brush up against her as he came in and headed for the kitchen.

He had to keep her under control.

She had been sleeping on and off most of the day. In between cigarettes and fits of agitation and disbelief she told herself over and over it would work out. She wrote notes to Phil; asking him-- pleading with him-- to stop drinking. She crumpled them all up and threw them away.

This was not the time. *Or was it?*

The phone from the bedroom was still nestled in to the brown shag carpet along side the couch. The cord had been twisted into a maze of loops. She was nervous, anxious and in shock to say the least.

The Vodka was in the cupboard above the refrigerator. He pulled a glass out of the dishwasher. It was dirty. It didn't matter. He could hear footsteps move from the living room down the hall in the apartment above him. The ice cubes clinked as they hit the bottom of the glass. Reaching in to the refrigerator he pulled out the last of the orange juice. He shook it and the splattering sound of a few drops of orange juice against the cardboard carton brought a discontented frown to his lips. He twisted the lid from the plastic gallon jug of Relsky Vodka.

The slider opened and she stepped out on to the patio. He took a hit from the bottle.

Click.

Click.

She drew in a hit from a Winston Ultralight as she set the lighter down. Within seconds he could smell the burning cigarette. Rusty got up and stretched. The toilet above him flushed and water ran down the drain pipe to his right. No one wanted to say a word. The everyday sounds they never seemed to hear were amplified; screaming out to break the awkward silence. He took another hit from the bottle. He could taste the plastic. The footsteps above him moved back into the living room. He could hear the screech of the recliner spring above him.

He poured.

The Vodka draped over the ice cubes like an executioner placing a black cloak over a condemned man's head. And the crowd was cheering for a quick execution.

She put the cigarette out, stepped in through the slider and plopped back down on the couch. He sat at the table and patted Rusty on the side. The dog's white leg came up and fluttered as he rubbed the scruffy fur. She knew he would drink until he passed out. It was like any other Thursday night.

Still no one spoke.

At least he had gotten rid of that fucking Mustang. Maybe now they could just go on. If they just pretended it never happened, *did it?*

As quick as she sat in the sofa she jumped back up. Hoping her obvious movements would break the stalemate. At least he could ask her what she was doing.

Nothing.

She disappeared for a few seconds and came out from the bedroom with an electronic alarm clock and set the alarm for 8:00 AM. On Friday mornings he had a sales meeting at 8:30 AM.

Murder myself, Murder I am.

He worried.

That fucking ticket.

He had to tell her about the ticket. If it hit the news and she didn't know about it, she would probably get hysterical and who knew what would happen. But alcoholics and the co-dependents they live with know how to leave well enough alone. She didn't need to know *right now*.

Hear no evil.

Speak no evil.

16

Friday morning I rolled over in my mother's guest bed and looked at the digital clock radio on the nightstand.

6:00. Good grief.

I knew my brother-in law- Tim would be up by now. He loved mornings, *I hated them*. I could hear footsteps upstairs in the kitchen above me. The coffee pot clanked across the sink and the pipe in the wall behind me sang to life as someone filled it upstairs. I groaned and rolled over.

Then I remembered.

I jumped out of bed and got dressed. Upstairs in the kitchen my mother sat at the table. For nearly 48 hours she had been calling every single person, agency, associate and colleague who may have possibly heard from or seen Rich. Her face was swollen and her eyes red from crying all night. Right now she wasn't crying however, *for now*. Her friend Diana finished putting grounds into the filter and slid it back into place.

"Hi Jon," Diana whispered, "She hasn't slept all night; she has been writing things down and crying. She'll be ok today — just go find Rich."

I stood in the kitchen wondering what to say. Seeing your mother in this condition is never fun for anyone. I felt like it wasn't even her and if any of us said the wrong thing or brought up the wrong subject that we may send her into a sobbing fit again. Tim and my sister, Colleen had just come downstairs. Everyone danced on eggshells. My mother had a pen and a notepad with dozens of pages and phone numbers and notes folded over it.

"Hi," my mother said looking up from her notebook. Her voice seemed kind of upbeat.

"Did you hear anything from Rich?" I asked, knowing what the answer probably was but felt like it was the best question to ask at the time.

"No," she said softly.

She drew a deep breath and almost started crying again. She took another deep breath to gather herself.

"You and Tim are going to go over the North Cascades Highway all the way to Moses Lake?" she asked.

"Yeah—I am sure he probably just went off the road somewhere and he might be stuck in the seatbelt or something—if he wrecked the car pretty good he might be fine; but just stuck. Don't worry; we'll find him and have a good laugh. Remember when he tried to turn the Volvo into a boat?" I tried to be positive.

Mom looked up from her pad and tried to smile. Even through all of the turmoil of the last 48 hours she still tried to acknowledge my sometimes senseless wit.

"We are going to stop at all the gas stations and little stores and see if we can find where he last used his credit card and stuff," I continued.

Mom dropped her pen on to the table and leaned back in her chair.

"Ok, be careful. You're dad is going to fly his airplane over the same area and see if he can spot a red car from the air somewhere," she stated strongly.

Although my parents had been divorced for 15 years, and rarely interacted, my dad was always ready to help anyone who needed it, this included. Diana's husband Denny was also going to ride his motorcycle straight to Moses Lake and then retrace Rich's route back from there; hoping to find some skid marks off the road and Rich's large frame captured in his seatbelt, but alive, off the road somewhere.

"Why don't you get some sleep, Karen?" Diana asked, rubbing my mother's back gently.

"No, I'll be fine," Mom answered.

She bounced back and forth between trying to be strong and positive to shaking her head and crying.

Tim reached under the counter into the cupboard and poured half of the coffee from the pot into the giant size insulated mug he always carried. I grabbed a smaller one and filled it up. Tim and I quietly snuck outside to have a cigarette.

Huddled next to the garage door outside in the gravel driveway Tim and I began plotting our strategy.

"Fuck, your mom is NOT happy," Tim started, "do you think we'll find him somewhere?"

"Shit. I don't know," I answered.

"He never drives that Mustang like he does his Subaru, I doubt he went onto the gravel roads with it, but he might have."

I took a drag and exhaled. Tim and I both looked at each other for some sort of positive sign, but neither of us appeared too hopeful.

"I think he just got lost, we've been on so many roads where he had no idea where we were but said 'we just keep heading one direction until we find a familiar road.' I don't know—but he has never really been in the North Cascades off-roading before. I hope he didn't run in to some dope grower or something. Fuck. Who knows?" I wondered aloud.

"I'm going to laugh when we find him on some road in the middle of nowhere, out of gas and out of cellular range," Tim added, smiling.

Behind the house, on the lake; we could hear a grebe serenading the coming morning sun. Down the driveway a car engine roared up the road toward the stop sign. We looked at each other, hoping that between the trees and bushes that lined the driveway we would catch a flash of red and see Rich's Mustang. But, the car turned right and disappeared around the lake.

"Do those cellular car phones even work up there?" he asked and flicked his cigarette out onto the gravel.

"Beats the shit out of me," I answered.

I turned and opened the front door to head back in.

My mother was still sitting at the dining room table. She handed Tim a gas credit card and got up to pour out the cold cup of coffee sitting in front of her. She never really liked drip coffee. But it seemed every time she turned around someone was trying to help he or comfort her offering to do something or asking if she needed anything; or, by filling a mug of the brown sludge and handing it to her and then asking if she needed to get some sleep. It just seemed like the right thing to do.

She tossed it into the sink.

"Where exactly are you guys going? DO NOT go up to people's houses or anything," she warned, "I am sure he would have used his Texaco card and got gas somewhere. Maybe you can find it. Don't get lost either. We don't need to have to come looking for you also."

"We won't," Tim replied, "We'll put up the flyers and see if we can't find him somewhere, Karen."

There were so many roads and small towns; Sedro-Wooley, Concrete, Darrington, Twisp. We weren't even sure where to start looking. It was like searching for a needle in a haystack.

*   *   *

The buzzer from the alarm startled Sharon up from the couch. She looked toward the front door. She was finally starting to get calmed down. She had slept off and on for the last nine hours, waking at every sound, going out on to the patio for a smoke and then clutching a pillow on the sofa. The chain was still across the top. Rusty wagged his tail and headed for the door. She slid open the chain and let him out. He was a pretty smart dog and the neighbors all recognized him.

She liked living here.

It was quaint and it was pleasant. He was making good money and apartment life was soon going to be a thing of the past. She liked flowers and despite asking the apartment complex manager if she could plant flowers in the bark along their patio, she had not yet got around to it.

But why bother?

They were going to be buying a house somewhere up here on the Plateau soon. She could plant all the flowers she wanted once she owned her own home. She really liked wildflowers and wanted to landscape with natural grasses and river rocks. She thought flowers would accent the curves of the river rocks nicely; especially against red brick pavers or railroad ties. Houses were going up everywhere on the Issaquah plateau and they were about ready to settle in to one of them.

But he might have fucked that all up.

She pulled down a white bathrobe from behind the closet door and slipped it on. She needed to get some coffee going.

Face down on the table he still wore the gray shorts and bright shirt from the day before. The Vodka bottle was empty and the orange juice carton was tipped over next to the sink. It was his day off so he didn't need to dress for work but he had to at least look presentable for the meeting.

And he had to go to that meeting.

They had to keep things normal.

He had wiped the car down and no one had seen them. They wouldn't find the car for days, he assured her; and it could be weeks, months or years if they ever did find anything. If they just kept up appearances, everything would be alright. This could be the best thing that ever happened.

They could start fresh, start new. He had gotten the truck back and gotten rid of that car. No one saw him, no one came looking. It was going to be ok. Just keep doing what we do and change nothing.

Maybe this was the wakeup call he needed to *finally stop drinking.*

He groaned and lifted his head from the table.

She started a pot of coffee.

His head felt like an axe had been driven into it. He gripped the Nuprin bottle and flipped the lid off on to the floor. He threw his head back and tossed four or five pills in toward the back of his throat and leaned down next to the faucet, tilted his head sideways and turned the water on. He pulled back and drove his hands toward the cold stream and splashed it into his hard face.

"We're going to need to get out of here for a few days," Phil said, quietly, staring out the kitchen window into the back yard of the apartment.

Gray clouds framed the dark green evergreens on the hill behind them. He drew a deep sigh.

Sharon's stomach jumped up into her throat. Her neck stiffened painfully.

"Get...out?" she said, barely stumbling through the words, stunned at the idea.

"You said if you got rid of the car and got it wiped down, that we just needed to act like nothing was wrong," she demanded, half screaming and half crying.

"I KNOW!" he yelled. "I KNOW what I said, But--"

"But what?" she asked as she reached in to the pocket of her hoodie draped around the dining room chair for a lighter.

He just stared.

"But *WHAT?* Phil?" she plied again as she opened the slider and sat down on the milk crate perched on the littered patio.

Cigarette butts overflowed both of the small brown ash trays. She grabbed one and turned it upside down into the coffee can she left out for just that purpose.

"I'm going to take a leave of absence from work, too," he stated coldly and turned to face her. He grabbed the hand towel from the oven door handle and dried his hands.

"*What?!*" she blurted.

She turned and stared in to the apartment.

"We need to just stick this out god dammit! You need to quit drinking and just stick this out! How the *fuck is taking a leave from absence going to help anything?*" she was nearly crying.

He stood upright, not really sure how she was going to react when he told her.

"Fuck this Phil! You said you just needed to wipe it down and ditch it; you said no one was going to find out what happened;-- that this kind of SHIT happened all the time!" she cried.

He stood silent and closed his eyes.

This is such bullshit.

"I got a fucking ticket, yesterday," he said coldly.

"So, what? People get tickets all the time. Pay it... *Where?* On your way back--" she stopped suddenly and her face drew upwards and met his, "Not in fucking Darrington, *Oh God.* Not in Darrington?"

"I got pulled over in that Mustang. Right after I washed it, on Sammamish Parkway," he said.

"*You what?!*" she screamed as she extinguished her cigarette in the now empty ashtray and quickly lit another one. Her hands trembled as she brought it and the lighter up to her face.

A ticket.

A fucking ticket?

"You got a ticket in that fucking Mustang? Jesus fucking Christ, Phil!! Do you know what that means? You son of a bitch!" she cried.

It would only be a matter of time now. She was scared. The asshole should have told her last night. She wasn't going to go down for this.

And she knew that *he knew* that.

That scared her even more.

If he didn't like what she was doing or how she was reacting would he grab that double barreled Stevens and go after her?

This was her husband. How could she think that?

They sat in silence for what seemed like minutes.

He had to keep her calm. He had to make her believe that if the shit hit the fan that he would take the fall. If she thought any different he knew she would turn.

And turn fast.

He had to think. He had to think clearly.

Keeping her calm made sense. He couldn't keep her at *gunpoint*. He had to make her believe that she had 'an out' if it all came down. That would keep her calm and in control. He told her to tell the truth if and when they got brought down. He would tell them the exact same story and she would be ok. He did it; not her. She had no reason to panic. He had to get that through.

But, if she was scared, she needed to tell him and tell him now. He knew he would be forever looking over his shoulder. He didn't want to forever be looking toward her also.

She had an out.

She needed to know that. He kept repeating.

Just stick it out.

Maybe evidence would point away from them altogether. If the ticket ever came up he could say someone had brought the car to the dealership to trade it in or sell it. That he had just taken it on a test drive to assess its trade in value. He nodded his head to himself.

Yeah, that's what happened. That's why I was driving that car.

He paced back and forth behind the kitchen table. It was coincidence they were camping in Darrington, too. He was just missing.

He should have taken the fucking car away from Darrington, somewhere, anywhere, and dumped it.

Fuck.

If they didn't figure out the ticket for a few days or weeks, they may not even realize he was missing *before the ticket was written.* Maybe the real estate guy went missing on May 4th or May 5th or May 15th—who knows? They didn't know how this was going to play out.

His desperation started to scare her.

"Listen, we'll go stay in motels for a couple of days, just to see what happens. If this thing hits the news or if they track that ticket, you can go. I'll take off and hide for awhile and contact you. But I need to know you are with me on this. Please, Sharon, I need to know you are going to stick this out, if not, *tell me now.* Tell me right fucking now and I'll go turn myself in. If you can't stay with me on this, tell me now," he repeated.

His tone went from one of demanding loyalty to crying for her forgiveness and support and then back to demanding she do as he say. If he couldn't make her do it, he had to plead with her to do it.

He had done it before. Cocaine. Rehab. Getting the shotgun from his sister's house the summer before. He knew what buttons to push to get what he wanted. He just had to push them in the right order.

Sharon didn't want her life to change. She wanted to go back in time and not get that damn truck stuck. She wanted things to just stay the way they were—without the drinking. She wanted to move into a house on the plateau and plant flowers. She wanted this to have never happened. And the easiest way out of this seemed to be to give it a few days and *pretend it never* happened.

"Of course I am with you. I love you," she answered, falling for his pleas, "I've always stood with you; *but this*? You have to STOP drinking. When we get a new place and start over—no more," she began to cry "no more drinking like this. *Look what it does.*"

"I know, I know," he said with the most sincere and remorseful voice he could muster. Inside his grin was widening.

He had her.

He had her right where he wanted her.

He left before she could change her mind. It was 8:20 AM and the meeting started at 8:30 AM.

He was gone.

He wouldn't be back for at least an hour and a half.

This was her chance.

She was willing to stick it out with him, but the ticket. That damn ticket might bring them here. She didn't know what to do. If she left and *he* found her, *what would he do?*

It was one thing to be a good, loyal wife, but what would he do if he found *her*, before police found him? She could call the police right now and they would be there within minutes. She could call them and they could go get him at the sales meeting and this would all be over. But so would the life she so desperately wanted. He would be gone, and probably gone for good. There would be no house on the plateau, no flowers and no garden. No more vacations; and Rusty? What would happen to her dog?

She simply did not know what she was going to do. Whatever it was, she only had a couple of hours to decide.

*   *   *

Somehow we had to narrow down where Rich had last been seen. Tim and I decided to head north on Interstate 5 to Mt. Vernon and re-trace the North Cascades Highway and then on to Moses Lake if need be. It seemed to make more sense than searching through every Podunk town along the way. In Mt. Vernon, we pulled in to the first gas station we saw.

I jumped out of his red and black Chevrolet Blazer and looked down at the flyer my mother and her friends had received from someone at Duvall Realty the night before. 'Have you seen Rich????' blazed across the top in medium sized black letters. Below them, a black and white portrait of Rich which had been taken for real estate ads he often placed. I stopped in the middle of the gas island and a gray Honda honked politely and nearly ran me over. I moved out of the traffic lane and stood, motionless in front of the entrance to the convenience store and stared at the flyer.

It was fully light out now and I glanced up across the rolling green dairy pastures toward the North Cascades off in the distance to the east. I didn't want to look at the poster, I just wanted to put them up and get looking for Rich. I was sure we would find him broken down on some obscure logging road somewhere.

"I tried to take a shortcut," Rich would say, "and then I hit a huge rock and blew out two tires. I've been here for two days!"

178

We'd laugh and add it to the list of adventure stories we had been accumulating over the years.

Then reality would hit.

Rich is gone?

A brief description of where Rich was last seen covered the page below the photo and asked people to call the office with any information.

What a waste of time, I thought.

He's stuck off the road somewhere and we need to find him.

I had seen these kinds of flyers in gas stations, truck stops and places before.

Did anyone ever read them?

Whenever I looked at them I always figured the person was dead, and I would stare and ponder how they met their end. I never imagined I would be handing one out.

I asked the clerk if we could post a couple near the restrooms and by the front door, she said it was no problem and asked what was going on. As I began, she grabbed the last few days' charge card slips and began looking through them.

"Duncan?" she said, "D-U-N-C-A-N?

"Yes!" I leapt toward the counter and leaned over to see what she had found.

"Ok— that's not it," she said out loud "no---no---no--"she continued through the whole stack of slips.

I stood at the front counter and explained to her how Rich had gone on a trip and not returned. How he never lost contact with my mother for more than an hour or two at a time. She would look up occasionally from the slips and nod. I explained how he had a cell phone and a pager. How he probably just got stuck; or lost; or broke down on some obscure road somewhere. I explained how he often went on trips like these. The entire time she nodded at me, pretending she really cared what I was saying and that I was probably right about what happened.

The entire time I pretended I was probably right, too.

"Nope. Sorry hun'," she said as she snapped the metal box containing the slips closed.

I took one last look at the flyers tacked near the restrooms; they were straight and uniform; not shoddily attached. The one on the front glass door seemed a little crooked, so I grabbed the tape and realigned it.

The smallest details mattered.

I imagined how, after we had found him, somewhere; that he would have dozens of people calling the Duvall Realty office stating that they had seen the man on the flyer, although he would now just be going about his daily business, the people who saw these signs a few days from now would not know that. They'd think they had just found a missing guy or something. It would be like a good gag. Remembering how I had broken down crying the moment I heard Rich was missing, I thought about how stupid I was going to look in front of my co-workers.

I returned to the Blazer in time to see Tim toss his smoke down and climb in. I grabbed the coffee cup off the top of the dash and we said not a word as Tim pulled the Blazer out on to the highway. If we didn't talk about it, it didn't seem like it was really happening. But then suddenly, out of nowhere, I would think it *couldn't* be happening.

Rich is just stuck somewhere.

Then we would start talking and joking again about where this story was going to rank amongst the adventures with Rich.

Tim had been married to my sister for a little over a year and had been dating her for a year and a half before that. He also had been on trips with Rich out on the gravel roads east of Duvall and experienced his fair share of swamped out engines, flat tires and loose spark plug wires that had stranded Rich at times. This was nothing out of the ordinary.

Except the fact that he had not called. *That was weird.*

But, (we both traded turns convincing the other) cellular phone coverage was not that good out here. We were not in Rich's usual back country. He was far less familiar with the roads and much more likely to give in to his adventurous curiosity in search of the next great 'off-road' short cut.

But in his Mustang GT?

Every time we came to a fact that did not make sense, like a broken record, we buried it in our favorite stories of getting lost or stuck with Rich.

As we continued up Highway 20, the open green pastures slowly gave way to scattered Douglas fir stands. Few stores or gas stations were on the route. We stopped at the occasional tow truck yard, service station and even antique or collectible stores just to place a flyer and see if Rich may have been in there.

We knew that once we found a point that he made it to from Moses Lake, we could narrow the search area down. As it stood, Rich was likely stuck somewhere between Moses Lake and Duvall.

But where?

We needed to find someone who had seen him or his car. As we made our way up the highway the story of his disappearance became shorter and more refined when we told it to the people wherever we stopped. Our routine became more efficient as we went along. I would ask if we could post the flyers and while doing so, Tim would ask them to look through credit card slips. Anyone in the store we saw we would show them the flyer and ask if they had seen Rich or his car. The more focused we became on the routine; the less we dwelled on Rich's fate.

Every couple of hours we would call back to Mom's house and see if he had showed up yet or if anyone had heard anything. Tim was doubly nervous as my sister was due to give birth at any time and if she went into labor, we would have to abandon the search for now and race back home. After each call our hopes would be dashed, and worse, we would have to break my mother's heart and tell her we hadn't found anything either. Just as we hoped they would get good news, she hoped we would find him somewhere; or find someone who had seen him.

It had now been more than 48 hours since Rich did not answer her desperate pages and phone calls. If he was stuck in the woods along some road, he would probably be hungry or thirsty. At one of the stops, we picked up some water and a can of Fosters Lager; he would really want that about now we figured. The more times we told each other we were going to find him, however, the less and less we began to believe it. We had no idea if we were even searching in the right area. He could be succumbing to hunger or thirst somewhere 200 miles away or 200 feet away. *We had absolutely no idea.*

Maybe we should just drive to straight to Moses Lake and come back this way? But that would take hours.

*   *   *

The sales team at Evergreen Ford had set another record for sales during the month of April and Phil's team had led the way. Driving from Pine Lake down to Issaquah where he worked took about fifteen or twenty minutes. He wasn't sure exactly, how well his supervisor would respond to him needing to take a leave of absence. They were in constant contact with his parole officer and somehow he needed to make it go as smoothly as possible. Never mind that Sharon was now at home wondering about that *fucking* ticket.

Maybe he should have waited to tell her. Fuck.

He really wanted to just pull over into the closest store and grab a couple beers. But he knew that might be disastrous.

He had been so successful at the dealership, that two months earlier, he was finally able to purchase the brand new 1990 Ford Ranger. It was the first time he had ever owned a new car and he loved it. His 1976 Torino had been on its last legs and the dents from running it off the road or in to fences or parked cars when he was drunk really made it look bad. It was hard to pull into work as the top sales team leader, in that bucket; and he knew it. Nothing said success to others more than a new car or truck.

Much like alcohol, cars had become part of the American culture. He really wanted to own one of the new Mustang GTs, but even with his substantial employee discounts it was still a little out of his reach.

A few minutes later he pulled in to the dealership lot and strode inside. His sales manager showered praise on Phil and his team during the meeting. But, instead of relishing in the spotlight during the meeting, he slunk to the back and hoped no one would even notice he was there. As the meeting progressed, he realized more and more that the world was just moving on. No one had come looking for him at the dealership; no one had called asking about him.

Everything was normal.

When the meeting ended he stood up and received the usual congratulations and positive affirmations handed out after such a stellar month. His sales manager noticed he wasn't quite himself in the back of the room and quickly moved beyond the small bunch of salesmen to where Phil was still sitting.

"Great job last month, Phil!" he said and slapped Phil gently on the back.

"So, how was Monte Cristo?" asked Mike, his sales manager, as they turned toward the door exiting the conference room.

"Oh…, well…, we ended up going fishing in Moses Lake instead," he quickly responded.

"Moses Lake? Wow. That's kind of a different part of the state, huh? I thought you were going up there near the North Cascades or whatever?" Mike quickly pointed out.

"No, No — Moses Lake. Yeah — the fishing was great. Just a quiet trip to unwind, you know," Phil reiterated.

"Well, I'm glad you had a good couple of days off — but I'm glad you're back. We need to get this month off to a good start. Tomorrow's the first Saturday of the month — boy I'm glad you're back!" he said.

"Yeah…, but we got some bad news last night, can I talk to you a minute? In private?" Phil asked.

"Sure, Phil; what's going on?" Mike turned toward Phil as he opened the glass door to his office.

"Well, its Sharon's mother, Helen. We got some news that she is going to need a major surgery and she needs Sharon to take care of her and I…, I am going to have to go with her to Spokane and help. It'll just be a week or two — three at the most."

He looked downward to the floor and itched his neck; he knew he had to act disappointed and ashamed at having to take some time off.

"I thought she lived here in West Seattle?" he asked.

"No, no—she moved to Spokane some time ago, I am not sure when— but anyways, I am going to need to take a leave of absence, if that's OK with you, of course," he continued.

"Well, of course, I mean you are one of our best salesmen, here, we don't want to lose you—how long do you need? Anything we can do. Yes, just tell me how long you need," he replied.

"Just a few weeks, that's all. Thank you, thank you so much," Phil exalted, stunned at how accommodating his boss was being.

"Do we need to call your parole officer or anything? I mean, if she calls here looking-"

"No, no. I'll take care of that. I have a meeting with her next week, so I'll let her know. It's no problem, really," Phil replied. The last thing he needed was having his parole officer mixed up in this.

"Ok, Ok. I just want to help, as best I can. You have been doing great this last year, so…"

"Thanks, Mike—Look I have to get going right now, but I'll check in with you as soon as I can—soon as I know something, about Helen, I mean," Phil said as he walked toward the lobby.

He was still stunned that his manager had been so accommodating. Even more, he didn't want to give up the life he was beginning to build.

But what had he done?

He was so mad at himself; he was well liked and respected at the dealership and he fucked it up because he couldn't *not drink*. When this was over, he'd never drink again, he swore to himself, he'd never drink again.

As he left the dealership a warm feeling rushed over him, he had gotten some time off and didn't attract any unwanted attention; moreover, he had convinced Sharon to stick it out with him. He had wiped the car down and left it in Darrington without a hitch.

Every minute that passed by was a minute closer to being able to resume his normal life again. He and Sharon could pack up some clothes and head to a motel. It would be like a mini-vacation. No phone calls, no one knocking on the door, no bullshit. The last 48 hours had been extremely tiring and stressful; he could get Sharon and disappear for a while. When this all blew over, he could come back to work and start over.

He smiled.

And then he remembered that fucking ticket.

And Sharon, alone in their apartment.

At least he hoped she was.

*   *   *

At about noon, Tim and I started to climb up the pass. The buildings and stops along the road became sparser and sparser. The corners of the highway became more and more severe and we decided we should stop along each one and at least look down the edge over some of the steeper drops lining the corners where a car could have spun off the road unnoticed. As we drove, we scoured the road in front of us for any signs of skidding tires or broken car parts from an accident.

Anything.

As we passed each road that connected to the highway I began writing down the names of the roads so we could check them off on the way back; assuming we had time before it got dark to drive down them. Gravel roads, driveways, forest service roads; anything. We quickly realized how important it was to find out where he might have last been seen. For all we knew we could be going all the way to Moses Lake. He could have turned on to a road 200 miles east of here and gotten lost and then broke down in the middle of the flat sage country of eastern Washington. And here, we were going to search every road in the North Cascades? Maybe, we thought, we should just go to Moses Lake and then come back this way, maybe he's just stranded along the highway? But for two days? The State patrol or someone would have seen him by now.

Maybe we should start going down these little roads and quit putting flyers up, he had to be somewhere where there was no cellular phone coverage.

It just made sense.

What if he didn't come up the North Cascades highway at all? What if he actually took the more direct route over Stevens Pass to the south or even decided to just stay on I-90, further to the south still? What if he got almost all the way home and took some stupid shortcut he had found in his Subaru and repeated the same mistake he had done when he flooded out his Volvo? What if he was stuck 200 miles south of here? This was fucked. Time was running out if he was hurt and stranded.

What if.

What if.

What if.

"FUCK!!!" I screamed and pounded the dash.

"What? What it is it?" Tim shouted and pulled the Blazer over onto a turnout along the winding highway. He peered in the rear view mirror and then quickly behind us.

"Did you see something?" he said.

His hands rested on the steering wheel and he slumped a little forward looking at me, quizzically.

184

"No, no, I'm just--" I answered, "just frustrated. I mean, where the fuck are we going? What are we looking for? This is fucking crazy."

"Eh," Tim said as he lit another smoke, "we just got to keep stopping at the little gas stations and shit and find where he got gas, he had to have gotten gas somewhere. We'll find it and then we'll know where to start looking at least."

It sounded so simple. But he was right.

17

Phil opened the door to the apartment and tossed his keys down on to the coffee table.

She was still here.

He paused, and then immediately he reached on to the coffee table and picked up the keys to the Ranger. He wasn't completely sure if she would stick around and the last thing he wanted if she ran was to be without a car. He had left her to take the car back to Darrington; but that was before she knew about the ticket; and now he had left her alone in order to go to his sales meeting.

And she stayed.

He still thought he had to keep an eye on her. She was acting a little weird, but why wouldn't she be? It was going to be hard to battle between the paranoia and rational behavior.

He finally convinced Sharon they could go stay in motels for a while and see if the cops traced the ticket back to him.

Maybe no one even noticed that guy was missing.

Maybe he was on a long trip and wouldn't be missed for days.

Maybe they would never trace the ticket to him and this would all just blow over.

He had been repeating these things to her since it happened. One thing was for sure—if he got through this he would never drink again. He and Sharon would move into a little place somewhere and forget all about the guy in the red Mustang.

As he turned for the door he, again, felt a shot of pain rip through his lower back. He grimaced and reached for the wall to brace himself.

It really hurt.

He went in to the kitchen and poured some orange juice into a small plastic glass they had brought in from the camping trip. He stared at the bottle of Vodka on the counter next to the sink. His back hurt too much. He needed something to get through these next few days. He would *tone it down*, he thought. Just drink enough to keep the pain at bay but not so much that it derailed his thinking. He poured two shots into the glass and affectionately watched as the vodka swirled through the orange juice like lovers embraced after a long time apart.

She'll understand.

They just needed to pack up for a few days and get the hell out of this apartment without anyone knowing they were even here.

BANG! BANG! BANG!

The knock on the door caught him off guard. His eyes expanded fully open. He froze.

Sharon ripped off the blanket wrapping her on the sofa. She jumped up and looked at Phil for direction. They stared at each other. Neither of them took a breath.

The knock at their door sent shots of adrenaline through them both.

"PHIL... SHARON?" they heard through the door.

She recognized Marjorie, the neighbor upstairs. They both let out huge sighs of relief.

What the hell did she want?

Phil stood behind the door as Sharon opened it up just a pinch and peeked out.

"I'm just waking up; Marjorie, what do you need?" Sharon said through the cracked opening.

"Oh, I'm sorry; I just wanted to see how your camping trip went. Didn't you go up to Monte Cristo, by Darrington or Granite Falls or something?" she asked innocently.

With that, Phil jerked the door open, surprising her.

"Hi Marjorie, no, we ended up going fishing in Moses Lake," he corrected her.

He bent to pick up a decorative pillow that had made its way in to the foyer. He didn't want it to look weird that he was behind the door so he acted like he had been doing a little housecleaning. Sharon shrunk away.

Moses Lake?

"Oh, Moses Lake? I thought you said you were--"

"Moses Lake. Fishing. It was great," Phil cut her off, "Listen, I've got to get this house cleaned up, thanks for stopping by."

And he closed the door.

Sharon looked at Phil with a puzzled look on her face.

"Moses Lake?" Sharon immediately asked.

Phil tossed the pillow haplessly on to the couch.

"If anyone ever asks, we went to Moses Lake. That's how it has to be," he demanded.

He grabbed the blanket Sharon had been using and folded it.

"I told my sales manager we were in Moses Lake the last couple of days and that your mother needed someone to come and take care of her in Spokane while she has surgery. He completely understood, when this all blows over, we'll move into another apartment here somewhere, and I'll go back to work. Simple," he finished, placing his hand reassuringly on her shoulder.

"But what about the people we saw in Darrington?" she asked, not convinced.

He purposefully avoided the question.

"Look—people we know, they just need to think we went to Moses Lake—that way when they find that car or they ever come up with anything else, no one would think that it might have been us. Just *trust me,*" he reiterated.

"I have this under control."

He tossed the tumbler back toward his lips and the drink hit the back of his throat. He looked at her for some sort of reaction and she just turned away.

Good.

"I need to go get some boxes so you can pack this stuff up so we can get it in storage," he said as he lowered the empty glass to the kitchen counter and glanced at the refrigerator.

Sharon looked up at him, "I'll go get them, I've--"

"No!" he said cutting her off, "*No fucking way!*"

He wasn't going to let her go anywhere; she needed to stay in his sight or here in the house. She was not leaving. No way. Not until he knew she meant what she said. Not until he knew she was still on his side.

She had heard that tone before, and she knew what it meant. It was a test. A test to see if she was loyal. At this point, she needed him to know she was still with him; it was easier to just let *him* go.

She did not want to hear him tell her again how it would all blow over, that no one could tie them to the red Mustang. She didn't want to hear how the guy might not be missed for days. That it hadn't even been on the news.

That was Wednesday; it was Friday and still not a word. The cops didn't even know on Thursday. Maybe he's right. Maybe this will all blow over and things can get back to normal.

"Ok...Ok...I'll just start getting things together to move first," she acquiesced.

Then the phone rang. Both of them jumped and stared at the receiver.

A paranoid wave rushed over both of them. Is this how it's going to be every time someone knocks on the door or the phone rings?

He motioned for her to get the phone and dove toward the blinds behind the sofa. He gazed out into the parking lot to see if any cars had pulled in that he did not recognize.

His pulse raced and his jaw clenched up.

The shotgun was back in the bedroom closet but he knew he could get to it, quick. If they were already here and trying to get him to surrender, he would get to that shotgun.

He strained to look as he scanned left and then right, what was that car doing there? He peered up at Sharon as she picked up the receiver.

"Hello," she said softly.

"Hi Sharon, how was the trip?" It was Phil's sister, Jody.

"It's Jody," she mouthed to Phil without actually saying it.

"Hi, Jody. Uuhhh....it was good," she said into the phone and looked back at Phil for what to say.

"I'm not here--" he mouthed back silently, "we are going to Moses Lake for a few—tell her that," he whispered to Sharon as he got up from the sofa, away from the blinds.

"Oh, good. Was Phil behaving?" Jody laughed into the phone. Phil's older sister knew the struggles Phil had with drugs and alcohol, but she always remained loyal to her younger brother. She checked up on him often.

"Yeah...he was ....fine," Sharon mumbled into the phone.

"Tell her--" Phil whispered again, "tell her we are going to Moses Lake."

"Uhhh...yeah...it was good, in fact, Phil is taking a couple more days off and we are going to Moses Lake, Phil wants to do some fishing, it will be good to get away some more," she said, her confidence growing with each word.

"Yeah—Phil's been good, he's been working a lot so, you know, no reason he can't take a vacation for a few days, you know."

"Well good. I'm glad he's happy with that job, selling cars; who knew? And he's so good at it," Jody said, proudly.

"Yeah, well, I've got to get some stuff packed up, Jody, Phil should be back shortly and then we're headed out. Do you want me to have him call you?" she asked.

Phil began waving his hands at her wildly and shaking his head.

"No!....No!" he whispered, "God damn it!—I do not want to call her."

"No that's ok. You guys just go have fun, Moses Lake, huh? How fun. I'll talk to him when you get back, just keep him under control, if you know what I mean," Jody laughed again.

"I will, Jody. Bye-bye," and she hung up the phone.

Sharon cautiously looked up at Phil.

"She said to just call her when we get back. What are you going to tell her about taking a leave of absence? What is she going to say then? Do you think she'll suspect something?" she quizzed Phil.

"Who knows? Let's just-" he paused and shook his head slightly.

"Let's just get through these next few days and we'll see. I'll take care of my sister," he said.

Despite the shock of the last 48 hours, her confidence was growing. She had just talked to someone who didn't know what had occurred up in the woods outside of Darrington. Everyone else in the world just seemed to keep on going like nothing had happened.

Her belief that it was going to be ok continued to grow.

Phil sat back down at the kitchen table and grabbed a bottle of Vodka.

"Look, we'll just go stay at the Motel 6, across the freeway down in Issaquah. Everyone thinks we left town and we can keep an eye on the apartment. Believe me, if they figure this thing out, there will be cops everywhere," he stated confidently.

She went in to the bedroom to pack a few things; Rusty followed her in and laid down on the bed. She opened her drawers and grabbed some sweats and a hoodie, if they were going to be staying in a motel, she may as well be comfortable. In the closet she pulled out a small duffel bag. Leaning against the wall inside the closet she *noticed the shotgun.*

She thought about the man in the red Mustang, someone was missing him; someone was missing him right now. She turned away from the shotgun and refused to look at it again. She closed the door to the closet and wished that damn shotgun had stayed at Phil's sister's house.

When she came out to the dining room with the small duffel bag, Phil was in the bathroom. The Relsky bottle sat on the table with the lid off. A small glass filled with ice and orange juice sat next to it, half drank. Her heart sank.

Even after all this?

190

There was no sense in fighting about it now, the last thing they needed was a long drawn out fight about the same old shit. If she brought it up now they would surely fight and never get to the motel. Desperately she wanted to get to the motel and just relax and not jump every time the phone rang or every time a car pulled into the parking lot in front of the apartment.

She picked up the tiny blue plastic cap and screwed it to the top of the bottle and put it into the duffel bag. The door to the bathroom creaked open and he appeared.

"I have the Relsky in the bag, we can get some more at the liquor store on the way, and some ice and chaser, too," she suggested.

She had him right where she wanted; nothing makes an alcoholic happier than alcohol. If she were going to get any rest at all to try and figure out what to do, she needed him off her ass for a little while.

He had her right where he wanted, believing this was all going to go away.

Together, they headed out the door to the truck and piled in.

Twenty minutes later they were in downtown Issaquah.

*   *   *

The small town of Winthrop was only a few miles away and Tim and I were beginning to get hungry. Neither one of us had eaten in almost 24 hours; it just never seemed to occur to us that we needed sustenance. Having found nothing to lead us to Rich, we seriously doubted whether we even had the right approach.

I had never driven over the North Cascades highway but remembered my father telling me how he had driven his dune buggy over it right behind a Jeep carrying Governor Dan Evans of Washington when it opened in 1969. This was not the introduction I was looking for.

Winthrop was a quaint town. It was lined on both sides of the street with small gift shops and antique stores. Its western themed structures had been designed and implemented by the same designer who had orchestrated the Bavarian theme of Leavenworth, Washington, 115 miles to the south. We found the only gas station in town and Tim pulled the Blazer in to the pump island.

I jumped out and removed my hoodie, it was getting a little warmer out and the clouds that had followed us up the pass were well behind us now. Tim grabbed a flyer off the stack perched on the dashboard and headed in. I walked a few feet away from the pump island and lit a smoke. The gas station seemed an unlikely place for Rich to have stopped. No convenience store, not even a beverage counter. Not surprisingly, Tim reappeared from the tiny gas station rather quickly.

"That guy's been here every day, all week. He never saw a new Mustang, especially not a red one. He said he would look through the credit card slips later, but he was kind of busy," Tim kind of laughed, "what an asshole."

Beyond Winthrop was the small town of Twisp. I had been to Twisp once, when my father had flown us over for lunch when I was eight or nine years old in his Piper Tri-Pacer.

"There we go," I stated as we pulled into town, "a Texaco."

The Texaco station appeared to be brand new or newly remodeled with a fairly good sized convenience store attached to it. This looked more like the kind of place that would draw Rich in for gas, smokes and a Big Gulp. Tim grabbed the flyers off the dash again and we headed inside.

"How you doin'?" the clerk asked as we strode in the door.

We had done the routine so many times that we moved with a purpose. If they hadn't seen Rich, we needed to get the flyer up and move on. We weren't even halfway to Moses Lake yet and it was going to be dark in five or six hours. That meant we probably wouldn't be able to search up some of the roads we jotted down on the way. A few stops before, we even stopped asking the clerks to look through the credit card slips right then; we merely asked if they would look at the end of the day and call the number on the flyer if they found anything.

"I was just hoping you could help us," I asked the clerk, "my step-father was supposed to be driving through this area a couple of days ago and he never made it home."

"Oh my gosh," she gasped, "I'm so sorry."

"We were just wondering, he was driving a brand new red Mustang GT, it had personal plates on it that said 'DUVALL'," I continued.

"YEAH!" she exclaimed, "that bright red Mustang, big guy? Real-estate agent or something like that."

"TIM!" I hollered across the store; trying to be polite but unable to contain my excitement, "TIM! He was here."

Tim strode across the store—

"Can you look through your credit card slips; I know he would have used his credit card. We really need to be able to prove he was here," Tim asked.

I was shaking. This meant we knew he had at least made it here. We didn't have to keep going to Moses Lake. He had probably gone down one of the side roads we passed on the way here and broke down or got a flat or something.

RICH WAS ALIVE! He had to be.

She fumbled through the credit slip file behind the counter. I fumbled through my pockets for some change, I needed to call Mom right away. This was fantastic!

"Here it is," she said and held the slip up in the air.

Tim and I both stared at it and immediately recognized Rich's illegible signature and the name on the imprint.

It was for $16.02.

He had bought gas and a large fountain beverage. I darted outside to the phone booth and dialed the operator to make a collect call. It had been a few hours since we last checked in and maybe my dad had seen his car somewhere and they were already sending a rescue to some obscure forest service road. Maybe he had even gotten it fixed and was already at home. I was sure my mother was already furiously lecturing him about taking those stupid shortcuts and he must feel horrible for making her worry so much. It was all going to work out.

What a story this will be. Stuck in the woods for two days!

"Mom, we found a credit card slip!" I exclaimed into the phone. "Have you heard anything? Is he back?"

"No," she said quietly, "where did you find the slip?"

"We are in Twisp, at a Texaco," I replied, hoping she would share in the joy of finding the slip.

But no one had heard anything.

His car hadn't been spotted from the air.

He hadn't arrived home with stories of a wrong turn and a flat tire and poor cellular service.

All I had was a credit card slip.

*　　　*　　　*

Even for a Friday night, the Motel 6 parking lot in Issaquah was unusually busy. Two vans full of kids blocked the entrance to the check-in lobby. Sharon pulled the truck around them and searched for a discreet space to park in the back.

He had been drinking the entire afternoon since they left the apartment. She felt much less paranoid here at the motel, but the truck was in Phil's name and would easily be traced back to him.

The front of the motel faced Interstate 90 and the rear faced Lake Sammamish Parkway and beyond it, Lake Sammamish.

The rhododendrons planted along the parking lot had flourished in the mild-wet climate of western Washington and she backed the Ranger in the far corner so that it was nearly covered by the flowering bushes. The only way someone searching for the truck would see it was if they specifically pulled in to the lot of the motel. Many of Phil's co-workers and his sister lived in Issaquah and since they had just told them all they were fishing in Moses Lake, it seemed prudent. She did not want one of them noticing his new truck and catching them in a lie. But after turning and looking back at how the truck was parked, she relaxed.

Phil stayed in the truck and began mixing the Vodka and the orange juice in one of the clear plastic cups they picked up at the liquor store.

She sidestepped her way through the vans and into the lobby area. The clerk handed her a registration card and she filled it out and handed the clerk her credit card. The clerk smiled, entered her information in to the computer and slid a room key across the counter.

The room was clear in the back of the complex as the clerk decided to place them as far away from the screaming kids as she could. Everything was working out perfectly. She just wanted to get in to the motel room, relax with a drink and take a hot bath.

As she opened the door to the motel room, Phil quickly jumped out of the truck and strode across the lot to the door. He had a drink in one hand and the bottle of Vodka in the other. Flopping down on the bed he began laughing.

"Go get the shit out of the truck," he demanded loudly. He was getting buzzed.

"Why didn't you bring it in with you?" she asked.

He glared at her. His jovial attitude quickly turned sour.

"Never mind, Sharon. You FUCKING stay here. If that phone rings—DON'T ANSWER IT!" he demanded.

She was confused, they were finally in a safe place and he was already turning into an asshole?

She needed a drink.

He ducked out of the motel room and cautiously scampered to the truck. As he crossed the parking lot she watched as he turned and looked left, and then turned and looked right and repeated the whole sequence across the lot. He opened the door and pulled the green duffel bag out and discreetly moved back toward the door of the motel room.

Once through the door he turned, locked the door and placed the chain across the security lock. He moved to the small window and drew the curtains closed. Carefully he pulled each corner in place to fully cover the entire opening.

She went to the tiny bathroom and turned on the water, placing her fingers in the flow from the nozzle. It smelled of bleach and cheap cleaning solvents. A hot bath and a Screwdriver would be heaven. Staring at the water as it filled up the tub; she could hear him unzip the duffel bag. Intently, she stared at the water filling up the tub. For a few moments, her head was not filled with the devastating events of the last few days, for a few moments she sat on the edge of the tub and watched as bubbles rotated through the crystal clear water.

It was clean and pure.

Phil appeared in the doorway to the bathroom just as she turned the nozzle off. His shoulders sagged forward and he held his drink in his wrist cocked to one side. He was getting really drunk now. One thing she knew was that once he started to get a little buzz going, it wouldn't be long. But he could either turn into a raging lunatic or simply sit quietly in front of the television and drink himself in to a stupor. She hoped for the latter.

"What is it Phil?" she asked, once she climbed into the tub.

"*You,*" he slurred.

She sat silent, staring for ten or twelve seconds.

"*You,*" he said again, a little louder, "you got... the fucking truck... stuck. *You did.*"

He looked at her puzzlingly.

She knew when he started this to just wait it out. There would be no arguing, if she tried to object he would yell and scream and put a fist through the wall. That was the last thing she needed.

Why couldn't he just go lay down?

"I told you it was the wrong...I told you it was the...the wrong fucking road," he slurred.

She looked down at her tired legs and then back up toward the doorway, he was gone. She heard him sit on the bed and toss more ice into the plastic cup. The television quietly turned on and she could hear him searching the channels. He found the local news and the bed squeaked as he jumped up to turn the sound up. She jumped out of the bath and joined him on the edge of the double bed, dripping wet; and stared at the television.

They remained motionless. Motionless for thirty minutes except for the sound of ice hitting the edge of the plastic cup as he tossed back the Vodka.

Nothing.

No stories of police looking for a missing man.

No stories of police looking for a man who had gotten a ticket in red Mustang. No stories from Darrington, no stories from anywhere that had anything to do with them. She knew it would come on sooner or later. Sooner or later someone was going to report the guy missing and they would be looking for his car.

What then?

18

A small group of teens gathered in a vacant grocery store parking lot about a block west of the Red Top Tavern in Darrington; laughing, joking, and skateboarding. Darrington is a very small town and with not a lot to do, those over 21 years old spend the evenings in the taverns longing for days past when logging was still a viable economic resource. Teens and kids wandered the streets looking for something to do. Anything new in the town always attracted attention. It was almost 9:00 PM and, except for the taverns, the town was about to close.

Just another Friday night in Darrington.

Except for the hot red car parked in the lot.

This was cool.

One of the girls in the group, Jessica Knoop, remembered seeing the car pull in and park there yesterday afternoon. She noticed the back window was broken out and couldn't believe someone would leave a car like this sitting overnight. She thought the guy she saw probably went to the bar, got too drunk to drive it home and just hadn't gotten up out of bed to come get it yet. He was probably sleeping off one hell of a hangover to leave this car here.

It had to be brand new or close to it.

What an idiot she thought.

Jon Keehner

Next to the Seattle Times box on the sidewalk, a number of kids laughed and carried on. Occasionally, one of the teens would look in the car to see if something in the car was worth stealing; but someone would say something and the 'would be' thief or vandal would pull away, stating they were 'only kidding'. As the evening wore on, the kids got braver and braver; one of them even opened the door and sat in the car wondering what it would be like to drive it. Soon another got in the passenger side and within minutes everyone was climbing in and out of the car. It was something new, something to do on a Friday night.

Jessica felt a slight sense of shame; she felt a little bad for the guy who had parked it here, he looked nice, he probably just had something come up and couldn't get back to get it. It bothered her to see her friends and others who she knew (but did not consider friends) mobbing over this car like this.

"COPS!" someone yelled as the Darrington Police patrol car turned in to the parking lot.

"So what?" another voice laughed, "It's probably just Norm, he's cool."

The kids quickly jumped away from the car. Even though they all knew the officers on the force, no one wanted to push their luck.

The patrol car pulled up perpendicular behind the tail of the red Mustang and the spotlight mounted to the door of the patrol car lit up the Mustang. The kids all backed away from the car and started ogling as to who was going to get busted for what.

The officer stepped out, "What's going on here?"

"Just chillin."

"Yeah—just hangin' out."

"What's up with you?" someone laughed out from the crowd of kids gathered.

The officer reached into his breast pocket and pulled out a notepad and pen and jotted down the license plate, "D-U-V-A-L-L".

"That's hard to remember—huh?" someone belted out.

They laughed.

Some of the kids began to wander off into the night looking for something better to do than hang out with the police. The officer looked at them with a grin and turned back to sit in the front seat of the patrol car.

He pulled the radio microphone off the dash and rolled up the window so he could talk with dispatch without the hearing all the banter back and forth from the kids.

Jessica stood watching the officer through the window as he talked on the radio. He flipped the red and blue patrol lights off and she could hear the engine whirring now that most of the kids had moved on. Her friends

197

wanted to take off also but she somehow felt compelled to stay, she felt bad for the guy who owned the car and was very interested as to why he had left it here since yesterday. Through the rolled up window she could barely hear the dispatcher on the other end talking back to the officer. Quickly he turned his head sideways and she heard him ask for dispatch to repeat the last line. He muttered something back into the microphone and flipped the red and blue flashers on the roof back on.

The parking lot lit up like a disco.

It was nearly blinding. Immediately the spotlight came back on and scanned across the car and came to a stop on the license plate again, the officer jumped out of the car and pulled out his notepad again — his voice became stern and loud, he was very serious now —

"I am going to need all of you folks to stand up against the wall here, nobody is in trouble — but I need to get some information from everyone."

The door on the patrol car was open and she could hear a blaze of police codes coming through the radio from the woman on the other end.

"Did anyone see the driver of this car?" he stated very clearly and deliberately to the on-lookers now assembled along the wall in front of the grocery store.

"Anyone at all?"

Jessica looked toward the officer and hesitated for a moment.

Fuck.

So he left it overnight. So what? She was starting to feel a little bad — the last thing she wanted to do was get the guy in trouble. She was just worried that his car was getting thrashed. She didn't really know now if she even wanted to say anything. Would the guy be mad at her?

Shit.

"I did," she finally said, raising her hand, "I saw him leave it here yesterday afternoon — what's the big deal?"

Across the parking lot a few people came outside from the tavern to see what the action was all about. The siren in the distance was drawing even closer, red and blue flashes reflected off the building behind the small crowd and the roar of a patrol car could now be heard racing in to the scene.

"Ok — I need you to come sit back here for just a minute — you aren't under arrest," he said as he opened the rear door to the car, "but I need you to just take a seat for a minute — is that OK?"

With a surprised look on her face she peeked back at her friends and sort of laughed and shrugged her shoulders at her friends while she walked toward the patrol car.

What the fuck have I done?

The officer lowered the power window a bit and helped her sit down; she pulled her legs into the rear seat area and quizzically gazed at her friends while the officer closed the door.

A Snohomish County Sheriff patrol car whipped into the parking lot and two deputies jumped out of the car and met the Darrington officer in the middle of the lot. The kids along the wall were mostly quiet now — making small talk amongst themselves and pointing at the girl in the back of the police cruiser. The two deputies and the officer talked quietly and shined their flashlights on the car and then on the license plate. Her knees were getting tight in the back of the car.

The Darrington officer pointed to the kids along the wall and then pointed his light to the back of his patrol car. One of the deputies climbed back into his car and got on the radio while the other deputy opened the trunk and removed some orange cones from the back. He, along with the Darrington officer moved toward the red Mustang and began placing cones around it. Once the cones were in place the deputy pulled his note pad and moved near the kids along the wall.

Inside the sheriffs car the deputy on the radio hung up the microphone and joined the other deputy with the kids. One by one they began taking everyone's name, date of birth and contact information down; the second deputy began questioning the youths as to what the names of those who left earlier were and who they saw in or not in the car at anytime. In the back of the patrol car, Jessica let out a sigh and couldn't believe they were making such a big deal about a car left overnight in a grocery store parking lot.

Across the pavement near the tavern, onlookers were smoking cigarettes and making small talk — *what have these kids done this time?*

The Darrington officer opened the door to his car and jumped in the front seat turning the map light on and retrieved his note pad and pen. He looked into the rearview mirror at the stressed out young girl in the back seat.

"Are you OK?" he smiled back to her trying to reassure her that she was not in trouble. He could tell she did not understand so he turned sideways in the seat and put his arm up along the seatback under the plexiglass divider.

"I need you to tell me everything you can about the driver of this car, to the best of your recollection. What can you tell me about the driver — what time did he park here, do you remember? Let's start with that?"

"It was yesterday afternoon, I was walking home and I saw that car — I mean that car is hot — you know?--and I thought it was my friend — and I was — like-- wondering how he got that car," she drew a deep breath and tried to calm herself down, "so I yelled at the guy and when he turned I realized it wasn't Roy—the friend of mine that I thought it was—and—he just ignored me—so I kind of laughed and said 'oops' and he just went down the street."

"Have you ever seen him before? Did he say anything to you?"

"No—he just kind of ducked away and went down the sidewalk."

"Was he white? black? hispanic?"

"White."

About how tall was he?—taller than you? Shorter than you?"

She sat back in the seat and threw her head back and exhaled loudly closing her eyes.

"Its OK—you're doing fine. About how tall?"

"Well he was taller than me, by—I don't know—an inch?"

"And how tall are you?"

"Five -nine."

"So he was five-nine maybe five-ten? Was he stocky? Thin? Average?"

"He was kind of buff in the arms—and short—sandy blonde hair—almost like a soldier cut or something?"

"How old do you think he was?"

"I don't know—25 or 30—maybe a little older—I can't really remember."

Outside the deputy's collected the names of the kids who were still there and the ones who left. None of them had seen who parked the car. After twenty or thirty minutes and a stern lecture about car prowling, the deputies let the kids leave. Most were now bored with the whole event and couldn't believe that a car left overnight was that big of a deal. Don't the cops in this town have anything better to do?

The Darrington officer wrapped up his questions and took down her contact information. He explained that it would be best for now if she did not discuss what she saw with anyone—and that it might be helpful to write down anything else she remembered. He explained that he may need to get a hold of her tomorrow for some follow up questions, but probably not.

"Why is this, such a big deal?" she asked as he opened the rear door to let her out.

"Well—the guy you saw get out of the car was reported missing yesterday—and he may have just drank too much and not wanted to drive home—I am sure he will turn up—this is just routine with a missing person -- its just procedure, you know. Have a good night."

*   *   *

Sharon couldn't believe he hadn't passed out yet. They had watched the five o'clock, six thirty and eleven o'clock news. Flipping back and forth between the channels as quick as it took to scan the stories and then back to another channel. Knowing that at any moment the story might hit the news.

But still, nothing.

He finished the Vodka off hours earlier and moved on to shots of Jack Daniels. The half-gallon she purchased at the liquor store earlier that afternoon was nearly gone. Time seemed to move so fast.

Why isn't this on the news?

The waiting was beginning to kill her. In some ways she hoped someone had reported him missing or something. At least they would have an idea of what the situation was.

But no news at all.

It must be good for them, but she just didn't know. She tried not to think about it anymore; whatever was going to happen was going to happen.

But she couldn't stop.

Why did she let Phil bring the shotgun? Why didn't she just leave it at his sister's house? If she had just refused to go camping in the first place none of this would have ever happened.

And that fucking road, why did she have to get the truck stuck? What if the road to Monte Cristo hadn't of been snowed in, that man would have just kept on going.

The ring of the phone startled her out of her daydream; she had just nearly fallen to sleep. It was loud. She had forgotten how loud motel phones rang.

The phone?

Her heart raced. It raced like it did when Jody called earlier. Were the cops outside? Waiting for them to come out? Had someone seen the truck? Was it Jody?

Had she seen their truck parked in the lot?

The phone rang again.

Just *don't answer it.*

But if it just rang and rang, they might knock on the door or worse. She had to answer it.

Phil jumped toward the window and peeked through the blinds.

But what would she tell Jody? Or Phil's boss? They were supposed to be in Moses Lake.

Shit.

The phone rang a third time. She had to pick it up. She looked at Phil for some idea on what to do, but he just stared out the window, his jaw clenched.

"Hello," she finally answered.

"Hi, this is Anita, from the front desk," she said, "is this Sharon?"

The only answer she could come up with was, "Why?"

"Well, sorry to bother you but you left your Visa card at the front desk area, and we've been so busy I didn't get a chance to call you yet. So, it'll be up here whenever is convenient to come pick it up."

She fell back on to the bed, and Phil grabbed the half-gallon.

She began to sob.

She thought she could do it, but this was too much. She thought the motel would be a refuge from the paranoia and the stress but it was no different. It was no different than sitting at home in the apartment and waiting for the police to show up and arrest them. She didn't know if she could keep this up.

He looked at her and took a shot from the bottle.

"It's going to be fine, baby," he said calmly as he twisted the cap off the Jack Daniels.

"I told you, they ain't got nothin'," he slurred, but remarkably coherent for how much he had been drinking.

"We got nothing to worry about, just relax. We'll know more in a couple days," he reminded her.

"But YOU!" She yelled at him and then quickly lowered her voice.

"You!—you son of a bitch! That fucking shotgun and the fucking booze. Why? Phil! Why? We should have never gone camping, we should have never taken that brand new fucking truck off-roading—you said we could make it through that fucking ditch! *And now?* And now—you just want to sit here and get fucking wasted? While I answer phones and get you booze? And that poor man in the Mustang. I fucking helped you! Jesus Christ, Phil! I can't take this. I can't take this anymore," she sobbed.

He set the bottle down and climbed on to the bed next to her and rubbed her arm. She never said any more. She just laid there and cried.

*　　*　　*

When the phone rang my mother jumped. How many more people were going to be calling and asking if we had heard from Rich? Every time my mother started the story over again I could hear the pain in her voice.

Tim and I returned from our trip over the North Cascades Highway and I was exhausted. I was not used to getting up at 6:00 AM but we were excited we had at least found a thread of hope.

My dad who had flown the same route earlier in the day had not seen anything from the air. But as he was by himself, it was somewhat of a challenge to thoroughly search the ground and fly at the same time. My mother was very appreciative of his efforts.

Tim and I sat at the counter in the kitchen strategizing what we were going to do tomorrow, Saturday. We figured we should go up through Arlington and Darrington this time and scour the side roads looking for Rich or his car. It was fairly well known that a lot of "strange" folks lived out in the area that were generally trying to avoid interaction with the rest of the world; and we also feared that maybe he had seen or found something he wasn't supposed to and someone had hurt him.

While we were discussing the next day, my mother's friend, Diana, who had been with her since Thursday morning handed the phone to my mother. She was now wearing off-white pajamas and the lights in the kitchen had been dimmed so that hopefully, Mom could get relaxed and possibly get some sleep.

I overhead her saying, "Uh-huh—yes…yes."

It didn't sound like someone calling and asking about Rich, it sounded like the person on the other end had some information. Everyone in the room seemed to notice also and it became deathly quiet.

"Yes, D-U-V-A-L-L, that's it! Where? …Darrington? Ok…" Mother's voice started to become excited.

Maybe they found him.

"NO! NO! NO!" she yelled into the phone.

"That's *not* my husband! NO! He's well over six feet tall and over 275 pounds!" she started to cry and continued, "how tall did you say? five foot ten??? Less than 200 pounds? *NO! That's not Rich! That's not my husband!"*

I looked at Diana, and from the look on my face she knew what we were all wondering—who was on the phone? Mother dropped the phone and clasped her hands to her face and dropped her head onto the counter and began to cry. Diana quickly picked up the phone.

"Just a minute," she said into the phone, "give us just a minute."

Diana stood there, rubbing my mother's back gently. We all sat in stunned silence. Mother pulled herself together after about 20 seconds. At that moment her voice sounded different. Her demeanor had changed. At that moment, through the questions and the hope and the small discoveries, she now knew that something bad had most likely befallen Rich. Someone who was 5'10" and less than 200 pounds had parked his car in Darrington on Thursday and abandoned it.

"Do you want me to impound the car?" the Darrington police officer asked.

"Yes! Yes!" my mother replied, "I want to see it. I want to come up right now and see it."

"Wait until it gets light out ma'am. Come up to Darrington tomorrow and just go to a phone booth and call 911, I'll come and get you."

It appeared that someone other than Rich had parked his car in Darrington, and just walked away.

Why?

19

Saturday   May 5, 1990

Mom sat upright in her bed. Occasionally she would get up and go sit in her office window on the top floor of her lakefront house and stare blankly at the darkness outside. She would wander back in to her bedroom and look for laundry to do.

There was none.

She went downstairs and dialed the 1-800 number to her bank and checked the balance. No one had touched the account.

But she knew that.

She continued down the stairs to the basement and checked on Colleen and Tim.

They were sleeping.

She went upstairs and checked the thermostat.

72.

Exactly where she set it an hour before.

She repeated the monotonous routine all night, a way to pass the time before her friends Denny and Diana would come over to get her and Tim to go see the car.

She had to see the car.

At around 5:00 AM she saw Denny and Diana pull into the driveway. Tim was already up and outside having a cigarette.

Friends and relatives were quietly strewn about every empty space in the house, wrapped in blankets and sheets. She didn't even know who was there and who wasn't. Fully dressed for an hour already, she quietly slipped outside to greet them.

The trip to Darrington from Duvall was about an hour and fifteen minutes. They pulled into an empty parking lot and found a phone booth. Tim jogged across the lot to the booth and dialed 911. The dispatch operator told her she would send officer Pistole over to where the car had been found at right away. Tim turned back toward Mom and found her and Denny looking at pieces of red and gray plastic lying on the ground.

"This is from the Mustang?" Mother pointed out, confused, "How did this get out here?"

"It looks like its part of the dash; you know that part that goes around the radio? I don't know?" Tim shrugged and handed the part to Denny.

They all turned and scanned the parking lot for more parts from the car. Tim went over to the garbage can and found what looked like the knobs from the air conditioning and fan controls. They all stared at each other, puzzled.

A Darrington Police cruiser pulled into the parking lot and Officer Pistole climbed out of the car.

"This is where we found it, it had been here since Thursday, but we didn't run the plates until last night just before I called you," Officer Pistole began.

"What's all this?" Mother asked showing the officer the parts from the Mustang.

"Looks like the kids might have gotten into it and tried to steal the radio, or something. Was that found right here?" he asked.

Mother rolled her eyes and started shaking her head. Rich's car was being vandalized or broken in to, a few blocks from the police station and no one noticed?

She grew irritated.

"What time did this happen? Was it like this when you found it last night? Or did it happen after?" she demanded.

The officer stood there and merely shrugged his shoulder.

"One of the local kids did get a good look at him, though. Like I said last night, maybe you could ask her to do a composite sketch or something?" he noted.

"Aren't you guys doing that?" Mom asked, even more irritated.

"Well, let me tell you something, I don't want to be rude but it's just a fact. We don't have the resources to do that—isn't this a Moses Lake case?" he stated.

Mother became visibly irritated at this point.

206

"Well who is going to look for my husband, it's obvious something's wrong — he isn't the one who got out of the car — you even said yourself — who is going to look for Rich?"

"You know, we don't have time to go on searches, ma'am. We have drug dealers and growers all over this area and we spend a pretty good amount of time just trying to keep clear of them up here. In case you haven't noticed, we are a tiny town, I am sorry," he answered and made his way back to his patrol car.

They followed him a block or two back to the police station to get a copy of the police report.

"Can we do our own search?" my mother asked as he turned away from her.

"Be my guest," he answered shortly, "the car is at the county impound lot, in Snohomish."

Mom looked up at him and asked, 'Should we be coordinating a search and rescue or do you think we are looking for a body?"

"Probably a body, ma'am."

He closed the door to his office.

Mother stood there, stunned and frustrated. They drove back to where the car was found and she slowly made her way to where a number of plastic trim pieces rested on the asphalt. Methodically and deliberately, she gathered up the pieces from the car and placed them carefully into a white plastic bag.

The drive back toward Snohomish took about fifty minutes. During the entire ride she methodically stared and turned over every single piece of the car. After carefully examining each one, she replaced it back into the bag and pulled out another. Once she was satisfied the parts probably yielded no clue as to the fate of her husband, she stared out the window as the pastured farmland rolled by.

Soccer fields with kids playing matches and green rolling hills filled with dairy cows. Tractors moved equipment between barns and people went in and out of gas stations. Overhead, flocks of sparrows darted around power lines. A small airplane disappeared above the clouds.

She saw none of it.

*　　*　　*

A knock on the door startled Phil awake. He dove toward the closet where he had stashed the shotgun. Sharon hadn't heard it.

"Hello! Housekeeping. Hello?" the woman's voice came through the door.

"Not today," he yelled through the door, "we are staying—not checking out yet!"

She shot up in the bed and stared at his hands clenched on the shotgun. It scared her, she had seen that look in his eyes and this time he was sober, somewhat hung over, but sober.

He let out a sigh of relief and gently put the Stevens double barrel behind the chair. He opened the Jack Daniels bottle and grabbed a plastic cup off the floor. It was a Saturday; normally he would have sold one, maybe two, brand new Fords by now.

"You need to call the front desk and tell them we are staying another day," he directed her with a low, stern voice.

He took a hit from the cup.

Without removing the pillow she had placed over her face, she objected.

"Why don't I just go get the card and sign us up for another night, it'll just take a minute," Sharon suggested.

She sat up and threw her legs off to the side of the tiny bed. The blankets were coarse and the sheets lay clumped on the floor. She grabbed the wrinkled sweat pants draped across the chair.

"No, no fucking way. The card is still down there. You just call them and tell them you'll pick it up later," he demanded.

"They can just run it again," he finished and took a drink.

"What—you think I'm going to fucking run off? Now? *Fuck you!*" she yelled back at him irritated.

"I just don't want to see anybody, that's all. I don't want anybody to see you either. We'll just stay here and wait it out. Something's going to happen today. It has to. It's been three full days now, and nothin'."

He uncapped the bottle again and refilled the cup.

She just sat on the edge of the bed and stared at him.

"Really? Fuck, Phil. Really? You are going to start fucking drinking now? It ain't even one o'clock yet. Don't you think you should lay off right now?" she questioned.

"My fucking back is killing me, don't fucking worry about it. I'll be fine," he darted back at her with a deadly mean stare.

"You know, if I was going to fucking run off, I could have done it yesterday, while you were at the fucking meeting!" she stated, pissed off.

He turned and stared her down.

"So you've thought about it. *I fucking knew it!*" he argued.

"NO! I am just saying, you have no fucking reason to think I am going anywhere. Jesus, Phil!" she argued back, surprised that he would think that now.

208

"Then pick up the phone and fucking tell them we are staying another night, and we'll get the card later. *Fucking do it!*" he demanded.

His voice was getting louder and she feared the housekeeping staff would overhear, she looked at him, he stared back at her with his arm raised, holding the Jack Daniels right in front of his mouth, completely still.

Fucking asshole.

She rose from the bedside and picked up the phone. He threw the whiskey into the back of his throat. It was going to be a long day.

"We need to go to the liquor store," his voice changed back. The crisis was averted for now. It would be good to get the hell out of this room, though; it was supposed to be a relaxing retreat away from what had happened.

It was anything but.

20

The impound lot was located in the middle of the small town of Snohomish, Washington. A uniformed Snohomish County Officer stood near the gate he had just opened. He was expecting them but they were not allowed to enter the impound yard. The gravel lot was huge and surrounded by a chain link fence.

Barbed wire capped the top.

They searched around the lot for the Mustang. Most of the vehicles in the lot were large emergency response trucks and search and rescue vehicles from Snohomish County. They looked as though they hadn't been moved all winter. Mother stared at the trucks in disbelief.

A lot of good those things are.

In the far corner they saw the back end of the Mustang. A blue tarp and been draped across the top of it and orange lettering now filled the back window.

Mother wanted to run up to it feeling the familiarity of every time she would see that car pull in to the driveway. It meant Rich was home.

Not anymore.

But she didn't want to let go of that feeling, if only for once more. They could see through the fence that the back window on the passenger side was shattered and the area around the radio was damaged.

Her heart sank.

This was Rich's pride and joy; he would be crushed to see what condition it was in now. She wanted to cry, not for herself, but because she knew Rich would be hurt seeing his car like this. The windows were down and the shiny red exterior was unusually dull with road film; it looked almost a dingy rust color.

"It hasn't been processed yet," the officer stated as he approached. "You need to stay back."

"How many miles are on it?" Tim asked.

"We need to know how many miles--" my mother repeated.

"I do not know—the team will look at it; if and when it gets assigned— they are on another homicide scene this morning and that takes precedence over a *missing person,*" he claimed.

"I just need to look at the odometer!" my mother cried.

Mom wanted to see if she could narrow down the route Rich may had taken, as he religiously and without fail, reset the trip odometer every time he put gas in the car. If they could determine how much gas or how many miles it had been driven, it may indicate one way or the other how big the search area needed to be.

Again, the officer refused to grant access to the vehicle.

Mother was furious and upset. Her husband was missing. A man had abandoned the car a day after Rich was missing and after repeated attempts to get some agency or police or search and rescue to help her, they tell her they can do nothing. And now, they tell her she can't even look at the car herself because it needs to be processed? She began crying, Tim helped her into the front seat of the car.

She fished into her purse and pulled out the spare set of keys she had for the car.

"Do you at least want a set of keys?" she said softly to the officer half crying.

"We have a set, ma'am," he replied.

"NO YOU DON'T!" she cried aloud to the officer.

She was getting mad again.

"The keys were not in it last night—you don't have a set, these are the only other set. How are you going to get the mileage, ever? If you don't have the keys?"

With that she finally let go. Tears rolled down her face and she stared through the open window at the officer, her hand outstretched with the keys in hand.

He peeked around the lot and peered down at the gravel for a minute.

"No one will help me find my husband. *No one.* He's not like this—he would not be missing if there wasn't a reason," she cried.

The officer glanced around, paused and then turned toward Mom.

"You know what? Here, give me the keys and we'll look at the mileage," he finally agreed.

Tim parked the Blazer and they got out and went back over to the car.

Mom looked up at the officer.

"We are coordinating a search tomorrow. We just need to narrow it down as much as we can," Mother continued, as tears slowly rolled down her face.

He opened the door to the Mustang and placed the key into the ignition, the trip meter turned on, 0281.

281?

It was only 86 miles from Twisp to Darrington.

281 miles?

They were perplexed. This meant the search area had to be huge; Rich might have been anywhere when he and the man who had abandoned the car crossed paths.

281 miles.

Seeing the Mustang firsthand really gilded my mother's resolve. Another restless night and an early trip to Darrington and Snohomish should have taken a much larger toll. And perhaps it had, but she did not let on that way.

As soon as she arrived home she went straight upstairs into her office and began calling everyone on her yellow tablet to spread the word that volunteers were needed for a search in Darrington the next day. If she couldn't get the police to help find her husband, she would coordinate her own search. No one seemed to want to take this serious unless a body was found or an obvious crime scene where it looked like a murder had occurred was discovered. The government bureaucracies and agencies frustrated her, but she would not let them, or anyone else slow her down.

Word went out through the Duvall Realty network of agents, friends and colleagues to meet at Darrington at 8:00 AM the next day, Sunday. It was going to be cloudy but the rains were supposed to hold off until Monday. Within hours, over one hundred friends and volunteers had been contacted and were preparing to look for Rich.

Our original hope that he had just gotten lost or stuck somewhere had been dashed once the car had been found and someone obviously other than Rich got out of it and walked away. Even though Mom was horrified that first and second night, there had still been a thread of hope. Any hope of Rich returning home to her, got out of that Mustang and *walked silently down the streets of Darrington.*

The only person who had seen the man who got out of that car was a teen-aged girl named Jessica Knoop.

Mom would cry and mourn for what seemed like the most likely scenario; but then she would think, that maybe, somehow, the man in the car had stolen it from Rich and Rich was lost in the forested roads of the North Cascades trying to hike to safety; but he was tired, and he was hungry and he was losing the race of time.

But sometime during this day, everyone began to realize that this was becoming less and less about finding Rich alive and more about helping and supporting my mother as she battled forward for answers. And ultimately, to find whoever had taken Rich from her and see justice served; whatever that may be.

His last known location was getting gas in Twisp and because the car was found in Darrington, it seemed logical to search on and around the highway between the opposing small towns. But 281 miles on the odometer didn't add up any way you looked at it. The locals were known to be friendly, but most people knew that some of the residents of the area, in many cases, moved up there because they didn't want to be bothered or seen. Some, just because they liked the peace and quiet and others because they were engaged in activities they didn't want anyone else to see. It was looking more and more as though perhaps Rich, on some side road or shortcut had stumbled across something he should not have. Whether that was at a home or a residence or just out in the woods somewhere, did not matter.

Upstairs in her office, Mom and some of her friends began dissecting the Thomas guide she had of the area and photocopying a wide swath along the potential search area. Much of the land was public or under timber company control but a few large sections of private land also covered the area. Every time headlights would stream in to the room or a car would drive by on the street outside, Mom would jump toward the window, *hoping* that maybe he had been picked up hitchhiking or something, *anything*.

It was advised that groups of searchers three or four to a car should stay together. No one wanted the searchers to run into something alone or in small numbers like Rich may have. They estimated between 60 and 80 volunteers would show up in 20-30 cars. Sticking with the advice of law enforcement to keep three or four to a search party meant they need to create about 20-25 unique grids to search. With the amount of area between Twisp and Darrington, the task became daunting.

As they laid out the first hypothetical grids, it became very obvious that some of the search areas were all public lands with open access and some were as much as 90% private with gated or no access. And there was really no way to tell where gates might be; but hopefully, if the same roads would still be closed during the search, that were closed when Rich came across the highway, the search area would be reduced.

Next, they realized they really had no idea how many people would show and some may or may not be able to stay for the whole day; so rather than create 20-25 large areas, they went about the task of creating 50-60 much smaller areas, with the idea that if your search party 'cleared' a grid, you would return to Darrington and receive another area to search. This way some groups could stay all day and search four or five grids and other groups could come and do one or two as time permitted. It seemed much more reasonable and far more efficient.

For hours, Mom separated herself from the 'grieving wife' and made maps; and organized and talked to friends and relatives about the search.

She wanted the police involved and this was the only way she was going to get it done. Some of Rich's co-workers contacted the media outlets in hopes they could get some help or tips, but with nothing to report other than a missing guy, not many seemed ready to run the story. But the car had been found and someone had seen a man get out of it that was not Rich.

As Mom and her friends worked tirelessly through that Saturday, they waited with anticipation for the news to come on that night.

Maybe, just maybe, someone would run the story.

*   *   *

Phil and Sharon spent Saturday afternoon and evening drinking; waiting for the local news to come on. It had now been three days and they started to believe that maybe the guy in the red Mustang lived alone or was on an extended road trip or something. Maybe it would be days or weeks before they heard anything.

Maybe they wouldn't here anything at all.

In an instant the television flashed to the picture of a bright red, late model Ford Mustang.

Sharon trembled and took a deep breath.

"Good evening, in our first story tonight a development in the mysterious disappearance of Duvall real-estate broker Richard Duncan. Duncan was last heard from on Tuesday when he phoned his wife and said he would be home the next day via the North Cascades Highway. After purchasing gasoline in Twisp on Wednesday morning, his co-workers say he simply vanished, failing to return home as scheduled. Tonight, however, we learned that his 1988 Ford Mustang, like this one pictured here, was discovered in Darrington last night; but no sign of Duncan. Friends are currently organizing a search in the Darrington area

214

tomorrow. Anyone with information or knows the whereabouts of Duncan is asked to call the Snohomish County Police at the number on your screen ...Dennis?"

"Thanks, Kathy in other news...."

Phil quickly turned the television to the other local stations; he stared intently at the screen.

He sat in the cheap motel room chair, leaning forward with his elbows on his knees and a clear plastic cup clutched in his right hand. His expression remained unchanged.

She sat on the edge of the bed painting her toenails trying to keep the fucked up predicament out of her mind. Neither said a word. The channels of the television clicked and changed, back and forth. The only motion in the room was the bending of his right arm as he brought the cup up and down from his lips.

Nothing about the ticket.

He smiled.

"They ain't got shit," he finally broke the silence.

She still said nothing. Her eyes strained intently at the toes on her right foot. Her hand delicately guided the tiny brush over each toenail. He turned off the television; the chair creaked as he leaned backwards and stared at his wife.

"See, I told you. Nothing to worry about," he proudly stated.

"Nothing to *fucking worry about?* Jesus, Phil. What the fuck are you talking about?"

She capped the toenail polish and leaned back on to the bed placing a pillow underneath her feet.

"You knew they'd find the car—and THANK GOD they didn't say anything about the ticket-" she started with a sigh and an air of discontent about her.

"But nothing to worry about?"

"They ain't got shit," he stated again boldly as he reached into the brown liquor store bag for another bottle.

"They're fucking searching for the guy in Darrington tomorrow, did you hear that? They don't think he's missing for fuck sakes. They think they're looking for a body," she almost started to cry but held back.

"What about it?" he retorted back, "They don't even know if that real estate guy didn't park it there himself and meet someone else or who knows?"

"Yeah? Well what if that tow truck driver remembers you for some stupid reason? Jesus Phil. What about that?" she demanded.

"What?" he asked sarcastically, "Maybe I should go up there and make sure-"

"DIDN'T YOU HEAR?" she cut him off, yelling.

She pointed at the now silent television and blew gently toward her toes.

"There's gonna' be a fucking search tomorrow, Phil. Fuck. And you're fucking wasted. *Again.* You should have taken that fucking car somewhere else!" she lectured.

He slammed the cup toward the wall and quickly rose from the chair; he turned and stared right at her on the bed. She drew back away from him and ducked her head, squinting her eyes. He stood there, towering over her, motionless.

Brown droplets of whiskey ran down the wall like the rain sliding down the bow of a damp cedar tree.

"They ain't got nothin' yet. They got a car. That fucking car, I wiped it down, no one saw me. It's done," he stated sternly.

"It's not done, Phil. It's just fucking starting, that fucking ticket. That fucking ticket!" she couldn't hold back any longer.

She knew this wasn't going to be easy and she wanted it all to just go away, but it was being beamed into a million living rooms. He was supposed to stop drinking, they were just going to hide out and let it blow over.

But he kept drinking, all day.

And that shotgun behind the chair, what if the shit hit the fan, what would he do? Would he fight it out with police? Were they going to die like Bonnie and Clyde? This was supposed to be easy—but it wasn't getting any easier.

"Look, we'll go to a different motel tomorrow, people have seen us here, we need to just keep moving. We move enough that no one becomes familiar with us, even if they do figure out who to look for. No one will ever notice us," he said.

"Oh, that's fucking great, Phil! A life on the run. How long do you think it will take them to hunt you down once the police get involved? Are we supposed--"

"Us," he interrupted, "Us. Hunt *us* down," he corrected her staring into the back of her skull.

"Us. You. Me. What the fuck ever. Jesus!" she cried, "We can't go on the run Phil, we can't. They'll kill us."

"What do you want me to do then? Huh?" he yelled, "You want me turn myself in? They don't even know that guy didn't park the car there himself! Maybe he parked it there and met a friend and went somewhere. They don't know anything! Maybe that cop who gave me the ticket never put two and two together, maybe he does? Maybe he doesn't!"

"I DON"T KNOW!" she yelled back at him and then quickly covered her mouth realizing someone in the room next to them could overhear.

"I don't know," she continued whispering, "I don't know."

"Well I fucking do. We'll get up tomorrow and go to Eastgate or something, a new motel. Work isn't expecting me back for a while and my sister thinks were going to be in Moses Lake for a few more days. We just wait it out. If they don't find something, they won't even know if he just didn't park there and walk away," he demanded.

He fished for another plastic cup out of the bag and pulled some ice from the cooler they had brought in from the truck. The whiskey danced in and around the cold cubes.

"What else do you want me to do?! There is nothing else *we can do,* but fucking WAIT and see what the *fuck happens!!*" he yelled.

She rolled over.

She couldn't help worrying.

What if they find where the truck was? Or worse?

21

Sunday May 6, 1990

By 8:00 AM, the parking lot of the IGA in Darrington was nearly full of cars and people standing around looking at the gridded off maps. I arrived with my roommate, Tom and my friend Troy in his blue Toyota 4x4. I hopped out and went to where one of my mom's friends was handing out gridded maps. I knew almost no one, except for Rich's friend, Tom Penski. Despite my close relationship with Rich; I rarely interacted with his friends and co-workers. Tom was different however. To most of Rich's friends I always felt like the awkward reminder that Rich had married a woman 16 years older than he was with a daughter nearly Rich's age and a son who was- well...they knew. But on the few occasions I would hang out with Rich and Tom at the office they shared, Tom was always kind and never judgmental.

The parking lot had spots for about 60 cars and it was nearly three quarters full. People stood milling around the parking lot talking in small groups. Theories about his disappearance ranged from lost in the woods to picking up a hitchhiker to playing some sort of sick prank. There were men and their wives, even some teenagers as young as 13 or 14. The employees in the grocery store stood inside the glass windows and stared out at us like they were at a zoo watching some sort of exotic exhibit.

"Ok, if I could get everyone gathered around," a man who I recognized from Rich's office but I did not know finally started.

"Our goal today is to find Rich, and for no one else to get lost or run into something they shouldn't. I think everyone here knows what may have happened so I am going to be brief and lay out some guidelines. PLEASE stay safe. Rich's car was found here two days ago, he got gas in Twisp—a couple hours away from here. We have gridded off sections on these maps and we will give each car load a map, when you go to the area be sure not to go on private property, we don't want to cause a stir with the locals—if someone asks you to leave just make a note of the spot and we'll give that to police-"

"Why isn't there any search and rescue or police here?" a voice asked from the crowd.

"Well, right now Rich is a missing person and they have not gotten involved yet, hopefully we can find Rich or find some evidence or something to prompt them to get involved, but right now, we are more or less on our own," he answered.

"So, with that said, just be careful, if you run in to a situation—and NO ONE, PLEASE, no one go off alone or get out of sight. Stay in groups. We don't know what happened, so let's be careful. There is a list of things on the back of each grid that Rich may have had on him, you may find some of these items or even if you think you have—do not touch them—note the location and call police. I need to tell you—it is not outside the realm of possibility that someone could come across Rich's body--"

The parking lot became eerily silent.

"So if you do—do not touch it—if he looks like he might be alive or unconscious of course—help him—but if something bad happened, it's been almost five days—do not disturb anything—call police," he somberly instructed.

"So here is the plan, for those of you who just want to stay in a car—I know we have a lot of you who aren't in condition to go hiking into the brush—for those of you who fit that—take one of the maps that just has highlighted roads. We want you to cover as many miles of these back roads as you can in case Rich is stranded along one of them. Whoever ended up with his car may have simply stolen it while Rich was looking at something or just made Rich get out of the car way out in the woods somewhere. We need to cover a lot of road. For those of you who want to drive and search for evidence and then stop and look and get back in and keep going—we have maps set up for evidence search. Campgrounds, turn outs, anywhere someone might stop and toss stuff out of Rich's car. And finally, we have gridded off areas where we want people to get out of their cars and walk a gridline—literally searching every square inch of ground for, well, anything. If something bad happened to Rich, he, well, his body, may not be far off the road. These search areas are small, but they need to be thoroughly searched. Once you are done, or you need to go back home—I know some of you have to work or whatever, as soon as you're done bring the map back to here so we can keep track of what has been searched. Are there any questions?" he finally asked.

"Do you think Rich is alive?" a man asked standing behind me.

"What if he was robbed and left out there--" yelled another.

"Who would have hurt Rich?" yet another voice chimed.

"Look, we all know there are dozens of different scenarios, speculating won't help us find Rich—he's out there—somewhere—he might be hurt or freezing or starving—lets go find him," he finished.

I looked at Troy and Tom for some indication of what to do, but they merely stared back. This was my thing—and they were here to help in any way they could—but I needed to take the lead on what we were going to do.

I believed at the time that Rich had taken a side trip onto one of the many side roads along the highway. I had been with him so many times in which we were headed to a specific spot, but an obscure road had lured him in.

To Rich, they were like candy.

If it was a dead end (and most were) we would simply turn around and go back. But that was in his old Subaru 4x4 station wagon.

He never took the Mustang off road.

If something were tantalizing enough; he may have gone on a well maintained, gravel Forest Service Road, however. I imagined that he may have gotten out of his car to take a piss or take in a view along one of the main gravel roads, some of the viewpoints he used to show me were 50 or 100 feet off the road. He would never leave the car running as his larger frame and physical shape meant that if someone he hadn't seen was hiking along the road or something and took off with the car, he wasn't going to chase them down.

But it had been 5 days.

I remembered that there were 281 miles on the odometer, it made sense that perhaps he decided to take a side trip on one of the roads and could have gone as far as 40 or 50 miles in before something happened. On so many occasions we had planned a two hour trip through the foothills near home and discovered some new road or view that just kept pulling us further in. He always called Mom and told her we would be late, sometimes three or four hours late. Maybe he just figured he'd eventually get cellular service and never did, and he had to hike out.

Troy and I had gone on many a trip down roads like these before. I decided we should try and cover as much road as we could, we could drive fairly fast and if Rich was way up in the hills, time may be running out.

I grabbed one of the maps with the roads highlighted out a little ways up the North Cascades Highway and Troy, Tom and I piled into his pick-up and headed north out of Darrington. With so many people searching, today had to be the day we would get some answers.

At around 1:15 PM Mom woke up. It had been the first time she slept more than two hours at once in almost a week. The exhaustion was finally beginning to take a toll on her. She decided she could no longer sit and wait by the phone and asked Diana to take her to Darrington. Nothing was going to stop her from searching for Rich.

"Are you sure you want to go up there, Karen?" Diana asked as they piled into the car.

"The police won't do anything. Darrington police told me there was nothing they could do. Moses lake Police aren't going to search for someone 200 miles outside of their jurisdiction. Snohomish County has a murder scene they are working on—and they won't start search and rescue unless we can narrow it down further," Mom paused.

Diana looked over at her, her hand on the keys in the ignition.

"Yes, I am going to Darrington," she answered very deliberately; sitting in the passenger seat of her car.

The drive to Darrington was eerily familiar to her. It did not seem like five days had passed, for her it was like one long continuous stretch of time with tiny bits of sleep in between. She had no idea it was even Sunday, it did not matter.

She had to do everything she could to try and somehow, get some police agency *to help her look for Rich.*

*   *   *

The Eastgate Motel was a welcome change from the Motel 6 in Issaquah. Maybe new scenery would finally lessen the paranoia. It was always on the back of her mind that Phil's sister or someone from Phil's work would see their new truck in Issaquah and wonder why it was parked there if they were in Moses Lake fishing? This motel was eight miles toward Seattle and few who lived in Issaquah needed to come to Eastgate lest they were passing through on Interstate 90.

They had made a quick trip to the apartment to let Rusty out of the house, he had been there for two days but he was well trained and used the papers.

Around noon they packed their stuff in to the truck and after getting her Visa card from the desk and checking out, they went to the Safeway store at Eastgate, near Bellevue and picked up some beer and wine coolers.

They wondered if someone in the search that was going on in Darrington would come across anything. So far, this was nothing more than a mystery. A man was supposed to be home and he didn't show. She was overly familiar with that scenario herself. They hoped and prayed no one would find anything. As long as nothing was found, they knew they would be in the clear.

She lay in bed and watched him drink most of the day. He had picked up the cleaning kit for the shotgun while at the apartment and had it disassembled and strewn across the table. Every couple of hours she would switch the television station to the local news channel to check on any developments. She had picked up a real-estate guide in front of the liquor store and had been looking through it circling homes available on the Plateau that were in their price range. She forced herself to pretend that things were going to get back to normal.

"Do you think we need a three bedroom or a four?" she asked.

He set the receiver of the shotgun aside and looked toward her on the bed.

"Definitely, a four. I want room for my camping shit and a home office," he answered.

He too, was merely trying to play along; knowing that she was merely going through the motions and trying to pass the time away.

He was so drunk he didn't even care.

She knew it would be awhile before they would be able to do anything like that, but she was tired of dwelling on what had happened, if they were going to get through this she had to learn how to keep moving forward; and put the Mountain Loop Highway, behind her.

At 10:45 PM she glanced at the clock on the nightstand next to her. She did not want to miss the eleven o'clock news. Hopefully, the story wouldn't even make it on. If it faded away, they could stay in the motel for another day or two and return home to tell everyone about their fishing trip in Moses Lake. She could spend the week cleaning and doing laundry and start looking at homes.

No matter how hard she tried, it wouldn't vacate her mind.

It had scared the living shit out of her; she knew that somewhere, that man's family was horrified. But the more it crept into her head, the more she had to think about normal things. For the rest of her life she would know what happened and knew there would be a cost, she was forever changed and traumatized by what Phil had done. But nothing could undo those few minutes along that road, and while she cried for herself and the situation she was in, she also cried for that poor man.

At 10:55 PM she turned the television to the news; he had reassembled the shotgun and loaded it.

It made her nervous.

He hadn't moved from the chair all day except to piss and to answer the door when they had Chinese delivered a few hours earlier.

On the end of the bed she cleared away the half empty Chinese take-out boxes and crossed her legs underneath her. She wanted to hop outside for a smoke but her wandering thoughts about what happened sidetracked her and now it was nearly eleven.

She crossed her fingers and *hoped*.

"Good Evening, in a continuing story, friends and family of a missing Duvall man descended on the tiny town of Darrington today, searching for clues behind the man's disappearance."

She stared at the television screen, yesterday's report had only shown graphics and maps; now they had footage from the tiny town full of cars and people — the reporters had actually gone to Darrington?

She swallowed, hard.

He took a drink.

"Duncan was last heard from by his wife when he spent the night in Moses Lake," the reporter continued.

"Moses fucking Lake!?" she gasped as she brought her hand up to her mouth, *"Moses Lake!"*

He leaned forward and stared intently at the television.

"Holy fuck — why did we have to say we were in Moses Lake?!" she yelled and stared at Phil.

This was a fucking disaster.

He raised his arm and motioned her to be quiet. She sat there silent with her hand over her mouth.

"And apparently got gas in Twisp, Washington and has not been heard from since. Friday night, his car, pictured here, was discovered abandoned in Darrington. This led friends and volunteers to Darrington where they spent the day searching for clues in Duncan's disappearance. Jim Carter is on the scene in Darrington, Jim, what can you tell us?"

"Hi Dennis, well, not much. Over 200 volunteers descended on this tiny logging town set in the foothills of the North Cascades. At eight o'clock this morning they fanned out in twos and threes and searched, desperately, to try and find Rich Duncan or any signs which might provide a clue as to his whereabouts. By nightfall, however, most of the cars had left, this tiny town went silent again, and still, no word on the disappearance of Duncan."

She flopped back on to the bed, Moses Lake. She brought both hands to her face and screamed quietly into them and sat back up.

"Were any clues found in the car, Jim?" the news anchor quizzed.

"Well, yes, not in the car per se, but in a late development we received word that someone saw a man getting out of the car who did not fit, the, uh, the owners, Duncan's, uh, description. Apparently this man was much shorter, much thinner and did not appear to be Duncan."

His jaw clenched and he grabbed the bottle.

She sat stunned, motionless and tried to process what she had just heard.

Someone saw him?

A wave of heat rushed over Phil. For a second he felt dizzy and disoriented.

"Police are giving little details, but apparently a sketch artist is working with the witness who saw this man—and we should get a sketch soon and hopefully some leads or tips. Police say this man is not a suspect at this point because this is just a missing person's case, but they do want to talk to the man who parked the car here to see if he has any insight or information on the whereabouts of Duncan, Dennis?"

"Someone saw you ditch the car?!" she yelled, "You said no one saw you—*what the fuck is that?*"

He sat frozen and drew a slow deep breath.

"Fuck, Phil! Someone saw you! Oh my god, someone fucking saw you!—and fucking Moses Lake—what if your sister or whoever sees this and they think we were in Moses Lake—does anyone at your work know about what happened before?" she continued, incensed.

"No one, fucking knows. It must be that girl I seen," he stated coldly.

"Girl? What fucking girl? You never said anything about a fucking girl!" she demanded.

"I just saw her for a second, right after I got out and closed the door. She was walking down the street and she said something but I just kept walking like I didn't hear her," he said.

"And Moses Lake don't mean shit. He was there and obviously they know he made it to Twisp or wherever."

"I know that, Phil. But it just isn't good that they are tossing around the same town we are supposed to be in *right now*. And we told Marjorie we were in Moses Lake and you told your work you were in Moses Lake. *And your fucking sister!*" she continued.

"What if they tie that ticket to you? And he was in Moses Lake, like we said, and this girl, this whoever she is can identify you? What then? Jesus," she cried, "they find nothing in Darrington and now we're more fucked than we were *before!*"

Sharon began to sob again.

"They know he didn't park the car and leave now, they aren't going to let this go—fuck!" she screamed, "I can't fucking believe this. I just can't fucking believe this. Why the fuck did you do it? Phil. Goddamit. Why?"

For the first time she looked at him and wanted to know why. She had been afraid to ask, but now, she was losing control.

He was supposed to wipe the car down and walk away.

Now someone had seen him park the car.

She was scared and the shock and trauma of what she had seen was finally starting to lift. She didn't know what to do. She wanted to call her mother or at least call Jody, maybe she would know how to get out of this.

He stared down at the cup full of whiskey and ice.

"I don't know. I shouldn't have been drinkin' like that," he answered.

And took another drink.

22

Monday   May 7, 1990

Monday morning found Mom exhausted and worn out. The search in Darrington had provided no clues as to the whereabouts or fate of Rich. For days she had been calling and speaking with law enforcement agencies literally across the state. Agency after agency told her she was contacting the wrong jurisdiction or needed to call someone else. When Rich's car was discovered, abandoned in Darrington, she focused her efforts on the Snohomish County Sheriff's Department.

She didn't know what else to do.

She was stunned and in disbelief that the officer in Darrington had told her she was "probably looking for a body" yet the Darrington police could not do anything given the financial constraints most small town police departments face. When she finally did see a Snohomish County Officer at the impound yard where the car was impounded, he told her that resources were not yet available as a current homicide took precedence over a missing person. Both of these situations made reasonable, logical sense. But not to a wife whose husband has been missing for six days.

It seemed no one was going to help her. *The case was going cold, fast.*

Darrington Police did however, contact Snohomish County in order to see if Detective John Hinds could do a composite of the man Jessica Knoop had seen get out of the Mustang. Snohomish County Detectives had been fielding calls all weekend from my mother and others concerned about Rich's whereabouts so they were not at all surprised when the request came in.

Detective John Hinds was a veteran of the Snohomish County Homicide squad. In his forties, he had seen his fair share of homicide cases and knew that persistence and hard work usually paid off. He had developed his skills as an artist into a very useful tool for law enforcement.

Just after 9:00 AM Detective Hinds' phone rang on his littered desk.

"Hi John, this is Tom," the voice started.

He recognized the voice of his supervisor, Sgt. Tom Greene on the other end of the phone.

"Hi, Tom," he answered, "What have you got for me?"

"Well, I need you to do a composite over in Arlington," Sgt. Greene answered, "You know that missing person case out of Moses Lake?"

"Moses Lake? How are we involved?" Detective Hinds asked.

"That missing real estate guy, from Duvall. They impounded his car over the weekend in Darrington, and Darrington can't handle this. Well, we got a juvenile witness who saw the man who abandoned the car and word in that town has already spread like wildfire. I need to get a lid on this and get that composite done at least. Maybe you could call the wife? She has been frantically calling all weekend and dispatch just doesn't know what else to tell her. A uniform who met her at the impound told her the current crime scene we were processing had precedence--"

"They *what*?!" Detective Hinds cut him off.

"Yeah, I know—I've been catching heat for it already. Mondays just seem to catch the shit from the weekend, you know?" Sgt. Greene pointed out.

"And to top it off, Darrington P.D. told her they didn't have the man power to help her, they said since it was a Moses Lake case at this point that they were too busy."

"Alright, I'll call the witness and get over to Arlington and see what she remembers," Detective Hinds hung up the phone and dialed the number Sgt. Greene had given him.

He contacted the witness and after speaking at length with her mother they agreed to meet at the Arlington Police station to see if he could get a good sketch from her. It had been almost four days since she had seen the man but she was confident she could accurately describe him. Hinds wanted to get the sketch does as soon as possible. Details tend to fade with time, and more importantly, if the missing man had been harmed in some way, whoever had done so would not think twice about making sure a teen-aged girl from Darrington *wasn't around to identify him.*

Murder myself, Murder I am.

*   *   *

Outside of an ATM in Monroe, Mom grabbed her purse off the passenger seat and fished for the ATM card. She hoped and prayed that somehow money would be missing from the account and give some indication as to where Rich might be.

But she knew better.

As she turned on to the highway in Duvall to head north she dialed Snohomish County Police to find out if they were able to do anything to help find Rich.

"Hi this is Karen Duncan, again," Mom began.

"Hi Karen, find anything in Darrington?" Sgt. Greene asked, familiar with what was going on.

Detectives had not yet been officially assigned to the case and each time she would call, dispatch had to route the call somewhere; Sgt. Greene was the one they called upon.

"No, we didn't. Someone thought they might have found a campsite, but, I just don't know — what do I have to do to get someone to help me?" she asked.

"Well, at this point he *is only missing--*"

"Only missing?!" Mom raised her voice.

"Only missing? Then send someone to search, why can't you search — do something?" she cried. "You've got *an impound lot full of 'Search and Rescue' vehicles!*"

"Well, we will do everything we can, it's technically a Moses Lake case right now, but I am sending a composite artist to meet with the witness who saw the man get out of your husband's car. He is very good, hopefully that will help us get to the bottom of this," he answered.

"Listen, Rich would not have let someone take that car. That was his baby. He called me all the time, he has never, never, been missing or unaccounted for like this. You have to understand — he had appointments that he has missed and — why won't anyone help me find my husband? *Why?"*

Tears rolled slowly down her face.

"I know this can frustrating, but let's see what the sketch artist can come up with, and we can go from there," he said.

"So Snohomish County is getting involved, then?" she asked, wiping tears from her swollen face.

"Well, we are going to do a sketch and we'll see where it goes, that's all I can do at this point," he answered as politely as he could.

Mom was still confused and perplexed how someone could just drop off the face of the Earth and police would not do anything about it.

228

She hung up the phone and came into Monroe.

The ATM she regularly visited was becoming frustratingly familiar. She opened the door, paced over to the machine and inserted the debit card.

Nothing.

Fifteen feet away her car phone began to ring. She hurriedly made her way back to the car and climbed in.

Hello?" she said.

"Hi Karen, how are you holding up?"

It was her friend, Linda.

"Oh, just in Monroe at the ATM. Nothing," she said quietly as she pulled the door to her Volvo shut.

"Well, you knew that; he didn't run away Karen, you know that," Linda stated trying to be encouraging.

"I just don't know. I just don't know what to do now--" Mom started to cry softly.

"I've called the hospitals so many times the receptionists know my name. I've called every police agency between Moses Lake and Seattle; I've called every person I know that knew Rich. We tracked down where he got gas, they found his car; a man got out of his car that wasn't him! Two hundred people searched the woods for him. And still no one in an official capacity will help me find my husband. Why?"

She sat quietly in the car as the rain started coming down and tears streamed down her face again, *"What have I done that no one will help me?"*

"Oh, Karen, it's not you. Have you thought about calling the television news or the newspapers?" Linda asked.

"I don't know what good that would do, I don't want the police to get mad or think I am trying to make them look bad. I just want someone to help, this is ridiculous," Mom answered.

"I know; it's hard. Are you on your way back to the house yet?" Linda asked.

"Yeah, I am just leaving Monroe; I should be back up there in 20 minutes or so."

*   *   *

Mom sat at her desk upstairs in her office. She had collected the grid search maps from yesterday and wanted to look for areas where people weren't able to search because of gates or private property. She wanted to try and organize another search for later in the week. Her desk was covered with notepads, pens and envelopes with hospital phone numbers, police phone numbers and numbers of friends who said they could help on another search. Sitting and waiting for answers was driving her nuts, maybe she missed a hospital or missed some small town police agency or something.

Her phone rang.

"Hello," she answered.

"Hi, could I speak with Karen Duncan please?"

"This is her?"

"Hi Karen, my name is Essex Porter, can I speak with you for a few moments? I really believe we can help you."

The voice on the phone was deep and authoritative.

"Who are *you?*" Mom asked and switched the phone to her other ear.

"My name is Essex Porter; I am with KIRO TV in Seattle. I'm calling to see if we can't help get the word out about your missing husband. I am not looking to 'scoop' a story--"

Mom cut him off, "How did you get this number?"

"I'll be very honest with you Mrs. Duncan, your friend Linda gave it to me, she told me a little bit about what's going on — I am so sorry, I just want to get some information out there and maybe with a little more publicity, well…, when stories like these start to get airtime, I hate to say it, but the police tend to put more resources toward cases that get attention rather than those that don't. I don't necessarily agree with it, but that's how it is. And again, I'm not looking for an exclusive or something like that; I just want to help if I can and if you'll let me."

He paused, waiting to see how Mom would respond.

"What do you want to know?" she asked apprehensively.

"Well, can you just tell me in your own words, what happened? Start at the beginning, I'll do the rest," he replied.

"Well, let me tell you, I don't want anything added that isn't true and I am not trying to get anyone in trouble. I just want the police to take this seriously and help me find my husband," Mom almost started to cry again.

"I just want to help, Karen, just give me a chance," he asked.

Mom wasn't really sure about involving the media. But no one else was doing anything to help find Rich, she almost felt she was running out of options.

"Well, Rich went to northeastern Oregon on Monday to look at real estate. He spent the night and then on Tuesday night he called me from Moses Lake, at the Motel 6; and told me he would be home the next afternoon, which would have been Wednesday. Well, Wednesday afternoon came around, and no Rich. He was going to drive across the North Cascades Highway and then through Darrington and Monte Cristo to look at some recreation property," Mom began.

"Did you hear from him at all on Wednesday?" he asked.

"No, I don't think he has cell service up there. But anyway, I paged him all day and nothing. So Wednesday night I started calling hospitals and the King County police but they said they could not take the report because his last known location was in Moses Lake. So I called Moses Lake, and all they did was take a missing persons report."

"Ok, go on."

"And well, by Thursday morning I was really worried so I called my son and he came over Thursday night and he and my son-in-law, Tim drove over the North Cascades Highway on Friday and found that Rich had used his credit card at a Texaco in Twisp, very early on Wednesday morning. Well, by that time I had filed a missing person case with Moses Lake and because a case was open, the police in Twisp wouldn't do anything. On Friday night the car was found in Darrington and a young girl saw the man — but don't say anything about the young girl, I don't want to put her in danger — but she saw the man who parked it there and this man was five foot eight to five foot ten and less than 200 pounds. Rich is well over six foot and about 275 pounds so I knew it was not him. Darrington Police had the car impounded to Snohomish County, but they wouldn't help us either. The officer in Darrington even told me we were probably looking for a body at this point," Mom became increasingly irritated.

"They said that? That you were looking for a 'body'?" he asked.

"Yes, we told them we were going to organize a search in the area and I asked if we should be looking for a person or a body and he said 'a body'. So Saturday I went to see the car and it had over 281 miles on the trip meter and that is much further than Twisp to Darrington, so we don't know where the car may have been driven, it just doesn't add up. Well, as you know, we searched yesterday around Darrington and all along the North Cascades Highway and came up with nothing. But we had no help from Darrington police or Snohomish County or anything. It's not like Rich to just disappear, he would not do this. Something is wrong and no one will help me. I mean, Snohomish County is apparently doing a composite sketch, but, I don't know when that is going to happen, and I've called Snohomish County Police so many times I think they are tired of hearing from me. No one will help me find my husband."

The familiar tears began to roll down her soft face again.

"I am so sorry, Karen, this is obviously very upsetting for you, I don't want to keep you. I think I can get some help for you, ok? Just hang in there, please. Did they say when they were doing the composite sketch?" he asked.

"I don't know, maybe they told me, but its, its, just so much, that I…"

Murder myself, Murder I am.

"I understand, Karen. I think I have everything I need. Do you have any questions for me?" he asked politely.

"Can you help me find my husband?" she asked tearfully.

"I'll get this story as much attention as I can, Karen. Thank you. If you think of anything else, call me, anytime."

Mom hung up the phone and grabbed a tissue from the side of her desk. She sat cross-legged on her chair for a minute drying her eyes and went back to sorting maps and phone numbers.

*   *   *

Sharon awoke at around one o'clock and turned on the television. Next to her, he lay on his chest, arms extended above his head.

He was passed out.

She picked up her cigarettes and fished for a lighter. Gently, she sat back on the bed to put her slippers on. Every time she went out for a smoke it seemed he would stand by the window, staring out at her, watching.

She thought he was losing it.

"Where the fuck are you going?" he demanded in a low, growl like tone.

He didn't move.

"Just out for a smoke," she answered quietly.

"Don't let anyone see you, don't fuck this up. Don't fuck this up like you got the truck stuck," he slurred.

Always the truck.

Asshole.

She unslid the chain on the door and slipped outside. She peered in through the window to see if he was getting up, sometimes he came out to smoke with her, but lately he had been sleeping in longer and longer.

His back was still killing him and the prescription didn't seem to be working. He laid there motionless, it looked like he was going to sleep for a little while longer.

She lit the cigarette and scurried down the sidewalk away from the motel room. Slowly at first, and then at a brisk walk she made her way around the corner and out of sight. It was the first time in more than two days that she was more than ten feet away from him. She leaned against the cinderblock wall of the motel and took a drag. She wondered about the girl who saw Phil ditch the car.

Was there anything else he hadn't told me?

She was furious that he had not told her about the ticket until almost the day after it had happened but she understood him not wanting to

232

worry her. And it was entirely possible the girl doesn't even remember what he looked like.

But was she lying to herself?

She took another drag. She knew that everything was going to hinge upon the media coverage, if they let the story go, it would take the pressure off. She dropped her smoke and smothered it out with a quick twist of her slipper.

In the motel bed, he rolled over and the pain in his back startled him awake. He lifted his head and gazed around the room.

Where the fuck was she?

He remembered she had gone out for a smoke, but it seemed she had been out there awhile.

Sometimes she had two smokes.

He dropped his head back down to the pillow. He stared at the clock next to the bed. It was 1:20 in the afternoon. With a groan he turned and sat up, his spine felt like it was going to split in half, he turned and slipped the curtain aside. Adrenaline shot through his body when he looked outside the motel room. He dove across the bed toward the shotgun and popped it open to make sure it was still loaded.

He glanced at the nightstand where he had left the keys to the truck; he knew he should have hid them. They were sitting right where he had left them. He threw the bolt on the door and slid the chain into position. He pulled on his sweats and kept the shotgun close.

She was gone, that *fucking bitch.*

He slipped the curtain to the side again and peered out; he still could see no sign of her. He had to act quickly, he could pack the duffel bag and sneak the shotgun out to the truck, but his clothes were strewn about the room and he didn't have any cash, she had the bank card.

He knew he should have grabbed it before.

The half-gallon of Jack Daniels sat unopened on the table. He reached toward it without looking and cracked the top off with one hand. He dropped the lid and took a swig, right out of the bottle. Glued to his hand, the shotgun stood ready. He glanced around the room for the duffel bag and spotted it near the luggage rack. It was time to cut loose, he knew she couldn't handle it; he should have dealt with it earlier.

That look on her face right after he had done it should have told him.

As he turned to grab the duffel bag the door handle turned and the door pushed in to the lock and stopped with a thud. He took the safety off the shotgun and dove toward the closet.

"Phil?" came her voice through the door, "Let me in, it's me. I went to get a newspaper, across the street."

He jumped to the door and then peered out through the curtains. He couldn't see anything but Sharon, standing in her slippers outside the door. He slid the chain off and threw the door open. In one quick motion he grabbed her right arm and nearly dislocated her shoulder jerking her into the room. The door slammed shut and he replaced the chain.

"What the fuck are you doing?" he demanded.

"I just went to get a newspaper; you were sleeping so I didn't think you would care," she apologized.

"Don't you ever fucking leave this room without asking. Am I fucking clear on that? Fuck. I had no idea," he demanded.

"I just went for a walk, next door, Jesus," she replied unfolding the newspaper.

"Here look through these sections," she said as she handed a portion of the Seattle Times across the bed, "and we need to go somewhere, I don't care if we go to the park and walk, but I can't just sit in here and drink, we need to do something."

He tossed the newspaper aside and grabbed her by the arm again and pulled her in toward him. His eyes were cold and empty. She could smell the whiskey on him.

"I fucking mean it, if you think you're going to turn me in, think-"

"Fuck you!" she yelled at him jerking her arm away. "You fucking did this. You got fucking drunk and fucking got us into this fucking mess. *You. Phil. You.*"

She knew the risk of calling him out, especially about drinking. But this wasn't going like she thought it was going to. He had essentially been drunk for a week now, except for when he took that damn car back to Darrington.

But she had to start thinking about herself now.

If he wanted to stay drunk for the next month until this blew over, that was on him.

She had to keep her sanity, she wanted to call someone and just talk, but she knew he wouldn't allow that. In the meantime, she had to keep abreast of what the media knew and she had to keep him sober enough not to do something stupid, but drunk enough she could keep him under control.

It would not be easy.

The cabin fever was hitting them. They decided to head to Issaquah and just wander the stores or something discreet. Anything but this fucking motel room.

After a short drive into Issaquah he placed a baseball cap snuggly on to his head and made his way into the sporting goods store. He convinced her that if they needed to get out of the motel and get some air, they could at least go somewhere where he could wander quietly and pass the time. He wanted to get a few days' worth of food and supplies just in case that girl in Darrington remembered what he looked like well enough to release a composite sketch which resembled him in the slightest.

As he wandered in and out of the aisles lined with tents, stoves and outdoor gear he started to smile.

He loved camping.

He picked up a new butane stove, some packable camping utensils and a few butane cartridges.

Around the corner of the aisle she stood staring at camping and hiking magazines. It felt good to be out of that cramped motel room.

"Here, take these up front and get them and I'll meet you in the truck," he whispered and scanned around.

"What are you *looking around* for?" she asked.

"JUST FUCKING DO IT," he whispered harshly and gave her a mean stare.

"Fuck. Whatever, just go away," she quipped back.

He handed her the basket with the items in it and casually made his way across the store.

Camping gear? What the fuck?

She continued to browse at the magazines and wandered over to the clothing section. She had no intention of buying anything but she wanted to spend as much time in the store as she could. After browsing for a few minutes she wandered up front.

"Getting ready to do a little camping?" the clerk politely asked as he scanned the items through the check-out line.

She didn't want to get into any drawn out conversations that might prompt someone to remember her so she minimized her responses.

"No, it's just a gift," she replied.

"Yeah, these are great little stoves, this one is more for solo backpacking than general camping—but they're super lightweight," he continued.

She paid cash for the items and headed for the truck. She fished into her purse for the keys and realized Phil had them, everywhere they went he demanded that he keep the keys. She was beginning to feel like a prisoner.

She opened the door to the truck and saw Phil crouched in the front seat out of sight.

"What the fuck are you doing?" she asked.

"Just get in," he demanded, "and look normal, like I'm not here."

As she opened the door an Issaquah Police car pulled in two spots down from where she was parked. Her heart felt like it was going to jump out of her chest. She took the keys from him and jumped in to the driver's seat.

He crouched even lower and grimaced in pain. His back felt like it was going to explode but he had to stay out of sight, if he sat up now right in front of a cop it might look weird.

She started the truck and threw it in reverse and almost hit the police officer as he walked behind the truck, he jumped out of the way.

"Sorry," she hollered back at the cop as she quickly rolled down the window.

The officer stopped and looked at her in her the side mirror. She waved and smiled and he continued in to the store.

Phil let out a huge breath.

"Just get the fuck out of here. *Fuck,*" he whispered.

She backed out of the spot and pulled away from the direction the cop was walking.

"What the fuck is wrong with you?" she asked looking over at him as he rose into a sitting position.

"My fucking back, its killing me from crouching down like that," he answered, "we need to bring the shotgun with us when we go out, again, this is bullshit."

"Why are you crouching down, Jesus. You have to act normal or someone's going to notice. Fuck! Phil," she argued, "And the fucking shotgun? NO! We can't go rolling around with that fucking shotgun. Are you crazy?"

The paranoia was beginning to drive her nuts. They were supposed to act normal and let this pass. But he was getting more and more paranoid and irrational. They sat in silence as she steered the truck on to the on ramp of I-90 back toward Eastgate.

This wasn't going as he said it would and maybe, she thought, they should try something else. But to even broach the subject could put her in danger. If he thought she wanted to get out of this, who knew what he would do. She battled back and forth as she carefully signaled in and out of traffic.

"Watch your speed! Watch your speed!" he yelled, finally breaking the monotony, "It's 55. You have to do 55!"

She glanced down at the speedometer, she was doing 56.

"And fucking signal! Every time. You have to use your signals!" he demanded.

Clearly, he was agitated.

He hadn't had a drink all afternoon. *It was time.*

She figured it might work in her favor to stop and get some beer, no hard stuff, but some beer. If she caught him before he got too drunk she might be able to talk to him without him flipping the fuck out. She had to try. Someone had seen him in that car — and the ticket. She could tell that ticket really weighed on him.

It weighed on her.

More than she was letting on.

23

Jessica Knoop and her mother pulled into the parking lot of the Arlington Police Department to meet with Detective Hinds. As she strode across the new asphalt of the parking lot she gripped her mother's arm tightly.

Nothing ever seemed to happen in Darrington and now she was the only person alive who had seen what could be a murder suspect. No one had any idea who or why the man was driving the car or even why he parked it there. What was known, was that the man who owned the car had not been heard from for nearly two days before she saw the man who abandoned the car. No one knew where he was from, where he was at, if he knew he had been seen getting out of the car and if Jessica was now in danger. Would he come after her and try to clean up any witnesses?

Gossip was nothing new to Darrington and everyone knew who had seen the guy. It wouldn't take much for someone with less than good intentions to roll into Darrington and discreetly find and silence her.

She was scared.

Her mother was scared.

But the one good thing about how quickly rumors spread throughout the tiny northwestern logging town, was that if anyone showed up asking who the girl was that saw the guy get out of the Mustang, the whole town would know someone was asking, rather quickly. And therefore, so would she.

She and her mother quietly walked through the front doors and asked the receptionist to see Detective Hinds. A metal door to the side of the lobby opened; Detective Hinds introduced himself and invited them in.

They went through a long hallway to a conference room at the end of the hall. Inside, placards of facial features such as eye shape, face shape, noses, mouths and hairstyles were laid across the table.

Detective Hinds knew the situation the young girl was in, but the best way to bring her out of danger was to get an accurate composite of the person of interest and identify him. He would need to explain to her the seriousness of the situation she was in, but experience had shown him that it was best to do so after the sketch was done. If she became even more nervous or scared it may inhibit the accuracy of the sketch. He needed her to relax, focus and feel comfortable.

"Hi Jessica, how you feeling?" Hinds asked calmly.

"I'm good—it's a little unnerving, but I'm cool," she nodded her head.

Jessica was very strong, and on the outside she was able to maintain her confidence. Of all of the kids in Darrington to see the man—she was probably the best equipped to handle it. She was honest, well-mannered and rarely intimidated by anyone; but this was a potential murder suspect, and even she still felt a little scared, deep down.

"Ok, what I want you to do is just try and clear your head a little bit and go back to when you saw the red Mustang. Now picture the man you saw..." he started.

"What stood out to you the most?" he asked.

"His eyes, I remember his eyes, they just seemed—I don't know, creepy. He just stared at me for a second and looked away," she answered.

He pulled the collection of placards containing eye shapes and flipped them through to the beginning.

"Ok, let's take a look through these and tell me if you see some that look like his, we can always go back and change them, we'll move on to facial shape and other features in a minute, but for now, let's just focus on the eyes," he continued.

She flipped through the placards and remembered how the man in the car resembled one of her friends. In fact, that was what had initially got her attention. She focused intently on each one and identified a pair which probably looked close.

"Those," she said, pointing down at the placard.

Over the next few hours she and Detective Hinds flipped through book after book of facial features, as the time wore on she became more and more relaxed. Facial shapes, mouth size and shape, eyebrows, they went through them all and detective Hinds created multiple different faces. She would look at them intently and then small changes would be made. Detective Hinds was very impressed by her confidence and thoroughness.

The sketch would most likely become a very key component to the case if it were to ever be solved. After many long hours, they finally settled on one.

"That's him," she stated confidently when they were done.

"That's him."

"Good, we'll get this out to other agencies and media outlets. Now, I don't want to scare you, but you need to be very aware and cautious until we get this guy. Anyone acting strange or out of place- you need to call 911 right away. I would suggest you keep a low profile, I know a lot of people – kids in town know it was you who saw him," he cautioned.

"I'll be fine, I know what's going on," she answered.

She got up from the interview room and made her way outside.

Although composite sketches sometimes look nothing like a person of interest, to the person of interest themselves they become a strong source of paranoia. They start to put doubt in the minds of a perpetrator and doubt in the minds of anyone who knows who the perpetrator is. Sometimes they go nowhere and sometimes every person in the county claims to have seen the guy in the sketch; he's their neighbor or ex-boyfriend or weird uncle. And when tips start to come flooding in sometimes the person of interest begins to act abnormally, further drawing suspicion to themselves.

Detective Hinds was now hunting a man down. He had the first tool, the first volley to throw at whoever had taken Rich.

He looked down at the sketch.

"Hello," he said confidently, "Nice to finally meet you."

*   *   *

After working most of the day Monday, I drove up to mom's house. I had missed work on Friday and Sunday and although my employer, Kevin Epps, fully understood the situation, if there was nothing going on with finding Rich, he needed me at the shop. I did not realize until years later, that Kevin did not need me at the store to help *them*. He knew that being at the store, trying not to fester on what had happened to Rich, would *help me*.

I pulled into Mom's house and parked carefully along the edge of the gravel driveway. There were four or five cars I did not recognize. It seemed everyone felt the need to come over and help in any way they could. Whether it was cooking or cleaning for my mother or helping her organize the next search, people came and went all day and night long.

When I went in I was surprised to see a small gathering around the television in the living room. Although I routinely watched the news and monitored the newspapers; Mom rarely did. She knew better than they did what was going on, why bother? But right in the middle of the couch sat my mother, glued to the television. It was nearly eleven o'clock so I slipped along side the couch and sat down on the carpet.

"Good Evening, in our top story tonight new developments in the disappearance of Duvall real-estate broker, Rich Duncan. Essex Porter is standing by at the Snohomish County Police Department, Essex-what do we know tonight?"

"Good evening Steve, well yes I am here in Everett at the Snohomish County Police Station where a composite sketch has just been released of a man police desperately want to speak to."

We sat staring at the screen as the reporter stood talking in a long brown overcoat and microphone. As he spoke, the picture faded from him to the composite sketch.

Everyone in the living room gasped.

It was definitely not Rich.

The black and white composite finally put a face to the man who may have harmed Rich. Mom just stared, and I expected her to cry, but she didn't.

She sat staring.

As the face hung silently in mom's living room, I realized this man would probably become a part of our life, forever. This face, whoever it belonged to, had replaced Rich.

Inside I raged.

"Again, this man is not a suspect but a person of interest. If anyone recognizes him, they are asked to call Snohomish County Police at the number below," he continued.

"I spoke with the missing man's wife this afternoon and according to her, Duncan was to return home on Wednesday afternoon but never showed. After tracking down where he purchased gasoline in Twisp, Washington. He simply vanished. That is until his car was discovered, abandoned in a Darrington parking lot. That is when the witness who helped police construct this composite sketch saw the man exit Duncan's car and simply walk away. Over the weekend, volunteers searched the Darrington and North Cascades area for clues to his disappearance, but found nothing. Now, police are hoping that this man can help fill in some answers, Steve?"

"Thank you Essex, so let me ask, what are police doing to find this man?"

"Well Steve, so far, very little. According to Duncan's wife it has been difficult to get one agency to actually take the lead on this investigation. As it stands now, Moses Lake Police are the only agency with an open investigation. But Snohomish County is becoming more and more involved, but, for now, Snohomish County has not opened an investigation, although they are looking for tips or leads on the composite sketch. With so many jurisdictions involved, it seems missing persons cases get shuffled around. But after speaking with Duncan's wife, this is not the kind of man who would have just run off or disappeared like this, he has no history of similar behavior; in fact a number of co-workers and others I spoke with at Duvall Realty, where Duncan was employed were all very insistent, this is not like Duncan to just vanish. Steve?"

*   *   *

"*Oh my god, Phil. It looks just like you,*" Sharon clasped her hand over her mouth again.

"We need to call your sister. Oh my god. We have to call Jody," Sharon cried.

"The fuck we do. That looks nothing like me," he said.
But he knew better.

"It looks enough! Jesus! Phil! How long until that cop that gave you the ticket puts it together? What about that tow truck driver? If he even thinks it looks like you and he just calls the police—on an off-chance? That it might be? Are you kidding? It's on every fucking channel!"

"Shut up! Just shut up!" he screamed and smashed the wall beside him.

His fist put a dent in to the drywall nearly an inch deep.

"Fuck! What are you doing? Someone is going to hear you! Fuck! Phil!" she screamed back.

"Lets call Jody, she'll know, please, Phil, please!" she began to cry.

"What the fuck is she going to do, huh? What the fuck is she going to do? Tell me to turn myself in?" he yelled back.

"Well, maybe-"

"Maybe what!" he stood up from the chair and went toward the closet.

"Maybe what, maybe I should turn myself in? Is that what you want?"

He reached in to the closet and pulled out the shotgun.

"No way. No fucking way. If you can't handle this I'll go into the woods for a few, no one will recognize me if they don't see me. No one is going to think that fucking sketch is me!" he yelled and checked to see if it was loaded.

She was horrified.

"No baby, no, I am just saying, put the gun back down, it's just me,…please, Phil."

She sat on the edge of the bed gently crying. He sat back in his chair and popped another beer open. He set the shotgun right next to him between the chair and the damaged wall and thought about that girl in Darrington who had seen him.

That little bitch.

He looked out between the curtains.

"Fuck. We need to get out of here, we've been here for two days and if someone here was watching the news. *Fuck.* We need to go to another motel and I can't be seen. No one will recognize me from that sketch but someone might see me and think it's me—I need to stay out of sight. FUCK!" he yelled and buried his sledgehammer like fist into the wall next to the other dent.

He threw his right arm across the table and sent empty beer cans flying.

"Calm down, baby, calm down," she started as softly as she could.

She had to defuse the situation. She was sure the guests in the next room had heard and who knew what they would do.

"Ok, Ok, another motel, let's just pack up and get out of here, just stay calm and quiet, and let's just go, ok?" she begged.

"We ain't callin' my sister. Clear? She stays out of this. I fucking mean it. Sharon. DO NOT CALL HER," he demanded.

His shoulders slumped downward and she could tell he was calming down. But they had to go; at least he finally had broken the ice about turning himself in. But they had to get out of there, and fast.

She gathered up the clothes from the floor and in the bathroom and stuffed them into the duffel bag. He pulled the take down pin from the shotgun and broke it down into two pieces so it could slide into the bag unnoticed. Within minutes they were dressed and ready to go. As quietly as he could he opened the door and peered outside.

Nothing.

She followed him out the door toward the truck.

"Give me the keys, Phil. Goddamit. You don't need to keep them," she argued, irritated.

They climbed into the truck and headed down the street, they had seen another motel about a mile away and it was kind of off the main drag, not many cars or people would be coming or going unless they had business at the motel. She turned off the highway and into the reception area.

"SIGNAL! Fucking use your turn signal!!" he yelled pumping his fist into the dash.

"Ok...Ok...Phil, calm down, it's ok. I will. I'll use my signal, every time, please, just calm down," she pled with him while rubbing his leg gently.

He had to calm down, last time he became this agitated, it wasn't good.

He crouched down in the truck ignoring the pain. She hopped out and took the keys with her. He was too stressed to argue. In a few minutes she returned with a room key.

"We're around back; I told them I was alone. You can't be seen or they will know something is up," she told him.

She pulled into the parking spot directly in front of the room window. The lights on either side of the room were off. They were either empty or sleeping, but she didn't care.

He had to slip in unnoticed. He unfolded himself from the truck and slipped in through the door. She watched both ways to see if anyone was watching.

He arranged the tiny table and two chairs so he could sit watching through the blinds and have a place for his beer and shotgun. She tried to toss the duffel bag quickly into the closet hoping he wouldn't notice, but it didn't work. He quickly got up and pulled the two pieces of the shotgun from the bag and reassembled them. She pulled off her jeans and put her sweats on. He handed her a beer and she sat back on the bed, sitting up with her back against the headboard.

She snapped the tab back on the can, "I just want to ask you something," she started as softly as she could.

He stared out the window, frozen. He knew what was coming. But if he was going to keep her from turning him in, he had to appear reasonable, he had to appear that he was willing to listen; and then show her how her idea wouldn't work.

"What. What do you want to know?" he asked quietly and took a swig off the beer.

"Just, just tell me, tell me in your own words, what happened up there, why did you do it?" she asked.

She began rubbing his shoulder.

"I told you, it was like... I just, I just go into survival mode. I shouldn't have drank so much. You know. That spot, where we—that spot is right by the other one. Where-"

"I know—I know."

She cut him off and continued to rub his shoulder.

There was no point in making him relive the past.

244

"Maybe if you just told them that. I mean, there has to be cases, I mean you've been so stressed out, maybe you could just tell them, I mean, really, how much time would you have to do? Three? Five? I mean, it was an accident. They don't know what happened."

"It was no accident. And I ain't no whiner," he fired back, starting to get mad.

"Calm down... Calm down," she continued, "How much time would you have to do?"

"I ain't turning myself in. Do you fucking hear me?" he started, "I'd be lookin' at 20 maybe 30 years and with good time I'd do 15 to 22. No fucking way. I'll be 55 or 60; maybe even older when I got out."

"Yeah, but when you stabbed that kid in Seattle you thought they were going to 'throw away the key,' remember? You ended up getting less time than you were doing before."

"This ain't like that."

"And when you went on that bender, right after you got out, they *didn't even revoke your parole.*"

He was unmoved.

"Someone up there is going to figure out who you were and get to that tow truck driver. We have to do something, Phil. We can't keep moving from motel to motel, eventually we have to go home and try and act like normal, but this is crazy, everywhere we go you look at everyone like they are recognizing you or they know, I mean... it has to stop."

"I just need to stay out of sight for a while; they won't keep showing that sketch for more than three, four days tops. Maybe no one ever figures it out," he said.

"Maybe they won't, maybe no one from your work or your sister or nobody ever will, but we can't take that chance. I don't want to be looking over my shoulder, wondering when it's all going to come undone, Phil. Jesus," she argued.

He could tell this was becoming too stressful for her; he had to come up with another plan. If he kept her living like this she was going to crack. He thought he could take off into the woods for a week or two and stay completely out of sight. But if he was going to leave her alone she had to believe this was going to work.

"What if I take off for a week or two?" he began.

"Take off? Where?" she asked.

"I've been thinking, ever since we went to Buffalo Bill's; people who know me aren't going to think that sketch is me, but someone might see it and then see me 10 minutes later and think — well you know. I just need to stay out of sight. And maybe someone at work or at the apartment might think it's me; who knows? Maybe they will."

She stared at him in silence.

"We could move out of the apartment and move somewhere else, Bellevue, Lynnwood, Seattle maybe. Start over. I could go up to Snoqualmie, camp out, you could box up the apartment and tell them an emergency came up, like with your mother or something and we have to vacate. Rent's already paid; they won't think anything of it. I camp out for a week or two, and if no one ever puts that face to me, I come back and we start new. I'll just tell Evergreen that I can't come back; a month or two goes by and I get a job at another dealership. I know if we get past the first two weeks or so, this will go away."

"And that *fucking ticket?*" she asked.

"I don't know. If it comes down to it I just say the guy was in for a test drive at the dealership or something. Whoever killed that guy must have done it after I test drove it. *I don't know,*" he argued.

"What do I do if they come to the apartment or they come looking for me?" she asked.

"They don't have *you*, if they figure it out, I was alone in the car, and you had nothing to do with it," he tried to convince her.

"I don't know," she said.

She looked down, shaking her head.

"Look, this is the only way I think we can do this, if they come down on me, just tell the truth. You had nothing to do with it. Just give me a chance, two weeks. Just give *us* a chance. I'll get help *I promise*. Just, please, let's try this."

He was nearly crying

It was in these weak and vulnerable moments that she really fell for him.

They were just too far in between.

24

Tuesday   May 8, 1990

On Tuesday morning, Mom sat down at her desk and stared out the window into the driveway. She was going to begin preparing more detailed maps for the next search after going to check on the bank accounts to see if someone had or were now trying to use Rich's credit cards. She had become more and more frustrated with the police and she considered going directly to Everett to the police station to plead with someone in person. Hopefully, the fact that someone at Snohomish County cared enough the day before to do a composite sketch meant they were taking this more seriously. The phone had been ringing every few minutes with people trying to be supportive and find out if there was any new news on Rich. Every time the phone rang a faint glimmer of hope would rush through her that it was Rich. But inside, she knew she would probably never hear his voice again.

"Hi Karen, my name is Detective John Hinds with Snohomish County Sheriff's Office."

"Did you find my husband?" she asked nervously.

"No ma'am. But I did finish a composite sketch last evening and we distributed it to media outlets and law enforcement in the region. How are you holding up?" he asked.

"I saw that sketch on the news. *That's not my husband,*" Mom quickly cut to the heart of the matter.

"Yeah, I think we are very certain of that at this point," he politely answered.

"No one will help me, I mean it's frustrating. It's been almost a week," Mom started.

"Well, why don't you tell me what's going on and maybe I can help find him," he asked.

"Well, I've told this story so many times now, it's just; I know Rich wouldn't just disappear like this. He is not that kind of person. We had a trip planned to Hawaii this summer and we were putting in new carpet on Wednesday and he needed to be here for that. He didn't just take off."

Mom paused for a minute to gather herself.

"So, when did you last speak with him?" Hinds asked.

"It was on Tuesday night. He was at the motel 6 in Moses Lake. He was supposed to be home Wednesday afternoon. I waited up all night and paged him and paged him and nothing. He always answers my pages. On Thursday I tried to report him missing but King County wouldn't help because he was last seen in Moses Lake. Moses Lake just listed him on the teletype as missing."

Mom took a deep breath.

"On Friday, my son and my son-in-law drove over the North Cascades highway and found where he used his credit card to buy gas in Twisp. Friday night I got the call that Darrington Police found his car. But they wouldn't do anything besides call Snohomish County and have it impounded--"

"Ok—I'm caught up. I did speak with the juvenile witness who saw the man who parked your husband's Mustang in Darrington. And Karen..., I just want you to know... that I agree with you 100%. There is something going on that I need to investigate. Technically this is a Moses Lake case but at this point I think we should be able to take over, I just have to clear it with my Sergeant; I am going to find your husband for you, Ok? Finding your husband is going to be my job until there is nothing left to investigate. Just, let me clear it with the Sergeant."

Mom hung up the phone and sat in her office staring out the window. She hoped someone would finally take the reins from her and find Rich.

*   *   *

Detective Hinds knocked on the wall outside of Sgt. Greene's office.

"Come on in John, did you call Mrs. Duncan?" he asked as he sat back into his reclining office chair.

"I did. And she is very frustrated as you might imagine," Hinds began.

"Well, you know how these multi-jurisdictional cases can be—and a missing person—none of this is easy. What do you think?" Sgt. Greene asked.

"I think there is something to this, but until we get an ID on the man who left the car there, it's going to be tough," Hinds answered and sat down into the chair across from Greene.

He put his elbows on Greene's desk and leaned forward.

"But I'd like to run with it if I can."

"Do you think this is ultimately going to turn into a homicide investigation? What's your gut telling you?" Greene asked.

"Well, this guy, Duncan, he was a pretty stable guy from what I can tell, I mean he wasn't in trouble, no family problems, he has money and no ones after him, at least from what I could get from Mrs. Duncan. So, yeah, I bet this is going to eventually end up a homicide or a cold case. But that sketch should generate something, I know one way or the other this will probably be over fast; or filed away. If it doesn't wrap up in a week or so—well...." Hinds answered.

"We haven't got anything else right now, so, I think, yeah—I think you should go with it. Call Moses Lake though and make sure they are ok with you taking over on it, if they say yeah, and I have no doubt they will, take it and find this woman's husband for her," Greene concluded.

As soon as Sgt. Greene had approved his taking of the case, the dispatch office was told to forward all inquiries about the case to his phone. The composite sketch of the suspect had been completed and distributed the day before and hit the news in the greater Seattle area the night before. He sat at his desk looking over the notes of the case and soon his phone started to ring.

"Detective Hinds," he politely answered.

"Hi there, (cough) sorry," the woman's voice on the other end was obviously old and very gravelly.

It seemed in murder cases that received a lot of media attention that the first tips always came from the elderly. Sitting at home and watching the comings and goings of others, convinced something nefarious is afoot with their neighbors. But, much to their credit, a lot of cases have been broken open by the old man or woman that no one ever noticed was watching. He even actually valued their input, but as a detective, you just never knew.

"My name is Patsy, and I think I know the man who owns that car *(cough, cough)* in Darrington," she stated quietly.

A dog barked incessantly in the background.

"Ok. Can I get you to speak up a little, ma'am? Please?" Hinds asked.

Almost from nowhere, he produced his notepad and clicked open his pen. He leaned forward on his desk and prepared to take notes.

"Sure, sorry. *(cough)* excuse me," she stated a little louder.

The barking continued.

Detective Hinds took down her name and contact information.

"My daughter is dating him. You know. I told her this guy was a louse. And OH YEAH, *he's a weirdo*, let me tell ya.' And. Well, she isn't really dating him *(cough)* I mean she met HIM. She never seems to meet anyone good. You know what I mean?" she labored through the words.

"Okay," Hinds said slowly, "What's his name?"

"Well, I have it written down somewhere, let me find it. SHUT THAT DAMN DOG UP!!" she screamed away from the phone.

"You see, she had spoken with him on the phone *(cough)* and I told her she should know something about him. That man. Driving that fancy car. Did you catch him? *He's very dangerous*," she asked.

"No, ma'am, but how do you know it's the same man. What kind of car did he drive? Is your daughter there with you?" he questioned.

"Well, no. She doesn't know I am calling. She isn't here right now, *(cough, cough)* but I know it's that man. It's the same man. She didn't want me to call you."

"Yes, go on," he said writing down notes.

"So my daughter met him, somewhere, on the phone a few times. And he's weird. Oh, yes, I'll tell you in a minute. And he wanted to meet her. And I told her 'you should know more about him before you go meet him' but *(cough)* she never listens. Well she went down to the restaurant, here in town to meet him for lunch. And oh my Lord! *Is this guy weird.* On Thursday, the day that car got left in the parking lot at the old You-Serve. You know right there next to the Red Top, the tavern. I like the Skyline better, but... but; anyway. And he *(cough)*, he told her he was over in Omak, you know, across the pass; you know that is a really nice drive; I would never live there, but I it might be nice for someone. You know."

Detective Hinds took a deep breath and leaned back. This was going to be a long day.

"Well, I told her NOT to go meet this man, ok, here it is, *Cory Cooper*." she said.

"Can you spell it for me?" Detective Hinds copied the name onto his notepad.

"That's the guy. So, *(cough)* she met him at the restaurant *(cough)* and he had been looking for real estate over in Omak, I think she said," she paused, "or maybe it was Oregon? I don't know, but he was weird. So my daughter starts to figure out that this guy is just a little off, you know what I mean? WEIRD. And he tells her that he will buy her a new Volvo if she would marry him. And when she told me this I said 'WHAT! MARRY him?' and she said, 'no, he didn't ask me to marry him, he said he would if we did,' and I just couldn't believe it. But when she got back she was scared. I mean SCARED! You know what he did?" she waited for a response from Detective Hinds.

Hinds just waited.

"He paid for lunch and when no one was looking *(cough)* when no one was looking, he unzipped his pants and tried to show her his....his *(cough)* you know, his male ....." she gasped.

"His penis? Ma'am?" Detective Hinds quizzed.

"Yes! HE exposed his...I mean right there in the restaurant. *(cough, cough)* Can you believe that? And she is so scared of him now. She gave him her phone number and I think he knows, I think, yeah, I think he knows where we live now. And how to find her. *And if a man does that?* And I heard this guy in that red car was a real estate guy and it has to be him."

Detective Hinds interrupted her—"Well thank you ma'am, I'll take a look into this and see what I can find out."

He set the receiver on the cradle and looked across the station room. Quickly he glanced over his notes and the phone rang again.

"Detective Hinds." he answered.

"Oh yeah, *(cough, cough)* I have his phone number. Its 555-6562. He's really weird."

"Thank you. I'll let you know what I find."

He hung up the phone.

Before she could call back again he picked up the receiver and called the Moses Lake Police Department and asked for Officer Jenkins. He explained how the car driven by Rich had been found in Darrington and asked if he could take over the case. Not surprisingly, Officer Jenkins agreed and wished him good luck.

*   *   *

My mother had been calling the Snohomish County Sheriff's office repeatedly since Rich's Mustang had been discovered a few days earlier. Sgt. Greene asked Hinds if he would please call her again, and take point on the investigation. Detective Hinds had been convinced by her the day before that something was not adding up, and he was happy to at least let her know that someone was listening, and taking action on her husband's behalf. On Tuesday afternoon he called Mom back.

"Hi, Karen, this Detective John Hinds, Snohomish County. How are you holding up?" he asked politely.

"Have you found my husband?" she asked demurely.

"No, but since I spoke with you yesterday I have been 'officially' assigned to this case. I realize that it's a missing person at this time, but--"

"But you know Rich didn't just vanish. You believe me?" she cut him off.

"I've worked a lot of cases over the years, Karen, and I just think, well, I think something is not right here. Yes, I definitely believe you. I think you are spot on. But we just need to work together and we'll get to the bottom of this, whatever 'this' is," he tried to reassure her.

"You think he's dead?" she asked and almost started to cry, but held back.

She felt it was time to be as strong as she could until this was over. She needed to be strong in order to bring Rich home.

"Well, like I said, I've seen a lot of these cases, sometimes they just walked away and come back—and I don't think that's what happened here—sometimes we find out what happened," he paused, "and sometimes, Karen, we may never know what happened; you need to prepare yourself for that. I will work every lead I get on this, I will work it as hard as humanly possible, but sometimes we just never get the answers we want. But for now, I am on this, 100%. Finding your husband or what became of him is my job, 24 hours a day and 7 days a week. I'll be on this."

After five agonizingly painful days, it finally seemed someone was officially assigned this case. From the first night, waiting up all night and watching for headlights in the driveway, to calling every emergency room between Moses Lake and Seattle, to trying to convince different law enforcement entities across the State that someone should be looking for her husband, to visiting his car and discovering a strange, unknown man had parked it and abandoned it, to coordinating a grid search of a 200 square mile area; all on no sleep and with no answers and without her partner in life who was nowhere, who had simply vanished; finally; *finally* someone with some authority was looking for Rich also.

She should finally be able to relax a little, to let herself unwind for just a tiny bit. But Rich was not home, he was nowhere. And although she was extremely relieved that someone in law enforcement was finally helping, she would not let herself rest, or relax or be patient.

She now became more focused.

Detective Hinds gave her his phone information and told her to call whenever she needed, as often as she needed.

He knew the burden placed on families and friends and relatives during the first few days and how much relief his assistance could bring. Working homicide never allowed him to meet the victims, but he always knew the families. It was tireless and stressful and sometimes a little thankless. But this is what he did, and he would do it well. His experience told him that once a case starts to get the type of attention Rich's case was beginning to receive in the media, that he had about 48 to 72 hours of really 'hot' time. Tips would pour in, leads would develop and if nothing became of the case it would probably grow cold until someone discovered a body. Then he would have to inform loved ones as best he could and hope something breaks again.

He headed home to get some rest and planned to return to the station in the morning and start looking in to the only lead he had; a man who exposed himself to a woman in a restaurant.

*   *   *

Tuesday night in downtown Seattle was a change of pace from the suburban motels Phil and Sharon had been living in for the past few days. He sat scrunched down in the passenger seat of the truck and wore a navy blue baseball cap pulled down as low as he could. He needed to get a backpack capable of carrying enough supplies for a week or two in the woods.

Potted trees and brightly painted iron railings failed to cheer up the dreary maze of concrete, asphalt and noise of the city. Mirrored glass streaked upwards toward the Seattle sky above the matrix of squared corners and stairwells. Hot dog wrappers and paper cups drifted along the busy sidewalks. Crowds of people huddled at every corner waiting for the crosswalk signal to move them from place to place. Drowning out the squeaking brakes and accelerating engines a horn deeply wailed as the ferry from Bremerton pulled in to the dock near the waterfront. Occasionally, a light salty breeze cleared the rank smell of car exhaust and filled Sharon's lungs with the rich aroma of freshly pressed espresso. It seemed there was a cart on nearly every corner.

Everywhere, signs of some sort told you where to go, where not to go, what to do, and what not to do. Some of them screamed out with lights and colors; others drew you in with subtle texture and hue. Street signs, business signs, traffic signs, window signs. Even some of the people sitting along the sidewalk or standing near the traffic lights held cardboard signs.

The surplus store on First Avenue had dozens if not hundreds of customers a day and he figured it would be a great place to blend in. Unlike Issaquah or Bellevue, the clerks wouldn't be asking a bunch of stupid questions trying to be friendly. He could buy his stuff and get the fuck out.

She searched the busy downtown street for a parking spot. Every bus stop was full of people waiting for the Metro. Pigeons darted across the packed sidewalks waiting for someone to drop a French fry or anything edible. So much was going on it felt safe; the last thing anyone was going to do down here was look at him in his black sweats, green fatigue jacket and navy blue cap. On the streets, people were everywhere.

And no matter who you were, *you were nobody.*

No one wanted to know what you did or who you were or where you had been. No one cared. It was a great place to disappear, but a horrible place to *be.*

In the woods he could avoid people, and the few people he interacted with would know what he wanted them to know. Just like the city, he could be anything he wanted. A war hero, an avid outdoorsman or a successful real estate businessman. Everyone believed him. The woods were a great place to be what *he wanted to be.*

She circled the block in the maze of one-way streets and packed crosswalks until finally someone signaled they were pulling out of a rare spot along First Avenue. She pulled past the spot and backed in to parallel park.

"Ok, go get what you need, I'll be right here," she stated.

He reached over and took the keys from the ignition.

"You just stick with me," he said sternly.

"Jesus, Phil. You're fucking losing it," she argued back and reluctantly opened the truck door and stepped out in to the noisy streets.

She could hardly wait for him to be gone; she knew it would be easier without his paranoid delusions all the time. But for now, she just acquiesced.

The couple walked through the glass doors into the surplus store. It was adorned with huge handwritten signs directing customers to the latest shipments of survival goods. Aisle after aisle of woodland camo and fatigue green military clothing was strewn about the shelves. Deployed tents, netting and camping equipment decorated the dark wooden rafters of the old shop. Fluorescent lights hung from the ceiling emanating a slight buzzing sound. It was remarkably quieter than the busy streets outside.

He grabbed a shopping cart and headed to the left most corner of the store. He didn't want to miss anything he might need so this had to be very methodical.

She stayed a few feet behind him doing her best to avoid being noticed, not by the few customers in the store, *but by him.* She just wanted him to get the supplies and get him out of her hair. No more drunken nights in front of motel room TV's waiting for the news; no more walking on eggshells and waiting for that shotgun to come out and no more lies about how this was going to go down.

He calmly went down each and every aisle; MRE's, Sterno fuel (in case the stove malfunctioned), a rain poncho and even some topographical maps of the area. As he placed them in to the cart he explained to her the usefulness and background of each item. Why he needed it and what would happen if the item malfunctioned. His knowledge of outdoor survival surprised her.

They had been camping together numerous times, but this was different; this was going into the woods and living off 'the fat of the land' he explained. With every detailed explanation she smiled and nodded, it felt normal to her. She felt like they were just shopping for camping equipment and there was no one looking for the man in the sketch. For a few short moments, Darrington, Jack Daniels and that shotgun were a fuzzy dream, she didn't want the shopping trip into the surplus store to ever end. This was how she remembered Phil, telling stories about camping and hiking.

It was nice.

He gathered the bags up from the end of the check-out line and turned out toward the door.

It was going to be ok, she thought. The delusion was overriding her sense of impending doom, at least for now.

"We should go grab dinner somewhere," she joyfully remarked as she took the keys from his outstretched hand and unlocked the truck.

She reached through the passenger compartment and unlocked the passenger door. He flipped the seat forward and put the bags behind the seat. Her short lived delusion came to a quick end.

"Are you fucking *stupid?*" he quickly shot back, staring at her as he draped his sore body into the front seat.

"We need to get to the fucking liquor store and get back to the motel. *I fucking told you, I can't be seen!*"

She snapped back to reality, the normalness of walking through a surplus store listening to her husband's extensive knowledge of survival gear could only last so long.

Of course they couldn't be seen.

Of course they had to go back to that fucking motel room and sit while he drank all afternoon. *With what he had done six days ago, the entire Seattle populous was looking for whoever had done it.*

There was not going to be a normal ever again.

No matter what he said and no matter what lies she told herself.

He would be gone tomorrow.

She deliberately signaled and pulled out onto the street, he slunched down a little and pulled the cap down as low as he could.

"What? You think we can just drop into a restaurant somewhere and dine? What the fuck are you trying to do? You hope I get caught, don't you?" his voice was low and terse.

"What are fucking talking about?" she demanded, "That is such bullshit! I just thought we could grab dinner somewhere, I mean I'm not going to see you after tomorrow for, what? Two weeks?"

She was irritated.

"And you better not fucking talk to anyone; your mother, my sister. *No one.* Just get our shit packed up and ready to move. Put it in the storage unit and then go stay with your mother," he continued.

She turned and looked at him and then slammed on the brakes nearly running into a man entering the crosswalk as she was turning right on to the freeway entrance.

"Fuck. Watch where you're fucking going!" he yelled at her again.

"What am I supposed to tell my mother when she asks where you went and why we moved out of the apartment and you aren't around?" she yelled.

"Just tell her I went camping with some friends, she's not going to care, she never liked me anyway, I'm sure she'll love having you all to herself for a week or two. That old bitch never liked me," he droned.

"Fuck you, leave her out of this. She has always supported you, with all the fucking bullshit and the drinking.-And the cocaine rehab? Leave her out of this!" she screamed back.

"Just tell her something, I don't give a fuck. But DO NOT TELL HER what happened. If you tell her, it's over. Do you get that? It's fucking over. I know what she'll fucking say," he demanded.

"I won't tell anyone, Phil. Jesus! If I was going to tell someone I would have done it by now," she yelled back.

"Oh, so you've thought about it then, huh?"

"Oh my fucking god! We keep having the same fucking conversations over and over. NO. I am not going to tell anyone. We wait, we see what happens and in two weeks we start over. I get that. You need to either trust me or don't!" she was nearly in tears as she screamed back at him wondering if he believed her.

She wanted to throw him out of the truck right here along the freeway. She wanted to pack his gear and take him up to the spot he was going to camp this very minute.

She didn't even know if she believed herself anymore.

*　　*　　*

An hour later they returned to the motel. The cinder block walls of the motel room were frigid. He had left the heat off when they left. It was unseasonably cold and the room felt damp. She turned on the heat and they settled in to their evening routine.

He sat in the chair drinking Jack Daniels and fondling his shotgun while she laid on the bed struggling to find some way out of this and back to her normal life. Short of a time machine, nothing was going to get her back there now.

She opened the Nuprin bottle, downed five of the little pills and cracked a beer open.

The news was going to be on shortly. Had they identified the man in the sketch? Did the ticket finally come up? She grabbed the television remote and pointed it at the old tube TV on the wall across from the foot of the bed. With a static pop it came to life.

"Good evening, new information tonight on the strange disappearance of Duvall real-estate broker Rich Duncan. A new search is going to be conducted in the same area this weekend. Live from Duvall, we have Devon Reading standing by. Devon?"

"Thanks Steve, yes, I just received word from co-workers here at the office of Duvall Realty that another search is being organized, possibly Friday or this Saturday. However, the search is going to focus more to the south of Darrington and further east toward Twisp, Washington."

"Are their clues that are leading searchers to those areas, Devon?"

"Well Steve, police are rather tight lipped about this at this point up until today the case was being treated as a missing person but new information is leading police to believe that this is, in fact, a homicide case, but exactly what that information is, we just don't know at this point and police are keeping very quiet on this one as of now. As you know hundreds of friends and family searched the Darrington area on Sunday; and Monday night, a composite sketch was released of a man who police are very interested in speaking with, but as far as we know that man is as of yet, unidentified and police are still asking viewers to call in if they think they know who this man is or even if think someone they know even resembles this man. Live from Duvall, I'm Devon Reading, Steve?"

"Thanks Devon."

"New information? What the fuck?" she gasped, "I think they know, Phil. Goddamit! I bet that tow truck driver finally figured it out. Oh shit."

She grabbed her hoodie from off the chair and pulled her shoes back on.

"Fuck, we need to get the fuck—we need to—fuck, Phil!" she panicked, "why don't we call Jody, she'll know what to do—they fucking know, Phil!"

Phil sat in the chair next to the small bed not moving a muscle.

"I told you, we aren't calling Jody!" he yelled, "they don't know who I am yet—if they did they would have put my face all over the screen."

"Yeah but they're going to search south of town on, what? Friday or Saturday? They are going to find-; I bet it's starting to-" she gasped and started sobbing again.

"Calm the fuck down, we knew they were going to find something sooner or later, just relax, and stick to the story. Move the stuff into storage, I avoid being seen for two weeks and we move in to a new place, the only way they are ever going to know is if you tell someone," he looked at her with a deadly stare, his eyes cold and unrevealing.

"Just keep your fucking mouth shut while I'm gone. It's just two fucking weeks."

He pulled his back pack from the bags of supplies he had brought in from the truck. The room was littered with survival food, fuel canisters, maps and supplies. He carefully studied the topographical maps for a place to hide. He wanted to avoid well known camp areas and disappear completely into the woods where no trails or other attractions would draw anyone into the area. He took a drink of whiskey and unfolded the second map.

His finger traced along I-90, "There," he said aloud.

The forest service road he found had no campgrounds or other sights along it, it appeared to be nothing more than an access road to the logging that had gone on in the area a few years before. It was also only a few miles from a local truck stop, he could move in and out of the truck stop unnoticed to get supplies as he needed and collect the daily newspaper to keep abreast of developments in the case. It was perfect.

He sat back in the chair and smiled. He triumphantly refilled his plastic cup and went about carefully positioning the supplies into his backpack.

From the bed she carefully watched him. She was glad to be getting rid of him for awhile but whether he liked it or not, this was now *on her*. She was the one who had to give notice at the apartment, she was the one who had to pack up all their stuff and move it into the storage unit. All the while lying to her mother as to why she was staying with her while she moved.

And Jody?

What was she going to tell Jody if she stopped by the apartment? She knew he was just on vacation and if they were going to move out of the apartment certainly that is something Phil or her would have told Jody.

"What am I supposed-"she stopped abruptly, "never mind—I'm just thinking out loud."

She didn't want another argument with Phil; she just wanted him gone for awhile. And with him gone, her destiny was finally going to be in her own hands

He glanced up at her for a second and then back to his camping gear. For the first time in days he seemed content and focused. He poured himself another drink and spent the evening hammering down whiskey and beer. By eleven o'clock he was so drunk and she was so exhausted, they didn't even watch the news.

None of it mattered.

25

Wednesday   May 9, 1990

The police station house was relatively quiet for a Wednesday morning; detectives and crime scene investigators had just finished processing another murder scene from the weekend and after the long hours of taking statements, photographing the scene and collecting evidence, detectives and staff often caught up on paperwork and rest.

The composite sketch Detective Hinds had done Monday night had run on local television news two nights now and copies of the sketch also had appeared in Tuesday newspapers around the area. Hinds was confident the sketch would start bearing fruit soon. So far though, the only lead was the man who exposed himself.

Detective Hinds was passionate about his profession. Although on the outside he always remained calm and steady, he worked cases thoroughly; whatever he found, wherever the evidence led him.

At 9:06 AM his phone rang.

"Detective Hinds," he answered.

"Hi, this is Dan Williams, I work with Rich Duncan--" the voice was higher pitched and soft.

"What can I do for you Dan?" he asked.

"Well I just wanted to run it by you that we, um, some other co-workers and I, that we were going to go up to Darrington and, and, um, keep searching for Rich and we thought we should let you know we'll be in the area, just in case—well—you know—we just wanted to make sure it was ok?" he quizzed.

"That would be helpful, please if you run into anything you can't handle, or you find a body-- dial 911 right away; but sure, the more help we can get the better," Detective Hinds responded.

Detective Hinds grabbed his notepad, "Give me all your names—and just be very wary, you can't go on private property, you need to be careful—there are some—well, how should I say—there are some unique people that live in that area simply because it's kind of out of the way and they don't want to people on their land or whatever. And you should also know that there could be a marijuana growing operation or some other activity that they may not want you to see—just use common sense and exercise some caution and good judgment, alright?"

"Yes, sir; we will, we are just going to, you know, we are just going to put up more flyers and, and, and kind of ask around some more, if you know what I mean," he answered awkwardly.

Hinds depressed the receiver button to hang up and let it back up again to follow up with Island County on his exposure person of interest.

Time was everything in a murder case and despite the fact that most leads and tips went nowhere; he had learned that you never really know which lead is going to turn into a break in the case and which ones don't. A good detective followed every trail until it went cold, thoroughly, and carefully.

"Island County Sheriff, this is Tingstad," the man answered after only one ring.

"Hi there, this is Detective John Hinds at Snohomish County Homicide, I am doing a follow up on a missing person and a name has come up—Cory Cooper?" he asked.

"Ever had any run ins with this guy? He may have been in Darrington last Thursday, and the report, well; the reporting party claims he exposed himself in a restaurant to her daughter during a lunch," Hinds continued.

"No- name doesn't stand out right now. Times must be a little slow, eh?—they got homicide chasing down a guy who exposed himself?" Detective Tingstad joked.

"Well, this is one of those- well the missing person is pretty stand-up, the man's wife is convinced he didn't just take some time away-"

"They always are," Detective Tingstad interrupted.

"Yeah, but I got a feelin' on this one, it just doesn't add up yet. Technically it's a missing person and this guy, this 'Cory Cooper' may have been driving the missing man's car the day after he went missing. I've got another witness who gave a composite of the driver—if I can just get him tracked down. I'm running a D.O.L. photo request to put in front of the witness but I wanted to give you a heads up in tracking this guy in case we need to go pick him up," Hinds responded.

Hinds hung up the phone and entered 'Cory Cooper' into his database. Two addresses came up on the screen, one in Mukilteo, Washington and another across Puget Sound in Clinton, a small town on Whidbey Island. The criminal database came up empty. If Cory was the guy, this was his first time, at least getting caught. He put in the request for a D.O.L. photo and sat back in his chair. He pulled the composite sketch from his desk and stared at it.

Are you Cory Cooper?

*   *   *

Mom woke from her nap and got up out of her bed. She looked at the empty spot on the king size poster bed where Rich usually slept. She went into the closet and stared at his clothes. Her hands caressed a pair of blue jeans hanging on his side of the closet. His belts hung from the wall; and carefully, she readjusted one of them so they all lined up perfectly. Over the last few days, in between phone calls and trying to eat something and trying to sleep when she could, she had done all of his laundry, ironed all of his shirts and carefully organized his sock drawer.

Twice.

She did laundry at four o'clock in the afternoon when she couldn't tell the story of how Rich had just disappeared to whoever called again. She did laundry at three thirty in the morning after lying awake in her empty bed wondering for hours where he had gone. She did laundry to try and take her mind away from thinking and obsessing over who had gotten out of Rich's car days earlier and left it, abandoned in a parking lot.

It had now been a week. It frustrated her that it took until Tuesday to get the police to do anything. She still could not believe that King County would not even take a report when she called as soon as he was missing.

When she thought about the possibility that they may find him, and find out what happened to him; and if in some way he could have been helped if they had just taken the report sooner, and started looking sooner; she became angrier and angrier the more she thought about it.

But the fits of anger were short lived.

There would be time for anger later.

For now, she needed to remain well organized and focused; despite the emotional hurricane enveloping the last week. She closed the closet door and got dressed. Sitting around and stewing wasn't going to solve anything. It was not going to find Rich.

The drive into Monroe was much the same. Like laundry, it had become an escape from the phone ringing, everyone in the house and all of the questions about 'How are you doing, Karen?' 'How do you think I'm doing?!' she wanted to scream every time she heard it. But she knew they were only trying to help and comfort her. She had always been there for her family and friends and it was hard to give off the persona as a pillar of stability.

But she knew she had to.

If they were going to find Rich it was only going to be her persistence and determined will that made it happen. If she quit putting pressure on law enforcement, the media and everyone else who wanted to find Rich, then she felt they would give up also. It was a lot to bear.

She pulled up to the ATM and removed the card from her purse. She hoped and prayed that something would have changed, that maybe something had happened and he was stuck somewhere out of contact with the outside world but had needed money and used the ATM. She inserted the card and entered the PIN.

Nothing. Nothing had changed.

No inquiries, no withdrawls.

Nothing.

She placed the card back into her purse and returned home, for the first time she didn't feel rushed to get home; she didn't feel as though someone were going to be calling with information about Rich. She wondered if this was how it was going to be from now on.

What if they never found anything?

Could this be how it ends?

Could he just disappear—the last known fact that a man, 5'8" to 5'10" about 200 pounds with sandy blonde hair and a crew cut ditched his car in a parking lot and walked away? Was she going to spend the rest of her life wondering where Rich was and who the mystery man that had walked away from his car was?

Not if she could help it.

*   *   *

Detective Hinds went down to the newsstand outside of the police station and picked up the daily newspapers from around the area. His sketch had made the front page of the Seattle Times again and the bottom fold-out of the Everett Herald.

This kind of attention usually brought in a lot of tips, but it depended on how long the newspapers ran with the story. If facts and tips continued to roll in, they would stay on it; but if the trail went cold they would drop the story to the back pages and the tips would grind to a halt.

But the newspaper served as more than a way to get tips from the public. It was also a direct link to the man he had sketched. He knew that whoever was depicted in that drawing was looking also; he knew they were nervous and frightened about the likeness he had constructed. The more he could dig up about the man and the more facts he could make known, the more that man would get scared. And scared suspects made mistakes.

His only lead so far was a man who may have exposed himself to a woman at a restaurant in Darrington. He hoped today would bring more leads, and hopefully, the leads would turn out to be a little more sound.

It was just about lunch when the phone on his desk rang again.

"Hi John, I got a good one for you."

"Better than a man exposing his penis at lunch?"

"Oh yeah," Greene began, "Have you ever worked with psychic Alice Simon?"

"A psychic?" Hinds asked, "Are you serious?"

"Absolutely. Run her down and make sure this isn't some strange scheme to get attention or publicity," Sgt. Greene answered.

High profile cases often attracted anyone and anybody looking to garner attention by becoming involved in these types of cases. The media is a double edged sword in a lot of ways; but a very effective one. Hinds was also aware that there were many cases in which someone purporting to be a psychic or mystic or just wanted credit for finding someone who had been murdered had actually orchestrated the murder themselves. What better way to improve your standing in the psychic world then to murder a complete stranger and then lead police to the body later?

He made his way over to the coffee pot and then plopped down behind his desk and dialed the number.

"Hi Alice, this is Detective Hinds, I received a message you wanted to speak to me?" Hinds asked as politely as he could.

"Hi Detective, I am so glad you called."

Her voice was sweet and well enunciated as she continued, "Yes, I have been getting very strong premonitions about this Rich Duncan. He is dead. This I know."

"Oh, yeah? How are you sure of this?" he asked and clicked the end of his pen to begin writing on his notepad.

"Well, yes, let me tell you. He has sent me a message—at first I didn't even know who this was—two nights ago, yes, he told me, he said, 'Alice—tell them I was shot!' and I tried to stay with him but I didn't know who it was. You know, this happens a lot—the medium does not

264

choose when or from whom to receive from—they choose us. But, yes," she paused.

"What else did you 'hear'?" he asked trying to keep his skepticism at bay.

"That is all I received from him but, yes, I tell you, I can tell you what I see. I see water….and trees…..side of a hill up against a tree….."

"Uh-huh…" Hinds scribbled furiously across his pad.

"…loose rocks….small creek nearby and fresh water….two people…no coat….no wallet….pockets empty….."

Her voice became so soft he could almost not hear her.

"……composite is accurate but suspect is slimmer. He had in his wallet an insurance card, a Visa and his wife's photo…..yes, she is 46 years old with brown hair—but she dyes it to remove the gray…..a lot of love….a lot of love. Oh no…..oh, sorry Detective; it's gone now. I can't hold them forever they come when they want, but these are some of the strongest feelings I've had, yes, in a long time," she finished.

"Ok, I'll keep this stuff in mind Alice; I don't want to lead you on, any help- if that's what it is- is useful, but I must profess, psychic powers are not something I am a believer in," Detective Hinds informed her.

"Oh, yes, I understand, Detective, so many aren't. But I assure you, *I am* an actual medium. If I have any more feelings I'll let you know, keep them in mind," she said.

Her voice was soft and eloquent, but other than that, Hinds was not impressed. He dropped the receiver back on to its cradle.

A tree?

A fresh water creek?

That's all there was between Twisp and Darrington.

Trees. And creeks.

He had no sooner finished the thought when the olive green phone on his desk jumped to life again.

"Hinds," he answered quickly and grabbed his notepad.

"Detective Hinds?" the woman on the phone asked.

"Yes, this is Detective Hinds, what can I do for you?" he replied.

"This is trooper Linette Fancier with the State Patrol, we got a call from a motorist; Paul Bullard, that he saw a body on the North Cascades highway--" she said, her voice direct and unassuming, "none of the regular patrols crossing the highway reported seeing anything or finding anything, but Mr. Bullard is quite adamant about what he saw. Perhaps this might be related to your missing person's case?"

"What did he relay to you?" he asked opening his notebook.

"Well, Mr. Bullard claims he saw a body near the summit of Highway 20. His wife and he were traveling westbound from Winthrop, and he was a little rattled, but he was quite sure of what he saw," she answered.

"When did he see this? — recently?" he asked.

"I have not taken a statement from him at this point; my supervisor felt we should hand this off to the appropriate county agency, which in this case would be Okanogan, Skagit, Chelan or Snohomish as we are not exactly sure which jurisdiction he was in at the time. But given the nature of your missing person's case we felt it was prudent to contact you first," she stated.

"Ok...ok...," he agreed.

Detective Hinds glanced down at the information he had written on his tiny spiral notepad and smiled.

Being a homicide detective is far and away one of the toughest jobs in the world. The people he works for are most often dead. On rare occasions they are discovered alive, but not often. In order to be effective, one has to be able to keep the humanity of the situation at front, always remembering the victim was someone's friend, spouse, parent or child and at the same time stay separated from it, to follow the facts and the leads *wherever they went*. He smiled, because he finally had a lead that wasn't a psychic and wasn't a man overly proud of his genitals.

Finally.

The green phone had made its way across his desk through the piles of notes and manila file folders and now sat right in front of him. The cord hung off to one side. Hinds dialed Paul Bullard. No answer.

He loosened his shirt collar and removed his jacket. The weather outside was still a little cool for the time of year but the office had a way of warming up during the afternoons. And he liked to be comfortable as he settled in to the thick of a case. He grabbed his notepad off of the desk and strode over to the north end of the station hall. A large map of Snohomish County and adjoining counties was laminated and affixed to the wall. He traced his finger up Highway 20, past the summit and estimated eight miles. This was clearly in Okanogan County.

He went back to his desk and thumbed through the law enforcement agency phone book he kept in the upper drawer.

He lifted the receiver and called the Okanogan County Sheriff. He notified Sgt. Fitzhugh of the situation and asked if they could notify patrols in the area to check out the turn-outs along Highway 20 for a body.

He pulled the composite sketch and the photo he had received of Rich Duncan and paced down the hall to the copy room. He made ten copies of each and put the stacks on the left corner of his desk. Once completed, he

266

faxed a copy of the composite and the photo of Rich to the Okanogan Sheriff.

It felt like this case was moving somewhere.

He checked the fax room to see if the faxed photo of Cory Cooper had come back in yet. He needed to get it in front of Jessica Knoop and see if this was the guy she had seen. It seemed unlikely, but maybe Cory Cooper was hitchhiking back from Omak, and Rich Duncan stopped to pick him up, from all accounts, Mr. Duncan was a friendly, helpful guy and maybe he stopped to pick him up. Something happens, maybe Cooper makes advances toward Duncan and a struggle ensues. Cooper kills Duncan, dumps his body along the highway and takes off with the car. He keeps the car long enough to impress his potential next victim; Mrs. Jays' daughter, abandons the car and hitchhikes out of town.

It was the best fit for what he had so far.

No faxes had come in for him yet. He returned to his desk and carefully studied Highway 20. It looked as though there were about 35-40 miles of highway which might fit the area Mr. Bullard had seen the body in. He needed to narrow it down. He went back to his desk and tried him again.

Still no answer.

26

Phil quickly gathered up the stuff strewn about the room. For the first time in a week he was out of bed before she was. His head hurt, he rarely got hangovers but last night he really hit the whiskey. Checkout was at eleven and he didn't need some maid coming into the room and recognizing him.

Nothing on the morning news said anything about a ticket yet. As far as he knew, they still didn't know who they were looking for. His temples pounded from all of the Jack Daniels and his back was getting worse.

She was getting on his nerves. All she wanted to do was point out how things were unraveling around them. But they had not discovered the ticket and they had no evidence, nothing.

She was remarkably quiet.

"This is the best thing—it's gonna be okay. You'll see," he began.

"I know," she softly replied.

He grabbed her arm violently.

"I need you to keep your fucking mouth shut. Are you with me?" he demanded.

She jerked her arm away from him. "I know! I'm just going to pack up the apartment and take care of things. Don't worry. I know."

She just wanted him gone. Last night was the first night he actually seemed focused. But the more he drank the more his ramblings scared her. It was *him* the police were going to be after if they ever figured it out.

The further away from him the better.

No matter where this was going, she needed to get some things handled. The apartment had to be packed and moved and she needed to find a new place to live. She had no idea how she was going to handle his sister, or her mother. But for the first time in a week, it would be how *she wanted it.*

No more yelling and screaming, no more second guessing every move she made, no more accusing her of wanting to turn him in. The more she thought about how agreeable he was, the more it worried her.

What was he up to?

As she watched him clean up the motel room and organize the supplies, she began to wonder if he could somehow pin this on her. His demeanor was too happy; did he know something she didn't? She had watched every newscast that he did, she had read every newspaper. She thought back over the last few days, had he contacted police and set her up? She shook her head, *what am I thinking?*

She went over to the closet and picked up the shotgun, "Where do you want me to keep this?" she asked.

He started laughing, "Are you fucking with me? That's staying with me."

"What do you need it for now? Jesus!" she wondered aloud.

But she knew the answer.

Her clothes were scattered about. Empty half gallon bottles lay dormant on the floor. She tried to pick them up and put them in the garbage; but the motel's tiny waste baskets were smaller than the bottles themselves. She retrieved a trash bag out from the camping gear that was still tossed in the back of the truck and continued cleaning up.

She hadn't done laundry in days. It would be good to get back to the apartment and do some laundry while she packed. She worried if the cops ever tied that ticket to him, they would show up there in force. But it had to be done.

He sensed what she was thinking. Any little shred of hope he could give her would keep her from falling apart. If she started to think this was going to fall on her she might just go to the cops first, but if she knew she had nothing to lose by just keeping quiet, well, maybe she would.

"If they come, you just tell them what happened, it was me; not you."

He stopped packing and stared directly at her.

"You have nothing to worry about, if they come, they come. If they don't, I'll be back in two weeks and we start fresh. We never talk about it, we never bring it up. These things go unsolved all the time."

"I know, Phil. You don't have to keep telling me. I am not going to tell anyone. I'll tell my mother you are fishing and I'll tell your sister I came back early. I'll tell her you might be getting a new job — in Seattle or Lynnwood or something," she answered without looking up from the clothes on the floor she was gathering up.

"Yeah, there are lots of car dealerships in Lynnwood I could work at, lots of apartments, too. And if they ever do get my name or anything, you just stay out of sight and pick me up — two weeks and we disappear. You'll see. No matter what happens, you're going to be fine," he said as he finished stuffing MRE's into his backpack.

"You know, if they find something, they aren't going to let this go, for a while. And that tow truck driver, it still worries me, he might just remember, I'm, I just — do you think we should have moved it?" she asked looking up at him.

"We can't go back and second guess now, what are you saying? We keep going over this. Whatever happens; happens. There is no way we could go up there, not now. Are you fucking stupid?" he looked at her irritated.

She shook her head and bit her lip. There was no point.

"Let's just get out of here, before the maids get here," she answered.

It didn't matter what she said, he had his mind set and she had hers. Soon he would be gone and she could do as she pleased.

They drove east from the motel for about 40 minutes. I-90 traffic loosened up quite a bit once they passed through Issaquah and began the slow gradual ascent toward Snoqualmie pass. The split level homes and suburban expansion was replaced by thick emerald green forests and the tall granite peaks of the Cascade Mountains. He said very little during the drive. Both of them knew where the other stood on the issue. Last thing she, or he, wanted; was an argument.

At Edgewick Road she pulled off the freeway and turned left back under the freeway and passed Ken's Truck Town; the last gas and convenience store before the Interstate began a steeper and more steady climb upwards to the pass.

"Turn here, go up the Middlefork Road," he gestured calmly.

The truck made a right hand turn and the pavement gave way to gravel. The sound of the rocks and pebbles whirring under the tires and clinking against the chassis of the truck reminded her of the drive out on the Mountain Loop Highway in that fucking Mustang. Once again she found herself driving along the whitewater of a Cascade river under his direction.

She hated that sound now.

After about 25 minutes on the gravel road Phil motioned for her to pull the truck off the gravel road near a beautiful swirling pool on the river. She gazed down at the deep green water boiling and churning around the smooth boulders of the river. The rush of the river howled like a winter wind. She used to love the sound of the river, the low drowning roar; the soft splashing.

Now it made her sick.

The trees, the river and the snowcapped peaks in the background reminded her of where they had been camping the week before; when his "survival instincts" had taken over.

The shotgun was packed away in the backpack. She didn't want to believe he would ever harm her. It made her sad that she even thought it. But her own survival instincts made her very wary. He opened the door and reached into the bed of the truck to grab the backpack.

She cautiously opened her door, the trucks engine gently purred against the backdrop of the gently running river. Somehow, she felt safer with the truck running. The shriek of a raven broke the silence. She looked behind her above the diamond tips of the tree tops expecting to see the black corvid suspended in the sky, but she could not find it. Deep inside the cedar canopy it shrieked again and its wings thumped like a heartbeat as it disappeared to the north.

He threw the pack up on to his shoulders and winced slightly as the weight of the backpack sent a sharp jolt of pain through his back.

"Two weeks. Remember, you won't see me when you get back here, I'll be watching through the binoculars and if I see anyone with you, I won't come out. Come back in exactly one week," he began, "I'll be across the river. I'll call you at the apartment in five or six days or so. I can probably hike back to the truck stop and get newspapers to see what's going on."

She hugged him gently, "I'll be out of the apartment by the weekend. It's going to be fine."

"Don't talk to anyone. Just avoid everyone you can. Stay ALONE," he directed.

He didn't want any stray cars to come by and see him heading into the woods so he kept the goodbye as short as possible.

She jumped back into the truck and turned around and headed back toward the freeway.

He paused for a moment and took in the beautiful surroundings. It was markedly quiet and peaceful. The sound of the river reminded him why he loved being in the woods so much. A few hundred yards up the road the map showed a small footbridge across the river and a trail that turned south away from where he wanted to set up.

The wind was coming gingerly out of the southwest; here in the foothills of the Cascades the weather in May was somewhat unpredictable. Some years it was consistently in the 60's and some years it never got above 50. One thing he could count on was rain. It was only a matter of how much.

He came across the footbridge and crossed the river and nearly slipped on the waterlogged cedar planks of the crossing. Once on the other side he turned north off of the trail. The thick ferns and mossy understory made travel wet and difficult. He carefully placed his feet so as not to break any of the soft, rotting, fallen branches. He didn't want anyone to be able to track him.

Now out of the sunshine in the shadow of the peak to the west of him, it was much colder. He stopped and fetched his fatigue jacket from the top of the pack. The sun wouldn't officially go down until about eight thirty, but in the shadow of the mountain, he needed to be set up by seven or seven thirty.

As he hiked through the layered forest he imagined how he would set up his camp; the tent under a large overhanging branch, a clothesline to dry wet clothes and a small fire pit. The spot on the map he picked was near a pool in the river where he figured he could fish. It was far enough from the road that he could have a fire at night and not be noticed, but he would not be able to have a fire during the day as the smoke would give away his position. Out here, he was in his element. No one was going to come in and arrest him, no one knew *exactly* where he was, not even Sharon. He could set up camp, build a fire and tear in to the Vodka he brought with him.

No one bitching about what was going to happen.

No one bitching about what they should be doing or should have done.

It was perfect.

*   *   *

The truck stop was quiet. For the first time in days Sharon could simply park the truck, get out of it and go in to a store without having to worry about his paranoia. It didn't matter if she was noticed by other customers or clerks in the store. She could make small talk; ask a simple question, anything she wanted. The weight she had been carrying was now 12 miles behind her, up a gravel road; probably drinking Vodka by now.

Toward the back of the store she casually picked her way through a rack of cheap sweatshirts, hoodies and t-shirts with 'Seattle' or 'Washington' silk-screened across the front. She was in no hurry. She could look as long as she wanted. She picked up a soda and asked for some Winston Ultralights at the front counter.

"Is that everything?" the clerk asked.

"Yes, thank you. Boy, what a nice afternoon?" Sharon smiled back.

Just the simple act of conversing with another human being was suddenly easier.

"Yeah, it's been nice the last few days. After that cold spell, it didn't seem like winter was ever going to end, did it?" the clerk asked.

Sharon looked down at her name tag; Joyce.

"Well you have a great day, Joyce. Thank you," Sharon politely stated and walked back out to the truck.

As she approached the truck two men came quickly around the corner and nearly knocked her down. She jumped to her right and caught her soda just as it was about to fall to the ground.

'Oops, I am sorry. Excuse us," one of the men said and they kept moving in toward the glass doors of the front.

The shot of adrenaline nearly stopped her breathing. She stood on the sidewalk a few feet from the truck, and blankly stared.

It was nothing. Just a normal thing.

She opened the door to the truck and pulled her tired legs inside. She turned on to I-90 and headed back toward Issaquah and then up to Pine Lake. Phil wanted her to pack and get everything out of the apartment and in to storage as quick as she could. When they figured out about that ticket that would be the first place they went.

If they figured out about that ticket.

It was never far from her mind.

Collapsing on to the tiny sofa in the apartment, Rusty wagged his tail and nudged his head into her lap. She had stopped at the grocery store in Pine Lake and picked up a dozen or so boxes to start packing, but she was exhausted. She didn't have to pack, she didn't have to go to the liquor store, and she didn't have to do anything she didn't want to.

"Just a minute, Rusty. Just a minute," she said stroking his head.

The apartment was cold. Blankets, pillows and laundry baskets were scattered about the room. An empty Jack Daniels half gallon sat on the table where he had left it Friday night.

It seemed so long ago, it was hard to imagine that they had only been gone five days. Rusty had been using the papers but they didn't suppress the odor of a dog that had been locked inside. As she lay on the couch she peered around the room with her eyes. The blinking light on the answering machine immediately caught her attention. She remained motionless trying to ignore the tiny blinking light.

But she couldn't.

She rose up from the couch and sauntered across the room to the small computer desk in the corner where the answering machine sat. She pulled her hands up to her face and rubbed her eyes while taking a deep breath.

It just seemed to never end.

She had hoped once he was gone the pressure would go away. She was fine at the truck stop and the drive back. But something as simple as a phone message was still an agonizingly difficult process. It was probably nothing; *or maybe it was his sister wondering why his face was on television.*

Or worse.

But waiting was not going to do any good.

She pushed the listen button on the machine and clenched her fists together as she brought them toward her face. Rusty sat and stared at her.

"Sharon, this is your mother. Where are you? How was camping? Anyway — call me when you get this. Love you dear. Bye-bye."

She let out a huge sigh and patted Rusty on the head. She quickly realized that the sanctuary she had been seeking was still a few stops away.

It wasn't here.

She didn't have to clean or pack right now.

"Come on Rusty, let's get out of here," she called to the dog.

She opened the front door and Rusty darted outside. She got to the truck and remembered the cab full of boxes. She had to at least get those inside. The boxes were awkward to carry but not heavy, she wanted to avoid anyone seeing her moving them in. Rusty jumped in to the open door of the truck and waited as she made two or three more trips. Once she was done she locked the apartment and got into the truck.

Her mother lived in West Seattle, about a thirty minute drive down I-90, but with evening traffic it might take her closer to an hour. If she was going to get any rest it would be with her mother. She made her way down off the Plateau and steered the truck back onto the freeway and headed west toward Seattle.

Sharon's mother, Helen, wouldn't be expecting her. As far as she knew, they had gone camping for a few days. But this was her mother. She wouldn't have to tell her anything yet. She just wanted one night. One night of rest without listening for sounds outside the door. One night without arguing with a drunk. One night without wondering and thinking 'what if?' or 'what if we do this?'

274

Just one night.

She sat slumped in the cab of the truck; exhausted weaving in and out of traffic. Crossing Mercer Island she stared out at the waves pushing their way across Lake Washington as she navigated the narrow lanes of the floating bridge. Boat houses, docks and the masts of winterized sailboats clogged the shoreline. In the distance ahead of her to the west she could make out the hazy jagged teeth of the Olympic Mountains. A stiff breeze pushed the truck gently out of her lane and snapped her from her daydream. The floating bridge rose gently above the water and in to a short tunnel. Once through, she could see Rainier Valley where she and Phil had managed the apartment complex for a brief time when he first got out of prison.

What a shit hole.

I-90 curved right and then left. To her right skyscrapers reached toward the cloudy sky as downtown Seattle came in to view. She reached for a smoke and gently rolled the window down. Her stress level was already beginning to come down; West Seattle was only a few minutes away.

*   *   *

Detective Hinds stared out the window into downtown Everett. Rays of late afternoon sunlight danced in and out of the stale gray clouds rolling in over Puget Sound. He sipped his latte anxiously waiting to hear from Paul Bullard. He had hoped for a few more leads from the composite sketch. Surely someone had to recognize this guy but in all honesty, he could be anyone.

The best lead he had was a potential body somewhere off of Highway 20, directly on the route between the last point Rich was known to have been, Twisp; and where his car had been abandoned a day later, in Darrington. He called the witness several times and continued to be directed to his voice-mail.

Hinds loved the view, although the station was a few blocks off of the water, he could still see Puget Sound in between the menagerie of concrete and brick buildings stretching out to the west of the station. He tossed the empty latte cup into the trash can and went back to his desk. He dialed the number again. Finally, Paul Bullard answered the phone.

"Hi Paul, this is Detective Hinds with Snohomish County, how are you?" he began.

"Oh my gosh. Hi. This must be about that body. Huh?" the voice responded. The man on the other end spoke slowly and overly enunciated every other word.

"Yeah, I need you to come down to the station if you can and I'd like to get a written statement if possible, I need to narrow down where it was *exactly*. Because I--"

Paul interrupted him, "Oh my gosh, yes! It was on the North Cascades Highway. Do you think it has anything to do with that missing Duvall guy? Oh, my goodness. It was right there on the highway."

Hinds tried to interject, "Well I need--"

He interrupted again, "Oh, wow. My wife and I were on the way back, oh my gosh, and we were coming up the hill and there was an avalanche-"

"Where at, specifically? Any landmarks, mile marker?" Hinds jumped in again.

"Well it was coming up the pass," Paul stated in a surprised tone.

Hinds paused. This was not going to get done over the phone.

Clearly.

"You know, why don't we do this—can you come down to the station and we can take your statement and then--"

"Oh, of course!" he replied jubilantly.

"Of course I can, do I need an attorney? Hah! Hah! Just kidding!" he laughed and continued, "Can my wife come? I mean, how about next Thursday or Friday—I can take the afternoon off--"

Hinds nearly dropped the receiver. There was never a dull moment.

"Well, I think it would be easier if you came alone, but I really need to start narrowing the search area down, we can't have a body lying out along the highway somewhere until next Thursday or Friday. Do you think we can do this tonight?" Hinds pressed.

"Oh my goodness! Tonight? Well yes, *this is related* isn't it? Oh, my gosh. Yes, I'll be there about 6:30!" Paul excitedly replied.

Hinds hung up the phone and pulled the Thomas Guides of Snohomish and Okanogan counties back out of his desk. He made his way to the copy room and photocopied the portions of Highway 20 in each county and returned to his desk to highlight the route. Quickly he realized it was going to be a jurisdictional nightmare.

The North Cascades Highway was about 18 miles north of Darrington in Skagit County; it headed west and then north into Whatcom County. After passing Diablo Lake and Ross Lake the highway turned south back in to Skagit County for a few miles and briefly entered Chelan County before eventually ending up in Okanogan County.

Because Rich's last known location was Okanogan County and because the car was found in Snohomish County; there was no point in involving the other counties until he had found something. He also knew that if a body was discovered, the homicide case would revert to whichever county the body was discovered in, further complicating matters. But none of that mattered; he needed to find out what Bullard had seen.

A half hour later a uniformed police officer strode in to the detectives area with a thin, smaller framed man behind him. The man had short dark brown hair and wide thick framed eyeglasses. He was wearing a button faded yellow shirt and paint stained blue jeans.

"Detective Hinds?" the officer asked, "this is Paul Bullard, and he says he has an appointment with you."

Detective Hinds stretched out his arm to shake the man's hand as the officer turned for the door; for a moment his outstretched arm hung in the air as Paul Bullard gazed around the station staring at the whiteboards, newspaper clippings and old wooden desks strewn about the space.

"Oops, sorry...Paul, Paul Bullard," he said taking Detective Hinds hand, "This is amazing! Oh my goodness!"

"Have a seat."

Detective Hinds grabbed an old wooden brown chair from the desk next to his and spun it around so Paul could sit next to him at the desk and look at the map.

He then pulled his tiny pad from his shirt pocket.

"So, tell me what happened?" he began.

"Well, my wife and I were headed over the North Cascades Highway last Thursday—do you think it's that real estate guy?"

"Lets just keep going and I can answer some questions once we're done here," Hinds responded.

"Anyway, we were going across the pass and just on the other side, toward Winthrop—beautiful town by the way—Winthrop."

Hinds took a deep sigh.

"And we're driving, you know, Oh my gosh, the regular—the speed limit. And, just as we came around the second—or was it the third? Well, somewhere up there," he twirled his hand and pointed away from the desk, "and rocks started coming down into the road right in front of us! Oh my gosh! And my wife started screaming and you could hear them hitting the car; it was like CLUNK! CLUNK! And I jammed on the brakes and we stopped and I got out to see if I had these huge dents in my car—AND THEN more rocks started to come down so we took off out of there," he finished speaking very quickly, almost out of breath.

"And....the....body?" Hinds inquired.

Paul Bullard took a deep breath, "Oh yeah, and so we are headed out of there because I didn't know how big that avalanche was—so we drove a ways down the road—maybe a mile maybe ten miles I don't know," he laughed, and began to speak fast again, "and we came to this turn out and I think we knew the avalanche wasn't down there so we pulled into a turnout and this man......this man was lying right in the middle of the turnout! I almost ran him over-"

"Slow down," Hinds interrupted, "take a breath."

"So I drove around the guy and both my wife and I looked out the window and we know he was dead."

"Did you get out of the car and look or did you see him move at all—did you get a look at his face?" Hinds asked.

"Oh my gosh, NO! We just wanted to get out of there. First the avalanche—and then a body along the road? Oh my gosh, NO! We left and went straight up the road."

He was nearly out of breath again.

Hinds sat back in his chair, relieved that he got what he did from Paul Bullard without showing his frustration. He moved his pad aside and positioned the photocopied maps in front of Paul.

"Can you show me about where you were when you saw the body?" he asked, pointing at the highway on the map.

"Well, let me see."

His finger traced the highway.

"So that's the summit there..." his finger was three inches to the right of where the summit actually appeared on the map.

"No, the summit is technically, right here," Hinds corrected him.

"Ok, so we went this way along the highway about...HERE!" he pointed gleefully.

Hinds followed his finger to the west of the summit.

He was going the wrong way.

Hinds sat back in his chair and took a deep breath.

"Is that not right?" Paul asked pathetically and slumped back into the wooden chair.

"No, no—you're doing fine, we just have to get you oriented on the map—this happens, don't worry."

Just then his phone rang.

"Why don't you go get a Coke or something and let me take this—the machine is just down the hall," Hinds asked, hopeful that a momentary break would help clear Mr. Bullard's train of thought.

He picked up the phone.

"Detective Hinds."

"Hi, this is Karen Duncan. I am just calling to--" Mom began.

"Hi Karen, how are you holding up?" he asked.

"Well, I just, I just wanted to see if you had anything?" she asked somberly.

"Well, nothing significant yet, Karen. We are getting some tips from the media coverage and I am working on those but I can't say at this time that anything major has come up — but we are working this really hard, we will find him," he continued.

"Well, I just remembered something and I don't know if I told you but I want to make sure I tell you everything I know — but," Mom continued, almost crying; "but Rich's business partner called me and he said he thought that Rich might have just walked away — and — I know that he didn't! I KNOW HE DIDN'T. And I told Mike to stuff it but I wanted to make sure, you knew — you knew that he didn't just walk away."

"I know he didn't, Karen. I know — don't let that stuff worry you. I am working this case 110%. You call whenever you need," he said.

Rich's associate, Mike, had called Mom and suggested that the police thought maybe Rich just walked away from it all. Grief hits people in different ways; maybe Mike didn't want to believe Rich was dead and had to hold onto the possibility that he was alive somewhere. Maybe Rich needed to get away from the stress and hired a guy to park his car in Darrington and he'll be back when he's not stressed.

Mom became furious and didn't believe it for a second but knew that withholding any details, no matter how ridiculous could cause detectives to lose their belief in the strength of her insistence that Rich did not run away. She cautioned Mike about telling anybody about that theory, that he had better keep it to himself.

"Well, just so you know — so that it doesn't look like I am hiding anything — Rich had tickets to Frankfurt and tickets to Hawaii in his briefcase. But those were for us to go on later this summer."

"No worries, Karen. I know this is hard. As soon as I hear ANYTHING that amounts to something I'll call you; but call me whenever you need," he finished.

"Oh yes, one more thing while I have you on the phone — what was Rich wearing the last time you saw him?" he asked.

"A white button up shirt, he always wore one, and blue jeans and white tennis shoes. I mean, he could dress nicely, but when he was traveling, it was all about comfort, that's what he always wore and I know that's what he was wearing because he was only going for one day," Mom answered.

Hinds jotted the information down on his pad. Paul Bullard appeared back at his desk and continued to look around with amazement at the station. He took a drink from his Coke.

"Karen, I have to run, I'll touch base with you tomorrow. Unless I find something important."

And he hung up.

Paul stood in front of him staring, not saying a word like a puppy that accidentally missed the newspapers on the floor.

"Sorry," Paul apologized, "I got lost down the hallway."

"You know," Detective Hinds began, realizing that his witness had no idea where on the map he had seen the body, "this could be related to my case, and I really need to—well if there's a body out there somewhere, related to my case or not, we need to find it. I am going to check with Okanogan County and see if they may have found anything, and if not, I really need to take you in person and show me where," he said convincingly.

"Oh my gosh! Sure, Sure. I can do that, when will you know?" Paul asked.

Detective Hinds rose from his desk and motioned Mr. Bullard toward the station entrance, "I'll know here in an hour or two, I'll call you."

"Ok—um—do you think you could show me out of here—I don't remember where I came in at?" Paul confessed.

Hinds stared at him blankly for a few seconds and not wanting to come across as rude to a potential witness, he motioned for a uniformed officer to come over and show Mr. Bullard how to get out of the building.

Just then his phone rang again.

"This is Detective Hinds," he answered.

"This is Sgt. Fitzhugh, Okanogan County," the voice began, "Just wanted to update you—we searched the areas you requested and found nothing. Some of the areas were technically in Chelan County so we didn't cover everything."

"Yeah, I spent the last couple hours with the witness and we had a tough time pinpointing the exact location on a map," Hinds reported somewhat disappointed.

"You think there's anything to the guy's story?" Sgt. Fitzhugh asked.

Detective Hinds learned during his tenure as a detective that cases are not solved by guessing which witnesses actually saw something and which ones were unrelated. Always follow where the leads take you and cases get solved.

"Well I don't know exactly what Mr. Bullard saw or didn't see, but I get the feeling he saw *something*. I think I am going to bring him over in person tomorrow and search the area with him and see if it jogs his memory a little bit," Hinds answered.

"Alright, I'll see if I can get some deputies to help, we can meet you at the summit," Fitzhugh said and hung up the phone.

It was seven o'clock and Hinds leaned back into his chair. He glanced down at his notes and briefly recounted the statement from the woman whose daughter had the run-in with the man at the restaurant. He then re-read what Alice Simon had told him. Paul Bullard was his best lead, maybe it all fit?

He stretched and got up from his desk. The station house was quiet as he strode down the hallway to update Sgt. Greene on the case so far.

"Knock-knock," Hinds said as he tapped on the doorframe outside of Greene's office.

"Come on in John, what do you have?" Greene asked.

"Well, not much."

Hinds loosened his navy blue tie and sat down in the chair across from Sgt. Greene.

He set the stack of papers on to Greene's desk and pulled out his notepad. Two uniformed officers wrestled a suspect past the door; the young man was yelling he wanted a lawyer.

Be careful what you wish for, Hinds thought to himself.

"Go ahead and close the door," Greene motioned.

"Here is what I have right now; perhaps Duncan left his motel in Moses Lake, gets to Twisp and pulls in to a gas station for gas and a soda. The clerk at the Texaco remembers that Duncan was alone. He heads up the North Cascades Highway and somewhere he comes across the man who abandons the car two days later. Maybe he pulled into one of the turnouts to pick him up hitchhiking, the man attacks and kills Duncan but during or shortly after the attack Mr. Bullard and his wife come across the scene. The man panics and takes off before he is seen in Duncan's car. He waits awhile and goes back to move the body out of the turnout. Duncan is a large man so he probably doesn't move him off the road very far. Two days later he uses Duncan's car to impress his date in Darrington, after he loses control and exposes himself, this guy hitchhikes out of town."

"But where--"

"But where was the car Wednesday night?" Hinds cut him off.

"I know;—the car had 281 miles on it. Twisp to Darrington is only 122 miles. Where are the other 160 miles? So I pinned some routes out of Darrington, if you assume he took the car somewhere and then straight back he could have gone about 80 miles."

"So that narrows it down, to only about a third of the state," Greene interjected.

"Well, this Cooper guy, he had an address in Clinton, if he drove all the way around through Anacortes and then back, there is still 60 miles unaccounted for."

"You think he joyrided the car for 60 miles?" Greene asked.

"I doubt it, I think if you killed Duncan and you are going to stash the car back in Darrington; and remember, the witness saw the car enter town from the Arlington side; I think you are going straight to somewhere safe, you clean it up and wipe it down and bring it right back," Hinds stated.

"Alright, what cities are 160 miles, plus or minus, round trip from Darrington?" Greene asked.

"I came up with a few; to the north, Bellingham is almost exactly 160 miles round trip; if you draw a circle to the south and west, Poulsbo, Seattle and Issaquah is about the farthest out on the eastern side," Hinds declared, "I think our guy lives in western Washington between Bellingham to the north and within this line between Poulsbo and Issaquah to the south."

"We need to find the crime scene—or a body—if we don't find something solid to take this from a missing person to a murder—we are going to run out of time," Greene pointed out, "You think there is a body out there? Or do you think Duncan is walking away?"

"Like I said, I spoke with the wife, this guy didn't walk away."

"Find me a body," Greene finished.

"I think my best lead is taking this Paul Bullard over the highway in person tomorrow and see if he can find where he saw that body."

Hinds went out through the hall and back toward his desk. He picked up the phone and dialed Mr. Bullard to have him meet him at the station early in the morning. The story wasn't completely clear yet, but he had to find that body. It seemed the most likely scenario.

*   *   *

In the shadow of the mountain, cold darkness draped over his camp. His tent was perched tightly under a low hanging cedar. The small fire crackled and popped. Perched on a small log he sat in the glow of the fire and went through his supplies. High above, the lone sound of a small airplane temporarily offset the rushing of the river 100 yards to his right. Through the thin clouds and tinted moonlight he could make out stars in between the branches of the forest. It was cold, but at least it didn't look like it was going to be wet.

Satisfied that everything was in order, he settled in around the fire. He removed a bottle of Relsky vodka and popped open the cap. No need for cups out here.

The pain in his back just didn't seem to be going away. His prescription pain medication, Carisoprodal, was almost gone. He thought he should have refilled it in Issaquah before he left but he couldn't take any chances. He did have a little weed in there with it, though; along with his fishing license tucked in to keep dry.

He rubbed his diaphragm.

The scar was still visible, even in the mild glow of the fire. About the size of a dime, the rough textured skin was a permanent reminder of his commitment to serve in Vietnam. When he enlisted in 1971, the recruiters had required that he obtain parental permission before they would take him in. His father demanded that he wait and his mother simply did not want him going to war. So he took the .22 from the house and shot himself in the stomach to show how serious he was. Luckily, and amazingly, he did little permanent damage to himself.

His mother signed the release.

He was used to taking things to extremes to get what he wanted.

After it happened, he worried the Army medical staff would notice the self inflicted wound and raise some warning flags. But they never did. Weeks later, still only 17 years of age, he was in basic training.

It was that simple.

When he was in elementary school his parents decided he needed more discipline and so they sent him to the Cliffside Preparatory School in Shawnigan Lake, British Columbia. The first time he got in trouble he left and made it all the way to a relative's house. His mother insisted he return to the school and finish. He hated that school. But after a year and a half, he finally refused. And his parents relented.

The vodka slowly took its desired effect and he smoked a pinch of the weed he had brought. He wiped the shotgun down and occasionally pointed it into the darkness. The fire burned down to a soft orange glow. He rose up from the log he was using as a chair and grabbed his lower back.

"Fuck," he said in pain.

He grabbed the bottle of Vodka and chugged as much of the throat searing liquid as he could. He lowered the bottle, shook his head quickly and swigged some more. He fished for the bottle of Nuprin in his pack and tore the cap off. Quickly he downed seven of the tiny caplets.

It was going to be a long couple of weeks.

The fire was almost out; he peered into the darkness for fallen branches or logs. He should have gotten wood in the daylight before he set up camp. No worries, he had a brand new winter weight sleeping bag and a gallon of Vodka, he could hunker down in the tent with the shotgun and his battery powered lantern and read the newspapers he had grabbed earlier. He unzipped the tent and hunched over to climb in.

Fuck my back hurts.

On the front page of the Journal American the composite sketch stared back at him under the light drizzling in from the fluorescent lantern. As he lay on his back, the paper suspended above him in his arms, he shifted and turned trying to get the pain to settle down. He stared at the curved hairline across the forehead of the drawing; the flat-top haircut and the prominent upper lip.

Murder myself, Murder I am.

That ain't me. No fucking way.

He flipped back to the sports section to see how the Phoenix-Utah series was going. He loved the NBA playoffs. But football was his true passion, and despite drafting Troy Aikman the year before, his Cowboys were unable to put together a winning season. He was disappointed when they used their first round draft choice on a tiny running back out of Florida a few weeks earlier.

He flipped back to the composite sketch.

And stared.

He shifted his weight again and bunched up his fatigue jacket to carefully place under the small of his back. Nothing he could do relieved him of the pain. It just wouldn't go away.

Outside, the fire was nothing more than a smoldering pile of dead cedar. The smell of the smoke was familiar and comforting in a way. He pulled a Winston Ultralight out of the pack he stashed in the corner of the tent and nearly knocked the shotgun from its perch against the tent wall.

She hated it when he would smoke in the tent.

She hated a lot of the things he did.

27

Thursday May 10, 1990

"Good morning Mr. Bullard, thanks for taking the time to do this.

Can I get you a soda, coffee or anything? The uniforms make the coffee every morning, and I must say they do a--" Hinds was interrupted by the ringing of his phone.

He moved across the desk area and reached for the phone.

"Detective Hinds."

"Hi Detective Hinds, this is Alice...Alice Simon. How are you today?" Alice asked.

Hinds was surprised that the psychic would be calling him again.

"I'm good, what can I do for you?" he quizzed politely.

He placed his free hand over his opposite ear to hear what she was saying. Mornings were sometimes noisy in the station and the other phone conversations and officers catching up and strategizing for the day drowned out Alice's soft voice on the phone.

"Well, I am still getting very strong feelings about this Rich Duncan case, I really can't afford to drive over the highway, despite what you might think, we do not make a lot of money in this profession--"

"I didn't think that at all," Hinds interrupted her, smiling.

"Some of us make money reading palms or running some type of scam—I'm not that kind of person, that's not what I do, I just get these really strong feelings, and I didn't ask for this ability, but I get these really strong feelings."

She paused for a minute to give Hinds the opportunity to ask for her help.

He waited patiently and glanced at Paul Bullard.

"Well, I am going to Winthrop today to see if I can help in some way. I know he is near the road, I just know," Alice stated convincingly, "He is underneath something — I see more trees — green--"

"Alice...Alice, I don't mean to cut you off. But I ....I need...to; well, it just so happens I am headed that way myself, today," he said.

He was sure he would regret telling her, but he had a feeling she was harmless and if she did have something to do with this, he could at least keep tabs on her.

"I tell you what, why don't I meet you around lunch time in Winthrop, and you can tell me then, that is the only free time I'll have," he explained.

"Oh, that would be most wonderful, Detective. Thank you. I drive a white Honda Accord four door. There is a little diner right as you pull in to town. I'll be there. Thank you so much."

Alice hung up the phone.

Hinds dialed Sgt. Fitzhugh in Okanogan County to let him know he was on his way.

Within minutes of leaving Everett, Paul Bullard began peppering Hinds with questions about murder investigations, crime scenes and the like. Hinds was used to the sort of questions Bullard was asking as his job was somewhat of a mystery to most, despite the common portrayals on television. Hinds loved how most crimes on television seemed to be solved by the overwhelming brilliance of the lead detective when in fact; most crimes in the real world were solved by unrelenting persistence and a few lucky breaks along the way.

They traveled through Arlington and Darrington and turned on to the North Cascades Highway about 18 miles north of Darrington. From here they traveled the winding two lane highway north and then east around Diablo Lake and toward the summit. The jagged peaks of the North Cascades towered above them. It was partly sunny and not too cool, but cold enough to keep the windows up on the unmarked police cruiser. Bullard was sure the turnout where he and his wife had seen the body was on the east side of the summit.

As they came around the final bend before the summit Paul Bullard sat up stiff in the seat and focused along the side of the road.

"You know, none of this looks familiar. We were coming the other way, but, gosh I don't know," he remarked.

286

A few moments later they hit the summit and found three or four Okanogan Sheriff cars parked in the wide gravel turnout. Hinds slowed the car and pulled in to the turnout. He pulled up alongside where the deputies were standing outside of one of the patrol cars and rolled down his window. Hinds drew in a deep breath of the clear mountain air.

"Hi there, I'm Detective Hinds, how are you guys?" he said.

"Yeah, we're good, we're good. Sgt. Fitzhugh asked us to come up here and meet with you to see if we could help and all," one of the deputies answered.

"Well good, thank you very much. We don't have much yet but once my witness here finds the turnout where he believes he saw a body a few days ago, I would certainly appreciate the help searching," Hinds said.

He rolled up the window and pulled out on to the highway. The Okanogan Sheriff's cars pulled out behind him and followed.

"Well, how far do you think it was from the top here any idea?" Hinds asked.

He took the final drink from the coffee they picked up in Arlington 90 minutes earlier. It was cold.

"Well, I mean, I don't really know. I think I'll just have to see it," Bullard answered nervously.

"Well, in terms of time, was the summit five minutes away, 20 minutes away?" Hinds asked as patiently as he could.

"Oh, my gosh. Well......I can't...I...oh my gosh. I am so sorry. I just—I think it was. Well-" Bullard stumbled through every word.

"It's ok, this happens all the time, we'll just drive down the highway and if something looks familiar, just say so and we'll stop. Don't worry if it's not the right spot, just relax," Hinds suggested.

Hinds was amazed at how his juvenile witness who had seen the person of interest get out of Duncan's car was so calm and collected while preparing the composite sketch and this adult man was having trouble finding where he had seen a body with his wife. Bullard shifted in his seat as Hinds steered the unmarked down the highway. In the rearview mirror three Okanogan County Sheriff cars trailed along behind.

Hinds stared upwards along the highway wherever the slopes abutting the road were vertical enough for an avalanche or rockslide to have occurred. They continued down the highway for nearly 30 minutes before the road began to level and straighten out.

"I'm sorry, we must have passed it, oh my gosh, we were going the other way so none of these look familiar. I'm so sorry," Bullard apologized.

Hinds turned the car around and headed back up the pass.

"No worries, I know how hard it is to find—well—I know what you mean about traveling the other way. It's amazing how the same drive can look so different going the opposite direction," Hinds reassured him.

Hinds was very good at gleaning information from all sorts of witnesses no matter how nervous or how stressed they may be. But he knew he could be in for a long day.

"Ok, just let me know when you see something familiar. We are in no hurry, just relax and focus," he said.

The once blue background of the mountainous peaks faded into gray as low clouds crept across the summit. Bullard strained out the window for any landmark or terrain which looked familiar. As they passed turnout after turnout he became visibly more stressed.

"Oh my gosh," Bullard started, shaking his head; "I'm so sorry. It was sunny out that day and the weather, it's like it makes it look different. I must look like an idiot right now, I'm so sorry."

"It's ok, this is just part of the process, I think what we'll do this time is put you in with one of the deputies, maybe riding in a different car or something or maybe you're nervous with me, let's just try a change of scenery. I have seen this dozens of times, Paul. Don't worry yourself. We have lots of time."

Hinds pulled the cruiser back into the turnout at the top of the pass, the deputies pulled in behind him. The wind was picking up and it was now getting colder despite the early afternoon sun fading in and out of the clouds above.

Hinds approached one of the deputies and explained the situation to him. The deputy understood and agreed to let Bullard ride with him down the pass a second time. He suggested they stop at each turnout and let him get out and see. Hinds peeked at his wrist watch and decided he would head straight to Winthrop so he could call Sgt. Greene and perhaps connect with Alice Simon. Surely someone had to have some idea of who the man in the sketch was by now.

*   *   *

The guest bedroom at Sharon's mother's was comfortable but the single sized mattress was old and somewhat worn out. Every time she would turn or shift, the springs would squeak and crack.

Her mother was glad to see her but Sharon refused to tell her what was going on. She didn't know how to do it without worrying her mother too much. Her mother understood that something had happened with Phil; maybe they had gotten in to a fight while fishing in Moses Lake or something. But her mother also knew to sometimes just let things alone.

She was there for her daughter whatever she needed. And if Sharon needed a few days away from her husband, she was happy to have her. Helen never liked the idea of her marrying an inmate, and now it turned out *her mother was right*.

The night's rest refreshed her, but no amount of rest was going to erase what had been done. She hoped that without Phil around, the time would pass easily and she would figure a way out of this mess.

But it didn't.

No doubt it was easier. She could go outside and smoke or go to the bathroom without answering questions about where she was going and that she wanted to turn him in. She didn't have to avoid being seen and make sure she talked to no one. Without Phil around maybe she could just get through this. She could pack up the apartment and see what happened.

She hugged her mother and put Rusty back in the truck. An hour later she pulled back in to the parking lot of the apartment. Nervously she peered around and didn't see anything out of the ordinary. She thought about knocking on the neighbor's door to see if they said anything about anyone looking for her, but she also just wanted to get the apartment packed up and moved in to storage.

She opened the door and went inside. After spending the evening in her mother's meticulously cleaned residence, the shambles of her apartment seemed to overwhelm her. She glanced down at the deer sculptures on the desk. The pictures tacked to the walls.

It was all coming to an end.

She loved this apartment. She loved living in Pine Lake. He had a good job and things were going well. She thought he would finally stop drinking after denting the truck and nearly wrecking the Torino a few months earlier. She knew it was tough for him, but things were starting to look up. His job was paying him far more money than he had ever earned.

Why did this happen?

She milled around the apartment for nearly an hour reminiscing as she looked over their belongings. She had wanted to plant flowers out front and redecorate the living room. But now that was over. For a second, she would think she should just clean up and stay there, that this wasn't happening. But she knew. And as the time passed she knew it could be any moment and the police would be knocking on that door; or worse.

Rusty lay down in his usual place. As far as he was concerned they were back home.

She went out on to the deck. The ashtrays were overflowing with butts, just as she had left them nearly a week ago. She lit a smoke and remembered that first night when he dropped the car off in Darrington and snuck in to the deck.

This was going to blow over, he said.

And then he told her about the ticket.

A fucking ticket?

She should have just convinced him to turn himself in then. But it never hit the news; no one was missing that man.

It seemed.

No one.

At least that's what they thought.

And now that girl who had seen him ditch the car helped make a sketch. It wasn't going to be long before that tow truck driver or someone else remembered seeing him that night in Darrington.

She took the last drag from her cigarette and stuffed it into the pile of butts. Two or three fell off the small table on to the patio. She lit another one and sat back in the tiny camping chair.

Fuck.

She thought about how much easier it was not having to deal with his paranoia but longed for her own apprehension to subside. How long was it going to be like this? Wondering when the police were going to figure it out. She had gone through the possible scenarios so many times in her brain that she was getting a head ache again.

Then the phone rang.

She stared over at the sofa. Her heart raced again. She hated this.

The phone rang again. It was loud.

The neighbors would certainly hear it ringing and see her truck out front and wonder why she wasn't answering it.

The phone rang again.

She grabbed an ashtray and went inside. No point in worrying about smoking in the apartment if they were moving out.

"Hello," she answered.

"Hey. It's me. Are we good?" Phil asked.

She was somewhat surprised to hear his voice. He said he would call in a few days but she had just dropped him off yesterday. It must have taken him an hour or two to hike in to a phone.

"Yeah, I'm just packing up. What's going on? Why are you out of the camp?" she asked.

"I just wanted to get a newspaper and shit and see if there was anything new. Get a couple beers while I was here," he answered.

"Where are you?"

"At that truck stop. I hiked for awhile and then a guy gave me a ride."

"A ride? A *fucking* ride? You need to stay out of sight! Jesus Phil!" she demanded.

"Look, don't worry about it, I told him I was just doing some fishing and hiking. Guy didn't think anything about it. Fuck. So is everything packed?"

"No, I just started," she said.

She closed her eyes and squinted her face as she realized she had just said the wrong thing.

"WHAT THE FUCK HAVE- What the fuck have you been doing?" Phil yelled and then dropped to a whisper not wanting to attract any attention at the phone booth.

A stray feral cat darted across the asphalt and disappeared under one of the eighteen wheelers running in the lot.

"I just started; I stayed at my mom's last night," she answered quietly.

"Jesus fucking Christ! Did you tell her? You better not have fucking told her!"

"No...no...I was just tired and worn out, I wanted to try and relax and I don't know if the cops are going to bust in here at any moment or what. Jesus!" she quickly fell back into her subordinate role.

"If you fucking tell her Sharon! If you fucking tell her!"

"What!? What Phil?! This is your fucking fault. You fucking did this," Sharon began to cry in to the phone.

"I am fucking here packing our apartment and you are up in the fucking woods, drunk no doubt. Have you been fucking drinking yet?"

Phil tried to talk over her.

But she continued.

"No. You fucking listen, this is bullshit. I haven't told a fucking soul, Phil; about what you did! No one. I can't fucking handle this....But I will, Phil. For you. For fucking you! See what your drinking has done? Again?! I'll fucking pack up this shit hole and get us the fuck out of here. But you did this, not me!"

She slammed the phone down and hung up. She picked up the receiver and slammed it down again, and again harder and again. She sobbed and cried and wondered if he would get a ride down here right now. But she didn't care.

The phone rang again.

"What!" she answered.

"Look, just get the fucking house moved out. That's it. My fucking back is killing me so I grabbed a couple of beers so I didn't have to drink all the Relsky back at my camp. I got to go; it might take two or three hours to get back up there if I can't hitch a ride. Just stick with it, don't fucking tell anybody. Do you fucking understand me? No one. I'll fucking call you tomorrow afternoon and you better fucking answer. I'll call at four o'clock.

Did you hear me? Four o'clock. My back is fucking killing me and it just won't go away."

"Yeah, yeah I got it. Four o'clock," she answered.

She hung up the phone.

With him gone, she felt like she could handle this. But every time she started to get used to being in charge of her own daily routine, he showed up like an unwanted guest. No matter what she decided to do, she had to at least give notice to her landlord.

She stood up and headed out the door and walked down to the manager's office. The door was open to her office and cautiously she walked in.

"Hi...I'm Sharon from F 104. How's it going?" Sharon began.

The manager, a young woman in her early twenties turned in her chair and smiled.

"Good. Good. What can I do for you? Did you see we are coming in on the 25th to get bids on new water heaters? They should be in and out, it will just-"

"That's fine—but the reason I am here is Phil got a new job and we are going to need to move out," Sharon interrupted her.

She just wanted to get this done and get packing. Being at the apartment made her head hurt. Moving was not going to be quick and it was hard to make herself stay. She just wanted to go. Anywhere, but that damn apartment.

"Uh oh! Well, let me look up your lease."

The manager swiveled around in her chair and rolled over to the file cabinet in the corner of the office.

"So, a new job? Wow! That must be exciting? Huh?" she smiled as her fingers tabbed through the files.

Sharon shifted back and forth from one leg to the other. Nervously she looked out the window as a car pulling in to the lot and parking had caught her attention.

"Here it is!" the manager finally exclaimed.

"Hillman. Right?"

Sharon nodded.

"Looks like you are on a month to month."

She paused and looked up at the calendar on her office wall.

"And it's the 10th; so 20 day notice is no problem. Let me get a notice to vacate and you just need to sign it. Wow. A new job? That must be exciting!" the manager repeated.

Sharon shrugged.

The manager scribbled across the page and turned the document to face Sharon. Quickly, Sharon signed it and turned for the door.

*　　*　　*

The phone booth on the main street in Winthrop was cramped and well worn.

"Hi Tom, anything on the Duncan case yet?" Hinds asked.

The receiver barely hung on the cable between it and the phone. Hinds wasn't even sure if the connection could be maintained. Delicately he held the wires next to the receiver so they wouldn't bend.

"No, no tips or anything. How about you- find anything of interest yet? Did you find where your witness saw that body?" Greene asked.

As Hinds began to speak a logging truck crawled along the street next to the phone booth throwing up dust and diesel exhaust. Hinds turned quickly and struggled with the receiver. He heard a couple of clicking noises as he jerked the cord to keep the connection going.

"Hello? Hello?" Hinds yelled in to the phone.

"I'm here," Greene answered.

"Sorry...anyway...no, he is not even sure where he saw it. He's up with a couple of Okanogan uniforms right now. I came down here to see if I could find that psychic lady. I promised her I would meet her. But I don't know. Funny thing about her though; she knew I was coming to Winthrop today. Weird eh?" Hinds stated as he looked down the road at an approaching car.

"Really? That is a little strange. Well, let me know what you need. The wife called again. She's still pretty shook up, but I told her you were working it, working it real hard," Greene finished.

"Yeah—I can barely hear you. I'll check in later," Hinds hung up the scarred receiver.

He made his way back to his unmarked patrol car and pulled his notebook from his pocket. The radio squelched out that the search party believed they may have found something on one of the turnouts about 12 miles back up the highway. Hinds dropped his notepad back in to his breast pack and turned the car up the highway to meet the Okanogan deputies.

Finally, maybe they had something.

A few cans of Coke and what appeared to be a torn shirt matching the description of what Rich was last wearing was found in one of the turnouts. If this was where the murder occurred, Paul Bullard may have in fact stumbled across the act mid-stream and the suspect may have then returned and disposed of the body in that area.

It was extremely steep, rugged and thickly forested. From his previous experience working homicide he had a feel for where killers tried to hide bodies and this fit perfectly. Based on Rich's description, he knew someone wouldn't be able to drag his 275 pound body very far, not without hurting themselves. For the first time in this case Hinds felt they might be close in discovering what had happened to the real-estate broker from Duvall.

When he arrived at the scene he found Mr. Bullard still sitting in the front seat of one of the patrol cars.

"Is this where you saw the body?" Hinds asked Mr. Bullard through the window as he walked up.

The window was still up and he stared at Hinds through the glass. Once he noticed it was Detective Hinds he smiled and waved. Hinds motioned for him to roll down the window and he asked again.

"Is this where you saw the body?"

"What?" Bullard asked.

"Is THIS where you thought you saw the body?" Hinds asked slower and more succinctly.

"Oh, yeah...but...no. I don't think this is it," Bullard answered.

"What did they find?" Hinds asked.

As he did, a deputy appeared from down the rocky embankment.

"They found some-" Bullard started.

As soon as he saw the deputy Hinds walked away from Bullard and toward the deputy.

"Anything?" Hinds asked.

"Well, we pulled in to this turnout to see if it helped the witness recognize anything and we found what we first thought was some litter; a couple cans of Coke and a torn shirt that matched the description of what the victim was last known to be wearing. Your witness thought this was it at first, but now he doesn't seem to think this is where he thought he saw the body," the deputy informed Hinds.

Hinds remembered that Mom had told him that Rich really liked soft drinks and maybe these Coke cans were related. He didn't know for sure, but then again, they never really do.

"Well, this is the best lead we've had. Let's at least do a quick grid search and see what we can find, is that ok?" Hinds asked the deputy.

"Sure, that's why we're here. If you think something might be here. Let's do it," the deputy answered and made his way over to where the others had crowded around.

Quickly the uniformed officers mentally gridded off the embankment running downhill about 40 or 50 yards and fanned out into the underbrush to search. An hour later they had methodically moved from one side of the hill to the other.

Nothing.

Hinds was ready for lunch, he asked the deputies to keep searching the different pullouts along Highway 20 and he and Bullard were going to head back in to town and grab some lunch.

Just before Detective Hinds and Mr. Bullard came into Winthrop, Alice Simon's car passed them heading the other way. Hinds felt strongly about where they had just searched and although he did not believe in psychics, he was curious as to what she might add to the investigation, if anything. He signaled her to pull over and invited her to join them for a late lunch in Winthrop.

A few minutes later, Paul Bullard, Alice Simon and Detective Hinds seated themselves in a booth toward the back corner of a small café. Through the giant glass window fronting the booth they could see the main street through Winthrop.

"You know, I'm having very strong feelings here. His body is somewhere here. It is really strong," Alice began as they settled in to lunch.

"Oh, yeah?" Hinds asked.

"Yes, I think I can help you locate his body, I think it is close," Alice continued.

Paul Bullard looked up at Alice in disbelief. He wiped his mouth with his napkin and said nothing.

"Well, you can follow us up the highway, I mean, certainly if you find where the body is, well....what can I say?" Hinds kind of laughed.

If anything, Alice would be another set of eyes if they did find an area to search. He believed her to be mostly harmless.

After lunch, Alice followed Hinds and Bullard toward the location of the search party about eight miles out of Winthrop. He pulled the unmarked into one of the gravel turnouts and asked Paul Bullard to wait in the car. He walked back to Alice's car behind him and asked her to wait as well. He then turned and walked twenty or thirty yards to where the deputies were now finishing lunch. He purposely parked out of earshot from the deputies so that he could speak with them without Alice Simon overhearing.

"So what did you find? I heard duct tape with hair on it, or something?" Hinds asked.

"Yes, we also found some broken glass, black tinted glass at the scene also," one of the deputies answered.

"Where was that at?" Hinds asked as he pulled his notebook from his breast pocket.

"On the Blue Lake Trailhead. About six miles from here."

"How many side roads are there between here and there?" Hinds inquired.

"Oh wow. There are probably 15 or 20. There are trailheads and campsites everywhere. A lot of those little roads branch off you know, just a few hundred yards off the main highway," a deputy answered.

"Ok...so I think we'll just head back up the highway ...again...and see if Mr. Bullard can recognize anything definitive. Now, I also have another thing I'd like to try. Don't look... but the woman in the car behind me claims to be a psychic," Hinds began.

The deputies all kind of looked at each other and smiled at one another.

"I mean, she appears to be harmless, she is another set of eyes; but, I am going to let her lead and see what she finds. It'll be interesting to see if she finds the area you found the ripped shirt or the road where the duct tape and glass was found, you know? If she drives past it we'll turn in and head to the sight, she'll see we've turned and she'll follow," Hinds finished and walked back toward Alice's car.

"Ok. So, if you'd like; we'd like to follow you up the pass. If you get a feeling or something just pull over and we'll search. How does that sound?" Hinds asked Alice.

"Oh, yes. That would be wonderful. I really believe he is close," Alice replied.

Hinds climbed in to the patrol car and Alice pulled out ahead of him. One by one the parade of patrol vehicles followed Alice Simon up the highway.

The speed limit was 55 MPH but Alice steadily drove at 40. They wound up the hill and Paul Bullard strained and poured his eyes over every turnout they passed. Every 500 yards or so signs stood marking trailheads up small logging roads. Ten minutes up the road Alice darted off the highway and jammed on her brakes throwing up dust and gravel into one of the many turnouts along the highway.

Paul Bullard gasped.

Detective Hinds raised his eyebrows and nodded, quite surprised. Alice had pulled in to the turnout where they had found the ripped up shirt earlier. Alice sat in her car motionless. Hinds climbed out and went up to the side of her door where she had rolled the window down.

"What do you have?" Hinds asked.

"Something occurred here. I don't know though, It's not really clear but I feel a lot of energy here. I am positive something happened here," Alice replied.

"All right, we'll mark this spot; let's keep going," Hinds suggested.

After about 15 minutes later the highway made a sharp hairpin and turned back north in the dark shadow of the Early Winter Spires; a remarkably scenic granite peak along the highway. It was nearly completely dark out. A few hundred feet beyond the hairpin Alice stopped and pulled over on to one of the gravel turnouts on the south side of the highway. For about three or four minutes she just sat there.

Hinds watched, curiously.

She then turned her car to the left and parked off the highway. They had passed ten or 12 of these turnouts already. A weathered cedar board with engraved letters indicated: BLUE LAKE 2.2 MILES.

Alice climbed out of her car and strode back toward Detective Hinds' patrol car as the Okanogan deputies pulled off the road in behind them.

"Here!" Alice yelled, "Something happened here."

Hinds turned the ignition off in the patrol car and walked back to the deputies.

"I'll be goddamned," the deputy said as he exited his patrol car.

"Is this it?" Hinds asked.

"It sure is. We found some duct tape over there next to those rocks with what looks like human hair on it. Over about five yards to the right we found a pile of broken glass. It's all in the evidence bags now," the deputy answered.

Hinds remembered that Duncan's car had the back side window broken out of it and that the window was broken somewhere other than where they found the car in Darrington as there was no glass on the ground or in the immediate area of the car.

Hinds opened the trunk to the car and removed his camera. He took several photographs of the scene and sketched out the exact location of all the items. The search party made another search of the immediate area as best they could in the dark. The temperature was dropping quickly and it was getting cold. After helping search for an hour or so, Alice Simon let Hinds know that she needed to get back to the west side of the mountains. He wasn't sure what to make of Alice Simon but he was very amused that she found the two places in which evidence had been recovered.

It was nearly 10:00 PM and still they had not found where Bullard thought he had seen the body. He was getting hungry again and Hinds promised Sgt. Greene he would update him again today, so they climbed back in to the car to go back to Winthrop while the deputies continued the search along the Blue Lake Trailhead. Maybe Greene had received some more tips or other information.

Hinds pulled out on to the highway and headed east again. Fifteen minutes down the highway Paul hollered at Detective Hinds to stop. Now that it was dark like when he was coming across the highway the Friday before, he was convinced he had found the turnout where he had seen the body.

He was positive.

Murder myself, Murder I am.

Detective Hinds radioed the search party to head to his location.

"Are you positive?" Hinds questioned Paul Bullard.

"YES! I don't know why, but now that it looks like it did, I remember, that low overhang- right there!" Paul Bullard pointed over to his right.

He excitedly jogged down the road about 50 feet.

"And this is where the avalanche started again, right here!" he yelled back at Hinds.

Finally.

As the patrol cars began filing down the hill, Hinds directed them off to the opposite side of the road. He asked two deputies to cordon off the area to keep anyone from turning in to the turnout. It was very likely that he had finally found his crime scene and there was no need to take any chances.

Hinds walked to the edge of the turn out and shined his flash light down the thick bushy hillside. The hill dropped almost straight down but not so steep that someone couldn't drag a body down it. In fact, the steep slope and thick understory made it a perfect place to drag a body. With very little effort someone could drag a person as large as Duncan down quite a ways from the highway. The radius of the turnout where the hill dropped off was nearly 200 feet and the floor below was probably 80-100 feet down.

This was going to take awhile, but if Duncan was down there. He was going to find him.

Tonight.

28

Sharon stared at the empty boxes in the living room. She sat down in a dining room chair and dropped her head in to her hands, her elbows resting on the kitchen table. She looked around the dark apartment. After a few minutes she forced herself up and across the room to the light switch. Laboriously she flicked the switch on.

Nothing had changed. The mess was till there. And now the musty odor of unfinished laundry seeped across the carpet.

The empty bottles of whiskey, the splash mark where he had thrown one of the plastic cups full of Coke and Jack Daniels had dried in to dull brown stain on the wall next to the slider. She moved deliberately from one room to another flicking on every light switch in the dwelling. She drew in a deep breath and sat down on the bed. Rusty whined and wagged his tail. She petted him and flailed herself backwards on to the empty mattress. The bedding and pillows were still folded out on the sofa. Besides the boxes strewn around the rooms, the bedding was the only progress she had made toward packing.

Her head hurt.

For twenty or thirty minutes she lay on the bed and ran the scene through her mind, over and over. Outside she heard a car pull in and park.

She didn't even care.

She didn't want to know.

She pulled herself from the empty mattress and went in to the medicine cabinet and pulled the bottle of Nuprin down from the shelf. After swallowing eight pills she grabbed her smokes from the dining room table and went back out on to the patio. The ashtrays were still overflowing. She grabbed them both and emptied them into a white plastic garbage bag.

It was a start.

She lit her smoke and sat, watching. Outside it was quiet. She looked around at the well manicured landscaping of the apartment complex grounds. She stared out at the evergreen trees in the distance and then followed the hilly landscape south to north where the green band met the sky.

She loved it here. It was perfect.

And he had fucked it all up.

Daydreaming took her mind off of it. For five or ten minutes she just sat staring, wondering what life might have been like here. She lit another smoke and petted her dog. No matter what she did she just couldn't start packing. She didn't want to stay, not by any stretch of the imagination. She knew they had to get out of there.

But it was hard. She was torn apart.

She wanted to sit on that patio and remember it just one more time, just one more smoke on the patio and then she would pack all of the boxes and load them in to her truck and go rent a storage unit somewhere.

In just a little while, she would pack all of the kitchen stuff; the pots and pans and plates and utensils. The toaster, the blender, the microwave and the cleaning supplies under the sink. The dry food in the cupboards and the canned foods under the counter.

All of it.

She would move on to the bathroom and empty the medicine cabinet in to another of the boxes. She would get a Sharpie and label them so when they found a new place it would be easier to unpack. She would gather all of the clothes and the towels and the bedding from the closets. She would remove the pictures from the walls and pack them with the decorations and wooden sculptures of animals he loved so much. She would empty the file cabinet and the desk and the entertainment center. She would disconnect the stereo and speakers and the VCR and all of it.

She would do it all, *in a little while.* After she rested on the sofa for a bit, or had another smoke.

Her head still pounded.

She made her way in to the bedroom and decided she should start in the kitchen. When she went to the kitchen she decided it would be easier to do the bathroom first.

She needed a Sharpie.

She went back to the bedroom and dug in to the drawer of the computer desk. Inside she found old pictures of happier times. For an hour she sat and looked through each one. She went back to the kitchen and grabbed a ball point pen and began writing the names and the dates and the places on the back of the photos. She stood up and sighed. It was time for another smoke.

At around 5:00 PM she realized the news was going to be on soon. She grabbed a wine cooler from the refrigerator and went back to the living room. She shoved the pillows and folded bedding to one end and sat down on the sofa. A stack of empty produce boxes blocked her view of the television. With a groan she rose from the sofa and tried to slide the stack of boxes over to her right. They didn't budge. Frustrated, she wrestled a bedspread off of the floor that had fallen down off of the sofa and draped itself over the white wooden footlocker he used to store the shotgun in. It was blocking her efforts to slide the produce boxes out of her way. She kicked it out of the way and slid the boxes over, they tumbled to the floor and as she jumped to try and catch them she tripped over the tangled bedspread and hit the floor herself. She lay there for what seemed an hour.

Crying.

She was done; she began to realize that this was not going to work. She couldn't do all of this by herself while he was in the woods drinking and smoking dope.

Wasn't that where this all started?

As she lay there she began to think about the new house on the Plateau and buying new furniture. Vacations, new cars and summer camping trips. She was not going to give up this easily. She could do this. She knew when she married him it wouldn't be easy. She wanted to just give up, but she couldn't. She just couldn't give up on her dream. They just needed to let some time pass, to see what happened.

For a second she realized she was lying to herself. But lying to herself was the only thing that made her head stop pounding.

Maybe this was a good thing that he was gone in the woods. She could do this her way and not have to listen to him bitch about how she was packing and where to get the storage unit or what time of the day was the best to move their belongings out unnoticed. All while he would be getting himself shit faced drunk.

She rose up from the floor. The blood rushing to her head made her dizzy. She made her way in to the closet and began pulling her clothes from the rack and sorted them on the bed. She missed the five o'clock news daydreaming on the floor. But it didn't matter.

She could do as she pleased.

She realized for the first time that she had made a choice and not had to suffer his wrath. She opened another wine cooler and figured she could spend the evening getting shit sorted out and things that were going to be thrown away she could get to the dumpster. That would be easy; that would make some room in the apartment and it wouldn't seem so cramped. She took a deep breath and sort of smiled, it was going to be alright. It was going to be a good night. She had a few hours to kill before the news.

She tried to make herself busy.

At 11:00 PM Sharon settled on to the couch, she managed to empty out a number of items she was going to throw away and folded a lot of clothes and towels; but she hadn't packed a single box. No matter how hard she tried she just kept getting side tracked. It wasn't that she didn't want to get the hell out of there; it was that she didn't want to pack it up, she just couldn't focus. Every time she heard a noise outside she would dive to the blinds to see what it was; and then go have a smoke and start over.

The cycle continued all night; until the news finally came on.

"Good evening. In our top story tonight the search continues for a missing Duvall man. Rich Duncan was last seen eight days ago in Moses Lake; his car, this red 1988 Mustang GT was found abandoned in a Darrington parking lot six days ago. Police have released this composite sketch of the man believed to have last driven Duncan's car but police are still asking for your help in identifying this man-"

Sharon winced as the composite flashed across the screen of her television.

"A search over the weekend provided no clues in the disappearance of Duncan but we did learn tonight that another search is going to be conducted on Saturday. This search is going to focus on the area south of Darrington and also further east toward the town of Winthrop along the North Cascades Highway. Police have few clues in the case but Snohomish County spokesperson Eliot Goodal did have this to say: 'We are actively investigating the disappearance of Richard Duncan and need the public's help in identifying, this man. He is a person of interest and was last seen driving Duncan's car. Anyone, and I mean anyone, who may have information about the identity of this man is encouraged to come forward. Snohomish County Detectives have numerous leads in this case and we are pursuing them vigorously at this time.' Again, anyone with information is asked to call the Snohomish County Sheriff; Jean?"

Every time she watched the news she hoped somehow that she would watch and there would be no mention of the man in the red Mustang. But every time it was the lead story and it seemed every time they were inching closer and closer to figuring out who had done this. Now they were going to search south of town. And if they did, would they find where her and Phil had camped?

Her head flushed.

She and Phil had never thought of that.

She remembered that they had packed up in a hurry that night and it was dark. She couldn't remember if they might have left anything that could tie them to it.

A piece of paper like a business card or pay stub used to start the fire?

Did one of Phil's business cards fall out the door one of the dozens of times they had opened it? And that tow truck driver, if he realizes its right where he towed Phil out...

Fuck.

What happens when they find the campsite?

They never thought about the camp and evidence or something that could tie them to it.

It just kept swirling in her head.

Or had they talked about it? She couldn't remember. But would she?

Of course she would.

But why didn't they?

They had thought of everything and talked about it all. It was going to work.

Until he got that ticket.

That fucking ticket.

But still nothing about the ticket. No knocks on the door, no stories on the news, no phone calls; *nothing.* Maybe Phil was right?

She fumbled for a cigarette. She was so tired of this, she couldn't remember. She started shaking.

Was this just paranoia?

Or maybe she really did have something they hadn't thought about. This could be important. She needed to talk to Phil, but he was nowhere to be found. For all she knew he was probably shit-faced drunk around the campfire by now.

Asshole.

Sharon paced around the dining room table and then in to the bedroom and back out. She went back to the patio for another smoke. On the way past the refrigerator she grabbed the last of the wine coolers left over from the camping trip. Her head was racing. Where the fuck was Phil. What should she do?

She nearly dropped the wine cooler on to the kitchen floor when the phone rang.

She didn't want to answer it, but not knowing who had called would be worse than dealing with whoever was on the other end. It was probably her mother calling to check on her after her out of the ordinary overnight the day before. She pressed the cigarette into the ashtray and strode in to the phone next to the couch.

"Hello," she answered.

"YOU'RE BACK!" Jody gleefully cheered in to the phone.

Sharon could tell right away by her tone that she still had no suspicions about Phil's fishing story in Moses Lake.

"Hi, Jody. Yeah- I'm back. I mean- we're back. Yes," Sharon spoke in to the phone.

"How was it?" Jody asked.

Sharon had to calm herself. What was she going to say when Jody wanted to talk to Phil?

"Um…it was good. I don't know."

Jody had spoken with Sharon hundreds of times on the phone. She could tell when something was going on with her and Phil.

"Well, let me talk to my brother for a minute? I'll straighten him out!" Jody laughed.

Jody sensed that Sharon and Phil had probably gotten in a fight or disagreement. Many times in the past she just needed to calm Phil down a little and smooth things over. She was good at it.

Sharon took a huge breath and just held the phone to her ear. She couldn't think of what to say and that made her even more stressed.

"Uh…Phil?" Sharon finally asked.

"Yeah — is everything alright?" Jody asked sounding more concerned.

"Did you guys get into it or something?" Jody continued

Sharon again did not know how to respond. When her and Phil had disagreements before it was always easy to just tell Jody what was going on, but this was different.

"He's not here," Sharon said as calmly as she could.

"Oh, no…are you sure everything is ok?" Jody asked again.

Sharon started to cry. For at least a minute or more she just sat on the sofa amongst her shamble of an apartment and cried while Jody tried to coerce her into telling her what had happened. Finally she just didn't know what to do.

"Did he leave? Mad? Is he drinking somewhere, Sharon?….Sharon?" Jody kept asking.

The last nine days raced through her mind, she didn't know what to do or where to even begin. She didn't want Jody to over react but how could she not. At least she had been through this with Phil once before, but that was a lot different. He was younger then and had so much less going on. Now he had a good job and a home and- she couldn't figure out where to begin.

"Sharon!...Sharon!! What's going on?" Jody pled through the phone.

"I don't know where to-"

Sharon could barely hold back her sobs.

"I don't know where to even fucking start, Jody. It's bad. So bad," she began.

"What is it, is Phil alright?" Jody asked sounding much more worried now.

"Well, he's not hurt or anything-" Sharon replied.

"Where is he?" Jody demanded again.

"He's out near Edgewick, camping....Hiding out," Sharon answered.

"Hiding out? Hiding out from what? Did he go on a bender?" Jody asked.

"No. its worse. Much worse," Sharon cried.

For a minute she just continued to cry. Jody knew this was serious but she needed to keep Sharon calm and figure out what had happened.

"Oh shit. Did he hurt someone? Did he get in a fight?" Jody asked her voice much lower and more serious.

"He can't do that. He's on parole; they are going to put him back in if he keeps getting in fights, god damn it!" Jody continued.

Sharon let out a deep breath.

And then another.

Jody sensed it was worse than just a fight. Sharon would have told her about a fight.

"Did he wreck that new truck? For crying out loud Sharon, just tell me. He's my brother! What the hell happened?" Jody demanded.

Sharon, again reached in to her mind for the right words.

The words that would lessen the blow.

But there were none.

No words existed which could lessen the devastation she was about to become a part of.

"Have you been watching the news?" Sharon finally blurted out.

There was no easy way to tell her.

She just needed to say it.

"The news? What do you mean? What about?" Jody asked confused.

"That missing real-estate man from Duvall?" Sharon finally stated.

The phone went completely silent. Sharon sat there in silence, her breathing labored and fast.

Jody was speechless.

"Oh...my...God... That....that wasn't Phil, Sharon. Tell me God that wasn't Phil! Oh, my God. Not again. No, Sharon not again!" Jody cried.

"I don't know why he did this!" Sharon blurted out.

Murder myself, Murder I am.

It was as though the flood gates had been opened. For hours Sharon tried to make sense of what had happened and how and why. No matter how hard they tried to turn back the sands of time with denial and bargaining, they couldn't.

It was done.

29

Friday   May 11, 1990

Detective Hinds normally had Fridays off, and after being up until three in the morning, he was wrecked. After finally finding the turnout that Paul Bullard was convinced he had seen a body they searched for three hours in the dark with flashlights and electric lanterns and found nothing.   But this was the life he signed up for and he was committed. At nine in the morning we went in to the station to brief Sgt. Greene on his progress.

"Morning Tom," Hinds said as he tiredly made his way into Sgt. Greene's office.

"Well, what did we find on the North Cascades Highway? Anything pan out?" Greene asked.

"Well, we did find some duct tape with hair on it and a pile of broken tempered glass which might match Duncan's car. I won't be able to tell until we compare it to the glass that's left in the car," Hinds began.

"Speaking of the Mustang. The press is really starting to run with this story and his wife is calling every day. She is not going to let up any time soon. Do you have enough gas in the tank to keep working this?" Greene asked.

"Sure, if you want to keep me going," Hinds answered.

"Bjorling finished processing the car and there were no prints. *None.* Somebody wiped that thing down clean. He did find some white hairs; he thinks they are probably dog hairs, kind of wiry and short. He also recovered some 'Winston' brand cigarette butts. Wife said Duncan smoked Kent III's and these are definitely not those."

"Why don't I head down to the impound yard and take another look now that forensics is done. I can take some of that glass we recovered up on the North Cascades Highway and see if we can rule it out or not." Hinds suggested.

"I think I'll go over there with you and we can grab Bjorling too; that way if we see something worth re-examining he can take it in to evidence. Give me 'bout an hour and we can head over there," Greene replied.

Hinds went back to his desk to transpose his notepad into his desk computer and compile a progress report. He was dead tired but if they could get it in to the press that the person of interest maybe smoked Winston brand cigarettes and had a white dog; that could root out a lot more tips.

So far he had a flasher in Darrington, a guy who saw a body in the road but didn't report it for five days and a psychic, who, whether he wanted to believe it or not, was remarkable at finding whatever signs she could find.

An hour later Detectives Hinds and Detective Bjorling along with Sgt. Greene made the thirty minute drive to the Snohomish County impound yard to the red Mustang one more time.

Inside the impound yard they found the car in the northeast corner under a tarp. Hinds pulled the keys from the ignition and opened the rear hatch. He brought the plastic bag full of black glass fragments he had recovered the night before with him to the passenger side of the car. Carefully he scooped out some of the broken glass in the rear of the Mustang and placed it on to a white sheet of paper. He then meticulously set it on the hood and poured some of the broken fragments from the bag out next to the other pile.

Clearly, they were of different tint and color and the fragment pattern and size of the chunks was much different. A laboratory examination would be needed to rule them out as coming from different pieces of glass, but Hinds was fairly certain *they were not a match*. Whatever had happened at the trailhead off the North Cascades Highway, it had had nothing to do with the disappearance of Rich Duncan.

For another couple of hours the three detectives poured in and out of the car, under seats, under the hood in the trunk area and still nothing. Hinds had been working the leads for nearly two straight days now and it seemed they were no closer to finding Duncan.

On the way back to the station Greene and Hinds began to face the fact that without any more leads or tips; this case was going to go cold and go cold fast. Next to having to inform a family member that a loved one had been murdered, letting families know that they had exhausted all leads and the case was going cold was one of the most difficult conversations he ever had to have. The prospect of not knowing what had happened to their wife, husband, son or daughter was immeasurably different and as devastating as the news that a loved one had died. A few hours later, exhausted, Detective Hinds headed home.

*   *   *

Passed out on the couch amongst the empty boxes and folded laundry Sharon had been asleep for nearly 12 hours. Startled, she jumped up from the couch and looked around at the mess that had become of her apartment. He had been gone for two days now and without his constant berating of her every move she thought she could get it sorted out. But now Jody was involved. She had no idea how she was going to react, but at least with Phil up in the woods, she and Jody could figure it out, together.

Something had woke her up, but she wasn't sure.

The phone was ringing.

She leaned toward the end of the cluttered sofa and moved a pile of pillows off of the telephone. Once again her heart rate jumped and the lump in her throat nearly made her vomit. She felt dizzy and disoriented.

This is fucking ridiculous.

She shook her head and gazed upward at the ceiling.

"FUCK!" she screamed.

The phone suddenly stopped ringing.

She glanced over at Rusty still lying under the kitchen table. As soon as she made eye contact with him he simply wagged his tail twice and stared at her.

RING!

Shit.

Who ever it was wasn't going to quit now. It had to be Jody she thought. Maybe she had figured out what to do, maybe she had a way out of this fucked up mess her brother had gotten them in to.

It rang again.

"Hello?" she reluctantly answered.

"What are you doing? Where were you?"

It was Phil.

She let out an audible sigh. She prayed that he hadn't called Jody and found out at that she had told her.

"Fuck, Phil. What are *you doing?*" she asked.

"I hiked in for more beer again, my fucking back. It's just- I don't know. No matter how I try and lay down it won't go away. Where were you just now, I called twice?" he asked, somewhat subdued.

She could hear the pain in his voice.

"I was just up late. Packing, you know," she answered.

"You just now woke up?" Phil asked angrily.

He couldn't tell that she was lying. Except for a few folded piles of clothes from the bedroom closet, the boxes piled up in the living room were as empty as her resolve.

"*Fuck you.* I packed all goddamn night, it's almost done but there is so much to do. I don't think you realize-"

"*WHAT?!* You aren't done yet? Jesus fucking Christ. You need to be out of there, it's been over a week! If that ticket comes back they are going to- FUCK!" he yelled.

"I KNOW, Phil! But it's not that easy, do you just want me to throw all this shit way? What?" she argued.

"I fucking told you to get packed up and out- I've been up here since Wednesday—this should have taken you a day maybe a day and a half. What do you have left? *FUCK!*" he yelled again.

"Phil I-"

"Shut up and fucking listen—we need to be the fuck out of there NOW. I can't be there—it's too risky. Get what you can into the storage unit and dump the rest. I don't know if I am going to be able to stay out here, we might have to go back to the motels again or something, I don't know. I just can't sleep, can't get comfortable- nothing," Phil commanded.

He reached back and rubbed his lower back. It was throbbing.

"I'll call you tomorrow at eleven—I'm sure I can make it one more night but get that fucking apartment emptied out and you'll probably have to come get me tomorrow," he continued.

"*Tomorrow?* I can't get this all done by myself by tomorrow!" she argued.

"What the fuck? You have had two fucking days! Fucking get it done and I'll call you tomorrow at eleven! DO you fucking understand me?" Phil yelled again looking around the truck stop.

The parking lot was mostly empty but in the distance behind him she could hear the roar of trucks moving along Interstate 90 a few hundred yards away.

Sharon couldn't believe he wanted to come back after only two days.

"DO YOU HEAR ME?" he yelled again.

"Yes," she quietly muttered.

"Just get it fucking done!" Phil yelled and slammed the phone down on to the receiver.

310

She sat on the couch and held the phone to her shoulder. Blankly she just sat, staring at the empty boxes.

Go get him tomorrow?

As much as she tried she could not find any answer that made sense to her. The drinking, the screaming, the paranoia. It was too much. The last two days had been the first time in over a week that she didn't wonder what he was going to do every time he moved or looked in her direction. It was bad enough that every car door slamming outside or every time the phone rang, her body flowed with adrenaline and apprehension. But at least with him gone she felt she could maintain without having to constantly wonder when it was all going to come crashing down.

Now he wanted to come back.

All she could see ahead of her was more drinking himself in to a stupor, more screaming and hiding in motels. How long would it take before she stopped jumping every time she heard a noise? And what was it going to be like when they finally did come for them?

Because eventually, they were coming.

And the only thing he could come up with was to hide in the woods and wait it out? While she packed the apartment?

He was leaving her out to dry.

She finally took the phone from her shoulder and placed it in the cradle. She stood and stretched, walking toward the patio and grabbed her pack of cigarettes off of the table. She slid the kitchen slider open and a cool rush of air sent shivers down her legs. Carefully she sat down on the milk crate, lit her smoke and gently rubbed her legs trying to warm them up. Rusty whined at the door and joined her outside. She looked around the beautiful green evergreens that surrounded the grounds. It had been cloudy and gray for a few days, but today the clouds parted, giving way to a scattering of deep royal blue sky above. For a moment, she almost found herself smiling.

As she smoked, she played with Rusty and gently pushed him around the patio and scratched him. For a few seconds, the camping trip exited her mind. It was just she and her dog, like it had been before. She put her smoke out and thought she might go to the store around the corner from her apartment and pick up a 'For Rent' magazine and begin looking for apartments. Quickly she realized how ridiculous that would be now. Now, that she told Jody what happened.

The secret was out.

There would be no going back. In a moment of weakness and exhaustion she had temporarily relieved herself of the painful burden she had been carrying.

She could never take it back.

Jody knew. And more than likely, Jody's husband now probably knew. Now she had to worry whether or not Jody was going to call the police. Tomorrow, when she picked up Phil she would have to tell him that Jody also knew what happened.

He will be fucking irate.

She quickly sat back down on the patio crate and lit another cigarette.

Her options were becoming more and more limited. No matter how badly she just wanted to curl up on the couch and sleep more of it away, she couldn't. Even if she refused to go get Phil, he would just call his sister and she would go get him, and then he would know and it would only get worse. No matter how many scenarios played out in her head there was no good one. Nothing good was ever going to come of what he had done, she had to accept this and start thinking for herself.

She extinguished her cigarette and called to Rusty.

"Come on boy," she said in a soft spoken but confident voice.

She grabbed her sunglasses off the table and fished another pack of smokes out of the half consumed carton, put Rusty in to the truck and headed to West Seattle to her mother's house.

*   *   *

Traffic poured out of the downtown Seattle streets toward Interstate 5 and Highway 99. A pungent mixture of diesel smoke and seaside air swirled through the city. It was Friday evening and attorneys Brendan Mangan and Leif Ormseth were just about to join a couple of colleagues at the Metropolitan Bar and Grill for some drinks. They had recently begun sharing an office as they developed and began their practices. Their front desk receptionist had left right at five to try and get ahead of the afternoon traffic which always locked the downtown Seattle streets on Fridays. Leif was waiting for Brendan to wrap up a couple of last minute things when the front office phone rang.

"Hi, I need some help." The woman's voice said softly.

"O...k..., what kind of help do you need?" Leif asked.

"I am not sure how to say this, but what if I saw something and I didn't have anything to do with it, but..."

The phone hung up.

Leif set the receiver down and glanced toward Brendan's office.

It rang again.

"Sorry, I am just really scared," the woman's voice was quivering.

Leif peeked in toward Brendan's office again but could not see him.

"My husband, he- *oh my god*- I don't know what to do," she said.

312

"Your husband did something and you are not sure what to do?" Leif asked, surprised at what he heard.

"He had been drinking really heavily, and then....and then....he's hiding in the woods now, he was in Vietnam. I ....I just..." she continued.

"Can you hold on, for just a second?" Leif asked and put her on hold.

Leif darted over to Brendan's desk to see if he was on the phone.

"Is this supposed to be funny?" Leif asked.

Brendan looked up from his desk.

"Is *what* supposed to be funny?" Brendan asked and set down the stack of documents he was reading.

"Your husband did something?? *You want to confess?* Ha! Ha! Very funny!" Leif said.

"What are you talking about?" Brendan asked.

Leif could quickly tell Brendan wasn't playing a prank.

"Oh shit. Pick up line one when I do. Listen to this woman. I think it's a prank but I don't know. I thought it was you," Leif said.

He went back to the front desk and picked up the phone.

"Sorry, ma'am. you still there?" he asked.

"Yes."

"Sorry, I needed to get a pen and paper. So what is your name ma'am? And your telephone number?" Leif asked.

"I ain't giving that out. I just need to know what I should do," the woman began sobbing.

"Well, ok. Why don't you tell me what happened and we can go from there," Leif answered.

He peered over at Brendan who was staring at him with his phone stuck to his ear from the doorway. He could here the woman softly crying. She didn't say anything.

"Ma'am? Are you still there?"

"Yes."

She took a deep breath and wiped her nose.

"Just give me a second," she said.

"A few days ago, well, ten days ago, my husband and I were camping and we got our truck stuck."

She paused again. Leif listened intently to the silence on the phone.

"And this man came to help us and-"

She drew in a deep breath and started to cry again.

Leif glanced over at Brendan again.

"I think this is real," Brendan whispered over to Leif with his hand cupped over the receiver.

"Ma'am, we can certainly help you. But I really need your name and phone number. From what you're saying the rules of attorney-client privilege would apply here, but this sounds like you might need to have someone represent you to go to the police," Leif tried to convince her.

"You can't turn me in, right? I mean if I give you my number the police aren't going to come to my mom's house, right?" she asked.

"No, ma'am. But I need to tell you, my partner and I may not be the right attorneys for this type of situation. I mean, we cannot say anything, ok; but what I'd like to do is get a hold of an attorney that I know that can help with this and then call you back," Leif said.

"Are you promising me- you won't call the police, I mean, I have to do something today. My husband is coming back tomorrow. He was supposed to be gone and I don't know what he'll do. You know. I mean, this has been on the news for the last few days."

She paused and took a few deep breaths.

"You know that real estate guy? From Duvall? That's missing? Well, I know where he is. My husband-" She began sobbing again.

"The guy in the red Mustang that they have the composite for?" Leif asked.

"Yes!" she sobbed.

"And I don't know what my husband will do. And he wants me to come get him tomorrow. I have to figure this out," she cried.

"Let us help you ma'am. I know an attorney who handles these sorts of things; he is very well known and very good. I am sure he can advise you, I just need to call him and then we will call you, but I need your name and number," Leif pleaded.

"*My name is Sharon,*" she finally answered.

Leif took down her number and hung up the phone. He looked shockingly at Brendan.

"Can you believe that?" Brendan asked.

"I think we should call John right away. He is the only lawyer I know of that might know how to handle this sort of thing," Leif suggested.

Attorney John Wolfe was one of Seattle's more well known and high profile attorneys. Leif called John's office and got no answer.

"Where would John be on a Friday night?" Leif quizzed.

"Maybe try some of the bars downtown; I don't know- F.X. McRory's, Metropolitan?" Brendan answered.

Leif dialed number after number and explained that this was somewhat of an emergency. After a few calls, John Wolfe took the phone.

"This is John, what do you need?"

*   *   *

A few hours later, Sharon grasped her mother's hand as the elevator door opened. It was cold in here and the nighttime janitorial staff had left a custodial cart in the middle of the long hallway leading toward the attorney's office.

Her mother agreed with her that this was the right thing to do. She did not want to go to prison. Somehow she had to get out of this.

Her blue jeans were stiff and tattered, the hoodie she had been wearing for the last few days draped across her tired frame. Her eyes were swollen from the ordeal she had been through over the last few days and once Phil fled to the mountains, she found comfort in her mother's strong courage and counsel.

Most of the office doors in the long hallway of the 61st floor were closed and locked. Only a small portion of the hallway lights remained lit during the off hours of the downtown skyscraper. A few doors ahead, one of the doors was propped open, light poured from the room into the dimly lit hallway.

The two women turned toward the door, and she lightly knocked as they entered, "Hello," she said mildly, "Knock-knock. Hello?"

"Hi there! We're in here," a man's voice hollered from the office inside, behind the empty receptionist desk out front.

The women slowly moved behind the desk toward the open door. Sharon took another deep breath as she entered to the room with her mother. The huge bay window behind the giant conference table framed the giant buildings of the Seattle night sky. She pressed her face next to it and felt the cold chill of the window and could barely make out the audible sounds of cars honking, engines whirring and sirens in the distance.

Downtown Seattle seemed so busy at night.

A man sat at the large conference table with a small laptop computer. Another man, wearing a freshly pressed suit and tie strode around the conference table in front of them and extended his hand toward Sharon and her mother.

"You must be Sharon," he said calmly.

She backed away from him and stared at her mother again, her heart raced.

"Yes," her mother quickly spoke, "She's Sharon and I am Helen."

Noticing Sharon's expected state of shock, the man quickly moved to reassure her.

"Its going to be OK, I think we can get this under control and get this sorted out. Can I get you some water, or something else? Anything to make you comfortable?"

Sharon and her mother pulled up seats to the conference table and Sharon laid her head onto the table, exhausted.

"First, let me introduce myself. I am John Wolfe and these two gentlemen are the men you spoke with on the phone earlier, Brendan Mangan and Leif Ormseth. You are here seeking legal advice. Anything you say in here is privileged and neither I, nor Mr. Mangan or Mr. Ormseth can ever repeat it to anyone unless you tell us you are about to go take someone's life. If that happens we are bound to contact the police because someone is in imminent danger. Does that make sense? So, just don't tell us you are *going to kill someone*, and everything else stays here."

"I explained it to her on the way here," the older woman said.

John Wolfe nodded and sat down.

"She knows, she just needs to get this straightened out," the woman began rubbing her daughters back.

"It's going to be OK."

"Well, good then, I am afraid, I have to ask, ma'am. If this is going to be confidential, you are going to have to wait outside while we talk with our client. Is that OK? We'll take good care of her, and if she needs to stop and take a break or something, she can come right out," Mr. Wolfe explained to her mother.

"You can wait just outside. Make yourself comfortable on the sofa. Whatever you need, right out there."

He pointed to the plush waiting area.

"So come in here Sharon, have a seat. So tell me what's going on, what happened?" John asked.

He, Brendan and Leif sat mesmerized as Sharon told them what had happened. John took notes on a yellow legal pad while Leif and Brendan listened intently to the woman's story. Off and on Sharon would break down crying. The further into the story she got the less the nightmare weighed on her.

After and hour and a half of telling and re-telling specific details John dropped his pen down onto the legal pad and leaned back in his chair. Sharon sat there, silent. Her eyes were swollen and physically, mentally and emotionally, she was a wreck.

"Well, I think for sure, and I think you know this. We need to let police know what's going on. But based on what you have told me, I expect I can get you immunity from prosecution in exchange for you telling police what you know. You may have to testify against your husband," John began.

"Oh god. Why did he fucking-" she threw her head down on to the table and wrapped her arms over top of her.

316

"But…there is this thing called spousal privilege. Even if you wanted to testify, your husband may be able to stop you," he explained.

"And they are most likely going to place a condition on the immunity based upon you telling the truth. If they catch you in a lie they can revoke it. So if there is something else. I need to know now. I can help you, but you have to tell me everything," John continued.

"And what if I don't say anything, what then?" she asked.

"Well, eventually, when he is caught. And it sounds like he very well may be caught soon, with a ticket and all that. You could possibly be charged with accessory. You see its one thing to not come forward when you are under duress from him. In other words, you fear for your life while he is around, but it's another thing to be free of him for a couple of days and not do anything. Does anyone else know about this? Besides your mother?"

"Phil's sister called last night; I told her what was going on and she thinks I need to go to the police, too," she cried.

"Well, they…your mother and your sister; or Phillip's sister rather; they are right. My advice is that we contact Snohomish County right away and negotiate immunity for you," John concluded.

"What's going to happen to Phil?" she asked looking up.

"Well, let me be blunt. I know he is your husband and all, and it sounds like he needs some help with what he's had to deal with. But, Sharon; with his past record, he could very well be looking at life without parole or even the death penalty. You need to think about Sharon right now. You. What's best for you," John answered leaning forward and folding his arms on the conference table in front of him.

"I'll have to testify? In court?" she asked reluctantly.

"Well, again. I don't represent your husband here. But this is very serious. Given what you have told me, he will have a lawyer and if I were representing him I would try and get the best plea bargain I could. I don't think this will ever go to trial. But if it does, yes, the prosecution will expect full cooperation for your immunity. But spousal privilege might stop that from happening," he answered.

"But, let me be very clear. This is a very serious situation. You said yourself they are going to be having another search and once they find the body, it's going to be all over the news for awhile. His sister knows what happened. Let me tell you. It's possible she may tell someone who may tell someone and if you wait, and they find that body, you won't have anything to bargain with for immunity. If they solve this, and I bet they will. You could face an accessory charge," John said as convincingly as he could.

Sharon sat in silence.

Murder myself, Murder I am.

Numb.

"I know this isn't going to be easy. The next 24 hours are probably going to be the toughest you may have ever faced. But somewhere, that man's family is wondering, and has been wondering for days now. I really think we need to call Snohomish County and get this taken care of. I'll be here with you through the whole thing," he said.

*   *   *

The phone didn't often ring at 10:30 at night at Detective Hinds home with good news. It usually meant a body had been discovered and he was needed. But given that he was on a fresh case, it was unlikely.

"Hi John, this is Tom. I think we finally got a break in the Duncan case. It's not good news though," Sgt. Greene began.

"What's going on?" Hinds asked.

"I got a call from an attorney...uh, John Wolfe, in Seattle. He says his client wants to come forward; she witnessed her husband killing Duncan." Sgt. Greene answered.

"Damn. I had a feeling this one wasn't headed for a happy ending. Let me guess- she wants immunity?" Hinds asked.

"Yep, and based upon what the attorney said, It sounds like it might be the best thing. Why don't we meet at the north precinct and we'll head down there," Sgt. Greene finished.

Hinds, exhausted from scouring the North Cascades Highway until 3:00 AM the night before, climbed out of bed and got dressed.

His job was to catch killers and he was glad they had finally caught a break and it looked like they were going to get someone for this, but at the same time he also had the tough job of informing family members of the victim. It was always the most difficult thing he ever had to do.

It never got easier.

And he never got used to it.

But now was not that time.

Now was the time he would move closer to catching whoever had murdered Rich Duncan.

30

Saturday   May 12, 1990

Detective Hinds and Sgt. Greene stood silent as the elevator climbed upwards for what seemed a minute or more.

It was just after midnight.

61st floor.

They moved slowly down the long hall toward the office. Inside, Attorney John Wolfe greeted them and took them through the office in to a small conference room. He indicated that his client wanted to provide details to a murder, but before he would allow her to provide those details, he wanted guarantee of immunity. Hinds called Snohomish County Prosecutor Larry McKeeman and he verbally agreed to the immunity conditions as long as Sharon was truthful.

Detective Hinds and Greene entered the next conference room to find a middle aged woman and her mother; along with attorney's Brendan Mangan and Leif Ormseth.

"Hi there, Sharon. I'm Detective John Hinds and this is Sgt. Tom Greene. I understand you have some information for us?" Hinds asked her as he sat in the chair across from Sharon and her mother.

"I am going to ask that you start from the beginning and we'll write down what is said and once your attorney here looks over it you can sign a written statement. We will need you to show us where the body is and we need help to find your husband, right away. We don't need him out there running in to someone else, ok?" Hinds continued.

Sharon nodded.

"So, tell us what happened," Sgt. Greene asked.

"My husband *shot* that real estate man-"

"Rich. His name was *Rich Duncan*," Hinds interrupted her.

Sharon looked down at the floor and put her hand up to her face and started crying gently.

"My husband shot, Rich; twice with a shotgun," she continued.

"What's his name?"

"Phillip, Phillip Van Hillman."

"Do you know where he is? Right now?" Sgt. Greene interjected.

"I can't get a hold of him, he is camping in the woods off of I-90 out by Edgewick. He's supposed to call me tomorrow," she answered.

"Does he know you're doing this?" Greene continued.

"No, not unless he talks to his sister. I shouldn't have told her," she said.

"And his date of birth?" Hinds asked.

"March 8th, 1954," she demurely responded.

Sgt. Greene stepped out of the interview to get an APB started on Phillip Hillman and get a report on his priors.

"Where did this occur?"

"It was on a logging road, just off the Mountain Loop Highway up near the Sauk River, outside of Darrington," she said.

"Do you mean the North Cascades Highway?" Hinds wondered.

"No, No. I know where that is, that's further north out of Darrington, we turned the other way when we were in Darrington," she answered.

Hinds quickly realized that Alice Simon and Paul Bullard likely had not seen anything related to this case at all, but he was not yet sure.

"And how do you know this was Rich Duncan?" Hinds asked.

"We saw it on the news. His picture. His picture was on the news," she answered and crossed her legs under the table.

Her mother rubbed her shoulder again.

"Can you describe Phillip for me?" Hinds asked.

"He's five foot eleven inches and weighs about 195 pounds. He is white of course, short brown hair and a flattop haircut. His hair has grown out, he hasn't had it cut in awhile. He has brown eyes and he is very muscular," she answered.

"Does he have any scars or tattoos?"

"He has a scar on his right wrist."

"Is he on parole or probation? Any trouble with the law before?"

Sharon sighed and looked toward the ceiling.

"He is on parole. For another murder and an assault after that. His parole Officer is Anne Prescott, in Bellevue."

Hinds couldn't help but shake his head.

Repeat offender.

"Do you live in Bellevue?"

"No, Phil works, well- worked at Evergreen Ford as a floor manager, in Eastgate. He was in Vietnam, he has combat experience, you know," Sharon answered as she sat back in the chair.

"You said he was on parole for murder and an assault? Where did these occur?" Hinds asked.

Sharon pulled a tissue from out of the box in front of her and wiped her nose.

"The murder was in 1974, a few miles outside of Darrington also. He showed me once where, where the other one took place-"

"The other murder?" Hinds confirmed, shaking his head.

Hinds let out an audible sigh.

"The assault was just a stabbing, the guy survived. It was in 1982 around the U-District, I think," she continued.

"Ok...so the second one was *just* a stabbing?" Hinds looked over at her attorney with an obvious stare.

Hinds paused, he was never shocked in the way murderers behaved, but he was often confounded and frustrated at how someone who had murdered before was back on the streets and would do it again. And this guy, it seemed, had done it right where he had done it before.

"And where did he do his time?" Hinds asked.

"He was in Monroe, Walla Walla, McNeill Island, Shelton and Reynolds work release in Seattle," she answered.

"Looks like he has done the full circle," Hinds remarked.

"So where do you live now? What's the address?" he asked.

"We live in an apartment up in Pine Lake outside of Issaquah. I am currently staying with my mother. I gave notice at the apartment and started packing- but. I don't know. You know?" she started crying and then wiped her eyes again and forced herself to stop.

"You live alone- just you and Phillip?" Hinds asked.

"Yeah, and our dog," she wiped her eyes again.

"What color is the dog?" he asked.

"He's a little white dog," she answered.

Hinds made a quick note about the dog. This fit with the few short white animal hairs they discovered in the Mustang earlier and Mom had told Detective Hinds that Rich never allowed her dogs in his car.

"Ok, so why did you decide to come forward at this time. This happened over a week ago. Why now?" Hinds asked as he sat back in the chair.

Sgt. Greene returned to the conference room and sat down next to him.

"Phil got a ticket in that Mustang. And all the news coverage and the composite sketch- Phil is worried he is linked to this. He's been so paranoid. Jesus," she began.

Hinds shook his head. He found it fascinating as to the different reasons people came up with to turn someone in for a crime. Sometimes they wanted revenge; sometimes it was because they felt it was the right thing to do. But most of the time, it was to protect their own asses from being caught.

This was no different.

"He wiped the car down completely and then took it to Darrington and left it in that grocery store parking lot. That's when somebody saw him and made that sketch," she continued.

"So where did he go when he ditched the car?" Greene asked.

"Our truck was still stuck up there- where…where he…the truck was stuck so he got a tow."

"From who?"

"I think it was Pine Tree Towing," she answered.

"Do you know where the clothes are that Phillip was wearing?" Hinds asked.

He and Greene had interviewed suspects together many times before and did an excellent job feeding off of each other with different lines of questioning to see if they could trip up the witness or suspect somehow.

"He put his shoes and the pants he was wearing that had blood on them and took them with him. He told me he dumped them somewhere between Issaquah and Darrington," she answered.

"Do you know where he dumped them?" Hinds asked.

"No."

"How did he arrange the tow?" Greene quickly jumped in.

"He called them the morning we got back from Darrington but he had to wait three or four hours in Darrington to get the tow because the tow driver had to take his wife to Everett to the dentist or something," she finished.

"What was he doing while he waited?" Hinds asked.

"He called me three or four times."

"How did he pay for the tow?" Greene quickly asked.

"With his Union 76 card."

The questions were coming so fast she had very little time to think in between them.

322

"What time did he get home from Darrington?" Hinds followed up.

"It was about midnight."

"What was he wearing when he left your apartment?" Greene asked.

"Sweat pants and a t-shirt, I think. I'm not positive."

"What time did he leave for Darrington?" Hinds asked.

"I think it was about noon or one," Sharon answered.

She looked worn out. The expression on her face quickly became very upset and her mother hugged her again as she pulled another tissue from the box on the table.

John Wolfe stood up and stared at the detectives.

"Let her take a minute, ok? She's not a suspect here, detectives," he reminded them.

"Can I go out for a smoke? I really need a smoke," she asked.

"Sure, let's start up again in...say...15 minutes?" Greene suggested. He peeked at his watch. It was nearly three in the morning.

Sharon got up and she and her mother headed down the hall for the elevator. John Wolfe called the building security to let them know to allow Sharon and her mother back in to the building. Hinds and Greene stepped out in to the hall.

"What do you think? Think she's being straight right now, so far?" Greene asked.

"I think so far, we'll see once we get to the details. But she is definitely rattled and upset. I'm just not sure why it took over a week to come forward, you know?" Hinds answered.

"Yeah, when she was asked why she came forward now- well..., you heard her," Greene pointed out.

"What did you hear back on Hillman?" Hinds asked.

"Just like she said. This is one bad dude. Murder one back in '74. It was in Snohomish County also. He was out on parole six years later and he went back for an assault two in '82 out of Seattle," Greene answered.

Hinds shook his head.

"How was this guy back out?" Hinds asked hypothetically.

He knew the answer.

Sharon and her mother made their way back up the long elevator ride and into the conference room.

Hinds and Greene both stood up as she and her mother came in and sat back down.

"All right, we need to know what happened now. Just relax and tell us everything you can. Ok?" Hinds began.

Sharon began to sob again.

"Sharon?...Sharon...look at me. Please," Hinds leaned forward again.

Sharon looked up and took a tissue.

"Just relax, you're doing the right thing here. Ok. We are finally going to be able to give this man's wife and his family some answers. They have been wondering and living a nightmare for the last nine days. Ok? You are going to help them right now and end this. You're going to be ok. I promise," Hinds continued.

He was a master at calming witnesses and getting the information he needed. Sharon once again calmed herself and took another deep breath. It was going to be a long night.

"Good. That's better. So we need to know why and how Phillip killed Mr. Duncan."

"It was with a double barreled shotgun. He shot him twice."

"So he shot him twice. Ok. This is very important, now. How long after the first shot was the second?" Greene asked.

"It was right away, Phil said he shot him the second time because he didn't want him to suffer," she said holding back tears.

"Was he alive after the first shot?"

"I don't know. I don't know. I really don't think so."

"What kind of ammo did he usually have do you know?" Greene asked.

"He has everything from bear shot to bird shot; I don't know what he was using."

"How much ammo did he have with him?" Hinds asked.

"I don't know; maybe ten or 15 rounds, in a plastic bag in the truck."

"How far apart were the shots?" Greene quickly asked.

"I think one or two seconds apart. They were very close together," she answered.

"Ok, so what happened to lead up to this? Why did Phil kill Mr. Duncan?"

Hinds stood up and stretched his legs by walking slowly behind where Sgt. Greene was sitting.

"He wanted the car," she answered quietly, almost ashamed.

"What exactly did he say? About taking the car?" Hinds asked.

"I didn't ask him until a couple of days later, I mean I was really stressed out and scared and he told me that 'My primitive instincts took over. We needed the car to survive.' I was scared that I was going to be next if I didn't do exactly as he said."

"Why do you think you were in danger as well? I mean this was your husband," Greene pointed out.

"Right after he shot that man, Mr. Duncan, he...he pointed that shotgun at me and told me to go get the 'blankety-blank shells.'"

"The fucking shells? Is that what you mean?" Greene asked.

"Yes. The fucking shells," she answered.

"I was so scared and I just wanted to go home. I was shocked," she continued.

"So then what happened?" Hinds asked.

"I went up the hill to where the truck was and I got the shells from the truck, they were in the plastic baggy. When I got back down with them he was standing over the...*the body*."

Sharon paused and clenched her mouth again about to sob.

She held it back.

"He said to get out of there, he didn't want me to see what he was about to do," she cried softly unable to hold back any more.

"Did he take anything from the body, the wallet, any money, his wedding ring, anything?" Greene asked.

"I don't know, I just walked down to the road. I wasn't there," she replied.

"Do you know what happened to the car phone, from the Mustang or Mr. Duncan's briefcase or overnight bag?" Hinds questioned.

"No, I think he got rid of that stuff on the way back to Darrington," she answered.

"Let's go back to before all this happened. How did you and Phillip run across Duncan?" Greene inquired.

Hinds, who had been pacing behind Sgt. Greene came back to the table and sat back down.

"It was about four o'clock on Wednesday, which was the second of May; we were camping maybe 12 to 15 miles outside of Darrington, almost to Barlow Pass. We decided to go four wheelin' and I was driving. Phil was pretty wasted. I went up this logging road and we came to a washout and I drove straight in to it thinking we could make it through it," she began.

"Did you take a right or left off the road?" Greene asked.

"We were headed away from Darrington and we took a left- it was about a quarter mile off the main road. I think it was about seven o'clock at this point. We tried to get the truck unstuck but couldn't so we walked back down to the main road to see if we could flag someone down for help. That's when this red Mustang drove up and the man driving asked if we needed help."

"Can you describe him for us?" Hinds asked.

"He was a bigger guy, maybe 200 plus pounds, maybe bigger. He had dark brown hair, brown eyes. He was well taken care of at home. He was wearing a lighter shirt-with pin stripes. He had white tennis shoes," she described.

"Did you notice if he had a wedding band?"

"Yes, yes he did."

"So then what happened?" Greene asked.

"We told him our truck was stuck and he said he would let someone know when he got to Granite Falls. He then took off," she said.

"He left? Heading toward granite Falls?" Greene asked.

"Yes, it was almost dark so I started looking for wood for a fire. About 45 minutes later he came back, he was headed toward Darrington this time. He stopped again and asked if maybe he could help pull out the truck with his Mustang," Sharon claimed.

Hinds and Greene looked at each other.

"Phil and I both said no, that wouldn't work. But he wanted to see where the truck was; maybe he could help push it out. He pulled the car off to the side and we went up to where the truck was parked," she continued.

"So all three of you together?" Hinds asked.

"No, at some point, I don't know when, but Phil disappeared. I thought this was weird because Phil would never leave me alone in the woods with a man he did not know. It took four or five minutes to get up to the truck. Once he saw it, he said he could not pull it out with his Mustang," Sharon stopped and twisted in her seat.

She took a deep breath and the pitch of her voice went higher. She was about to start crying again.

"When I got back down to where the Mustang was I realized the man was not right behind me anymore. I turned back and looked up the road. He was about 50 feet away with his back to me so I figured he was...you know..."

"Relieving himself?" Hinds filled in.

"Yes, so I turned down around the corner where Phil and I had been sitting waiting and I noticed that Phil's shotgun and a couple of beers were missing from where we were sitting."

Sharon started to speak very quietly and her eyes teared up again.

"And...And that's when...that's when I heard the two shots," she stopped and her mother grabbed her hand while she dotted her eyes with the tissue.

"I walked back around the corner up the road... and I saw... and I saw.... the man lying face down. Oh, god. And Phil was up the hill a little bit walking toward the man."

"Where was the gun?" Greene asked.

"In his hand, his right hand," she feebly stated.

"How far was he from the body when you first saw him, after the shots?"

"Maybe ten or 15 feet."

Sharon wiped her arm across her face.

326

"I yelled at Phil, 'What the fuck is going on?' and he just said 'He's done. He's done.' By now I was only about ten feet away from the man."

She paused again and brought her hand up to cover her face. She shook her head and rubbed her eyes for a minute.

"Maybe we should take another break?" Sharon's attorney interrupted.

"No, no...I want to get this over with. I'm tired and I just want to get this over," Sharon replied.

"Well, we're going to need you to show us where the body is and where this happened. This is going to be a while. If you need to take a break for a minute," Greene informed her.

Sharon put her head down on the table. Her mother grabbed her hand and caressed it. Sharon sat there, motionless except for a few short sobs.

"I'll be fine. Let's just get on with this," she said.

"OK. So he said, 'He's done. He's done.' Then what happened?" Hinds continued.

"I was about ten feet away and Phil just looked weird. Like I have never seen him. His jaw was clenched, very tightly and his eyes were very cruel looking and empty. That's when he said to go get the fucking shells. I just looked at him and said' What are you talking about?' And he didn't say anything and then he just said 'Go get the fucking shells!' He was walking toward me with the shotgun pointed at me. I was horrified. I knew I was next if I didn't do exactly as he said."

"Did you fear for your life at this point?" Greene asked.

"Oh, god yes! I just went up to the truck and got the shells out of the baggy and came back. That's when he said for me to go away, he didn't want me to see what he was about to do."

"Did you see what he did?" Hinds asked.

"No, I just walked toward the road and never looked back. I was afraid to turn around."

"When did Phil rejoin you?"

"After ten or fifteen minutes I walked back up the road and he had drug the body across the logging road on to the edge of it. The man was lying face down. I just turned around and went back to where the Mustang was. I was nearly hysterical at this point. I didn't know if another car was going to come or? It seemed like a lifetime but Phil finally came down, it was like 9:30 or ten."

"Was it dark out?" Greene asked.

"Yes, it was very dark; Phil got into the passenger side and made me drive back to our camp; up the road a ways away from Darrington."

"Where was the shotgun?"

"He had it between him and the door."

"Ok, so you headed toward your camp- what next?" Hinds continued.

"We got to our camp and packed up our stuff as fast as we could. We left our camp and continued away from Darrington to go home," she said.

"So you're headed toward Granite Falls at this point?"

"Yes, but about ten minutes up the road the snow was still all across the road. I slowed down and Phil just said to 'gun it' and I was so scared I did not want to argue with him, so I did. We made it about 40 or 50 feet into the snow and got stuck, the snow was almost knee high."

"So you were stuck?"

"Yes, and by now it was about 11:00 and Phil told me he needed to sleep so he climbed in the back seat of the Mustang and put our dog up front and I spent the next five or six hours digging out that car. At some point I was so mad, so mad at everything that I smashed the rear window out with the shovel."

"What was Phil doing during all of this?" Greene asked.

"He was sleeping, off and on. He had drank so much that whole day."

Through the vertical blinds in the conference room window, daylight began to illuminate the room.

"Look, let's take a break for a few minutes and I need to make a couple calls to get some help in Darrington, we can start up again in 15 or 20 minutes and I think we should have time to grab some breakfast out toward the precinct in Mill Creek, before we head up north," Greene suggested.

Greene and Hinds stepped out in to the waiting area and began calling the King County Sheriff to coordinate how they were going to arrest Phil. It looked like they were going to have to put together a team to go hunt him down in the woods.

Fifteen minutes later Sharon and her mother rejoined them in the conference room.

"Alright...so you get the car unstuck and head home through Darrington?"

"Yes, it was about five in the morning by now, we stopped in Arlington to get gas and Phil went over to the Safeway across from the BP station," Sharon continued.

"What did he get at Safeway?"

"He came back with milk and donuts. We then drove straight to our apartment, in Pine Lake," she said.

"Can you tell us exactly what route you took?" Hinds asked.

"I don't know the names of the roads but-"

Sharon's attorney disappeared into his office and came back with a Thomas Guide for Snohomish and King County. He opened it up and showed Sharon where Darrington and Arlington were on the map and then pointed out the area east of Lake Sammamish where her apartment was.

"Ok, we traveled down this road, Highway 9 all the way to the Woodinville-Duvall Road and then we took Avondale Road south until we hit the Eastlake Sammamish parkway and then up to Pine Lake."

"What time did you get back to your home?"

"I don't know exactly, I mean I was so stressed I just lost track of time. I think it would have been between eight and ten at the latest?" she replied.

"And that's when he wiped the car and took it back to Darrington and got the truck unstuck?" Greene asked.

"Yes, I just passed out on the couch. I was so tired; I didn't really wake up until he got home late that night or early Friday morning like I said."

"Ok, so what did you and Phil do for the last *eight* days?" Hinds asked.

"On Friday morning, Phil had to go to his sales meeting and he had been drinking most of the night. But he came home from the meeting and told me he had taken a leave of absence from work. He was so paranoid that we stayed in different motels, in Bellevue and Eastgate," she answered.

"How was he acting? Was he planning on leaving the area?" Hinds asked.

"He was drinking, heavily. And so paranoid. He wouldn't let me out of his sight. He kept saying that I wanted to turn him in. He made me take him to some outdoor stores and the Army Surplus downtown on First Avenue; he bought some maps and dehydrated food and stuff. Finally, on Wednesday he had me drive him to Edgewick, off of I-90 outside of North Bend. He said he was going to set up a camp and for me to come and get him in two weeks. If I came and he saw someone with me, he would disappear into the woods again and I should come back a week later."

"Well, at this point we need to get your statement in writing."

"I can type it up on my computer," Sharon's attorney offered.

"We can go grab some breakfast, but we need to get that body recovered right away. I have some deputies meeting us to go up to Darrington. Until we get Phil in custody you are going to need to stay with me. You cannot contact anyone or use the phone until this over. Ok?" Hinds said.

Hinds and Greene stepped out in to the hallway.

"What do you think? Is she telling us everything?" Greene asked.

Hinds continued toward the elevator doors and without even slowing his step he answered, "*Not a chance.*"

31

Cold spring air hung over the forested foothills of the Central Cascade Mountains near North Bend like the cobwebs from a bad hangover lurk in your head. It was Saturday morning and Phil slept even less than the night before. He was starving and his back was getting worse. The Vodka, the beer, the dope; none of it was relieving the low constant pain in his spine. He tried sleeping on his side; he tried wadding up his jacket and lying flat with the jacket bunched up in the small of his back.

Nothing worked.

Empty Vodka bottles littered the campsite like bread crumbs marking the path between the campfire and his tent. As the morning light drained away the blackness, a blue jay a few yards from the tent squawked and screamed every ten or fifteen seconds.

There was no way Phil would get any sleep now.

Under the canopy of the old growth evergreens the moist air brought chills to his exposed arms as he struggled out of the tent. He rubbed them furiously and surveyed the perimeter of the camp. The cedars and fir trees were so thick along the river where he was camped that he could only see maybe 50 or 100 feet in any direction.

It was cold.

Vigorously he stirred the embers of the previous night's fire until the scent of burning cedar floated through the cold, damp Snoqualmie forest.

It was remarkably quiet and serene. A pair of nuthatches chirped and danced around the littered twigs and pine needles covering the ground. Although it was nearly nine in the morning, the sun would not break the summit of the rock faced peak he was settled under until at least noon or one.

He reached back and tried to rub the pain out of his spine. Nothing seemed to work. It was time to get the hell out of here and stay in a motel for a few days.

The hike back to the store at Edgewick would take a couple of hours unless he managed to hitch a ride. He dropped his cigarette in the fire and hobbled down the trail toward the gravel road. He could leave the camp set up for now and once Sharon came and picked him up they could drive back up here and pack everything. Maybe it would be wise to just head out of town for awhile where the news wasn't covering the story of that fucking real estate guy; Oregon? Idaho? California?

Anywhere but here. If they just spent a week or two out of sight, then he could get another job and just tone down the drinking a little.

What a fucking mess.

Through the trees ahead of him a raven floated down from the sky and gently settled on the bow of a hemlock tree. To his right another branch fluttered and a magpie dropped and sailed to the ground with a screech. He stopped and watched as the raven dropped to the floor of the forest and hopped a few steps. Two or three magpies darted away from the raven and in to the surrounding trees. As Phil drew closer the raven cocked its head and screamed a warning to him; on the ground beneath the hemlock, Phil expected to see a deer; but instead he was surprised to see the remains of a coyote, a few days dead.

The raven had nearly picked the carcass clean.

*　　　*　　　*

Detective Hinds was exhausted as they finished up breakfast at the restaurant in Mill Creek, Washington. He had barely caught three or four hours sleep yesterday afternoon after his all-nighter searching Highway 20. When the phone rang last night informing him of the meeting downtown at the lawyers office, he knew he would be in for another long one. It seemed like one long continuous day.

Sharon excused herself and went to the restroom to wash up and splash some cold water on her face. Standing in front of the mirror she removed the large sunglasses she had been wearing even as they ate breakfast. Her face was red and swollen. Her eyes sank back deep in her head; pierced by the light.

It was almost over.

Staring, motionless in the mirror, she thought about Phil and what he had done. Detective Hinds assured her he would let her know the moment he was taken into custody. Her life was forever going to be different. She remembered the prison dances at Monroe and corresponding with Phil while he was locked up. She remembered when they got married and how excited she was when he got out. It was going to be different; he was going to be ok, he just needed a good woman to guide him along.

A woman who wouldn't tolerate relapses.

She broke down in front of the mirror sobbing.

She pulled a paper towel from the dispenser and ran it gently under the faucet. She placed it above her forehead and squeezed the moist brown paper. As the cold water rushed into her eyelids she remembered the camping trips along the Sauk River and how she felt safe with him.

How had it gone so wrong?

The door to the restroom swung open snapping her out of her trance. It was her mother.

"Are you ok in here?" she asked, "You look like shit."

Sharon gasped and struggled not to laugh, if only for half a second.

"I know; I'll be out in just a second. Let me clean up a bit," Sharon said.

Her mother rubbed her shoulder gently and went back into the restaurant.

She pulled another handful of paper towels from the dispenser and wiped her face. She looked in the mirror and wiped again. Just as she finished drying her face, the tears would start to roll down again. It was no use. She tossed the sunglasses back on her face and quietly made her way back to the table.

Detective Hinds and Sgt. Greene sat at the table quietly speaking; her mother was at the front counter paying the bill. She could sense they were talking about her but didn't know what about. She was too tired and broken to even care.

"Well, they are waiting for us at the north precinct, we will stop by there and I have to brief the other officers. It should take just a few minutes. You can wait in the car with your mother if you like," Sgt. Greene told her.

"After that we will head up to Darrington and then out the Monte Cristo Highway; as soon as you point out the location we will have an officer take you wherever you need to go, you won't be needed any longer."

Outside, the steady rain had taken a soft turn. The drive to Darrington was about an hour and if the body was located where she had described it would be another half hour after that.

Hinds opened the rear door of the cruiser and let her and her mother sit down. He jumped in the front seat next to Sgt. Greene. They turned onto the highway and headed north.

Hinds turned in the seat to talk with Sharon and her mother.

"And don't worry too much; if we don't get him in to custody this afternoon or tonight we can post an officer or have King County post an officer near your front door," Detective Hinds informed her.

This afternoon or tonight?

For just a second she felt like she was going to pass out. Her thoughts swirled around her tired and exhausted mind.

"What will happen if Phil runs?" Sharon asked leaning forward.

"Well, hopefully the officers executing the warrant won't allow that to happen. But sometimes, if the suspect sees something he doesn't like, he might," Hinds answered.

"Will they shoot him?!" she asked horrified.

"Well, if he's armed or poses a danger. That is possible. But look, these guys are trained to make these kinds of arrests. You let us worry about that," Hinds reassured her.

She gasped and put her hand to her mouth.

What have I done?

The drive to Darrington seemed to go by really fast. Sharon stared out the window and landmarks they passed subtly reminded her of the nightmare of the week before. They drove through Arlington and the BP where she had gotten gas; they came in to Darrington and turned right, south out of town. A Darrington police car joined the convoy. She gazed down at the Sauk River as they drove past and accelerated up the hill on to the gravel highway.

The trees were as dark and menacing as she remembered. She strained to look out the window with every logging road they went past. In what seemed like a minute, she recognized the stretch of road she had sat and waited for help. She could still see that Mustang coming up the road and the dark haired man who was so eager to help them get unstuck. She motioned for them to slow down and then to stop.

"Up there. About 100 feet, on the right," she said softly.

The green fir branches swayed and danced in the breeze above her as she looked toward the sky. She remembered sitting on the ground and waiting for Phil to come back down that road, and how the only sound she heard after those two blasts was the piercing call of that raven soaring above her, searching.

Detectives and the forensic team slowly walked up the narrow logging road as it climbed slightly uphill away from the Mountain Loop Highway. Forty or fifty feet up the road a burm had been cut into the road. Directly to the left of the road and old cedar stump and a deadfall lay just as Sharon had described it on the way up.

As they drew further up the road into the damp darkness the breeze shifted subtly and detectives recognized the dank but familiar smell of human decomposition. Another twenty feet up the road Hinds noticed where something large looked like it may have been drug across the logging road and down into a small depression to the right. A stand of juvenile maples lined the ring of the fern covered indentation in the ground. Ten or fifteen feet further Hinds noticed the end of a freshly broken branch. And then another. Someone had recently stripped the bows from a dead tree nearby. He was certain that Phil had probably broken some branches to cover Rich's body.

"Over here. I think we have it over here!" he hollered to the others.

He moved closer; careful not to disturb any evidence. The smell was nearly overwhelming. It was something that most detectives never got used to. Hinds reached in and carefully pulled away a dead cedar limb and then another. First he spotted the white striped dress shirt. It was heavily stained dark brown from blood and being in the rain for the last nine days. A member of the forensic team skirted the small depression and pulled another branch away. Hinds could now make out the familiar sight of waterlogged, blood-soaked denim. The body was in a very advanced state of decomposition, and clearly would not be able to be identified without the use of dental records.

As the forensic team fanned out and began gridding off the search area, Hinds began making notes. A few feet from the body they found a white Nike shoe, most likely Rich's. The area was littered with evidence; cigarette butts, empty beer cans and two red shotgun casings were found exactly near the area where Sharon had said the murder took place. In a large, rotted stump they also found a shotgun wad; indicating that the shot was so close, the wadding had passed clear through Rich's body and still had enough velocity to lodge itself in the wood.

Once the forensic team and the coroner began processing the scene, Detective Hinds knew it was time to make the hardest type of call he ever had to make. In most cases, informing the next of kin about a homicide is done in person. Sometimes the family has no idea anything has happened. One minute they are going about a normal life and then he shows up at their door and changes their lives forever.

Other times, the victim has been missing for years and when the call finally comes in, the family finally starts to get closure. Sometimes the killers are caught before the family even knows their loved one is gone; sometimes the killer is never caught and they never know what happened. But they all have one thing in common. Their wife or daughter, husband, son or brother did not die in an accident, from a disease or natural causes; they were murdered by another human being.

As Detective Hinds trod down the skid row to the main road he spotted a raven perched near a dead cedar stump. Curiously the raven had extended its wing fully parallel with its body and appeared to be *preening a wounded wing.* Hinds, tired and exhausted, drove back in to Darrington and called Mom.

"Hello?"

"Hi Karen, its Detective Hinds," he began.

Although Detective Hinds and all of the detectives had been very accommodating in taking Mom's calls during the past week, it was somewhat unusual that they ever called her. Her heart began to race.

"Well I have some news," he started.

"It's not good is it?" she softly began to cry.

"No, I'm sorry but, no its not. We have found your husband," he continued.

"Is he alive?" she asked with the strongest voice she could muster, but in her heart she knew the answer.

She had known the answer for over a week once they discovered someone else had been seen in Rich's car.

"No, I am sorry, but he has been deceased for some time. Near as we can tell right now, since last Wednesday."

Even though after ten days; and Mom expected the news; it was still devastating to hear it for the first time. The random and fleeting hopes that some strange event had occurred and he would be returned to her as an unidentified victim in a coma at some small town hospital or brought out of the woods after being nursed to health in some obscure mountain cabin he had wandered into lost or returning from some foreign land on an emergency trip that he could not tell her about.

Something.

Anything.

But he was dead.

"Do you know who did this?" Mom asked holding back her tears.

*   *   *

Nearly two hours after leaving his camp, Phil arrived at the truck stop at Edgewick. He went inside the store and grabbed a six pack of beer and a bottle of Nuprin. Outside, cars came and went at the gas island and the constant traffic in and out of the store made him feel confident that he could just blend in. The clerk placed his six pack into a brown paper sack and after getting some quarters he wandered out to the phone booth.

He pulled a beer from the sack and glanced around to see if anyone was paying any attention to him. Satisfied, he dropped a quarter into the phone and dialed his apartment. He took a swig of beer, mindful that no one would see him. He hoped the beer would offer some sort of relief as his back continued to ache. Every time the phone rang he grew more irritated.

Where the fuck is Sharon?

After ten or twelve rings he slammed the phone down. The quarters clanked down into the change container at the bottom of the phone. He peered around again as he dropped the quarters back in to the slot above and watched a large RV pulled in to the gas island. He dialed the number again as two pre-teen girls hopped out of the side door of the RV and giggled their way into the store. Again the phone rang and rang.

Fucking bitch is asleep still. Goddamit.

Again he slammed the receiver down. A brown Toyota pulled off the road and in to the parking space right in front of the phone booth. A young man about twenty hopped out of the car and stood a few feet from Phil. Phil smiled at him and pried the quarters from the change slot. He dropped them in to his vest pocket and moved toward the front entrance. The young man passed him and entered the booth; Phil peeked back at him and stared as he went inside. As he entered the store he made eye contact with the young lady who had sold him the beer earlier.

"Just waiting for my ride," he smiled at her as pleasantly as he could.

She smiled back and continued stocking the cigarette bin above the counter. He made his way toward the back and in to the souvenir section again, it seemed there were far less people back here out of the way. The clock on the wall indicated it was nearly 10:20. He glanced out the large glass window at the gas island and watched as the RV pulled out and headed up the road toward I-90. Pressing his face closer to the glass he could now see that the phone booth was empty again. Casually, he sauntered to the front of the store; it was now brimming with activity. He reached up and pulled the baseball cap further down on to his forehead, the last thing he needed was someone recognizing him from that damn composite sketch.

Across the parking lot to the west of the store he could see a truck pulled nose in to the mechanics shop and an older man in coveralls wiping his hands. A slight breeze had kicked up but it looked like it might finally be a halfway decent day. He looked forward to summer coming. He slipped in to the phone booth and dropped in two quarters.

That bitch better be up by now.

He held the receiver in between his ear and shoulder as he gripped another beer from the sack. Again the phone continued to ring. No answer.

That fucking bitch.

He wanted to slam the receiver down and smash the phone to bits. But with all the people coming and going someone would notice him for sure. He took a deep breath and grabbed his quarters from the coin slot at the bottom of the phone. He turned and went toward the east end of the store around the corner and to the north side of the station where there were no visible windows. Inside his vest pocket he felt for his pack of cigarettes as he sat down on the sidewalk and leaned up against the cinderblock walls.

Pain shot through his spine.

He thought about calling Jody but he had no way of knowing if Sharon had talked to her already and given her some sort of cover story; *or worse.* Sharon was probably up all night packing and maybe she had simply passed out and left the phone unplugged for some reason. He would give her an earful for making him wait in pain like this.

At 10:30 he pulled himself up from the sidewalk and walked to the phone booth. Cautiously, he stepped in and dialed the number. This time he let the phone ring for nearly five minutes. If she was asleep this might be the only way to wake her up. If Sharon didn't wake up soon and answer the *Goddamn phone* he would have to call Jody to come and get him. He wasn't sure what he would tell her but he could come up with something. Sharon, on the other hand, had better have a real good story for not answering the fucking phone.

He could feel a slight buzz coming on from the six pack, but with the amount of drinking he had been doing since being released from prison the last time, it took far more than six beers to get much started.

A few moments later an eighteen wheeler rumbled in to the lot and stopped only 20 or 30 feet away. The exhaust from the engine was so loud he could barely hear the phone ring; a few seconds later another car pulled in behind the tractor-trailer and honked. His frustration level grew and he slammed the phone down again. Just as he did he twisted in the booth and jolts of pain ran up and down his spine. Dragging that 275 pound man 30 or 40 feet up the hill where he buried him had damaged something. He was sure of it.

More and more cars came and went as he stood in the phone booth, watching. He just needed to get the fuck out of there and rest in a bed or go to a medical clinic; something. He dialed Sharon one more time and still, no answer. He took a deep breath and pulled the quarters from the coin box below and dropped them in the top of the phone. The dial tone blazed in his ear as he thought about what the hell he would tell Jody- and

337

further- what he was gong to say to Sharon when he finally got back to their apartment. Reluctantly, he dialed his sister.

"Hey, it's me," Phil said in to the phone.

Something about the familiar sound of his sister's voice made him smile.

"Phil?.....uh, hi, Where are you?" Jody began; sounding somewhat shocked to hear from him.

"It's a long story. I don't want to talk about it right now. Have you heard from Sharon?" he asked as he lit another cigarette.

Jody didn't want Phil to know that she knew what had happened, she was scared for her brother and wanted the best for him, and she knew he was in trouble, bad.

"No....I thought she was with you?" Jody answered.

"Eeehhh.....not right now," Phil said.

"What's going on? Where is Sharon at?" Jody asked.

Phil sighed.

"I really can't say right now. I just need you to call Sharon and see if you can get a hold of her. Tell her to answer the damn phone."

"Are you guys ok? Where are you?" she asked again.

"Look, its better if I just don't tell you right now. Will you trust me for once? Just get a hold of Sharon and tell her I am going to call back at eleven, alright? Please?" Phil begged.

"Alright, alright; I'll call her. If I can't get a hold of her call me back, Ok?" Jody asked.

Phil hung up the phone and turned to go back in to the convenience store. A few minutes later he returned to the phone booth and dialed Sharon again.

No answer.

He was becoming more and more irritated; it was almost eleven o'clock.

Maybe she was making a run to the storage unit.

The beers were wearing off and his back was already starting to throb again; he reached in to the pocket of his vest and took six more Nuprins. By eleven o'clock the truck stop was churning with activity. Cars were even beginning to line up while waiting for gas. He thought he might even be able to hitch a ride back to Issaquah and then hitchhike up the hill to the apartment; it was only 30-40 minutes away. He hadn't seen television in three nights now, he had no idea if they may have already known who he was and were now looking for him. But, he thought, if they knew who he was by now, they would have been at the apartment and answered the phone; it wouldn't be just sitting there, empty.

338

At 11:20 he dialed Jody again hoping she would just come and pick him up. He should have never gone in to the fucking woods, he thought.

"Did you find Sharon?" he asked when Jody picked up the phone.

"No, not yet. I called her but it just rings. *Where are you at, Phil?*" Jody asked again.

"I'm up at Edgewick, camping," he answered.

"Edgewick? You mean by North Bend? I thought you and Sharon had gone to Moses Lake?" Jody asked.

"It doesn't matter right now. I'll tell you about it later; my fucking back is killing me and I need to go to a doctor or something. I don't know. I can't get a hold of Sharon-"

"Phil, are you alright?" Jody asked.

"Yeah, why? I mean…, my fucking back is killing me…, why?" Phil asked nervously.

"Well, when did you last see Sharon?" Jody questioned.

"It doesn't fucking matter!" Phil yelled and hung up the phone.

Jody stopped abruptly and slowly set the receiver down. She looked at the King County Officer who had arrived at her house in Issaquah a few minutes earlier.

"He hung up," she confirmed.

"So he is at Edgewick? Right now? What else did he say?" the officer asked Jody.

"He is there, yes. He's in a lot of pain, his back hurts. Look, I can get him to turn himself in if you just let me talk to him," Jody pleaded.

"With a murder one suspect ma'am, I'm sorry. But if you tip him off in anyway that we are here or that we know, you could be aiding a fugitive, do you understand?" the officer replied.

"But, please! I just don't want him to-" Jody argued.

"I understand, we should be able to get him without incident, but if he resists- well," The officer continued.

Jody glanced at her husband. He shook his head and went downstairs to keep their children occupied.

"If he calls back, just try and keep him on the phone. DO NOT TRY AND TIP HIM in any way. Is that CLEAR?" the officer reminded her.

A few minutes later the phone rang again.

"I'm sorry. I just-" Phil began.

"If you need me to come get you, I will. I have to do a couple things first-"

"I need you to get a hold of Sharon! I'll tell you all about it later. Can you just call Sharon for me, please?" Phil asked.

"I'll try her again. Just wait right there- call me back in twenty minutes or so," Jody said.

"Twenty minutes?" Phil asked.

"I'll try her again- if I can't get her then I will come and get you, ok?" Jody replied.

"Sure- that works," Phil answered and hung up the phone.

He was sick of this little truck stop already.

Jody looked up at the officer again.

"Very good. Now, when he calls back, we really need you to keep him on the phone," the officer said.

The officer turned and went in to the living room to radio back to dispatch the status of the suspect. He sat next to Jody at the kitchen table for another hour. Phil called a number of times to see if Jody had found Sharon yet and each time he quickly got off the phone. It was going to be difficult for Jody to keep him on the phone without him knowing something was going on.

At 12:10 King County Police officers along with Washington State Patrol Troopers began assembling near North Bend. WSP Lieutenant Gary Trunkey took charge of the scene. King County Police Major Jack Beard lived across the lake from my mother and Rich and actually served on the Lake Margaret Community Board with Rich. When he heard of the impending arrest across his scanner, he immediately headed for North Bend.

At 12:15, Lt. Trunkey and Trooper Ed Holloway drove past the convenience store in an unmarked car. A few hundred feet past the store, another officer parked his patrol vehicle and circled back on foot in the woods to the east of the store across the street. He took up a position where he could watch Phil using the phone. Trunkey and Holloway returned to the store and parked behind the service station shop to the west of the store and out of site. Minutes later two King County Officers who had parked their patrols out of site down the road moved in and joined Lt. Trunkey and Trooper Holloway.

From this vantage point they observed Phil moving in and out of the store numerous times. They had been informed by Snohomish County Detectives that he often carried a green duffel bag with him and in that duffel bag, most likely, was a sawed off double barrel shotgun. As Lt. Trunkey watched Phil through his binoculars he could not see the green duffel bag.

An hour after Lt. Trunkey had taken up a position west of the service station; Major Jack Beard arrived on the scene in a civilian car borrowed for the arrest. Saturday afternoon meant the mini-mart was going to continue to be very busy. Customers and cars flooded in and out of the truck stop. Officers became very nervous about approaching Phil to make an arrest and worried the situation could elevate at any moment.

340

Somehow, they had to clear out the station in order to minimize the risk to innocent bystanders.

At around 1:25 the Washington State Patrol closed down both off-ramps leading to Edgewick road. This way traffic could leave, but no one could get in. As busy as the station was, the sudden lack of incoming traffic might tip Phil that something was up.

A few minutes later Phil came out of the convenience store and entered the phone booth again. Lt. Trunkey and Major Beard wanted to confirm that the man they were observing in the dark sweat pants and blue vest wearing a baseball cap was indeed the man they were after. The traffic flowing in to the mini-mart had suddenly stopped as they shut down the off-ramps from I-90 but dozens of motorists still loitered around the area. As Phil was on the phone to his sister, officers at Jody's house kept in radio contact with Major Beard and confirmed he was in the phone booth at that exact moment.

They were confident they had their man.

Major Beard and Lt. Trunkey drove the civilian car Beard had brought with him, past Phil at the phone booth. Inside the mini-mart they could see dozens of customers milling around and waiting at the cash register. They had to minimize the risk to the customers somehow. They pulled the car around the back of the mini-mart out of sight and radioed King County dispatch to call the mini-mart and have them lock the doors in case Phil tried to go inside and take hostages.

Around the front of the mini-mart, Phil hung up the phone and *went back inside* to wait for Jody to come and pick him up.

Inside, the phone rang.

"Ken's Truck Town, this is Joyce," she politely answered.

"Hi Joyce, please do not make any visible reaction to this phone call. This is the King County Police. This is not a joke or a prank."

"Uh...okay...." Joyce answered and peered around the store.

"Everything is okay, I need you to stay calm, I want you to go over to the front of the store and lock your front doors. We have the area surrounded and we are about to make an arrest on someone. Make sure you just stay calm and do that for me. Ok?" the voice said.

"Uhhh....sure," Joyce quietly responded and hung up the phone.

Joyce was stunned. At first she was extremely nervous, but it seemed kind of surreal.

"That was the police," she whispered.

"We're supposed to quietly lock the front doors."

"What?" Shelley asked.

"Apparently the place is surrounded. I don't know," Joyce answered.

Joyce Malone and Shelley Van Zandt had worked together in the convenience store of the truck stop for some time now. Saturday's were pretty busy times. Customers came and went all morning using the restrooms, pre-paying for gas and feeding hungry kids. But this was a first.

Shelley and Joyce moved to the front windows and looked outside. They could not see a police car or officer anywhere.

Was this a joke?

In the back of the store Phil wandered amongst the souvenir clothing racks. It was warm in the store and he thought it was funny how he sometimes took the little things, like heat, for granted.

Shelly moved over and locked the front doors.

They had no idea Phil was now inside the store.

Traffic to the mini-mart had been shut down for nearly ten minutes but a few customers had loitered near their rigs before heading inside. As Trunkey and Beard cam around the corner where they could now see the phone booth, Phil was gone.

Shit!

"Get them back on the phone and have them *unlock* those doors, *now!*" Beard commanded.

Inside a woman who had just paid for gas went toward the front door. As she pushed on the door she came to a sudden stop.

"Um, excuse me....*this door is locked,*" she exclaimed as she stared over at Shelley and Joyce.

"It will just be a minute," Joyce argued not really knowing what to say.

She and Shelley pressed their faces toward the windows of the store to see if they could catch any of the impending action outside. Again, they didn't see anything.

In the back of the store Phil twisted and rotated his hips as he stood about the circular racks of sweatshirts, t-shirts and hoodies. Still, nothing seemed to line the discs up to relieve the pressure.

"Uh....*you need to unlock this door. My kids are in my car!*" the woman standing at the door started to raise her voice.

Shelley and Joyce still had no idea Phil was inside the store and just as Joyce was going to explain that a man was about to be arrested, the phone rang again.

"Ken's Truck town, this is Joyce," she answered.

"Joyce, this is King County Police again, I need you to very calmly go unlock the front doors right away," the voice said.

"Is he-"

"Just go do it, right now please," the voice cut her off.

Joyce hung up the phone and grabbed her keys. Nervously she gazed around the store and wondered what the hell was going on. Should she get everyone out of the store?

Should she leave the store?

Phil meandered toward the front. He figured it would take Jody about 30-40 minutes to get here. He wasn't sure what he should even tell her. Out front he noticed a woman loitering in front of the doors and sounding somewhat irritated. It was nearly 1:40 now and if Sharon was dropping stuff off at the storage unit she would most likely be back by now. He decided he would give her another call before Jody showed up.

Outside he noticed the traffic at the mini-mart had finally begun to slow down. For the first time in a couple of hours the gas island was completely empty. He dropped a couple of quarters in the phone and dialed Sharon again. As he put the receiver up to his ear he turned to look behind him. A middle aged man was walking toward him from the service station across the parking lot. He turned and faced the phone as the ringing continued while he reached in to grab his smokes from his vest pocket. Just as he turned to look back at the service station the man he saw walking toward him walked right past the doors and was reaching in to his coat. Phil stared and couldn't believe his eyes as the man, now only ten feet away pulled a gun from his jacket and pointed it right at him.

"SHOW ME YOUR HANDS! NOW!" Major Beard yelled.

Lieutenant Trunkey came running around the corner from the other direction with his pistol drawn and trained right at Phil. For a second he just stared blankly, stunned. In his ear, the phone kept ringing.

"GET DOWN! NOW!...NOW!...GET DOWN!!!"

In an instant two King County Police cars and two Washington State Patrol cars ripped in to the parking lot and uniformed officers began piling out of their cars, all with guns drawn.

Phil dropped the receiver and put his hands slowly up.

From across the street he saw two more officers come running in; a couple of unmarked cars raced in to the lot and jammed on their brakes.

"LAY DOWN! RIGHT NOW!" Major Beard yelled at him again.

He crouched down a little and slowly walked toward Phil.

Phil stepped out of the booth with his hands still in the air. For a second he thought he could run, but he knew they would shoot him. A wide grin started to creep across his face.

He was the star of the show.

He could hear them yelling to lie down but the enormity of the situation had overcome him, he just stood there, watching, *and smiling*.

Behind him, Lt. Trunkey holstered his weapon and rushed in behind Phil and tackled him to the ground. Phil wasn't expecting to be taken down and he cried out in pain as Trunkey knocked him to the asphalt. With his knee in the small of Phil's back Major Beard jumped in and pulled Phil's arms behind his back and handcuffed him.

Phil lay face down on the asphalt with his arms cuffed behind his back. Officers immediately rushed in to the store to search for the green duffel bag or Phil's shotgun.

"Can I sit up? My back—it's fucked up," Phil pled with Major Beard and who just looked at him and said nothing.

Lt. Trunkey asked Trooper Phillips to read Phil his rights. Trooper Phillips knelt down and read Phil his rights while Phil groaned and struggled in pain. After he was done the trooper lifted Phil to his feet and placed him in the back of Officer Craig Wolf's patrol car.

A few minutes later Sgt. Richard Baranzini climbed in to the front seat of the patrol car Phil was sitting in.

"Did you receive your Miranda rights?" he asked through the plexiglass slider.

Phil appeared to be in pain as he shifted and struggled to get comfortable with his arms cuffed behind him. He bit his lip and winced in pain.

"Yeah."

"Is there anything you want repeated?" Sgt. Baranzini asked.

"No," he grimaced.

"Would you like to talk to us?" Baranzini asked.

"What about?" Phil whispered in pain.

"We need to find your camp and your belongings," Baranzini answered.

"Yeah, sure. You take a right up there and go down the Middlefork Road. Across the big concrete bridge and then a few miles past the little wooden bridge the road bends to the left. You'll see some big rocks along the road its back in the woods about 50 yards," Phil struggled.

"Is there anything in that camp that's going to harm my officers? Guns, knives, explosives?

"The shotgun is in the tent. They should be careful though, it is loaded," Phil informed him.

Baranzini exited the patrol car and conversed with the other officers asking if they were familiar with where Phil described his camp. A few minutes later he got back in to the patrol car.

"Do you think you could put these cuffs up front? My back is really sore," Phil asked.

"No," Baranzini answered.

Phil sighed.

"The faster we get this done, the sooner we can get you to Snohomish County and the sooner those cuffs will come off," Baranzini continued.

"Yeah, alright. What do you want to know?" Phil asked.

"Did you bring anything with you from the camp?"

"No."

"So we won't find anything in the store, we don't need to worry about a gun stashed or something that some kid is going to find?" Baranzini asked.

"No, I didn't bring anything from the camp."

"Well, how about you just show us where the camp is?" Baranzini asked.

"If that gets this done sooner, then sure, whatever," Phil answered.

After the arrest the State Patrol re-opened the off-ramp and the traffic streamed in to the mini-mart. Many of the officers now cleared the scene as they drove up the Middlefork Road to locate Phil's camp.

Detective Hinds was still in Darrington processing the murder scene so Detective Pince and Detective Gray were called to the scene of the arrest to transfer Phil to Snohomish County Jail.

Fifteen minutes up the Middlefork road Phil indicated where the camp was. Through the trees they could see the blue tent from the road. A King County K-9 unit joined the other officers processing the scene. A few minutes after showing officers where the camp was, Phil was transported to the Washington State Patrol Office in North Bend. After waiting a few hours to obtain a search warrant for his camp, Phil was finally booked in to Snohomish County Jail having been charged with first degree murder.

He knew how this went: They were going to charge him with the highest crime they could, try and scare him in to confessing, then, when they figured out they had no real evidence, his lawyer would plead him down to a lesser crime. He'd probably lose his parole and go back to prison. But like last time, he'd probably end up with less time than he had to do before he got paroled.

He'd been here before.

He'd served his fucking country.

32

For the first time in almost two weeks, Mom was able to try and go to sleep without the fear of the phone ringing. Soon she was to go about the task of holding a memorial service for Rich. But today, today she was done.

Her friends were staying at the house to field all of the calls that would come pouring in. The news story the night before went out on all four local news networks at five, six thirty and eleven. Sunday morning the Seattle Times had already put together a full page spread on the story. Mom wanted to get the memorial over with as soon as possible and then begin the struggle to move forward in her life without Rich.

Still in her pajamas trying to read, she tried to take her mind off the nightmare that unfolded in her peaceful life. One day she was shopping for baby clothes with her daughter and coordinating new carpet downstairs. And the next, a never ending descent into the unknown.

She could hear the phone ringing and her friends were fielding calls; then five or ten minutes later it would ring again. She needed a day away, so she asked her friends to screen them.

Surprisingly, at about 2:30 PM, one of her friends tapped on her door softly.

"Karen, are you awake?" she asked softly.

"Yeah, I am just reading, trying to get my mind away from it, from all of it," Mom answered.

"Well, I know you don't want to take any calls, but there is a man on the phone who really wants to *apologize* to you."

"Apologize?" Mom asked, "Who is it?"

"I don't know but he said he wishes he could have done more, when this, Phil or whatever his name is, he killed his friend, only three or four miles from where it happened with Rich," the woman answered.

Killed his friend? Three or four miles from where he killed Rich?

Mom rose up out of the bed. She was tired and worn out and in no mood to tell and retell the story of what had happened to Rich, there was time for that, later; but she was very interested in who might be on the phone. She made her way out of her bedroom and down the hall to her office.

"Hello," she said, "This is Karen."

"Hi Karen, I just wanted to call and say how sorry I am about your husband," a middle aged man spoke on the other end.

"Who are you?" she asked.

"Well, Phil Hillman, that's his name; Phil Hillman killed my uncle 16 years ago. Right up near the same place as he—as your husband," he answered.

"I heard he was in the system before, but, what happened?" Mom asked, listening intently.

"From what I understand, this guy and his friend had gone camping up there outside of Darrington. It was in July, July of 1974; about a year after this guy got out of the Army and back from Vietnam...."

Mother was stunned. She could hardly believe what she was hearing. An elderly man named Newton Thomas, had been killed by the same man now accused of killing Rich only 16 years earlier and it happened less than four miles from where he killed Rich. She heard from Major Jack Beard the night before, that the man they arrested at the truck stop had been in the system before, but she did not hear the details.

How could this man have been let out of prison?

After listening to the man recount the details from Newton Thomas' murder, Mom was shocked. The fact that the man who killed Rich had killed before was utterly incomprehensible to her. After enduring eleven days of torturous pain and exhaustion, the revelation of the fact that this man was not still in prison folded itself into a formidable mixture of anger and bargaining. She wanted to call Detective Hinds and find out the details of this man, but she was too exhausted. It could wait a day or two; she needed to get her strength back.

She lay back down in bed and tried to read, anything to sidetrack her wandering thoughts. She had been offered tranquilizers and other types of stress relieving or sleep medication but she was hoping to just force it from her mind, at least for a little while.

An hour later she was asked if she would take another call. She rose out of bed as she was unable to sleep anyway. The young man on the other end of the phone was James Sylte. He offered his condolences to Mom and began crying on the phone with her. Mom sat and listened as he recounted his story of how Phil had tried to kill him seven and a half years earlier. Over and over he expressed to Mom his shock that they had ever let him out.

They let him out twice?

In many ways, it mattered not that Rich's killer had killed one man before or a hundred. The senselessness was still the same. But after hearing that the State of Washington had let this man out of prison, not once; but *twice?* Mom was infuriated. If the State had simply required him to serve his sentence—even after giving him the first chance in 1982—Rich would not have been killed by Phillip Hillman on May 2, 1990.

Mom did not yet know how or why this man had been let out of prison twice before, but she vowed at that moment that she was going to do everything in her power to make sure he never walked free again.

*   *   *

On Wednesday, May 16, 1990; Phil was officially charged with First Degree Murder and held on $500,000 bail. Detectives and prosecutors now had to work together to prepare for a trial and eventually the sentencing phase. His attorney's believed that what he had done to Rich was so similar to what he had done to Newton Thomas in 1974, that this was clearly only worthy of a murder in the second degree conviction. Under the Sentencing Reform Act sentencing guidelines Phil would most likely be sentenced to 20-25 years and would be eligible for parole again in as little as 13-15 years.

The prosecution had a slightly different take on the matter.

Although Phil was initially charged with first degree murder, detectives began to investigate whether any aggravating circumstances existed which could be used to upgrade the charge to aggravated first degree murder. This charge carried two possible sentences in Washington State; life in prison without the possibility of parole or the death penalty.

Detectives knew immediately after Sharon had come forward to confess and provided them with his name that Phil had previous violent convictions on his record. After reading both case files, detectives

348

concluded if there ever was a case where life without parole or the death penalty was warranted, they believed strongly, this was one.

However, the previous crimes could not be used to *convict* Phil; the circumstances surrounding the previous cases would certainly be showcased during the sentencing phase if Phil was convicted; but in order to get that conviction, it had to be made on the facts of *this case*, and how a jury would view them.

Thus, in order for prosecutors to seek the death penalty in this case, they had to convict Phil of aggravated first degree murder. In order for the murder to be prosecuted as aggravated first degree murder rather than just first degree murder, one of a number of conditions outlined in the statutes needed to be present.

In this case, the condition which could most likely elevate the murder to 'aggravated' was if the murder was committed to facilitate the commission or cover up of another felony such as rape or robbery. It seemed prosecutors could clearly argue that Phil killed Rich in order to steal his Mustang. The first motive Sharon offered up when questioned, was that Phil did it 'for the car'.

Detectives now had three main areas of focus in this case. First, they had to solidify the first degree murder case they had by processing the evidence already collected. Second, they set about the task of investigating whether or not any aggravating circumstances existed in the case so that the charge could be upgraded. And third, they needed to prepare for the penalty and sentencing phase of the case by investigating the past crimes and interviewing friends, family and associates of Phil.

Additionally, detectives had to overcome 'spousal privilege'. Spousal privilege protects a person from testimony by their spouse. However, if a crime is committed *against the spouse*, then the privilege becomes weaker. Based upon her statement, it appeared that Phil had threatened Sharon with the shotgun and if detectives could make those charges stick, it could make it easier for a judge to allow her to testify. Without her testimony, aggravated first degree murder would be nearly impossible to prove.

The first place to start looking was at Phil and Sharon's apartment.

Detective Hinds along with Detective John Gray pulled in to the apartment complex in Pine Lake to execute a search warrant on Phil's truck and their apartment.

It was Friday, May 18, 1990.

Thirty minutes to the northeast at Cherry Valley Elementary School in Duvall, my mother and over 300 hundred of Rich's friends, family and colleagues filled the school gymnasium in memory of Rich. Mom's first grand-child, Joshua, had been born the night before.

Murder myself, Murder I am.

The Connemara apartments in Pine Lake was a relatively new complex consisting of a scattering of three story, 12 unit buildings. Phil and Sharon lived in unit # F-104. The 1990 Ford Ranger was parked out front of the unit as Sharon told them it would be.

The Detectives were looking for Rich's brief case, cellular phone or the key's to Rich's Mustang. These things could be used to show that Phil killed Rich to steal these items and thus, the murder would be 'aggravated.' Additionally, Sharon had given them permission to seize whatever items they felt were needed to tie Phil to the murder. Sharon provided them with a set of keys to the apartment.

Inside the one-bedroom abode, they found a lone table in the entryway with a rolled up newspaper and a cactus plant. The bathroom was directly across from the front door. To the right, the hallway led to the lone bedroom. Down the hall to the left, the living room was littered with stacks of empty produce boxes and liquor boxes. It was clear someone was preparing to move out. A small leather sofa sat covered in folded bedding and pillows next to a dark brown entertainment center. A few pictures were still hung on the walls and a large, white, wooden footlocker lay on the floor in front of the sofa.

Beneath a scattering of papers, candles and trash bags a white lace table cloth covered the dining room table. A pair of painted gold sculpted deer stood watch over the detectives. A carton of Winston Ultralights and a Bible were also found on the table. A thin, wrinkled, green paper about half the size of a standard sheet caught Detective Hinds eye.

He picked up the document and held it up to read it. It was dated May 3, 1990.

It was the traffic ticket.

Next to the ticket he also found an accident report although the date had not been entered. The accident report indicated that at some point Phil had a 1976 Ford Torino and had driven it off the road. Hinds wasn't sure if it had anything to do with the case but he took it in to evidence anyway. Hinds then went through a stack of unopened mail.

He moved in to the kitchen and found the cupboards mostly empty. No car phone handset, no keys, no briefcase.

Hinds moved in to the bedroom and found a small dresser with a battery powered lamp and a white ceramic box with credit card slips and business cards inside of it. Inside the ceramic box he found a credit card slip dated May 1 from a Unocal in Arlington. Arlington was only a short drive from Darrington. Another credit card slip was dated May 3, 1990 and was charged at Pine Tree Services in Darrington. It was the receipt for towing out the truck after the murder. Hinds took both of these in to evidence as well.

The drawers of the dresser were still filled with clothes along with boxes of shotgun shells and shotgun shells lying loose in the drawers.

On top of the dresser Hinds found a note written to Phil and signed by Sharon. It was very apparent that Phil's struggles with alcohol were well known by Sharon long before they went in to the woods with a shotgun, beer, cherry wine coolers, whiskey and vodka.

Phil,

Your marriage is going to be in a lot worse shape than your alcoholism & broken trucks- if you don't get your act together. You seem to feel I am exaggerating the problem- as you've pointed out your work hasn't suffered as to date. It's only a matter of time before your habit will affect your work, and the trust in our marriage has already been destroyed.

I feel you are clearly responsible for our troubles- yes you have an addiction to alcohol- but you also have a choice. These disasters that continue are going to end now before tragity (sic) has the last say.

In a drunken stupper (sic) you are going to kill yourself or some poor undeserving sole (sic) in a (sic) accident. Tonight you have already put another dent in the truck. You come home so drunk you couldn't even open the front door. I had to open it for you- & your (sic) driving –great- you are a fool.

I can't continue to live on the edge. You are thinking only of yourself & your god dam (sic) addiction.

If you can't beat this problem then think of getting help. You have Insurance now, check into a program so you can get dryed (sic) out.

I love you very much & I know you know this & I will support your sobriety- but not your addiction. Love is a complex process requiring hard work. I know you Phil & I know you want to do the right thing- you are strong & have great courage- please continue to fight for us.

I know you have today & tomorrow off- I will not be here for you today- I want you to consider your life and the direction you choose to go. I am taking the truck not to be mean but to save the truck from further damage in case you choose to drink.

Love,
Sharon

P.S. I see you also ran over the grass in front of our apt. great. (sic)

The date for delivery on the 1990 Ranger was February 12, 1990; Hinds concluded this letter was written sometime in the last couple of months at the very least. *Definitely after* his parole revocation hearing in February of 1989 in which Sharon promised his Community Corrections Officer Marsha Meadows, that she would *"not tolerate relapses."*

Hinds collected a number of business cards, deposit records and pay stubs and put them in to evidence. After a thorough and complete search of the apartment they concluded the briefcase, keys and car phone handset were not in the apartment. Detective Gray suggested he go to the apartment management office and see if Sharon or Phil had given written notice to vacate the apartment. Hinds moved outside to photograph and search the Ford Ranger.

A few minutes later, Gray showed up with a copy of a 'Notice to Vacate' dated May 10, 1990 and signed by Sharon Hillman.

After they finished processing the Ranger they packed up and headed back to Everett. The line-up was to occur at around 2:00 PM.

* * *

Putting a suspect in front of witnesses and asking witnesses to pick the suspect out of a group of six men of similar build and facial features was always a risky business.

Memory is a funny thing.

Some people involved in crimes remember the most insignificant and seemingly minute details: the color of someone's shoe laces or the fact that a thread was coming undone from a cheaply made windbreaker; yet they can't remember the persons face.

Sometimes they don't want to.

Other times they are scared to.

As soon as a key witness fails to positively identify an assailant defense attorneys begin ripping flesh off the witness's memory of events like sharks in a blood soaked sea.

Other witnesses are positive they have identified the suspect without a doubt. Turns out, they identified an off duty police detective or some dirt bag who was in jail at the time of the crime for letting his 15 year old step-son have a few too many scoops of old-time discipline. Then the defense attorneys start ripping chunks of flesh off *the entire case.*

Despite the compelling and overwhelming evidence in any given case, a witness who wrongly identifies a suspect will stick in a jury members mind more than a guy's wife who states she saw him kill a man with two shotgun blasts at less than ten yards.

352

And no one was certain Sharon wouldn't go back the other way between now and the trial; if she was even *allowed* to testify. It was one thing to put him in prison for the next 20-30 years with his wife taking the stand and looking him and the jury in the eyes and telling them she watched him pull the trigger. It was another thing to ask her why she's changing her statement and listen to her claims of police misconduct and persuasion and how she was scared and now she wasn't sure. They needed to have some insurance just in case a plea deal wasn't worked out and this went to trial.

But, everyone expected him to deal. He had made a deal before. In fact, the similarities to the 1974 murder were uncanny. Double barreled shotgun, alcohol, seemingly unprovoked victim, unknowing accomplice and most striking- only four miles away from where he had gunned down Rich.

Who says they don't always return to the scene of the crime?

At 2:00 PM Detective George Wilkins and Detective John Hinds entered the Snohomish County Jail to pick out participants in the line-up. It seemed easy but sometimes guys can't help but laugh or sometimes they try to look too serious and the line-up can be tainted. In most cases, guys may have done it before and it beat sitting around a concrete room with 20 or 30 other guys that have been telling the same stories over and over for who knows how many months.

Detective Hinds had the guards bring Phil to the doorway of his cell so he could check if he had shaved his mustache or not.

Hinds and Wilkins then began walking through the north wing of the 3rd floor to pick suitable line mates. Lawrence Faria was picked first. He was similar in build, quite a bit younger, but he didn't look it. He had a thick dark mustache and his hair was somewhat darker than Phil's, but he would do. If Phil's attorney didn't like it he could ask for him to be removed. There was no point in over thinking this.

Next they selected Michael Chapel. He was nearly the same age as the killer but a little thinner. His hair color was similar but somewhat longer. A number of the witnesses described the killers hair as being short, almost cropped into a military style cut, but again, if the lawyers didn't like it they could replace him.

After looking through the glass for a good five to ten minutes longer the detectives moved down the hall and into the service elevator and went to the 2nd floor. In the south wing they pulled Richard Clark. He was younger, almost the same age as the first line mate. He was much thinner and longer hair as well. His hair and mustache color was almost a perfect match.

Next, they selected Steven Blackburn and Robert Hurst from the work release unit. Just in case the lawyers objected to one of the choices, they also decided Detective Dallas Swank fit the description and would be made available as an alternate if needed. The inmates were transported to the line-up room in the basement of the Carnegie Building.

Phil, who was still complaining of severe back pain, was brought over in a wheelchair. Jail medical staff had cleared his medical condition and he was going to be returned to general population after the line up. Chairs were brought in so the line-up could be conducted from a sitting position and the wheelchair removed.

The seven chairs were placed along the wall and white cards about 11" by 14" were given to each inmate. Handwritten numbers from a wide black sharpie adorned the cards. In addition to Detectives Hinds and Wilkins, Detectives Brad Pince, Jeff Miller, Doug Pendergrass and Sgt. Tom Greene were present. Deputy Prosecuting Attorney Dave Kurtz was joined by one of Phil's attorneys.

Once the inmates and Detective Swank were seated, Phil's attorney asked that Steven Blackburn be excused. He then asked that Phil and Detective Swank switch positions so that Phil was in chair #3 and Detective Swank was in chair #4. After the line-up order was completed and the line-up deemed acceptable by the attorneys, the witnesses were moved into the lunch room to be instructed.

The first witness brought in to identify the suspect was Arlington resident Sandra Fink. She worked in a baby boutique in Darrington and on the morning of May 3, 1990 some time between 10:00 AM and 12 noon she believed a man fitting the description of the suspect was in the boutique. This would seem unlikely as Sharon claimed that at 10:00 AM on May 3, the day after the murder, he had just left their apartment in Issaquah to wash the Mustang. Further, he received the traffic ticket at approximately 12:43 PM nearly 80 miles to the south in Issaquah.

Her importance to the case was large however. In many cases, defense attorneys will argue that witnesses who may exonerate their clients are not brought forward enough, that police investigations are biased. Once police believe they have their guy, according to defense attorneys, they stop looking.

So here was a witness, who may have seen the suspect in Darrington between 10 AM and noon; if this were true then it seems unlikely he would have been driving the victim's car at 12:43 PM in Issaquah. The time to travel between Darrington and Issaquah is about two hours given the route the suspect's wife outlined in her statement.

In addition, 281 miles were recorded on the trip meter of the odometer. Rich was known to reset his trip meter whenever refueling. If this were the case and he reset it in Twisp on the morning of May 2, the route the Mustang traveled, Twisp to Darrington; up and back the Mountain loop highway down in to Issaquah the morning of May 3; back to Darrington to be in the boutique at 10 AM; back to Issaquah before 12:43 PM and back to Darrington that afternoon to be abandoned in the Serve-U grocery parking lot would have shown approximately 483 miles if the assumptions were true.

Given that detectives knew he probably wasn't in a baby boutique in Darrington on the morning of May 3, the chances she would actually identify the suspect were one in six. Even if she did by chance, pick the suspect, the mountain of evidence piling up against him would not be insurmountable.

Sandra requested that the members of the lineup say the phrase: "Do you have a garbage can?"

Once she was finished, she exited the line-up viewing room and filled out her identification sheet. She indicated that suspect #1 was in her boutique in Darrington on the morning of May 3, 1990 and that she was positive. Fortunately for suspect #1 (Michael Chapel); he was in jail during the 'baby boutique sighting.'

Next, tow truck driver John Fox Sr. entered the viewing room. He had written across the bottom of his identification sheet the words: "My wife said it was the Mt. Pugh trail."

As per instruction, each inmate would be instructed to recite these words in order. Detectives were fairly confident Mr. Fox could pick out the suspect as he had spent two or three hours with him.

Despite the fact they had signed credit card receipts it was important if it went to trial that Mr. Fox be able to positively place the suspect near the scene of the crime. Rich's body was buried under logs no less than 100 feet from where Phil's truck was towed out of a washout with the assistance of Mr. Fox; the day after the alleged murder.

It took John Fox less than ten seconds to identify the suspect. He even told detectives he did not need to hear any of them recite the words he had written; he was sure. He immediately exited the viewing room and filled out his identification sheet. He indicated inmate #3 (the suspect) was the man he helped tow out the night of May 3, 1990.

He was absolutely positive.

The next witness was King County Police Officer Jerry Hamilton. He was the officer who had written a ticket for no front license plate to someone driving Rich's Mustang on May 3 at about 12:43 PM on Eastlake Sammamish Parkway just north of Issaquah, where the suspect resided. The person driving the vehicle provided a driver's license matching the suspects name and the officer stated the picture on the license matched the person driving the car. Moreover, the signature on the ticket matched the signature provided by the suspect during booking. Officer Hamilton's identification of the suspect would help but the signature on the ticket, and the match to the drivers' license photo on the day of the ticket would more than likely convince any jury he was driving the car.

Officer Hamilton took his time and exited the viewing room. Upon filling out his identification sheet he had indicated inmate #4 (Detective Dallas Swank) was the person he gave the ticket to.

With one more witness to go, detectives were a little nervous. Jessica Knoop had seen a man get out of Rich's Mustang on the afternoon of May 3 in the Serve- U grocery store parking lot. She had also provided a description to a police sketch artist which was prominently displayed throughout the Seattle area news media. She entered the viewing room and carefully looked the suspects over. In a few minutes she exited and positively identified inmate #3 (the suspect) as the man she saw exit the Mustang in the grocery store parking lot.

The line-up went better than expected for the prosecutors. No major hang ups. Sandra Fink had not put the suspect in Darrington at the wrong time and although the case may have been stronger if Officer Hamilton had identified the suspect, it would not be a major obstacle as he interacted with dozens of drivers each day.

33

Prosecutors routinely meet with victim's family members when discussing the type and extent of penalty for these kinds of crimes. Although ultimately, prosecutors are forced to make the final decision on whether to seek capital punishment or not, the feelings and beliefs of the victim's family can weigh heavily on their decisions.

On May 22, 1990 Mom went to the Snohomish County Courthouse to meet with prosecutors and find out what would happen to the man who had taken her husband from her. She immediately asked what Phil had said had happened.

Detectives informed her that he had not said anything, under advisement from counsel.

The first thing detectives did, was to explain to Mom what evidence they had that explained what had happened to Rich.

They had a ticket Phil received less than 12 hours after Rich went missing. They had a witness (Jessica Knoop) who saw Phil park and abandon Rich's car; another witness (John Fox) who could place Phil less than 100 feet from where Rich's body was recovered. And most importantly, they had a witness (Sharon Hillman) who observed the killing and was with the suspect for seven days after as he attempted to elude law enforcement, although there would be a number of questions as to whether or not the defendant could block her from testifying due to spousal privilege.

Empty shell casings recovered at the scene of the murder were matched to the shotgun recovered from Phil's camp after his arrest. Dog hairs recovered from Rich's Mustang were consistent with hair samples taken from the dog found at the suspect's apartment. The prosecution could prove that he had taken a leave of absence from work and detectives had recovered the written notification that he was moving out of his apartment, although it was only signed by Sharon. This was not a case of an accidental shooting—this man was doing everything in his power to conceal the crime after he had done it.

In their opinion, the evidence added up to murder in the first degree; and if they found evidence of an aggravating circumstance then they would upgrade the charge. Phil's defense was arguing that no premeditation existed in this case. Premeditation is a key component in a first degree murder charge. Without premeditation, the charge would drop to second degree murder.

In addition, they cautioned my mother, as solid as the case seemed, the only witnesses to the crime were Phil and Sharon. A trial would not be for some months and it was likely the defense would come up with some very compelling arguments that a jury just might believe.

The defendant could argue that Rich loaned Phil the car before he killed him and that Phil had killed him for 'other' reasons. Additionally, it was very easy for attorneys to get statements thrown out that were made by witnesses early on in an investigation. Witnesses change their minds; remember things differently when under stress and the like. And it was also possible Phil could utilize the law which prohibits a spouse from testifying against them.

They could change their story and claim self-defense—that Rich had attacked Sharon; and Phil was merely defending his wife. When faced with the death penalty, defendants are compelled to try everything and anything the lawyer's advise.

When asked directly by prosecutors how she felt about the death penalty, my mother told them that she was not advocating for or against such measures.

That was truly, up to a jury to decide.

Detectives who worked the case, however, firmly believed capital punishment was in order in this case. He had killed before, and tried to kill again; those facts could not be used during the trial phase; in other words, the previous murder could not be introduced to the jury as evidence that he probably committed this murder as well. But, these facts could be brought up at sentencing, and detectives believed they had a very strong case and that once a jury convicted him and then subsequently became aware of his violent past, they would choose the ultimate penalty.

He had killed a man 16 years earlier and nearly killed another man eight years earlier. Both times he had promised officials responsible for his early release from prison that he would not drink alcohol. Doctors who treated Phil warned the State of Washington officials that he had to stay alcohol free.

At this point in the investigation, prosecutors needed to establish premeditation in order to maintain the first degree murder charge; and they needed to prove that the murder was committed to steal the car.

Detective's and investigators continued to press Sharon for more facts from the case. Her immunity was based upon her cooperation and her telling the complete truth. Additionally, they began to interview those around Phil as to what they may or may not have known.

After the prosecutors and detectives finished going over the facts of the case with my mother, she was not convinced the whole story was being told. A number of details did not add up. Details, which only those who knew Rich, would know.

In her interview with police, Sharon maintained that the murder took place some time after 7:00 PM. Mom explained to detectives very clearly that Rich was supposed to be home by 4:00 PM *at the latest*. She made this very clear in the missing person report she filed as well as in numerous conversations with Detective Hinds *long before Sharon came forward*. This meant that Rich would have been driving through Darrington around 2:00 or 2:30 PM in order to be home in Duvall by 4:00 PM. If he were any later than that he would have 100% without a doubt, stopped and called her or paged her.

Appointments and punctuality were one of the most important parts of Rich's character. He firmly believed that you should do as you say and say as you do. If circumstances beyond your control dictate that you are going to be late to an appointment or other commitment, the right thing to do is call as soon as you know you are going to be late. He preached this and *he lived it*. Mom told detectives that they could ask dozens and dozens of friends, colleagues and customers if any of them could name even one time in which Rich was going to be more than ten or 15 minutes late and did not call to inform them he was running late. Mom said they would not be able to find a single incident.

Not one.

Additionally, Mom pointed out that based on the credit card slip Tim and I had recovered in Twisp; Rich was in Twisp at 6:30 AM. The drive from Twisp to Darrington is about 90 minutes to two hours. Assuming he may have stopped along the way to look at some of the scenic points along the route, he should have been in Darrington by 9:30 or 10:00 AM. It is even possible he stopped for breakfast in either Twisp or Darrington although no record or witnesses indicate this, but *even if* he did stop for breakfast and it took an hour, this still puts him in Darrington at the latest plausible time of 11:00 AM or noon. There is no plausible scenario whereby Rich would have been in Darrington at 6:30 PM or 7:00 PM and *not have called her, paged her or left her a message that he was going to be later than 4:00 PM.*

Detectives understood what she was trying to say and they agreed with her that at this point, just the fact that he was in Twisp at 6:30 AM and then supposedly murdered more than 12 hours later when the trip from Twisp to the murder scene was less than a two hour drive, did not make sense to detectives either.

They reminded Mom that they could only present facts they could prove and that of the three people who will ever truly know what happened, one was given immunity to avoid being prosecuted as an accessory to murder based on her telling of the complete truth; another was going to be on trial for murder and the third, was dead.

The second detail that bothered Mom was that Sharon claimed Rich offered to help pull the truck out with his Mustang. This was preposterous in Mom's opinion.

Rich kept that car in immaculate condition. He took it through the car wash every chance he got and kept it parked in the garage at their house in Lake Margaret. He *would never* have offered to back the Mustang up a logging road and attach a chain or tow strap to it in an attempt to get a truck unstuck. This was another one of those scenarios, Mom pointed out, that detectives could ask everyone who knew Rich if he would *ever* use the Mustang to tow a vehicle. Again, Mom assured them that not a single person who knew Rich would find it plausible.

Lastly, Mom also found it troubling that Rich would have got out of his car and hiked 200 to 500 feet uphill when it was 'almost dark' to see if he could help 'push' the truck out. Although Rich was a very helpful and friendly man, he was a man of larger carriage and not in the most athletic of shape. By no means was he obese, but he was fairly overweight for his height. Having been with Rich in the woods four-wheeling, anyone who knew Rich would find it hard to believe that he would assert himself in such a physical way to help someone in their situation. He would have offered them a ride, he would have offered to call a tow truck – he would have facilitated getting them assistance in any way he could but he most likely *would not have done this himself.* He knew his own physical limitations and knew he would not be much help pushing a truck stuck in a washout.

These three details about Rich's character are things that only those who knew Rich would have known. They are also three very distinct characteristics that strangers, such as Phil and Sharon, would erroneously have made assumptions about.

Mom did not feel as though anyone in the office really understood what she was saying to them so she told them once again. Before she left she wanted to make three points very clear as they continued. In some ways, it seemed as though Mom had taken charge of this investigation. She was not going to go away quietly or without a fight.

First, most people have shown up late or not at all and failed to call at least once or twice.

Not Rich.

Second, a lot of people would use their car to pull someone out of a ditch or to get them unstuck in some fashion.

Rich would never have used his 1988 Mustang GT for such.

Third, most people would get out of their car and hike 500' to see if they could push a car out.

Rich was not an active and physical person.

These three facts convinced Mom that, in her opinion, neither Sharon nor Phil was telling the truth about what had happened. But detectives and prosecutors told her that the truth may never truly be known and they could only proceed with the evidence they had. Detectives agreed they should look further in to the story they had been told, but needed to focus on establishing premeditation and proving Phil killed Rich to steal the car. After hearing Sharon explain that Phil said he 'went into survival mode-we needed the car'; detectives would focus on proving aggravating circumstances.

Mom also questioned them as to why they had to give Sharon 'use immunity' when she had *multiple* opportunities to go to the police right after Rich was killed. The first opportunity being when Phil returned the car to Darrington and was away from her for more than 12 hours. The second being when Phil went to his sales meeting at Evergreen Ford. Investigators explained that without her coming forward, the case may have dragged on or even gone unsolved as they did not yet know about the ticket. In the end Mom was glad that the case was being resolved, and if it meant that the truth would never be fully known as to what really happened, so be it. She was appreciative of the hard work detectives had done to find out what happened to Rich and was equally supportive of the work prosecutors and detectives were doing to bring the man who had done this to justice.

Part of her hoped to learn at this meeting that somehow Rich had done something wrong. That he had interfered or involved himself somewhere he didn't belong. If this were the case, she could start to make sense of the tragedy. But as she processed what she heard, it slowly sank in to her that Rich had been killed for just the opposite. Not because he had done something to make someone mad or got in a conflict he shouldn't have; but he was killed because he may have stopped to help. No matter what her reservations were about the validity of Sharon's story, Mom did believe that one simple fact.

Rich stopped to help these people.

And the thanks he received for the kindness he offered these two stranded motorists was two shotgun blasts from less than 15 feet away.

One to the torso.

And one to the neck.

The complete utter senselessness of the killing was a bitterness that would never leave my mother.

Not even to this day.

*   *   *

The following week detectives brought Phil into an interview room to ask him how he came in to possession of the keys to Rich's Mustang. Prosecutors decided the best way to present this to a jury would be if they could show that Rich had his keys on his person when he died and that Phil removed the keys from Rich's body. If the defense argued that the keys were left in the car, the defense could also try and convince a jury that you can't steal a car from a dead man. It sounded ridiculous when detectives explained it to my mother, but even an implausible and unrealistic argument can raise just a tiny seed of doubt in juror's minds.

Especially in a potential capital case like this one.

If a juror does not want to see a man that they are presiding over their guilt or innocence get the death penalty, they can hold on to the tiniest and most unreasonable shred of doubt.

Once Phil's defense heard the line of questioning they quickly realized that the prosecution was looking for evidence of an aggravating circumstance. They obviously knew an aggravating circumstance could result in the death penalty. But the prosecution had not yet made it clear what they were after and was not required no notify them yet.

Given the mountain of evidence piling up against their client the defense refused to offer up any answer other than Phil could not remember where he got the keys to the Mustang. The keys would have either been taken from Rich's body, attached to his belt where he *routinely kept them* or they were left in the car. Investigators were going to have to get it from Sharon, if they were going to get it all.

On May 29, 1990 Deputy Prosecutor Gerry MacCamy, Detective Joe Ward and Sgt. Tom Greene met with Sharon again at her attorney's office to go over some of the facts of the case that they were not exactly sure about to see if she would testify one way or the other, about how the keys to the Mustang came in to Phil's possession.

They were also interested in whether or not they could establish if Phil had assaulted or threatened Sharon in any way with the gun. This would make it easier for them to convince the court that Sharon should be allowed to testify at trial despite the confusion surrounding Washington's spousal privilege laws.

In this case, prosecutors still had a very solid amount of evidence even if the defense could block Sharon's testimony. But if they could also charge Phil with assaulting or threatening his own wife, it might sway the judge to disallow defense attempts to block her testimony.

At 9:15 AM the three men sat down at the conference table in John Wolfe's office along with Sharon and her mother Helen.

"Hi Sharon, I am Gerard MacCamy and this is Detective Joe Ward- I believe you remember Sgt. Greene?" he began.

Sharon nodded.

"We'd like to ask some questions just clarify very specifically what you remember and what you would be able to testify to, if in fact you testify at all. Ok?" he continued.

"Ok," Sharon softly replied.

"So, it seems that Phil *never* pointed the shotgun directly at you in a threatening manner? Is that the case, now?" Gerry asked.

"Well, Phil has been calling me a lot. And his sister, Jody has been calling me a lot," Sharon began.

"Are they trying to get you to change your story?"

Sharon looked down at the table. It seemed like this nightmare was never going to end.

"No, Jody is not trying to make me change my story but she does think I am lying when I say I felt threatened by how Phil was acting and stuff. She said 'Phil would never do that,'" Sharon said.

"Alright, well, let's get right in to what we know for sure and what you are sure you can testify to. Did Phil always carry the shotgun with him or did he just take it out when he wanted to do some shooting. In other words, you said that he carried it for protection- did he always *carry it* with him?" Gerry asked.

"It was always with us, but in the truck. He would go get it if needed," Sharon answered.

"Did he keep it loaded or unloaded?" Gerry asked.

"It was unloaded when it was in the truck but he loaded it whenever it was outside of the truck," Sharon answered.

This fact could become important at trial and attested to the significance of her testimony. She stated that Phil *did not carry* the shotgun with him at all times while outside the truck. That it was usually left *in the truck*. This supported the idea of premeditation, as Phil would have had to go to the truck to get the shotgun and he would have to load it; two very specific actions prior to killing Rich. Whereas, if Phil always carried the shotgun with him, he would have had it with him and loaded, whether he was planning to kill Rich or not. It was thin, but it was something.

"Ok, at the time of the shooting, where was Phil holding the gun? What part of the gun?" he asked.

"He was holding it by the trigger part and it was pointing down," she answered.

Sgt. Greene and Detective Ward sat back in their chairs.

"Can you describe in detail, how he looked at you and what you perceived as threatening?" Gerry continued.

Sharon was not sure exactly what he meant. She peered at him somewhat confused.

"What do you mean?" she asked.

"Well, if you were to testify in court that you felt threatened by how Phil was acting after he killed Duncan, how would you describe those few seconds after, the time that made you feel as though Phil would harm you if you did not do what he said?" Gerry clarified.

"Well, he turned and faced me, directly. And his jaw was tight; his eyes were very piercing. I had seen this look before when he has been drinking heavy. He said to 'get the fucking shells,'" she described.

"Why did he want more shells?" Gerry asked.

"I thought that was in case someone else showed up, but he never said exactly why," Sharon answered.

"So why did you feel threatened? I mean, *I understand*, but a defense attorney is going to ask you why you felt threatened. What would you say?" Gerry asked.

"Before this, when Phil has been this way-"

"Been what way?" Gerry interjected without looking up from his notepad.

"When he has been close to becoming violent, I have learned to react to him passively, you know," she said.

"Has he ever physically assaulted you, even if you didn't report it?" Gerry asked.

"No...no. He has *never* harmed me. But he has put his fist in doors...- walls," Sharon answered.

"What made you think you were in danger?" Gerry continued.

"I could not say one way or the other that I was in danger, I mean…I was in shock, you know. I just knew to stay passive, like I've done before," she said.

Gerry glanced over his notes for a minute. Sharon sat in her chair, silent. Occasionally she would make eye contact with Sgt. Greene but she appeared uncomfortable.

"The best way I can describe it is that if I cooperated with Phil, he wouldn't shoot me- but I couldn't be certain," she added.

"Ok. After he shot Duncan did he reload the shotgun when you brought him the shells?" Gerry asked.

"I couldn't say one way or the other. I'm sorry but I just can't remember," she finished.

Gerry paused and stared at his notes. He was confident that if a jury ever heard her explain how Phil didn't always carry the shotgun and had to get it from the truck and load it, that he could establish premeditation. But he was not confident that she would ever be able to testify. If she wasn't convincing in the fact that Phil had committed a crime against her as well, the defense was likely going to be able to block her testimony.

Sgt. Greene was going to question her about the keys and some other facts that detectives needed cleared up, but Gerry MacCamy just wasn't sure she would ever be heard by a jury.

"Ok, you said in the first interview that Duncan talked to you and Phil, left and then came back a while later. When Duncan returned, who talked or had contact with Duncan the most? Was it you? Or did Phil talk to him more?" Sgt. Greene asked.

"I talked to him the second time more than Phil did," she answered.

"Ok, do you remember if Duncan locked the car when he went with you to look at the truck?" Greene asked.

Sharon looked toward the ceiling and sat back in her chair again.

"I'm sorry. I don't remember," she answered.

"When you walked back down to the Mustang, after Phil shot him. Do you remember if Phil had the keys or were they in the ignition?" Greene asked.

No matter how many ways they asked, it seemed she could not remember where the keys came from. Gerry began questioning her again and moved on to other aspects of the incident.

"If you were asked to describe what you thought Phil's 'state of mind' was that day- before he shot Duncan- how would you describe that?" Gerry asked.

"Wow."

She drew a deep breath and looked at the ceiling again.

"Well, he had been drinking Jack Daniels all day and throwing up. So he could drink more."

"So how drunk was he?" Gerry asked.

"He was coherent, but tipsy I would say," Sharon answered.

Gerry decided to change things up a bit.

"What do you know about Phil's upbringing, his teen-age years?" Gerry asked.

"Well, his parents are both dead-"

"What were their names?" Greene interjected.

"Malcolm and Nadine," she answered.

"Anyway, his dad was somewhat of a war hero. I did not know him but he put Phil down a lot. Phil wanted to join the Army you know, when he was 17 and they wouldn't let him. He needed permission to join up when he was only 17. He shot himself in the stomach to force them to sign the permission form," she described.

Gerry looked at his notes again.

"You mentioned his combat in the previous interview, what did he do, do you know what his job was?" Gerry asked.

"He rarely spoke of it but in the few times he did I remember him saying he carried a radio and jumped from planes or something. I know he loved the thrill- the edge- you know?" she finished.

"What do you mean the edge?" Greene asked.

"Of combat. He would join up again if there was ever another war," Sharon added.

"So the first four days after the shooting, where were you staying?" Gerry asked.

"We stayed in motels," Sharon answered.

"Do you remember which ones?" he asked.

"Uh...the Motel 6 in Issaquah and then the Days Inn at Eastgate and the third one was....I don't remember the name of it; but it was the second one...west of the SeaFirst Bank in Eastgate. I know it's white. That's all I remember," she answered.

"You said he had been drinking a lot. How much would you estimate?" Gerry asked.

"Oh gosh. I bet a fifth a day...at least?" she answered.

"Well, that will do it for now. Thank you for you answering our questions, I know it has been difficult," Gerry said as he rose from the conference table.

Detective Ward and Sgt. Greene followed Gerry outside and returned to the Snohomish County Courthouse.

After finishing the follow up interview with Sharon, investigators feared they would not be able to prove that Phil had killed Rich in order to

366

steal the Mustang. After discussing the interview with the prosecution team they decided the best course would be to get a statement from Phil to see what he would say.

The defense had been pressuring them to start working out a plea but before they gave up on finding aggravating circumstances they wanted to have leverage on Phil to put as much pressure on him as possible. They knew from the record that he had been calling his sister, Jody. Maybe if they interviewed her and got some insight on the crime, they could use that to aid in getting Phil to confess and he just might finally admit he took the keys off of Rich's body.

It was a long shot at best.

34

On June 1, 1990; Detective John Gray met with Phil's sister, Jody at her home in Issaquah. He told Jody they wanted to get some background on Phil and if this went to trial, her statements could help the jury understand Phil. At her request, Detective Gray wrote the statement for her.

She led the detective upstairs and put on a pot of coffee.

"Ok. Thanks for taking the time here, let's just start and ask how you are related to the- to Mr. Hillman?" Gray began.

"I am Phillip Hillman's older sister," Jody answered.

Nervously she sipped from the cup clutched in her hands.

"How would you describe your relationship?" Gray continued.

"I have maintained a close relationship with him," Jody answered hesitantly.

She wanted to stay positive about her younger brother.

"How would you describe him?" Gray asked.

"He is really brilliant and a nice, funny, great person- most of the time," she kind of laughed, hoping to ease the tension a little.

"Go on."

"Well, he is an alcoholic and cannot handle drinking. When he is drinking, he cannot stop."

Jody took another sip from the cup and hunched forward over the kitchen table.

"He gets obnoxious. He has always been nice around me- yet stubborn. You know? He has had a past problem with cocaine, in 1988, and I helped him get into treatment for that, but he did good."

"Has he stayed clean? From the drugs, I mean?" Gray asked.

"In the last six months to a year, I have not seen any evidence of drug use," Jody answered.

She was still not completely comfortable about answering questions, but she knew she had to.

"How often did you see him?"

"During that time,...oh... I see him or talk with him on the phone about twice a week," Jody answered.

"Ok, Ok. Tell me about what happened, this most recent event. When did you first learn about the shooting?" Gray shifted directions on the interview.

"I first heard about the shooting from Sharon, which was on May 10, late at night. She was just hysterical. I had to really calm her down; she was just in shock, still," Jody answered seeming to loosen up a little.

"When did you first speak with Phil after the shooting?" Gray continued.

"Well, it turns out, Phil called me by phone on May 5 or 6 and he told me he was in or he was going to Moses Lake fishing. I kind of thought they said they were going up to the Sauk in the North Cascades but I didn't really think anything of it, you know. I then talked to Sharon and she told me they were in Moses Lake, too. No mention of anything else. But, obviously that wasn't the case. But you know, I am sure they were stressed I mean, goodness," Jody answered.

When was the next time Phil contacted you?" Gray asked.

"Well, Phil called me again on May 12 at 10:40 AM. I remember it because for some reason I looked at the clock above the oven right when he called and it just kind of stuck into my mind. He said he was in Edgewick and he needed a ride to come home. I mean, I knew what was going on but, I mean, I just wanted him to turn himself in but I didn't let him know that I knew. So, I told him I would try and get a hold of Sharon and that's when I called the police," Sharon answered.

"What did you talk about, how often did he call?" Gray continued.

"He said he was in pain because of his back. I had a total of seven phone calls from Phil that day. He never mentioned being in trouble or doing any violence- only his back pain," Jody responded.

"Have you spoken with him since he has been in jail?" Gray changed directions again.

"Well, since he has been in jail, I have had at least 10 or 12 phone calls with Phil. I mean, of course I have talked to him. I love him, he's my brother, you know?" Jody answered and sat back in her chair.

"What has he said?" Gray asked.

"Well, as you might imagine he has told me about the shooting in Darrington," she said.

"Did he tell you what happened, that day? The day of the shooting?"

"He said that day he was drinking, that first he drank a half case to a case of beer and a couple of pints of whiskey since he got up that morning. He said they were four wheel driving and got their truck stuck in a ditch outside of Darrington. And that Rich Duncan stopped to help them. I mean he didn't know his name at the time obviously, but he does now; Phil said 'no' when Duncan offered to give them a ride. He said that Duncan left and came back later. Phil told me that he wished Duncan had never come back and it did not happen," Jody said sounding somewhat upset.

"Did he describe to you what happened, after Duncan returned?" Gray inquired.

"He said they went to look at their truck up the road. Sharon was first, followed by Duncan and Phil. Duncan could not do anything about the truck and so they walked back to the road. Phil told me that he then shot him."

Jody sat silent for a moment with a shocked look on her face.

"Did he offer any sort of reason why?" Gray asked.

"Phil said he had 'no idea why because Duncan, he…he was a real nice guy who was trying to help me,'" Jody answered.

"What did he say he did next?" Gray asked trying to keep the conversation moving forward.

"Phil told me he moved the body 30 feet up the road. I asked him if Sharon had to help him and he said no. You know he did say that he is very remorseful about this shooting and cannot believe he did it. I believe him," Jody said and moved to pour herself another cup of coffee.

"OK, there are some questions we need to ask based on what he has told us, so, first, where did he get the shotgun?" Gray continued.

"That damn thing. The shotgun is Sharon's and I told both Sharon and Phil, last summer, not to take the shotgun because it would violate his parole; you know? But Sharon said they brought the gun for protection in the woods," she answered.

"Does Phil do any hunting that you know of?" he asked.

"No, I don't think so. I mean Phil was not a hunter but he said he liked to hunt birds," she said.

Gray was surprised at how she had just told him he was not a hunter but liked to hunt birds. He made a short note on the margin of his notepad.

"Where did they store the shotgun?" he continued.

"They kept the shotgun at home unless they went camping. Last summer I had the shotgun at my house when I learned they took it camping. Sharon came and got the gun a couple three months later, in the fall of 1989," she answered and took a sip of coffee.

"Has he had any violent outbursts, since this last time on parole?" Gray asked.

"Since he got out of prison, I have never seen him violent toward anyone nor have I seen him destroy anything in anger. With the phone calls with Phil from jail he has said he knows alcohol changes him but he said he thinks something else is wrong with him or he wouldn't do anything like this. You know? It's so hard on us right now. I asked Phil if I could come to the jail and see him. This was about two weeks ago. Phil said 'no, not right now. I can't see anybody right now. I feel too awful and it's hard to live with."

"Alright. Well that should do it for now. Go ahead and read this over, if it seems accurate go ahead and sign it," Gray said as he placed the written statement in front of her.

After making a few minor changes and initialing them, she signed the sworn statement.

Most of what was in it would be considered hearsay in a court, but Hinds wanted to know what Phil had been saying and see if he couldn't use the statement to convince Phil to make a statement as well. His lawyer would probably try and stop it, but it was worth a chance. This was a fairly open and shut case as long as Sharon held it together until trial and *was even allowed to testify* to what she had seen. And given her immunity, and the thought of having it revoked and facing charges herself, she probably would. But it couldn't hurt.

*   *   *

Almost a week after interviewing Phil's sister, the defense offered to plead guilty at the arraignment scheduled for June 14. But only if the charge was second degree murder rather than first degree murder. Phil's attorney, James Kempton had defended Phil during the 1974 murder of Newton Thomas and believed strongly that the cases were very similar. He contended that if it wasn't first degree murder in 1974, then it wasn't first degree murder now. This case, like the one before, lacked the element of premeditation. The defense believed the sooner they could get this put to rest the better. The only way the prosecution would even consider this was if Phil made a statement before the arraignment.

Murder myself, Murder I am.

On June 7, 1990 Phil agreed to make a statement. It had been over a month since he had killed Rich and the defense felt it was best to just move this forward and plead guilty- but not to first degree murder. He dictated what he wanted to say as his lawyer wrote it out:

"There is no possible justification for what I did. My remorse is indescribable, but I'm sure the sorrow of the victim's family is worse. For my own salvation, I must find an explanation even though I know it will not justify my acts.

Vietnam keeps coming to mind. I don't want to sound like a whiner, but at age 17 I was placed in a combat unit in Vietnam. They found out I was not yet 18 so they sent me out of the combat zone for 3 weeks until I turned 18. I then spent one year in the 1st of the 7th Cavalry Infantry Combat Unit. Our job was to patrol the woods and when we found a trail that was used we set up an ambush on it and kill anyone that walked by. To an 18 year old this was at first extremely frightening to me, but as time went on it became exciting. Living on the edge was still frightening, but the excitement was also there. I honestly could not now count the number of victims I witnessed.

Today, if I am in the woods with a gun, that same Vietnam surge seems to come over me and it is once again survival time. As said earlier, this does not justify what I did. It only makes me feel more guilty for allowing myself to afford that wooded nightmare opportunity by going there. Particularly while drinking.

Your honor, I know I have a very serious and dangerous problem. Whether it's my fault or not does not matter.

On the date in question, I waited near the Mountain Loop Highway while Duncan followed my wife to our stuck truck. He was very nice and I did not consider him a threat. He wanted to see if he could extract the truck; I knew he couldn't; I was somewhat tired and quite intoxicated; so I waited with our camping gear. At some point I apparently picked up my shotgun and stepped in to the woods off the trail. I remember seeing Sharon walk by me- on her return I let her go by. I then saw Duncan come in to view. I remember just previously ducking behind a rock and crawling just like I used to do in Vietnam. When Duncan came into view, I was in my teenage Vietnam combat state of mind. As Duncan came down the road I was hidden in the brush just off the road, knowing then that I would kill him. When he approached, I shot him knowing it would kill him. As hard as I've tried, I cannot remember firing a second shot. In Vietnam we would pull our victims off the trail, dig a very shallow grave, put them in, and cover them up. I did the same with poor Duncan.

This happened in Snohomish County on or about May 2. This has been hard to write but I'm glad to get it said. My lawyer wrote this, but I dictated, discussed while written, read and indicate it is the 7th day of June, 1990."

Phillip V. Hillman

Once the statement was complete the defense told the prosecution that if they held to the first degree murder charge that they would not plead guilty. They would take it all the way to trial and that the wife would never be able to testify. The prosecution had no evidence suggesting where the keys to the Mustang came from. They had his confession at this point and the confession was clearly to murder in the second degree only.

Phil's attorney let them know that he would be waiting for their call to see what they would recommend for a sentence, and given the new sentencing guidelines put in place after the Sentencing Reform Act was passed in Washington, it should be a 'no brainer'.

The prosecution informed him that they would look over the statement and get in touch. They needed to speak with the family of the victim and after that, they would get back to him. The prosecution team decided to meet on Monday the 11th of June to discuss their options before consulting with Mom.

35

Gerry MacCamy walked in to the conference room at the Snohomish County Prosecutors office just after 9:30 AM. Detectives and assistant prosecutors were assembled around a long conference table. Phil's arraignment was three days away and they had to decide if they were going to increase the charge to aggravated murder in the first degree, move forward with the case as charged, murder one; or agree to drop the charge to second degree murder.

"Well, where do we stand?" Gerry asked.

"It seems to me we have him for murder two, hands down. Even if the wife is not allowed to testify, we know the medical examiner will say that Duncan was killed from two wounds inflicted by a shotgun. We recovered two empty casings at the murder scene and the ballistics lab can say these two casings were fired from the same shotgun which was recovered in a tent in Edgewick where the defendant was camping when we arrested him," one of the assistant district attorney's began.

"How can we link him to the camp?" Detective Hinds asked.

"Forensics was able to recover a complete fingerprint from one of the plastic vodka bottles recovered at the camp as well as statements from multiple King County Sheriffs deputies and a Washington State Trooper detailing how Phil told them he had been camping there," the assistant answered.

"We have a tow truck driver who identified Phil from a line-up that will testify that he towed Phil's truck out from being stuck in a washout roughly 24 hours after the victim was reported missing. The washout was only 100 feet from where we recovered the body," Detective Ward added.

Gerry had Phil's statement in his hand and was slowly reading it to himself, carefully scrutinizing every word.

"We have a ticket the defendant received in the victim's car, six or seven hours before he received the tow from, John Fox. A ticket that was given to him almost 100 miles from the murder scene," he continued.

"Didn't the Traffic Officer pick out the wrong guy in the line up?" Detective Pince asked.

"Yes, but that won't be hard to overcome, I mean, he routinely interacts with dozens of different drivers. I don't think a jury will think much of it. It was a routine stop 15 days before the line up," Gerry interjected looking up from the statement he was fixated upon.

"We also have a witness, a juvenile female who saw Phil get out of the Mustang when it was abandoned in Darrington. She *did* identify him in the line-up," Hinds said.

"And thankfully, the gal in the boutique shop didn't pick him out and mess up our time line," Detective Ward added.

"So where do we stand with the aggravating circumstances?" the assistant district attorney asked.

"Well, neither the defendant nor his wife has made any statement regarding the keys other than they both *don't remember,*" Sgt. Greene said.

"I don't think we are going to be able to get a jury to believe that he killed the victim to steal the car. They will probably see it as a crime of opportunity. It's risky- especially if this turns out to be a death penalty case," Detective Ward said.

"And the only premeditation we have is from the wife's statements and I just don't think we are going to be able to get her on the stand. I really don't. Especially now that she has toned down her belief that Phil was threatening her," Hinds added.

Without the additional charges against Phil whereas his wife was the victim of the crime; it would be a very tough case to be able to overcome the spousal privilege statute.

"Couldn't we argue that she is lying? I mean, when she was trying to explain why she didn't come forward sooner than nine days after the murder, sure, she was scared then. But now that she has immunity. She's not so worried about it. Wasn't her immunity based upon telling the truth?" Detective Ward asked.

"Well, I just don't think a judge is going to see it that way, maybe she was scared and now that he is in jail and locked up, she doesn't want to deal with this anymore. Who knows?" the assistant district attorney pointed out.

"So we haven't got a qualifying second offense and we haven't got premeditation-"

Gerry MacCamy slapped Phil's statement down on the conference table and stood up with a big smile.

"*I think we might,*" he smiled.

He lifted the statement up to read what he had underlined.

"It's a long shot, but we might just have enough to put a little pressure on them! And it's right here in his confession," he exclaimed.

Everyone in the room focused intently on Gerry.

"He says in his statement, and I quote; 'At some point I apparently picked up my shotgun and stepped in to the woods off the trail. I remember seeing Sharon walk by me- on her return I let her go by. I then saw Duncan come in to view. I remember just previously ducking behind a rock and crawling just like I used to do in Vietnam. When Duncan came into view, I was in my teenage Vietnam combat state of mind. As Duncan came down the road I was hidden in the brush just off the road, knowing then that I would kill him. When he approached, I shot him knowing it would kill him.' Unquote. He admitted he picked up the shotgun and then stalked his victim *knowing that he would kill him,*" Gerry finished.

"I don't know. Can premeditation be only a 30 or 40 seconds? Is that enough?" the assistant district attorney asked.

"Well, we can push them on it. We can show them we are serious and that we are not going to rely on the wife's testimony. I mean, we most likely are going to have to drop the charges against him for the assault on his wife anyway. We keep the charges at first degree murder and just inform the judge that if we find more corroborating evidence to substantiate an aggravating circumstance, that we may amend the charges to aggravated before trial."

That afternoon Phil's attorney called to discuss a plea bargain. His defense suggested Phil would plead guilty to second degree murder if the state would agree to recommend 23 years. With time off for good behavior this meant Phil would most likely only serve a little over 15 years.

15 years.

The prosecution did not agree. Phil's own statement he had made the week earlier essentially contained an admission of premeditation they argued. The prosecution countered by offering that Phil plead to first degree murder and a recommended sentence of 32 years. If they didn't want to accept this, then they were going to continue investigating to find aggravating circumstances and if it went to trial then the prosecution may up the charge to aggravated first degree murder which, if convicted, meant a mandatory life sentence and possibly the death penalty.

Phil's attorney was somewhat stunned. He argued that the circumstances surrounding this murder and the one Phil committed in 1974 were essentially the same. Phil was in the woods with a shotgun, drank too much and tragically; a man died. Phil obviously had an untreated condition which led to this behavior, but a premeditative killer, he argued, he was not. He did not kill Duncan to hide the act of stealing Duncan's Mustang and he certainly did not seek to kill Duncan in advance. More importantly, the defense argued. There is no way the wife will ever be able to testify due to spousal privilege, especially now that she had clarified her story regarding the threatening behavior Phil may or may not have exhibited toward his wife. Moreover, she was out of the picture unless the prosecution wanted to withdraw her immunity and try and put her up as an accomplice. The defense knew that would be an uphill battle for the prosecution as well.

The defense informed Gerry that they would be pleading not guilty to first degree murder and further, they would be asking for the defendant to be evaluated by a psychiatrist to determine if the statement Phil gave on June 7 was even admissible. It is entirely possible, the defense argued, that Phil was in no mental condition to give such a statement As far as the defense was concerned, the statement would be thrown out and if Phil suffered from some sort of psychological condition relating to his service in Vietnam then he would argue this at sentencing.

This was a case of a good young man wanting to do right by his country, a man who served his military and then was discarded by society after they were done with him. They taught him to kill, encouraged him to kill and then dumped him back in to the public where he did what he was trained to do, kill. If the prosecution wasn't careful he warned, Phil was going to end up in a psychological center receiving treatment.

Not to be intimidated by Phil's high profile attorney, Gerry argued back that if *he wasn't very careful with his client,* his client was going to get the needle.

Phil met with his attorney prior to the hearing and explained that it was unlikely that the prosecution would be able to have Sharon testify, but with all of the physical evidence piling up, it was very likely he would be convicted of second degree murder. He also explained that the prosecution was sticking to first degree murder because they felt the crime was premeditated based on Phil's own statement. He further cautioned him that if they went to trial and new evidence came to light, the State could up the charge to aggravated first degree murder which carried a mandatory life sentence and could even bring life without the possibility of parole or even the death penalty. His attorney felt the best strategy was to plead not guilty at this point and see where it went from here. The omnibus hearing would be some time toward the end of July and they could probably work out a favorable plea deal by then.

On June 14th, 1990, Phil pled not guilty to the charge of first degree murder. His lawyer petitioned the court to allow Dr. Donald Bonnington to administer a psychological evaluation to Phil to determine his state of mind during the confession on June 7th and any other factors which may be relevant to Phil's defense.

At the same time, the charges against Phil for assaulting his wife were dropped. The prosecution knew it was a huge blow to their case for aggravated first degree murder and might even derail the first degree murder charge. But detectives and investigators close to the case refused to be intimidated by the defense. They knew what had happened, they also knew that proving it was often difficult and presented many unique challenges, but they were not going to give up.

Not at all.

After the hearing, Gerry MacCamy phoned my mother to inform what was going on. He figured the press would certainly be reporting how charges had been dropped for assault and he wanted my mom to hear it from him rather than from the news so that he could explain in more detail what was going on.

"Hi Karen. How are you doing today?" Gerry asked.

"Well, I'm just going through some of Rich's financial affairs and trying to just struggle through it. What's going on? I usually don't hear from you guys unless there is some sort of news," Mom asked.

"Well, since we last spoke we re-interviewed Sharon and she kind of backed off her comments that she felt threatened by Phil," he began.

"What! Oh, of course. Now that she has immunity… if she *didn't fear for her life* and feel threatened, then why did she wait nine days to come forward!?" Mom asked angrily.

"I understand your frustration, I believe she was very scared, Karen; but when it comes to going in front of a jury and telling them that you felt your husband may kill you if you went to police is a lot more difficult then it sounds," he continued.

"Yeah? Well she should see what it's like to stare at your husband's clothes hanging in the closet and knowing he is never coming home and will never wear them again. She should see how difficult it is to sit in the window and stare every night wondering where he is! She should see-"

"I know, Karen, I know it's been tough. We are doing everything we can. We did decide to drop the charges against Phil for assaulting her," he said.

"So that means she won't be testifying?" Mom cried out.

"I really don't think this is going to get that far, I expected that we would plea this out, but I don't really know, now. He has a very high profile attorney. But I promise you, he's not going to get him off, we have way too much physical evidence for that. A lot of legal wrangling is going on right now," Gerry explained.

Mom was furious again. She wanted the nightmare to end when they caught the man, they had him red-handed. She wanted to believe that the case would be open and shut and that she could just try and move forward in her new life without Rich. But somehow it seemed it was falling apart again. The ten days of hell wondering where Rich was and fighting to get some official agency to even go look for him; only to learn that his killer had killed before and been let out by the State on parole and *now the case was falling apart?* What was going wrong? How could there be *any possible legal* means to escape justice?

"So is that it? She backed away from her original statement?" Mom asked irritated.

"No, I have some more news.-"

"Of course you do. Probably not good is it?" Mom asked irritated.

"Well, Phil did admit to the murder in a phone call to his sister and she made a statement about it, it is hearsay but it does help in some ways. We also got a statement from Phil, he admitted what he did but there are some parts of it that are a small concern," he continued.

"Hey, just lay it out. At this point what does it matter?" Mom continued.

"He claims he may be this way because of his combat in Vietnam," he said.

"WHAT? How does that matter if he admitted to it?" Mom asked.

"Well right now we don't know. He is going to be evaluated by a psychologist and then we'll know more. There is this thing, it's called Post-traumatic Stress Disorder, or PTSD. But don't...I guess *worry* is not the right word because I know this is very much on your mind; rest assured, we are doing everything we can to get him locked up for a long time. His attorney did try to get us to drop the charges to second degree murder but I absolutely said no way," he continued.

"*Second degree?*" Mom gasped.

"We said no. So, we will get him. Just let us do our job for now. Technically, you may hear through the news or something, that he did plead not-guilty today," he said.

"So this is going to go to trial?" Mom asked.

"Well, I don't think it will, but we need to prepare as though it will. As it stands now the trial won't be until the end of September," he continued.

"What do I have to do?" Mom asked.

"We'll help prepare you for that, if and when it comes to it. Don't let that add any more stress to your life right now. You may want to call or get in touch with the Victim Advocate at the county, they have a lot of help available to explain what to expect. OK?" he stated.

Mom just sat in her office chair and stared out the window.

"Well, I just wanted to keep you updated. And of course if something changes I'll phone you. But for now, just know he is not going to get away with this, not in any way. What you see and what you hear in the news is just legal jockeying, don't be surprised if the defense tries to make Phil available to the press so that he can tell his story, whatever that might be."

Mom hung up the phone and sat in her office chair. She worried somehow this man was going to get off with some sort of ridiculous sentence. She even wondered if they would let him off completely due to his 'state of mind.'

The trial, set for September 24th, was three months away. Mother prepared herself for what could be a lengthy trial. It could take two days; it could take two weeks. No one she asked would really offer up a definitive answer.

The Victim Advocate told her that it would be graphic, vulgar and difficult. Crime scene photos, defense witnesses trying to portray Rich as a large and threatening man, they had no indication of where it would go and what type of defense would be used.

Mom would need to stay through the whole thing, no matter how terrifying and grotesque it would become. It would not take long for jurors to figure out her relationship to Rich and they would watch her like a hawk. If she got up to leave or gasped at the wrong time or anything, it would factor in.

Her anger had begun to turn into strength however and she knew she would have to sit through it all, for her beloved husband, Rich, for her companion stolen away from her by a man who just seemed to kill without regard; and for poor Newton Thomas, beyond all of the sadness and tears, she even thought of him. He must have been a pleasant, sweet old man as well.

Who kills an 83 year old man?

She remembered the phone call from James Sylte, and how he described to her in detail how Phil stabbed him over and over again. He had even apologized for not being able to do more to keep this man in prison.

She would be there.

Every fucking day.

She would be there.

She would sit through the photos of her husband's ten day old rotting corpse. She would watch as the shotgun was paraded around the courtroom. She would listen to witnesses talk about how the killer was just suffering from PTSD, how he just drank too much. How, he was an alright guy, how he just made an error in judgment. How we should feel sorry for him. She would sit in the hardwood bench seats of the courtroom from beginning to end. And she would never waiver.

This she would do.

For Rich.

For Newt.

And for James.

36

On June 25, 1990, Phil was to be interviewed by Dr. Donald J. Bonnington of the Harvard Psychiatry Group at 10:00 AM. At around 10:20 the bailiff's showed up to escort him from the holding area he was in to an interview room. The appointment was scheduled for two hours. Dr. Bonnington was to interview Phil and determine if he was competent to make a confession or statement. If it was determined he was incompetent, it was possible his statement from June 7, 1990 in which he admitted the murder was premeditated could be inadmissible at trial.

Dr. Bonnington advised Phil that this interview was not confidential and that it could be used by the court with or without his permission. Further, the interview could be used to aid in his defense or sentencing and could also be used against him. Phil indicated that he understood this.

Dr. Bonnington opened the interview by asking what Phil thought of his confession.

"I don't like that they think its first degree murder- that I thought it out about killing this person. This is no different than the first time I killed, and that one was only *second degree*," Phil began.

Phil then digressed to the 1974 murder of Newton Thomas.

"I was up in the woods at the Sauk River- back from Vietnam about a year at that time. Something comes over me when I'm in the woods or in a tavern. It just comes, not pre-thought, but like a rush; I want to hurt this person. That's the part of the confession I don't like. Like, there *was no premeditation*," Phil stated.

"Do you mean this present charge?" Dr. Bonnington asked.

"Yes, I do."

"Well tell me about the first one," Dr. Bonnington began.

"In 1974 I was camping and drinking. I stopped by a campsite about a quarter mile from where I was camping. I got in an argument with the man there and I asked if he wanted a drink. I just wanted to say 'hi'; where was the good fishing?"

"And how did he respond?"

"He wanted me to get out of his campsite," Phil started.

"And how did you feel about that?"

"I didn't feel he had that right; felt I could do what I wanted to do in the woods," Phil explained.

"So then what happened?"

"I got my shotgun out of the car. It wasn't pointed at him. In the argument I could have shot him. He was an older man, no physical threat to me. I could have beat him up. At the time, it just kind of happened. I remember saying, 'Fuck this- I don't have to take this shit' and he said for me to get out. 'This is my campsite' he said," Phil continued.

"Why did you shoot him?"

"Basically, I'm an angry person. After I shot him, I hid his body in the bushes-"

"When was this?" Dr. Bonnington interrupted him.

He wanted to see if Phil was still able to separate the past from the present, it could be an important indicator as to his state of mind.

"This was July of '74," he answered.

"And how did this end?" Dr. Bonnington asked.

"Another camper then came down and had a pistol and held it on me while his wife went back to town for the police. I went to jail," Phil answered.

"So, this murder and the one you described, from 1974 are the same to you, is there anything that *is different?*" Dr. Bonnington asked.

Phil sat back in his chair and smiled.

"I didn't give them a confession. I was in jail three months, plea bargained for second degree murder," Phil pointed out.

"So how are these two events the same to you?" Dr. Bonnington asked.

"An act of rage. I got 20 years. I did eight years. Two years at Shelton and transferred to Monroe because I assaulted a guy in Shelton," Phil explained.

"Tell me about that."

"He was selling a guy in prison some shoes. I was to give the guy some pot so he could buy shoes. I got mad so I beat him up. In the service I was trained quite a bit and I got some on the street. I worked with the South Vietnamese Army and they were pretty aggressive."

Phil took a drink of water and Dr. Bonnington leaned back in his chair.

"Tell me about the incident in 1982, the second degree assault," Dr. Bonnington asked.

"In 1982, February of '82 I got out. I had an assault again in August of '82," Phil began.

"And how did you get caught for this?"

"The guy knew me and reported me," Phil continued.

"Did you hurt him?"

"When I stabbed this man he went to the hospital. Stabbed a couple of times in the chest area," Phil explained.

Phil paused and Dr. Bonnington sat silent, waiting to see where Phil would take the conversation when not directed.

"Tried the V.A. like I said, after McNeil Island. Part of the parole stipulation was that I get into an anger management program. I completed the anger management program at King County Hospital."

"So, what happened that night?" Dr. Bonnington continued.

"I'd been out of Monroe then about five months. I met this guy in a tavern that was next door to his house. We started talking, he invited me inside and we smoked a joint. A couple of weeks later I saw him again, he was growing pot in his basement. I got in an argument with him about roasting pot."

"What did you argue about?"

"I thought it had to dry naturally so I stabbed him while we argued."

"How did you feel when this went on?"

"It is hard to describe how I felt at this time. I really don't know. I wondered why I do these things."

"Did you ever talk to anyone about this?"

"I talked to Sharon and told her something was wrong. I'd been down to the V.A. to get some treatment for this- for my rage- but it took four or five hours to be seen. I got frustrated and walked out. I just gave up any idea of treatment. On that charge I got ten years on assault. *Ten years.* I did six years- two in Walla Walla and then requested a transfer to McNeill Island so my wife could see me."

"So you were married at this time?"

"I met my wife in Monroe, married her in Walla Walla. She lived near McNeill so they transferred me to that prison. I'd known her since 1978," Phil explained.

384

"Let's talk about your current situation, the events back in May. Tell me what happened," Dr. Bonnington continued.

"I purchased a four wheel drive truck. It was in a remote area. We had been drinking all day. We took a logging road off the main road. My wife was driving and she got the truck stuck. Then we knew we had to go to Darrington for a tow. I grabbed some of our personal things out of the truck and went about 200 feet to the main road and was going to stop a car for help. One of the things I took from the truck was the shotgun," Phil began.

He shifted in his chair. He reached up and itched his neck.

"This guy came by in a red Mustang. He offered to go into town and call someone and get us a tow. Five to fifteen minutes later he came back and asked if he could pull me out. He wanted to look at the truck to see if he could help. I stayed there and waited with the property and while my wife and he walked up to the truck."

"And what were you doing as they went to the truck?"

"I sat looking around in the woods. I recall grabbing my shotgun-"

Bonnington quickly interrupted Phil- "What were you thinking about- as you grabbed the shotgun?"

"I thought of Vietnam. I was just feeling it," Phil answered.

Bonnington made some notes on the margins of his report.

"Ok, go on."

"I saw my wife coming down the road. I was in the bushes then- she didn't see me."

"And what, at this point, did you know about this man, Duncan?"

"He said he'd give me a ride in to town. He was a nice guy. He was there to help us," Phil answered.

"Ok. Go on."

"I thought I'd scare her. She walked by me, but I didn't say anything. She didn't see me. Fifteen seconds later this man came down the trail. I was still concealed. I stood up and shot him."

Phil took a deep breath and continued, scratching his neck again.

"It was like Vietnam- where my mission was to ambush trails that were used. We would set up ambushes along the trail- shoot anyone coming along and bury them. I buried the victim- Duncan- in a shallow grave. When first time I saw him I had no thought of hurting him. The second time I didn't know I was going to shoot him until after my wife walked by. I shot him with my shotgun twice."

"How did you feel after you shot him?" Dr. Bonnington asked.

"Buried the body off to the side of the road after a lot of guilt, shame remorse. Every time after a crime like this, I feel that way."

"Then why not go to police, right away?" Dr. Bonnington inquired.

"I don't want to be caught. These crimes aren't planned out. My wife was in shock, scared, hurt. I thought at that time I'd go live in the woods," Phil answered.

"What did your wife do?"

"My wife stayed with me a few days afterwards. We stayed in a motel," Phil said.

"How was she acting?"

"She wanted me to turn myself in. She was afraid she'd become an accomplice to murder. I said if they questioned her to tell them everything. But it never came to that," Phil paused.

Dr. Bonnington continued to write on his pad.

"What did you do next?"

"The next day we had the truck towed out. We drove Duncan's car in to Darrington and had a ticket on the way for speeding. Then I wiped all the prints off. The day I shot him I took the car to Seattle. Then I went to the woods, camping there," Phil answered.

"What made you come back?" he asked.

"I hurt my back in the woods, ruptured disc or something. I couldn't make it in the woods. I hitchhiked into Edgewick and called her to come pick me up so my back might heal. But Sharon had already gone to the police. They arrested me then in Edgewick. They didn't arrest me at the campsite."

"Looking back, how do you feel about what happened?"

"I know right from wrong. I believe in the law. I have committed horrendous crimes, but there has been no planning. That's how it happens."

Dr. Bonnington tapped his pen on the table and paused for a minute. He then changed the direction of the interview.

"Tell me about yourself, your parents, your family and such," he asked.

"Both of my parents have passed. My father from a heart attack in 1986 and my mother from complications with emphysema, last year. I have two older sisters, Jody and Sunny- well, Allison. My wife is not allowed to see me as she is a witness for the prosecution."

"How do you think the prosecution is going to go?" Dr. Bonnington asked.

"I'll probably get life without parole. I wouldn't want someone like me out on the streets, liable to happen again," Phil stated matter of fact-like.

"Why do you think that is?" Dr. Bonnington asked.

"I am an alcoholic, except when I was in prison. I smoked pot and drank in high school. At 17 I entered the Army, signed up on the buddy system with a friend and volunteered for Vietnam. I only made it as far as the 10th grade. My parents wouldn't give me permission to join. My father was drinking very heavily at the time. I shot myself in the stomach with a .22 rifle. After that she signed."

"How was your relationship with your parents after that?"

"While I was in basic training they divorced and Dad moved to California. I didn't see him until after Vietnam when I was on furlough," Phil answered.

"How was your relationship before that? Growing up?"

"Since I was four or six years old, as far back as I remember he was either at work or drinking and passed out. He was an electrical engineer and owned his own company, he was very successful. I played football for ten years and my parents never came to the games."

"And your friends at the time?"

"My friends had less than me, but not the things I had. They had a good family. Mother wanted to send me to a boarding school in Canada. I didn't want to go. It was like a military school. Cliffside Preparatory School."

"What was that like?"

"Talking out of turn in class, you were beaten regularly. First time I tried to escape there, I walked ten miles, hitchhiked to the ferry, made it to my aunt's house. I called my mother but she wouldn't let me come home. I went back to school and they put us in gym shorts and beat me in front of the whole school."

"Did your father ever beat you?" Dr. Bonnington asked.

"No, no, he never beat me. He was a nice drunk. Mother never beat me either. This was about in the 4th or 5th grade. I was there about a year and a half longer and I said I wouldn't go back."

"How about other problems with the law, besides these major cases we know about?"

"I had trouble with a DWI and minor consumption, but no felonies. I did get into a lot of fist fights because of my temper. It comes in a flash, lost control, I couldn't do boxing, it was hard to hurt unless I'm in a rage."

Phil paused.

"I don't know who I'm enraged with," he quietly remarked.

"I had a number of suicide attempts after returning from Vietnam. I overdosed on Seconal," he continued.

"What was going on at the time?" Dr. Bonnigton asked.

"I was very depressed; I felt Vietnam was my last chance to make something of myself. Me and my buddy who I signed up with, we wanted to become heroes. But the people weren't behind us. I got an honorable discharge in 1973 for medical reasons, for suicide attempts. I am eligible for V.A. benefits."

Dr. Bonnington moved the topic away from Vietnam.

"How did you meet your wife?" he asked.

"Monroe had dances once a month and Sharon wanted to come in to the prison to see what it was like. We hit it off right away. I knew her for five years before we were married and we lived together for five months in 1982. I married her when I was in Walla Walla in 1983."

"I see in the reports you have seen psychiatrists before, how did that go?"

"I saw a shrink once a week for three years, Dr. Harrold Eggertson. And then a couple years more off and on. But it didn't help," he answered.

"Why do you think that was?" Dr. Bonnington asked.

"No feedback. I saw a psychologist at McNeill Island; I went in to group and talked. Every time I saw the parole board I had to have a psych evaluation. Nobody ever mentioned Post-traumatic Stress Disorder to me. I don't really understand it. One time my sister mentioned it though," Phil answered.

"I dream about Vietnam, not so much now. A couple times a year I daydream about it, when I'm not thinking of something else. Part of me is missing the action, the danger. I get bored and daydream," Phil returned to the subject of Vietnam.

"Tell me about after you were released this most recent time," Dr. Bonnington asked.

"Well, I was selling cars," Phil answered.

"Since your release?"

"No, I worked as an apartment manager also, in Rainier Valley. But it was all black, drug dealers and druggies. I would get threatened all the time because I was evicting people for not paying rent. That's why I got the shotgun, for Sharon, so that she had protection while I was gone," he answered.

"So then you moved and began selling cars?" Dr. Bonnington asked.

"Yes, at Evergreen Ford. I was a team leader. I was making between four and five thousand per month. But it was hard to deal with success. I'm not supposed to drink but success is hard to deal with," Phil began.

"Why is it hard?" Dr. Bonnington asked.

"People celebrate by drinking. I knew jealousy when I saw a nice honest person able to drink. I've never been a thief, have a lot of guilt and remorse over the people that I've hurt. I can't face my family yet. I feel terrible for the victim's and their families. I know how wives of victims must feel."

Phil shifted in his chair and leaned back. He let out a long sigh.

"How do you think they feel?"

"They want the death penalty for me."

388

"And what do you think is fair?"

"If I plead guilty to first degree murder that would be 388 months or 32 years before parole. But with my prior record, I might just get life without parole. I do good time in prison. I got my barbering, hairstyling and cosmetology license last time in Monroe. But in Walla Walla, they locked us in a cell for 24 hours a day."

"What did you like to do to pass the time?" Dr. Bonnington asked.

"What did I like to do? I read a lot of action stories, westerns, animals and wildlife. Sometimes I feel I could write, but I never do it. I don't know the why of all these crimes," Phil answered surprised at the question.

"Alright, now I need to just ask you a series of questions. Just answer them as you feel. There are no 'wrong' answers. Ok?" Dr. Bonnington explained.

"Can you count upwards by seven's starting at seven?" Dr. Bonnington began.

"Seven, 14, 21, 28,...35, 42,...49-"

"Ok, good."

"Can you tell me who the first President of the United States was?"

"George Washington."

"And who is the President now?

"George Bush."

"And before him?"

"Ronald Reagan."

"Ok, good," Dr. Bonnington replied.

"I am going to say a proverb, and just tell me what comes to your mind first," he continued.

"Don't cry over spilled milk."

"It's done," Phil answered.

"Don't throw stones in glass houses."

"Shouldn't criticize somebody for something you do yourself," Phil answered.

"If you found an addressed stamped envelope on the street, what would you do?"

"Mail it," Phil smiled.

"If you were in a crowded theatre and smelled smoke, what would you do?"

"Alert somebody," Phil answered again, surprised at the question.

"All right, that's it. Your counsel will get my evaluation as soon as it is complete. Thank you Phil, and hang in there," Dr. Bonnington said.

The doctor motioned for the guard and he left the room. Phil sat in the conference room for a few minutes until bailiffs escorted him back to his block.

Murder myself, Murder I am.

*　　　*　　　*

A few days later Detectives got word that an inmate in the same cell as Phil had some interesting information. Information which might indicate that *Sharon was lying.*

On June 29, 1990 one of the inmates in the same unit as Phil contacted his attorney and wanted to offer up some information about what Phil had been saying while in jail. Investigators were hesitant with these kinds of situations because they are very often difficult to present to a jury. Rarely do juries put much stock in what another inmate has said or done while in jail. However, these kinds of discussions can also create leads worthy of investigating that turn up useful evidence. Given the status of this case and how desperately detectives wanted to make sure this didn't get pleaded down to a second degree murder; they believed it may be worth their time to see what the informant had to say.

At 10:55 AM, Detective Joe Ward met with an informant who would only be named as R. Fortune and his attorney, Mike Nance.

"Ok. So how long have you known Phil?" Ward started out.

"I've been in the same unit as him since he was arrested, like a month and a half ago," Fortune replied.

Ward began writing notes on a blank piece of paper.

"You know, we kind of clicked as he's interested in boxing and basketball and both of us are in for…you know…'assaultive behavior,'" Fortune continued.

Ward sat there silent and deliberately stopped writing. He did not look up at the inmate but simply waited. After a few awkward seconds Detective Ward looked up at Mr. Fortune.

"Look, you wanted to talk to me to see if you had anything that we could use—I know what you want in return. Give me something and we'll talk, ok—you tell me what you've heard and if anything becomes useful- we'll move forward?" Ward stated bluntly.

"Yeah, yeah. I know how it works. Look, he told me that he owns a V-6 extended cab truck. He said he'd like to beat her-" he pointed toward the female bailiff who had brought him down to the meeting, "or kick her ass. He didn't like the way she spoke to another guy in our unit," Fortune began.

Ward continued to take notes.

"He said his wife was stupid- but he didn't explain why. He loves shotguns- man he talked about them a lot. He told me he had a double barrel break action that was sawed off and how to alter shells," Fortune continued.

At this point Ward asked him to clarify that a little bit.

"Well, like…he said that you can open them up and remove the pellets and replace them with like dimes or piano wire with pellets on the ends and in the middle. He laughed when he said he'd done it. It will 'cut a deer in half' he said," Fortune described.

"So what has he said about himself, how has he described himself?" Ward asked.

Ward was interested in how much Phil would talk about Vietnam or his military history. It seemed that if Vietnam was a big part of why he killed, surely he would be talking about it with his cohorts. But he had to be careful not to lead Mr. Fortune where he wanted him to go.

'Well, I don't know, he says his favorite movie is 'Creepshow'; you know; where someone kills two people in a store with a 12 gauge shotgun- and then he said something about how an Indian Spirit gets involved," Fortune continued.

"Did he speak of any other crimes at all?" Ward asked.

"No, not really. He said he'd done 14 ½ years for murder but he didn't really talk about it at all. You know, I mean, he's more focused on what he's gonna' catch for this one, you know?" Fortune said.

"Oh, yeah? What's he thinkin'?" Ward asked with a smile.

"He thinks he is gonna get between 20 and life. Even though I showed him on the Sentencing Reform Act chart where he is only going to get 32 years or 388 months," Fortune explained.

"Why do you think that's the right number?" Ward asked quizzically.

"Well, shit, because they are going to arrest his wife," he answered.

"Why does he think that?" Ward asked very interested in the response.

"Phil said 'That bitch' or maybe it was 'that cunt can't even peel a trick right," Mr. Fortune stated.

Ward felt he might have something here now, but did little to show it.

"He also said 'The guy acted like a John Wayne, that's why he's smoked- gone.'"

"So what does 'peel a trick' mean to you?" Ward asked.

"Well, peeling a trick is a street term for using a woman to lure a person or a man or whatever so that you can rob them," Fortune explained.

"I mean, he seems like a crafty guy. He said he should have done a bank job. His old lady was freaking the fuck out; he cleaned up the scene and jumped in the truck," Fortune claimed.

Ward was somewhat skeptical as Phil's truck was stuck in a washout but maybe he just misunderstood how Phil described it.

"So what is your overall impression of what happened based on what Phil has told you?" Ward asked.

"Seems to me, he set his wife up to appear as though she had car trouble, that dude stopped to help and because he acted like John Wayne...he got smoked," Fortune finished.

Ward wasn't sure what to make of it. In a lot of ways it was possible that Phil had said all this stuff but at the same time, jail culture is different and guys say stuff that isn't true to build themselves up. Whether Phil was talking big to Mr. Fortune or telling the truth, Ward could not say. But it did seem somewhat relevant. If it was true, it meant that Sharon was *indeed lying about what happened.*

37

On July 13, 1990 Dr. Bonnington provided the findings of his psychological evaluation to Phil's attorney. The omnibus hearing was scheduled for a week later on July 20, 1990. His findings could influence the judge to disallow the June 7th confession if Phil was not competent to make such a confession.

From his letter to James Kempton on July 13, 1990 Dr. Bonnington wrote:

"...Though tense in the beginning, this man became quite open with me. He understood the purpose of the examination and was willing to accept whatever the evaluation was. He does not feel that he is safe on the streets. He realizes that he has a problem that has not been treated due to his own frustration the one time he went to the V.A. He has had several groups in prison and in the anger management, but he has been unable to reach the source of his problem. He does not understand the disassociation that takes place when he is in the woods, but it seems to be a precipitating factor along with the drinking.

He believes he is an alcoholic and I agree with this assessment.

The only time he was not drinking since high school was while in prison after Vietnam. Apparently he had no serious felonies or police difficulties prior to Vietnam. After Vietnam, besides his suicides, he had a great deal of difficulty fighting, unable to control his rage and anger, feeling desolate, isolated and alienated from the general populace because of their lack of backing of the Vietnam War. He feels he had a chance of becoming a hero in Vietnam, but failed it. He has not until recently at the suggestion of his sister, had any idea of post-traumatic stress disorder. He is quite naive about this condition. He has had repeated dreams about Vietnam and daydreams about it and misses the action, the excitement, the danger and believes it has something to do with why he kills. His statement that he would not like someone like him out on the street as violence is likely to happen again, is good indication of the insight he has. This man declares himself to be dangerous on the streets again. He has been trained in lethal methods to eliminate his opponent.

He represents one of the tragic outcomes of the Vietnam war wherein he carried the lessons learned in the military into civilian life; the rage over his childhood abuse and his ability to kill converge, reinforced by the 'license to kill' given him in Vietnam. The precipitating factors of being in the woods (jungle) and carrying a weapon (shotgun), drinking (a loosening of inhibitions) and the pressure of an unknown male whom he sees as an enemy result in spontaneous and uncontrollable associations so that he is again in the dangerous and exciting situation of Vietnam. The result: He kills and buries the body. The recurrent dreams, the flashbacks and his loosening of reality with liquor all conspire to bring about a violent outcome.

These are not premeditated but are rather the result of intensive training of a lethal nature imposed on him by the service. His rage and anger over an emotionally deprived and abusive childhood solidified him as a proper candidate for the role he fulfilled for the government in Vietnam. He made an aborted attempt to obtain therapy at the V.A. but could not tolerate the frustration. His threshold for frustration is very low and easily overwhelmed. He hoped to be a hero in Vietnam and returned to a country whose people either ignored or decried his exploits. It is likely his violent felonies represent an attempt to both reclaim his status as a hero as well as to punish those he feels ostracized him upon his discharge.

Whether his post-traumatic stress disorder can be treated now after so long a time is questionable. His rage remains unaltered despite the anger management program and represents only the tip of the iceberg of his seething need to relive and re-experience Vietnam all over again. From a psychiatric viewpoint, one must take his life history into account in meeting (sic) out factors that mitigates his crimes.

It is curious that his diagnosis was not made for so many years and therapy directed to it. Three victims are the price of such ignorance... "

Ultimately, the evaluation was a win for both prosecutors and the defense. Dr, Bonnington had concluded Phil was competent enough to make the confession. However, Dr. Bonnington also concluded that Phil suffered from Post-traumatic Stress Disorder but doubted whether it was treatable.

Post-traumatic Stress Disorder as it relates to military combat was not new. It has been documented throughout history under a number of different names.

Shell shock.

Soldier's heart.

Combat fatigue.

Any of these terms may conjure up images of grown men sobbing in a blood filled trench and baying for their mothers' comfort. It is a side effect and a cost of doing business. The business is war; and business, is good. It is faked. It is real. It is undetected and hidden from friends, family and comrades. It is obvious to passers by. It separates the weak of mind from the true of heart.

It is sometimes misunderstood.

It is rarely understood.

Combat veterans across the globe and throughout the history of war have exhibited symptoms which the societies in which they came from (and have returned to after) have found to be undesirable.

However, depending upon the cultural view of war and healing, different societies have had different ways of dealing, coping and treating soldiers returning from war.

For example, American Indian tribes gathered and retold stories of bravery in battle. As young boys proved their worth to the tribe, their names were changed marking the significance of the moment. The community gathered together and retold the stories and the warriors may have felt as though they were transitioning from one stage to the next. It was a natural and expected progression.

In Rome, soldiers returned from lengthy, sometimes year(s) long battle campaigns and were forbidden from entering the city in uniform; they were to behave like citizens, not soldiers. Similarly, lavish ceremonies marked the change in role for the Roman men. Many were farmers or craftsmen with wives and children when they were called upon to fight in the Legions and upon returning, foul language, violent acts and other behaviors were frowned upon. In both cases, these societies recognized that a transition was taking place. Men as soldiers and men as part of the community were different roles and shifting between them may not always be easy. But it was clear that a shift was expected to occur.

Murder myself, Murder I am.

Comparatively, returning veterans from Vietnam were often ostracized and rebuffed by society. Treatments of this late sixties and early seventies culture are vast and readily available. But one thing appears to be clear, media coverage from the era focused on the idea that soldiers returning from Vietnam as a whole did not receive the same welcome from the general public as soldiers returning from other conflicts had received.

In post-Vietnam America, it has become known as Post-traumatic Stress Disorder. Or simply: PTSD. Post-traumatic Stress Disorder is characterized in the Diagnostic and Statistic Manual of Mental Disorders 4th Edition (DSM-IV) by symptoms of significant distress or impairment socially, occupationally or in some other area of functioning as a result of the exposure of the patient to some sort of direct or indirect trauma.

Specifically, a person must:
1) Have been exposed to a traumatic event;
2) The person must re-experience the event in at least one of several ways;
3) The person avoids reminders of the event and the avoidance must be manifested in at least three separate ways;
4) The person has at least two symptoms of increased arousal;
5) The three types of symptoms listed must be present together for at least one month causing clinically significant distress or impairment socially, occupationally or in some other area of functioning.

(Paraphrased from the Diagnostic and Statistical Manual of Mental Disorders 4th edition.)

The American Psychiatric Association (APA) first recognized PTSD in 1980 {Diagnostic and Statistic Manual of Mental Disorders 3rd Edition (DSM-III)}. The criteria for diagnosing PTSD were met with skepticism from psychologists, legal professionals and the general public as the condition is somewhat difficult to confirm. In addition, academics in the psychology profession worried that PTSD may be a sociopolitical construct and not a psychiatric condition.

Legal scholars and the general public who were often asked to pay for PTSD programs with tax money were concerned at how easily the condition could be malingered for financial gain. This concern climaxed in 2004 when 4.3 billion dollars were paid out for PTSD related disability payments. During the five years prior to 2004, veterans seeking treatment increased by 80% and disability payments increased by 149%.

It is no surprise the numbers increased as wars on two fronts were being waged (Iraq and Afghanistan). As more people became aware of

PTSD in general and more specifically, PTSD treatment options and the consequences of allowing the condition to go untreated; the stigma attached to those seeking treatment for PTSD may have lessened a little and likely also attributed to the increase in those seeking treatment.

It seemed unlikely that Phil would be able to use this as a defense but affirmative defenses such as these were becoming more and more common.

Especially if this was to become a death penalty case.

It could be very relevant at sentencing no matter how the case played out. It looked more and more like Phil's wife was not going to be able to testify and the case which seemed to be air tight in the beginning as an aggravated first degree murder was now in jeopardy of dropping all the way to murder in the second degree. Regardless of what name is given to the offense, it meant that he could possibly do as little as *15 years*.

As the saying goes, sometimes the best defense is a good offense; and now that Dr. Bonnington's report was part of the case file, Phil's defense made Phil available to the press. If this was going to go to trial, the more press coverage about Phil's time in the military the better. Vietnam had been officially over for 15 years by 1990 but the stigma and remorse of how society treated Vietnam veterans when they returned was a very relevant issue of the time. If Phil's defense could capture this, it could bode very well for them at trial.

The report from Dr. Bonnington came out on Friday, July 13 and on the following Sunday a full page, two part article was published in the Seattle Times chronicling what was known so far and trying to offer up some sort of insight on the killer and the victim.

Mom had been contacted by the reporters who prepared the article and she refused to do an interview with them. It had only been two months and although she was appreciative of how the media attention had played a significant role in bringing Rich's killer to justice, she was apprehensive at describing Rich's life and childhood so it could be compared to Phillip Hillman's. Reporters then contacted Rich's parents and other friend's of Rich who were more than happy to relate what they knew of Rich.

A picture accompanying the article showed Phil in his Army uniform as he graduated from basic training and lamented his tough up-bringing and alcoholism. The article also conceptualized the idea that his job in Vietnam was so horrific it must have made him this way. Most disappointing to my mother when she read the article was the continued assumption by the reporters that Phillip Hillman was telling the truth about his role in Vietnam.

What if he never really ambushed trails and dug shallow graves to bury the dead?

In psychological evaluations, doctors have to assume that the patient is telling the truth. Philosophically, this assumption is made because doctors believe it is in the patients best interest do so if the help they are seeking is going to do any good.

However, a court case is a whole different matter.

If the defense were going to use an affirmative defense they were going to have to prove these claims and not just use them to garner sympathy from the jury pool.

38

Investigators were not convinced about Phil's claim to have suffered from Post-traumatic Stress Disorder. No doubt he suffered and possibly continues to suffer from something.

Psychologists who examine patients like these admittedly can only base their diagnoses from what they are told, what they have seen and how, in their professional estimation, the symptoms fit the diagnosis.

However, Phil claimed on more than one occasion that he *may have* felt like he was back in Vietnam where his role was to kill Vietnamese and drag their bodies off the trail and bury them.

Investigators are trained to focus on minute details, body language, facial expressions and speech patterns. Interestingly, on more than one occasion, he prefaces this idea with "Maybe I" or "I may have..." suggesting he may not be being truthful. He may not want to commit to this idea fully and he is prepared to get "caught in a lie" so to speak. By prefacing it with "maybe" or "may have", he can get out of or retract the statement when needed.

Although this is common nomenclature when discussing ideas or philosophies where one uses this preface simply because they do not know the answer for sure. In this case, it seems pretty clear, either Phil killed Vietnamese and dragged them off the trail burying them in shallow graves *or he didn't.*

Investigators wondered; *why the preface?*

If he is simply lying about the extent of his combat role in Vietnam, this does not change the fact that he may have suffered from some sort of Post-traumatic Stress Disorder.

But how would it play out to a jury?

It seemed a jury would have far more sympathy for a combat veteran. And they would have to show that despite his service; perhaps he was not telling the truth about what he did in Vietnam. Perhaps it was merely a convenient scapegoat.

Further, it directly changed the role and impact the United States military may have had in this case. For, if the United States Army did not turn him into a killer through his mission and role in Vietnam, what did happen?

Was he prone to violence before going to combat?

Maybe he hoped the Army would provide him the opportunities to kill and when they didn't, he deserted the Army and began killing on his own.

Investigators needed to be ready with the facts.

If this was going to be a capital murder case, every tiny and minute detail had to be thoroughly investigated and prepared for trial. If the prosecution wasn't prepared, the jury could become sympathetic and relying upon requests for discovery from the defense was not going to be enough.

These kinds of fact finding missions were always tough. If the prosecution was going to try and disprove the facts surrounding his combat service, they would have an uphill battle with a jury.

First, they would have to avoid coming across as anti-military or anti-war. They would have to show that their attempts to sort out the truth from the fiction with respect to Phil's enlistment in Vietnam should in no way be viewed as an attempt to discredit those who served valiantly, honorably and with dignity regardless of the year served or the political conditions of the times.

They would have to persuade a jury, that in fact, it is quite the opposite. Hundreds, perhaps thousands of soldiers returned from Vietnam and experienced difficulties in processing or coming to terms with their own unique experience. Hundreds and perhaps thousands returned to the United States and suffered no ill effects.

No experience can be compartmentalized and each individual experience is unique to that person. Because each persons experience is unique, and because we as a society have created a system of laws whereby we judge the actions of our fellows, we examine written records and try and glean truth from them, whatever that truth may be.

In many cases we are unable to find any amount of certainty in truth. In other cases, the truth becomes crystal clear and pointedly reveals fact. In most cases, the truth lies somewhere in between these two endpoints, and just as the combat experience is unique to each person, the responsibility for that persons actions which can be placed directly or even indirectly at the feet of that combat experience varies for each person looking in from the outside.

It would be difficult to determine if Phil's role and mission in Vietnam was to *kill Vietnamese, quietly drag them off the trail and bury them* or not, but the available records could be examined and matched up with known historical facts from the Vietnam War to try and get a better picture.

With 100% certainty, combat soldiers in Vietnam were asked to fulfill missions which required the kinds of actions the killer has claimed to be influenced by and distraught over. Veterans in units like the 82nd Airborne, 101st Airborne during the peak years of combat; 1968-1970 were without a doubt running these types of missions.

But the 1st of the 7th Air Cavalry (Air Mobile)?

Other more obscure less popularized units and soldiers were probably also running such missions. Exactly how the defendant fit into all of this can only be discerned from the record. And even that, will always leave some amount of arguable doubt.

Records from the conflict in Vietnam are at times, incomplete. Enough books, movies and other forms of media have been produced portraying the conflict in Vietnam in a multitude of ways.

According to official United States Army records obtained through public disclosure requests, Phil enlisted in the Army on September 1, 1971 while still just 17 years old.

His father, he had told friends, was a 'war hero' and he wanted to be one also. Dr. Bonnington alludes to this in his report and Sharon even mentioned it in an interview with detectives.

In order to get the required signatures from his parents enabling him to enlist, the prosecution would explain how he reportedly shot himself in the stomach in a feigned suicide attempt. Fearing he may cause further harm to himself if he were not able to join up, his parents relented and signed the forms.

He attended basic training in Tacoma, Washington at Ft. Lewis and on the 5th of November in 1971, he became a Combat Infantryman (11B10). Because he was not 18 years of age he could not yet serve in combat operations in Vietnam.

Becoming a hero would have to wait, the prosecution would argue.

On March 14, 1972, six days after his 18th birthday, he was en route to the United States Army Pacific (USARPAC) Republic of Vietnam (RVN).

401

Two weeks later on March 28, 1972 he was assigned to Company C 1st Bn 7th Cav (AirMobile) which was part of the 3rd Brigade of the 1st Cavalry Division.

Finally, he would become a war hero, just like he told friends.

And this, the prosecution could argue, was a critical juncture in this entire story.

Problem was, to be a war hero, he needed a war.

And the war in Vietnam was winding down.

Almost a year earlier in June of 1971, Secretary of Defense Melvin Laird announced that responsibility for 90% of the combat operations in Vietnam had been given to the Army of the Republic of Vietnam. By March of 1972, all combat operations had become the sole responsibility of Army of the Republic of Vietnam units. The United States was still providing air support and cover. Most combat units had redeployed out of Vietnam. The sole remaining combat units left were the 196th Infantry Brigade and the brigade his battalion (1st Bn of the 7th Cavalry) was assigned to, the 3rd Brigade of the 1st Cavalry Division.

On March 30th 1972, the north Vietnamese launched the largest offensive of the entire conflict known as the Easter Offensive.

The only American unit involved was the 196th.

Although the 196th Infantry Brigade responded and supported efforts to repel the North Vietnamese during the Easter Offensive, the *3rd Brigade of the 1st Cavalry Division did not.*

According to the June 16, 1972 edition of the St. Petersburg Independent, the 3rd Brigade was providing "security for the Saigon-Long Binh-Bien Hoa complex in the capital military region."

On June 26, 1972, the remaining units of the 1st Cavalry Division were brought back to the United States.

Having only been in Vietnam for 90 days, the defendant was reassigned to C Company, 87th Infantry effective August 13, 1972. This unit had recently been reassigned as part of the 18th MP Brigade.

The last official ground combat casualty occurred on August 10, 1972 when D Company 3rd Battalion 21st Infantry went on a four day patrol and two soldiers were wounded in a booby trap. This final combat unit had been assigned to guard the US helicopter base at Da Nang.

No one was going out into the jungles to kill Vietnamese and drag them off the trails and bury them in shallow graves.

Only those with specialty jobs and those with less than six months of service would remain. Phil had been in country only four and a half months. He would be eligible to leave September 28, 1972.

Investigators knew it would be an uphill battle.

They could raise doubts as to the defendants claims regarding his role in killing Vietnamese but did any of these facts stand up and prove the killer did not, 'Kill Vietnamese and drag them off the tail and bury them?'

No.

Did any of these facts support such a role and mission by the killer?

No.

It was clear that a black and white answer was not going to be possible. But the prosecution certainly could raise doubts as to Phil's claim of killing Vietnamese and burying them.

The prosecution would then have to offer up more of a plausible scenario than Phil was just lying about his experience in Vietnam to try and get out of killing two people and nearly a third.

Each individuals experience is their own and despite records, accounts and debriefings, no one will ever to truly be able to conceptualize the Vietnam experience of another.

But, based on the military records, historical facts about ground combat operations in Vietnam from March of 1972 through August of 1972 and the personal details of the defendant from the time prior to his enlistment through his discharge in 1973, it is entirely plausible that *prior to his enlistment,* Phil's violent nature was growing and increasing.

After interviewing dozens of people who knew the defendant during childhood, junior high school, acquaintances and neighbors, investigators began to hypothesize that a number of factors may have combined to drive him toward the US Army and combat in Vietnam.

His alcoholic father continuously belittling him, his need to live up to the "war hero" status he felt his father had obtained. In some sense, if he were to go to Vietnam and kill enemy soldiers and save the lives of American brethren in arms he could come back and exorcise the demons placed upon him.

He could also satiate the need to kill and to be violent. He was good at it, this he knew.

He liked it. He enjoyed it.

No longer would he have to listen to the stories about World War II and Korea.

About how *his father's* generation knew what America was about.

How *his father's* generation knew that sacrifice and hard work would move the American way forward.

That the North Vietnamese were nothing compared to the Nazis and the Japs and the North Koreans.

How they knew what honor was, they knew what meant something.

They did not run around protesting wars—they volunteered to serve and to fight them to preserve the American way, his generation had landed on Normandy and Guam and was ready to invade mainland Japan.

His generation was not hooked on LSD or taking pot or having orgies on the lawn of an academic institution or government office.

His generation had honor and discipline.

He could finally get the monkey off his back. Only problem was, *the war was over.*

Prosecutors could argue he had missed most of the action. It was now August, 1972 and soldiers interviewed in papers across the country were pointing out what a joke the situation in Vietnam had become.

One returning soldier stated that "No one had been hurt or injured in his unit for over 8 months. If you weren't in the 196th, you had zero chance of seeing any action."

For many, this was a blessing.

For some it was disheartening. Having been assigned as a rifleman in C Company 87th Infantry in August of 1972 was almost a formality. They were all that was left, and they were now part of an MP Brigade.

He was excited when he first got there, to be assigned to a unit that might go do something- the 1st Air Cavalry; but they got orders to leave the country—it was over. The 1st Air Cavalry was leaving and because he had only been there for a couple months he was stuck. He spent the summer like he had spent the spring; *waiting.*

What did it matter? He was over here and his father and anyone else who mattered would know no different about what went on where they couldn't be.

If this went to trial, prosecutors would have to tear down the idea of a returning war hero. That would have been easy in the 70's, but it was 1990.

Prosecutors would have to tell the jury, that he *is lying.*

That he could tell stories about Vietnam however he wanted.

He could go back and tell off the old man with stories of how he had charged through the jungle taking fire and saving his buddies.

He could say whatever he wanted. *Whether it was true or not.*

One thing could be proven, that by November 15, 1972 he had returned to the continental United States and was stationed at Ft. Lewis. It would be another two months until he was assigned as an Auto Rifleman in Co C2 of the 39th Infantry 9th Infantry Division. Back in the States, his addictions weren't as easy to hide nor as tolerated as they were in Vietnam. Nick Hansen had signed a sworn statement in 1974 claiming that Phil was strung out 'on junk' in Vietnam.

Readjusting to life in the States wasn't as simple either. Sure, he could drink- and drink to oblivion if he wanted. For soldiers who came back two, three or even four years before this, it was different.

They had seen major combat.

They were in the jungles under fire and fighting to keep the war winnable. He had been guarding air bases and listening to everybody else's stories about war.

How the 1st Air Cavalry killed Vietnamese in the jungle, how the 9th Infantry waded through rice paddies and killed everything they could. They were just like the guys who had stormed Normandy or crossed the Rhine or who fought inch by inch through Italy.

Now, it appeared to investigators that he had missed out on major combat, but he could lie about that.

The Army of 1973 was changing and changing fast.

The draft was nearly officially ended. Reveille was a thing of the past. Soldiers did not need to rise up two hours before starting their work duties.

Mustaches were even allowed.

The Army had gone soft.

They wanted guys to go to college; they gave guys separate individual rooms.

Some of them even had peace symbols knitted into blankets sent from home.

Maybe his father didn't even believe the stories about killing Vietnamese on the trail or charging in to the jungles to save his buddies. Everybody back here knew the stories. The war was over before he got there. The papers said, The TV reporters showed. Every movie theatre across America ran trailers before movies exposing it all. Everybody was hooked on dope, a majority had half Vietnamese babies who were trying to get into the US and the rest couldn't stop the burning, dripping and itching every time they had to piss. *The sins of war in a foreign land.*

The old man knew.

Everybody knew.

So much for being a war hero.

What a crock.

And he didn't even get to kill anybody. It was January, 1973.

He could drink though.

He could drink.

By March 3, 1973 he had been dropped from the rolls and listed by the US Army as deserted. Sixteen days later he found himself in bed at Madigan Army Hospital in Tacoma, Washington after attempting suicide by overdosing on Seconal. Nothing had gone right.

How could this be?

After tearing apart honorable military service, prosecutors would have to win back the jury. They would tell about the awards and ribbons the defendant had won.

The first being the National Defense Service Medal. This was awarded to any member of the military during recognized time periods. For the Vietnam era, the period was designated January 1, 1961 to August 14, 1974. Recipients of this award do not have to be directly involved with combat operations or in any proximity to the conflict area. This award recognizes that a person was in the military during a designated major conflict.

Next, he received the Vietnam Service Medal. This was awarded to members of the military serving in Vietnam and "contiguous waters or airspace." Members of the military who served in Laos, Cambodia or Thailand in support of operations for Vietnam during specific time periods were also eligible.

In addition to the medal, the Department of Defense established thirty separate and distinct military campaigns defining the period of service for which the medal was awarded. The defendant received the award for the 29th campaign; officially designated 'Vietnam Cease Fire' (March 30, 1972 through March 28, 1973). The third medal, The Republic of Vietnam Campaign Medal, was identical in eligibility requirements as the Vietnam Service Medal but was issued by the government of the Republic of Vietnam — not the United States. Its use and wearing on the uniform was authorized by the Department of Defense and reception of the award is notated on official military service records.

He received an Overseas Bar which is presented for serving overseas in a combat zone for a total cumulative time of six months.

Finally, he received a Sharpshooters Badge with an Automatic Rifle Bar. These badges are awarded based on three skill levels: Expert being the highest; Sharpshooter in the middle; and Marksman being the third or lowest rank. A number of different bars can accompany the badge signifying which weapon was used to qualify with- Pistol, Carbine Rifle, and Automatic Rifle etc. None of these awards and decorations seemed to provide any more or less insight to the role, function and mission by which he served. But now that prosecutors had restored the military honor, how would they portray the defendant in closing?

After returning from Vietnam, they would argue, he could hear the old man laughing in his head. The alcohol didn't work anymore. He had wanted to go to exotic far away lands and kill *gooks*. He didn't want to sit in a hospital bed 35 miles south of his hometown and watch while his father laughed at how the US Army that he was a part of was soft, weak and pathetic.

The US Army had convened a Court Martial for his desertion but it had become abundantly clear to the staff and doctors at the hospital that they simply had another casualty of the 1972-1973 era of the Vietnam War: he was strung out.

They had seen it hundreds of times before and were trying to figure out the best method for dealing with the hundreds of cases they were going to see in the future. The post-Vietnam Army of 1973 was not going to tolerate drug abuse and addiction.

The "Old Reliables" University forming at Ft. Lewis to bring the next generation of soldiers into the post Vietnam cold war era had no place for addicts. There was no point in convening a Court Martial for this. Why make the plight of the Vietnam soldier any worse? Why put more destruction into the eyes of the media? Reporters during the war had done enough damage to the conservative military establishment. It was time to use the media to show how the military was changing for the better. How Nixon's vision of an all volunteer force would work using attraction rather than discipline. No one wanted to see or hear about a Court Martial convened to determine a junky could no longer function in today's Army.

No, the Court Martial would have to wait for different days. He would be generally discharged. Not honorably or dishonorably. It was easier to admit the old ways of the Army weren't working and let the last bit of evidence of it disappear into the cocktail lounges, rehab centers and AA halls across the country. On April 27, 1973 he was out of the United States Army.

Did Phillip Hillman serve his country honorably in Vietnam?

Without a doubt he was there.

But do his claims about setting up ambushes and dragging the victims off the trail and burying them in shallow graves seem plausible?

Unlikely.

Phil Hillman was not a war hero suffering from PTSD and haunted by the sins of Vietnam.

He was no monster.

Until he drank.

And now the only conclusion a jury could reasonably come to, was that Phil Hillman suffered from unquestionably difficult circumstances. But by his own admission, when he drinks he cannot control his actions.

There is no cure for alcoholism.

There is no cure for the childhood memories which haunt him.

There is no cure for wanting to kill so badly that you shot yourself in the stomach *at 17.*

There is no cure for *not becoming* a war hero.

407

Murder myself, Murder I am.

The one recognizable condition that Phillip Hillman *does have* which can be cured, is his inability to control himself from killing innocent people when the rage hits him.

And the cure for that is to put this man behind concrete walls, razor wire and armed guards.

And never let him out.

39

A few days later, mother received a phone call from prosecutors. They wanted to discuss the terms of a plea deal. The defense wanted the death penalty off the table and they were willing to plea this out. Perhaps they knew the defendant's combat service could not be substantiated. Maybe they weren't sure a jury would even care.

An affirmative defense was always risky.

Mom was stunned.

This meant no trial to sit through. This meant that she wouldn't have to spend her sleepless nights worrying about whether he would even be convicted. This could mean the end of this chapter of the nightmare. Finally, this man would be locked up for good.

On July 19, Mom and a number of Rich's close friends met with prosecutors at their office in the Snohomish County Courthouse. It had been over a month since Phil had given his statement and they had since interviewed Sharon a second time and Phil's sister, Jody. Investigators had thoroughly looked in to Phil's background and even spoken with an inmate in the same cell block as Phil. They now had a much clearer picture of what the defense was going to argue. Dr. Bonnington's report confirmed that Phil was competent to make the statement he had on June 7th, but it also speculated that Phil may suffer from some form of PTSD related to his service in Vietnam.

Gerry MacCamy started off the meeting by assuring the group that if they had to go to trial they had him hands down, without a doubt, on second degree murder.

Second degree murder?

What happened?

The first problem was spousal privilege. It was possible that the prosecution could ask the judge to allow Sharon to testify but it was extremely unlikely that the judge would allow it. Even if he did and they got a conviction months down the road, it would very likely be overturned on appeal. The law was very clear about allowing a spouse to testify against their spouse unless they were the victim of the crime or victim of a related crime. The charges against Phil for assaulting Sharon when he pointed the shotgun at her had been dropped.

Phil very much believed he was only guilty of second degree murder and not first, and most definitely not aggravated first degree murder. To him, what he had done to Rich was no different than what he had done to Newton Thomas. And if that was second degree murder back in 1974 then it should be second degree murder now.

They explained that it was also unlikely that they could prove an aggravating circumstance without Sharon' testimony. No matter how many times they interviewed witnesses, they weren't going to find the keys to the Mustang nor were they going to get Phil to admit he took them off of Rich's body. By now his lawyer had made it very clear to Phil what not to say. However, if the defense would only plead to second degree, then the prosecution would move forward with the aggravating circumstance at trial and also move forward with the death penalty.

But Phil's lawyer would know that they were bluffing, whether he would risk calling their bluff when his client's life was on the line was the only leverage they had. The defense would most likely put Phil's service in Vietnam on trial through his Post-Traumatic Stress Disorder diagnosis and if it didn't get him off on a lesser charge, it was very likely the jury would have enough sympathy that they would not sentence him to death. If they did manage to convict him of aggravated first degree murder, he would then get life without parole.

It was also possible that the jury would not view Phil's admission that he "apparently grabbed the shotgun" and then killed Rich minutes later as premeditation. It was possible they would come back with a second degree murder conviction. It seemed that if they could get him to plea to first degree murder then they would be coming out ahead.

Mom had listened quietly as the prosecutors explained the different scenarios. She was not looking for the death penalty but she firmly believed that life without parole was warranted for what he had done to

Rich. Not to mention what James Sylte had suffered and Newton Thomas deserved more justice than the seven and a half years Phil served for ruthlessly gunning down a defenseless 83 year old man.

Essentially this meant that they were compromising at murder in the first degree. The prosecution viewed this as a win. They were essentially getting the defense to *plea up* to first degree by forcing the defense to risk a lot at trial.

Mom and the rest of the group seemed satisfied. They didn't care what *label* the lawyers wanted to attach to his crime; first degree, second degree — tenth degree- what mattered was that he would never be free to do this again.

In order to get the plea, the prosecution continued, they would have to agree to recommend to the judge at sentencing, that Phil be sentenced to the upper end of the sentencing range. The days of the Indeterminate Sentencing Review Board were over. Judges now used a sentencing grid put in place by the Sentencing Reform Act (SRA) of 1981. Any crimes committed after July 1, 1984 fell under these new guidelines. The SRA created a grid whereby one axis took the offenders previous crimes and assigned the offender an "Offender Score"; the other axis factored in the seriousness of the current conviction. In theory, this type of sentencing created consistency in sentencing whereas criminals with similar histories received similar sentences for like crimes. Regardless of race, sex, age or status.

Mom asked the prosecutor to cut to the chase.

"How many years is that?"

Nearly all of Rich's friends stared intently at the prosecutor. He stood silently for a few seconds. Mom expected that he would get at least 50 years maybe even more.

"32 years," he finally said, "and with a third off for good time, we are looking at about 21 and a half."

"*WHAT?!*" mother exclaimed out loud.

"Karen, we know-"

"*NO WAY! And don't!... Don't you DARE!*" Mom cut him off.

After fighting with the police from the very beginning to get them to look for Rich to hearing a Darrington Police Officer tell her she was "probably looking for a body" yet still refusing to help to listening to John Sundstrom tell her about how Phil had killed a defenseless old man and then hearing James Sylte exalt to her how he could not believe they ever let him out after trying to kill him to now hearing he could possibly be a free man in as little as *21 or 22 years?*

This was too much. This was not going to stand and she would not go down without a fight or without telling them what she thought.

"Karen, we just think that-"

"No! *You listen to me.* You sit down and you listen. I know that this meeting is nothing more than a way for you to tell us what's going to happen before it gets out to the press. And I am so thankful for all the work that John Hinds and the other detectives did on this," Mom began.

Detectives seated in the conference room began to smile.

No one said a word.

"But 21 *years?* That's not justice. That's a joke. I have NEVER believed that this guy has told the truth about what happened. I still don't believe what his wife is saying and sure, she came forward and threw her husband under the bus so she wouldn't go to jail also. She said it was 45 minutes before Rich came back and he said it was 10 or 15 minutes. They said it happened at nearly 7:30 or 8:00 and that's a crock! Everyone in this room who knows Rich knows that is a crock."

Mom was taking control of the room.

"If you're going to take this plea bargain then you are going to listen to what I have to say. Somebody is going to hear what I have to say! And what about this guy, this "informant" what about that. He admitted that his 'wife couldn't peel a trick right'? And he got smoked 'cause he acted like a John Wayne? These people are lying about something-" Mom was beginning to get very upset.

"Karen, we know this but it's about what we can prove, we have him for second degree murder and they are going to plea to first, this is a win," One of the assistant prosecutors tried to interject.

"I don't care if he pleads to tenth degree murder- 21 years is *not enough!* There is no way Rich would have used his car to tow that truck out. There is no way he would have hiked up that hill to even look at that truck- and PTSD? That's such a crock!" Mom continued.

She took a deep breath.

"When you look at his statement he made when he killed Newton Thomas- did he mention having a Vietnam flashback? *NO!* If he were having a Vietnam flashback when he killed Rich then why didn't he kill his wife, too? If he saw nothing but Vietnamese coming down that trail then his own wife would have been a Vietnamese and he would have shot her, but he knew she wasn't! NO! Instead he *shot my husband!*"

Mom was nearly crying but she found the strength to keep going.

The room was dead silent.

"And there was no mention of Vietnam when he attacked that man in Seattle, he said 'A weird feeling came over him'; well yeah, he was drunk and had just been in a fight in a tavern, I bet he did feel weird! And you even looked at his military records- he lied in his statement when he said he was in that unit, the 1st of the 7th or whatever it was, for a year and it turns out he was only in it for a couple of months! That unit he said he was in was back in Texas by June of 1972. I just read about it!"

Mom had to stop and gather herself.

But no one in the room even moved or made a sound. They knew she was not finished.

"So if I have this right, he killed a man, a defenseless *83 year old man* who had spent his life helping others and his own doctors in 1982 characterize the murder by saying 'Phil got in to a fight with a 77 year old man'. *A fight?* What a bunch of bologna! And they let him out of prison— even though he beat the crap of someone in prison—they let him out - even though he had only been in there for seven years! Seven years for killing Newton Thomas. This after he walks away from the work farm for two days. *He escapes and they don't make him serve out his full sentence?* And then- and then when he gets out for that in less than six months he tries to kill James Sylte? That ALONE should have put him back in prison for life! Or at least for the rest of the 20 years he was sentenced to. He would still be in prison until 1994 and we wouldn't even be here. But instead, *his release date becomes earlier than it was before!"*

Mom was only getting started.

"But that's not good enough. No. He goes back to prison and gets married? And even though *every psychological evaluation* I have read in these case files says he has mental problems ranging from psychopathic deviancy to antisocial disorder to 'passive aggressive' behavior, they decide that after killing one man and nearly another, he just needs to keep away from alcohol, go to 'group therapy' and then they suggest he go to marriage counseling before he decides to have kids? *Are you kidding me!* This justice system is a joke!"

"Karen, if we could, there is-"

"*I am not finished. Sit down sir!*" Mom yelled.

"So now that he's back out on the streets again, his family is supposed to keep his parole officer abreast of how he is doing. And how did that work? He moves into Rainier Valley and goes on a cocaine binge. His wife knew and his sister knew. His parole officer decides to let him go to treatment, this according to the papers, because he 'turned himself in'. *Did that dumb broad even read his case file? I doubt it.* And then, speaking of the papers, one of his family members, probably his sister, but who knows? Someone says they didn't want him to go back to prison 'just for having a beer?' My God, are these people *insane?* His own wife knows what he did for almost ten days! And she could never have turned him in before? Not when he drove Rich's car to Darrington? Not when he went to some sales meeting? And his own sister knew he killed Rich on Thursday night- it was 24 hours before Sharon had come forward. If there is one thing clear throughout all of this it's not Vietnam, it's not people trying to harm him or hurt him in any way; in any of this! It's simple. This man is nothing more than a misbehaving little boy who grew up violent and when he gets drunk he reverts to a little boy having a temper tantrum. Only, now, he has a gun or a knife and he goes after people who are defenseless or *even people trying to help him like MY HUSBAND DID!"*

Mom was screaming now. Still no one even moved.

They all stared and listened.

"You know, I am sorry, I know you all have done so much to help, but this...this is NOT justice. 21 and a half years? No way! You know, when Newt was killed it seemed no one really even got to go to court and speak for him and James Sylte wasn't even contacted when this man was sentenced for trying to kill him. And now, the one person who can put this man in prison for life was given 'use immunity' for her cooperation and now *she can't even testify? AND she might be lying about the whole thing?* Look, I know you have done your best, and this is no ones fault, the law is the law. But I will not be a part of this. If you think you should take this deal and it is the best you are going to get then take it. But I will not sit by while this man tries to get out of prison ever. I will go to every parole hearing and I will write letters to every person that receives mail that can keep this man behind bars and I will work to get every single person whoever knew Rich, knew someone who knew Rich or even heard of Rich to write the judge letters and I will beg and plead for them to put him away for life, no matter what plea deal you have arranged. *This is not justice!* Not for Newton Thomas. Not for James Sylte and certainly not for my husband who the only thing he did that day was try and help these people," Mom finally finished.

"Well Karen, we understand how tough this has been. But we think this is the best we can do."

Mom had said her piece.

On July 20, 1990, Phil pleaded guilty to murder in the first degree. The prosecution had agreed to recommend a sentence of 32 years at sentencing.

*   *   *

A few days later Detective Hinds explained that Mom would have the opportunity to send in a Victim Impact Statement. It was a letter that the judge was required to read before sentencing.

"Can only I send one in? Or can my son Jon, and my daughter Colleen, can they send one is as well?" Mom asked.

"Anyone can send one in. Anyone who was impacted by this crime. The judge does not have to go with what the plea agreement is. He can

414

give what is called an 'exceptional sentence' if he thinks it's warranted." Detective Hinds answered.

'So, *anyone* who was impacted by this can send a letter to the judge?" Mom asked again.

"Yes."

"Can I campaign for people to send in letters or does the law require that the people do them on their own?" Mom inquired.

"You can send everyone you know an envelope already stamped and addressed to the judge, its ok. I have seen a few cases where the judge received dozens of letters. It can really have an effect," Hinds answered.

"And how much of an exceptional sentence can he give?" Mom asked.

"He can do whatever he feels is justified, but remember, Phil will be able to appeal it if it's out of the standard range. So even if he does give him an exceptional sentence, he might be able to appeal it," Hinds explained.

Mom stared out the window.

"You know Karen, I want you know we did everything we possibly could. If there ever was a case where...where the death penalty was called for, I think this is it. But sometimes we just can't get the sentence they deserve, you know," Hinds said.

Mom looked at Detective Hinds and smiled.

"I know you did. And I know you did the right thing in giving her immunity. I don't blame you at all. It was the right thing to do at the time. I just- I just wish we could get the truth," Mom confided.

"Truth about what, Karen?" Hinds asked.

"The truth about what really happened up there, that day. I don't believe it happened like they said it did. Rich *would never have offered to tow that car*. And he was supposed to be-"

"Karen, I don't believe it either. I have been involved in a lot of these cases. Sometimes we never even catch who did it; sometimes there are questions that we just don't ever get the answer to. At least we found your husband and got someone. Someone will pay for this. No matter what, a 32 year sentence is not going to be a walk in the park," Hinds explained.

"Well, keep me informed if anything changes and when the sentencing is going to be. I have a lot of work to do before then," Mom said and climbed in to her Volvo.

Over the next month and a half, Mom set about contacting every single person she or Rich knew to fill out a Victim Impact Statement. She began by networking through Duvall Realty and collected every name and address she could. She and her friends spent hours every week calling and contacting as many people as humanly possible. Mom kept a box of envelopes that she had already stamped and had filled in the Judges address with her at all times. Whether she was at the grocery store or the bank or going to dinner, she kept the envelopes with her along with the instructions on how to write the letter to the Judge. Whenever she saw someone who had heard the story of what happened to Rich and they were impacted by the story, they could send in a letter Mom explained.

She kept a checklist of names to make sure she had contacted everyone and during the last week of August and the first week of September she politely followed up with everyone on her list to make sure they had sent in their letter so the judge would have time to consider them before the sentencing hearing scheduled for September 12, 1990. Every envelope she sent out also included a couple of extras so that they could pass them along to anyone else who may have known Rich. By her figures she expected that the judge would receive at least 150 to 200 letters. She had created more than 250 envelopes and stamped and addressed them all by hand. By September 5th, she was out of envelopes. All she could do now was follow up and send more last minute envelopes as needed.

A few days before the sentencing, Mom got a call from the prosecutor, Gerry MacCamy. He explained that the sentencing was being delayed by two weeks because the judge had already received *over 200 letters* and more were pouring in every day.

Mom was not the slightest bit surprised.

Jon Keehner

40

Wednesday   September 26, 1990

The courtroom was nearly packed. Every wooden bench was full.

Onlookers had filled in at such numbers that the walls of both sides of the courtroom were full of people standing and looking toward the bench.

The proceedings were supposed to start at 2:00 PM and it was now 2:06. I stood in the left rear corner of the courtroom drenched in a long black trench coat. I knew from going to court before, that this was the best place to get face to face with the convict.

The room was warm and the windows high along the walls were beginning to fog up, the room was mostly quiet, especially considering 80-100 people had crowded into a room designed for 40-50.

To my right I saw a bailiff walk in and stand near the entrance to the courtroom, and then another took a position on the other side of the entrance. Then two more came through and extended their arms along the benches in an effort to keep the crowd away from the entrance. I heard the ding of the elevator and two more bailiffs came rushing out.

Then I heard the short footsteps and the rattling of chains.

Two more bailiffs came through the entrance; these guys were big, easily over 6′2″ and 230 pounds apiece. The source of the rattling chains finally came in to view.

He was about 5′8″ with sandy blonde hair. He looked nothing like the pictures in the paper or the composite sketch. He was wearing a green jumpsuit and taking very short steps as his ankles were chained tightly and there was very little slack between the two leg braces. His arms extended in front of him like small tree trunks. They too, were clasped very tightly in chains.

When he saw the enormous crowd who had gathered, he grinned. He knew he was only going to get 32 years and that he would be out by 2014. Sure it was a long time, but time was something he had done. He grinned and the room became so silent the only sound was the clink... clink... clink... of the chains as he made his way the 30 or 40 feet it took to get to the defendants table in the front.

For a second, I thought I heard my mother crying softly ahead of me in the center of the courtroom.

Then it stopped.

I squeezed through the crowd and slipped in next to her.

"ALL RISE!" the clerk ordered, seated just beneath the bench up front.

"The Honorable Daniel J. Kershner, presiding," she announced.

Daniel Kershner was the same judge who had sentenced Phil to 20 years in 1974.

"Be seated," he quickly stated as he sat in the judges chair and opened the proceedings.

"Let me be clear, this is an emotional process, and by the amount of attention this case has received and the number of people in my courtroom today, if there are any outbursts, I will have bailiffs clear this courtroom. Thank you."

The courtroom fell completely silent again. He read aloud the charges and confirmed that the defendant had, in fact, plead guilty under his own free will to the charges. He continued to read aloud the recommended sentence that the defense and the prosecution had agreed to.

32 years.

With 1/3 off for good behavior he would be out in about 21 ½ years. Most likely, with his parole being revoked for the 10 years he had been sentenced to for nearly killing James Sylte in November of 1982 his sentence for that offense would have to be completed before this sentence would commence in November of 1992. He would be eligible for release some time in late 2013 or early 2014. That seemed like forever to me, but he would only be 59 years old.

Based on the State of Washington standard sentencing guidelines this was in the high end of the range. Rich would only have been 55 if he had not been murdered by this man. It was unbelievable to me that in four short months the talk around the case had gone from seeking the death penalty to now what looked like a plea deal that would essentially be reduced to 21 ½ years.

418

2013 or 2014? That seemed like a long way off.

Judge Kershner then informed the court that Rich's friend, Barb Goldenberger would read aloud the statement my mother had crafted in between stuffing envelopes with Victim Impact Statements, sorting out her financial affairs and learning how to live without her husband.

Mom and Barb and her husband had spent hours and hours crafting the statement.

It was short and sweet.

The judge then shuffled through a short stack of papers and began speaking.

"The only real issue before the court at this point is whether or not the court; on its own initiative, should impose a sentence outside the standard range. Both the State and the defense are urging the court to sentence the defendant to the top of the standard range, or 388 months. The question is, do I want to declare an exceptional sentence or accept what the State and the defendant are proposing?" he began.

It seemed no one in the courtroom would even dare take a breath or exhale. It was dead silent.

This was indeed the question.

"In order to declare an exceptional sentence, I have to find that there are substantial and compelling reasons to impose such a sentence. There can be little doubt that substantial and compelling reasons do exist in this case," he continued.

The defense attorneys gathered around the front table started to shift in their seats.

"It seems abundantly clear to me, from reading all the information that's been provided, that Mr. Hillman poses a clear and unequivocal danger to society. I think if Mr. Hillman were released at this time, and not that that was even being considered, but were he to be released at this time, I think it's obvious that in all probability he would commit another violent offense. I think this case contains ingredients for substantial consideration of what the court's role is in a case of this kind. I've dealt with many cases concerning the Post-traumatic Stress Disorder, many of those related to the Vietnam experience, and I have, certainly accepted that as being a valid consideration when the court sentences someone that's apparently been subjected to Post-traumatic Stress Disorder. It's certainly something that I should consider."

He then paused and removed his reading glasses.

They are going to let this guy off because of PTSD?

I was enraged.

Smiles began to creep across the faces of the defense attorneys. Phil leaned back in his chair. It seemed it was going to work. This guy got him a light sentence before and he was going to do it again.

The judge rubbed his arm across his face and put his glasses back onto his face.

He continued, "The question as to whether or not it should induce the court to act one way or the other or to lessen the sentence is not clear. However, I think in the case of Mr. Hillman, I have seldom seen a more compelling case for the imposition of an exceptional sentence."

What? Holy shit! Where is this going?

The defense attorneys stared shockingly up toward the bench, Phil quickly leaned forward. Just like that it changed from looking like he was going to get a short sentence to maybe he wouldn't.

My heart raced and I felt my mother's hand grip mine so tight I thought I was going to lose circulation in my fingers.

The reporters in the front of the gallery scribbled away on their pads.

Phil shifted his feet and the chains clinked again against the chair. It looked for a moment as though he shook his head in disbelief. His attorney gently waved his hand in front of Phil, motioning him to be still.

"The release of Mr. Hillman back into society at any time would be tantamount to sentencing another innocent person to death. Mr. Hillman has admitted what occurred. There's no question about that. It's clear in the record what happened in this case. Nor is there any real dispute what happened in the prior murder case or the prior second degree assault case."

The judge stared directly toward Phil and leaned slightly forward, raising his tone just a bit.

Mother's hands were cold and her grip continued; she gently nodded in agreement with the judge.

"Even the defendant admits, and I respect him for much of what he has admitted because so many do not and never do admit, what took place. Mr. Hillman has assumed full responsibility for what he did," he continued.

Respect?

Responsibility?

It was like being suffocated.

Again, it seemed as though he were going to get a light sentence. It seemed as if the judge were taking Phil on a roller coaster ride, and we were all going with him.

"In addition to that, he's stated candidly that he, himself, believes that he's not safe to be at large; that he would constitute a clear and substantial danger to the public if he were at large."

The judge paused, and began to speak in a somewhat reserved tone.

"There is no need for me to go over the facts; the record is replete with what did occur. My conclusion is that the court should consider and should impose an exceptional sentence in this case--"

The courtroom subtly clamored as people looked right and left. The judge banged his gavel and the dull roar quickly subsided.

Mom had gotten it.

He was going to get more than 32 years.

But how much more?

How much had the days and nights of self-addressing hundreds of Victim Impact Statements and phone calls pleading with people to make sure they were mailed and in on time and collecting the names and addresses of everyone who knew someone who knew someone who knew Rich paid off?.

"—and further, because of the obvious future dangerousness of Mr. Hillman. Future dangerousness has been accepted by our courts as a valid consideration for an exceptional sentence. In view of the history of Mr. Hillman, it's so obvious and apparent that I don't think it needs much discussion that there exists a future dangerousness if he is released from confinement in the foreseeable future. So on the basis of future dangerousness, I'm going to impose an exceptional sentence, finding that there's substantial and compelling reasons to do so."

The judge again removed his glasses.

Phil's main defense attorney began shaking his head and he leaned and spoke into Phil's ear. He again motioned for Phil to maintain his calm demeanor.

Under the desk, Phil's leg began shaking, slowly at first; and then to a rapid 150 beats per minute pulse.

It wasn't going well for him.

"Before I do that, though, I'm going to also indicate that I feel there's a second ground. That the future dangerousness, in and of itself, which makes it obvious that the defendant could not be released at this time and probably never should be released because of his inability to control himself, which leads to the death of innocent people. Future dangerousness I feel is probably not contained as a statutory aggravating factor. However, I think it's clearly been accepted by our appellate courts," he continued.

Phil's attorney ran his fingers back through his graying, long, matted hair slowly until his hand came to rest on the back of his scalp, and he clenched the back of his head and let out an audible sigh.

The judge looked at him directly, as though he could foresee the appeal that would be coming. The judge leaned forward in the direction of

Phil and his attorney and his looks shot back and forth, directly into his attorney and then directly at Phil and then back again.

Back and forth, back and forth as he continued to address the court.

"But there's another ground that I think is particularly apropos in this case, and I'm not sure it's ever been used and I'm not sure it would be accepted by the court, but I think in this case there could be a good Samaritan exception which the court could and in this case would use to find a basis for an exceptional sentence. Good Samaritan situations create relationships between people, and the violation of those relationships," he leaned further forward, staring directly into Phil's eyes.

"I think, should be handled very swiftly and very surely by society."

The judge maintained, speaking very slowly and very deliberately; he then leaned back in his chair.

"I don't think anybody could really argue but that we should do whatever we can to try to increase the utilization of good Samaritan direction; that people should continue to and hopefully increase the utilization of good Samaritan direction; that people should continue to and hopefully increase their ability to act in an appropriate good Samaritan manner. Therefore, I think because of the special relationship, because of the nature of the---" the judge paused for a moment and recognized the importance of what he was saying.

"I'd call it trust and the position of vulnerability that someone puts themselves in when they act as a good Samaritan, all lead to my conclusion that there exists another independent ground for an exceptional sentence, and that would be because of the killing while in the process of performing a good Samaritan act. Therefore, I'm going to declare an exceptional sentence."

Phil reached out for the plastic cup of water placed in front of him. His hand shook for but a moment as he raised it to his lips.

"What that exceptional sentence should be has been a real problem for me because I don't know what guidelines there are to set that. Obviously, I think that any sentence has to assure that Mr. Hillman is not released until such time as age and just time itself has minimized the danger to the public. In my opinion, that requires a lengthy sentence. I should add that I don't feel I have the authority to sentence to prison without parole. I think that's reserved for aggravated murder, which that was not the plea here. I'm going to sentence Mr. Hillman to 840 months. That constitutes 70 years."

Immediately the sound of dull whispers and people shifting in their seats began to fill the courtroom.

My mother gasped.

70 years.

422

At that moment I looked around and I wanted to believe that Rich was standing in the corner, watching the proceedings. I wanted to believe that he was sipping on a Super Big Gulp through too small of a straw and looking down at his pager clipped to his belt. I wanted to believe, that 40 miles to the northeast; Newton Thomas got up off the dirt of that North Cascades campground, brushed the pine needles off of his flannel shirt and trousers and finished cooking his supper. I wanted to believe that this was the end and the pain and the suffering I watched my mother go through for the last four and a half months would disappear like the snows of early May melting back in to the Sauk River.

But Newton Thomas never finished cooking his pork and beans.

And Rich's pager wasn't going off.

My mother's tiny, tear drenched hand squeezed mine.

And the months of crying, and wondering, and asking why, and trying to be strong when she hadn't slept for days at a time, and having to tell the story of what had happened to her husband over and over had culminated into Mr. Hillman's fate.

Even though the attorneys and the prosecutors who didn't know Rich and had never met Newton Thomas had decided and agreed upon the sentence weeks earlier. Even though Phil was supposed to get 32 years and with good time, would get out in 2014. Even though the plea meant the sentencing was a formality, my mother, through all of the letters and impact statements to the judge; my mother got her message through.

Judge Kershner heard it, *and he agreed.*

"I feel that the sentence is necessary because there's no other assurance that Mr. Hillman would not be freed to continue his uncontrollable urge to kill, and therefore, the sentence will be for 840 months or 70 years."

"Your Honor, If I may-" Phil's lead attorney finally rose and blurted out. His hands outstretched; his palms pointed upward in the air in disbelief.

"You may," the judge politely responded.

"I feel the court based that upon no assurance that he would be controlled. I feel, with all due respect, Your Honor, that this totally ignores any assurance that may be available in ten years or 20, or even as the prosecutor suggests, and we concurred, 32 years," his attorney started, stunned and dismayed that the judge had gone beyond what he and the prosecution had agreed to.

"I think to totally eliminate any possibility for treatment and rehabilitation 30 years down the road, I think the court is reaching beyond what is necessary, and hopefully it's not in response to the public outcry over this offense, but I would suggest to the court that 32 years is certainly a long time and it certainly should be adequate to bring this man into such condition as the parole board would be the deciding party as to whether or not he should be released at that time, and I think to sentence him until he's 104 years old is exactly what the court said it was not allowed to do by life without parole."

Treatment?

Rehabilitation?

I couldn't believe what I was hearing.

"I think the court has gone beyond that and I feel that the recommendation of the State and the defense and also the entire basis for the plea which was entered was based upon the agreed recommendation of both parties, and I'm sorely distressed that the court has chosen to ignore that, as is Mr. Hillman, I'm sure."

He continued, looking down at his client for the first time since it became apparent his plea deal wasn't what he was going to get.

"As I say, that was the basis for the plea, and we're...." he paused before he said something he may letter regret.

"We express disappointment that the court has gone that far."

He shrugged his shoulders and shook his head.

Staring at the judge, hoping something would compel him to reconsider.

He had a deal.

It was supposed to be 32 years.

"Well," the judge began, sounding somewhat irritated; as a lawyer of his caliber must have known that an exceptional sentence was possible.

"Counsel, I did spend a substantial amount of time considering this case. The basis of my ultimate conclusion, I think, at least in my mind, was predicated upon common sense. I would find it very difficult to not sentence Mr. Hillman, in view of his history and in view of his inability to control his conduct which results in the death of people, that there is no sentence" he paused and took a breath, he tilted his head slightly back and chose his words very carefully, "Well the most appropriate sentence would be prison without parole. I don't feel that's available to me. The 70 years, generally, a third of that would go off for time for good behavior. Certainly he's going to be an old man, when he gets out of prison."

An old man? I thought to myself.

That's a gift that was taken away from Rich; Rich doesn't get to be an old man.

Rich was only 31 you fucking bastard.

I tensed up and my mother sensed it and gently shook my hand that had been clenched in her fist.

I then realized she hadn't won.

Rich wasn't going to come streaming into the courtroom, alive again. She knew this. When your husband, who you love very much, is taken from you, gunned down with a 12 gauge shotgun, gunned down for trying to help someone, no one can claim victory.

But she had taken a small swipe back at the man who did it.

A slap in the face that would see him rot in prison; not until 2014, like the plea deal; but until 2039.

The judge continued, "And that's the unfortunate, and that's tragic, but to enter into speculation at this point as to when he's going to be safe to be at large, I think is foolish. I think what the court has done is endeavored to protect the public primarily and to consider Mr. Hillman secondarily, and I feel that's what I've done. There are always unusual outlets for assistance, such as a governor's pardon or perhaps changes in the law as we progress to better understand the type of stress disorder that the defendant may have had, but at this time, a sentence even just of 32 years, again, taking a third off, we're talking service of maybe 20 some years. So I think that's all I need to say concerning your position and I just want to assure you that I've given a very substantial amount of time in trying to figure out what's appropriate in this case."

The prosecutor raised his finger to get the Judges attention.

"Mr. MacCamy?" he asked.

"Your Honor, I'll present an order in a few minutes regarding the defendant's right to appeal or collaterally attack," he quickly stated, hoping to end the discussion.

His smile was unable to be contained.

With that it was over. The bailiffs lining the rows of wooden benches extended their arms outwards to keep the crowd in place.

Phil got up from where he was seated and two bailiffs took either arm and began to lead him out of the court. His head was a little lower, his posture somewhat more demure than when he had pranced in 20-25 minutes earlier. As he came by us, my mother turned away from him and could not bring herself to look at him.

She had no expression she wanted him to see.

She had spoken.

She did not want to know what he even looked like so that she would not have a face burned into her memory.

I did.

Some day I will speak as well, you son of a bitch. And you will fucking hear me.

I stared right into his face, I am sure he had no idea who I or any of the people in the courtroom were.

Whether they were friends or relatives, wives or step-sons.

Murder myself, Murder I am.

He did not know and he did not appear to care.

The one thing they all had in common was being touched by Rich's kindness, his humor and his helpful nature.

41

In December of 1990, the first appeal of the sentence was filed with the court. Phil did not believe that it was within the legal framework of the law for a judge to give an exceptional sentence based on 'future dangerousness'. The entire reason behind the Sentencing Reform Act of 1981 was to increase the consistency of sentencing and to reduce some of the power vested in Judges through sentencing. The Legislature realized that some cases would undoubtedly come up where exceptions would be justified, but they wanted to make *very sure* that these would be rare and openly and transparently handed out.

Judge Kershner had sentenced Phil to an 'exceptional sentence' based on two factors. The first being 'future dangerousness' whereby the judge believed that a longer sentence was required because in all likelihood, Phil would still be dangerous to society if and when he was released 21 years later.

The second reason he gave for giving an 'exceptional sentence' was based on the 'Good Samaritan' principle. In this case, Phil had killed someone who was acting in a manner to help Phil. The judge explained the 'Good Samaritism' was important to societies and that by killing Rich while he was helping him would cause society to become less likely to help each other for fear of what could happen. Because of this damage to society, Phil should pay a higher price.

A month before, on November 7, 1990 the court entered an addendum to the court's findings and conclusions regarding the exceptional sentence. This was a formality as nearly every exceptional sentence is appealed. This document clearly laid out the Judges reasoning behind the imposition of the exceptional sentence.

The addendum written by judge Kershner explained that:

"The murder was a premeditated act of aggression directed toward an innocent victim who was acting in the capacity of a good Samaritan."

However, Phil claimed in his appeal that Judge Kershner justified the exceptional sentence based on 'future dangerousness' in addition to the victim's status as a 'good Samaritan.'

Mom knew that an appeal was coming but she had done all that she could do. It was now in the hands of the appeals courts. She could write no more letters; she could not even speak or be involved with the appeals process in any way.

It was truly out of her hands.

Nearly a year later, the Appeals Court agreed with Phil that basing an exceptional sentence on 'future dangerousness' was not allowed. The Court could base *the length* of an exceptional sentence on future dangerousness; but could not use future dangerousness as the *justification* for an exceptional sentence. The Court remanded the case back to Snohomish County for re-sentencing.

Judge Kershner had since retired but had agreed to come out of retirement to re-sentence Phil. It was clear that he could not use 'future dangerousness' as a justification for giving an exceptional sentence. It appeared that the Appeals Court had made it very clear that an exceptional sentence was not warranted in this case.

In December of 1992 Phil again had to come before Judge Daniel Kershner. The same judge who sentenced Phil in 1974 for second degree murder and had also sentenced Phil in 1990. Phil was confident his sentence was going to be reduced to the 32 years they had agreed to.

Judge Kershner, however, was not swayed by the Appellate Court and he again sentenced Phil to 70 years. He explained his reasons while Phil looked on...

"So, I'm going to find that the Good Samaritan doctrine all by itself, in and of itself, is sufficient basis and of such seriousness to support a finding that there should be an exceptional sentence and, the facts of this case I think give rise, because of the nature of the offense, that there should be a substantial amount of time imposed. I am relying upon the future dangerousness aspect of the

defendant's situation in determining what the nature of the sentence should be and there, again, I think that leads to the conclusion that it should be a substantial sentence. So I am going to declare an exceptional sentence based upon the Good Samaritan factor and I am going to re-impose the sentence of 70 years [840 months.]"

Phil was furious at the re-sentencing. He believed that the judge had completely disregarded the Appellate Courts ruling and had simply reworded the same sentence that the Appeals court had *clearly* rejected.

In 1993 he filed another appeal.

In the second appeal he claimed that, first; the trial court "used the Good Samaritan rationale as a decoy in place of 'the true reasons' for the exceptional sentence, future dangerousness."

He also claimed that Judge Kershner "harbored a secret intent to flout the decisions of this Court and the laws of this State." The Appellate Court summarily rejected this notion.

Secondly, he contended, again, that the victim's status as a "Good Samaritan" was not a valid aggravating factor. Again the court rejected his notion as they had decided that very thing in the first appeal. This time however, Phil contended that "the Good Samaritan aggravating factor imposes a 'Biblical standard' in violation of the constitutionally mandated separation of church and State." Here the court found that the "court did not rely on the Bible to justify its decision; rather the opinion merely cites the Bible as the source of the phrase "Good Samaritan."

Phil also contended that the 840 month sentence for first degree murder was clearly excessive because a similarly lengthy sentence would be authorized for *aggravated* first degree murder. However, the Appellate Court would only overturn a sentence if it "shocked the conscience."

The Court responded: *"Hillman has not challenged the finding that he presents an extreme danger to the public, which in part was based on Hillman's own statement that if he was out on the streets, it was 'liable to happen again.' Additionally, the crime here was egregious, involving 'Hillman's cold-blooded stalking and ambush of the victim' who was attempting to assist him. We cannot say that no reasonable judge would have imposed a sentence of 840 months in such circumstances."*

Finally, Phil claimed that the length of his sentence violated constitutional bans on cruel and unusual punishment.

To which the Appellate Court responded: *"Only punishment which is 'grossly disproportionate to the gravity of the offense' violates the state and federal constitutional guaranty. To be 'grossly disproportionate' punishment must be 'clearly arbitrary and shocking to the sense of justice.'"* The Court then referred to a previous decision known as 'Creekmore.'

"*In Creekmore, the appellant claimed that a 720 month sentence for his conviction of second degree murder constituted cruel and unusual punishment. The Creekmore majority referred to Solem vs Helm(1983) in which the United States Supreme Court stated that in the case of an accomplice to murder 'clearly no sentence of imprisonment would be disproportionate to the crime.' Clearly if any sentence short of death is constitutionally permissible for a conviction of second degree murder, the same must be said for a conviction of first degree murder. Given the gravity of Hillman's offense, we decline to declare his sentence 'shocking to the sense of justice.' Thus, we conclude that Hillman has not shown the sentence in this case to be unconstitutionally disproportionate.*"

On September 21, 1995, the Appeal was closed.

* * *

As of this writing, no other appeals have been filed and Phil's earliest possible release date is March 6, 2039.

He will be 85 years old.

Afterword

On May 2, 1990, Rich stopped to help a pair of stranded motorists along the Mountain Loop Highway, 90 minutes north of Seattle, Washington. Before the day was over, Rich would lie dead in the forest from two blasts of a 12 gauge shotgun. Hundreds of friends and family would begin searching for his body and inevitably, his killer. Less than two weeks later, his body would be found and his killer identified and arrested. Hundreds and hundreds of murders are committed in America every year. In most of them, the victim knew the killer.

Rich did not know his killer.

He had never met him before.

Rich allegedly stopped to help them get their truck unstuck.

What could Rich have possibly done to deserve this man's wrath?

Within days, details began to emerge. In 1974, a little more than a year after being discharged from the United States Army, the killer had murdered another complete stranger a scant four miles away from where Rich's body was found. The first victim was killed in a similar manner-with a 12 gauge shotgun. After the crime, the killer admitted he didn't like the "attitude" he was getting from his victim. His victim was an unarmed, 83 year old man.

Less than eight years later, in 1982, the State of Washington determined that he had been rehabilitated and was safe to be in society again. He had learned how to keep his body in top physical condition. He had learned new skills in prison, he could cut hair, and he could be a barber.

Scissors and a straight razor.

A skilled trade.

Although he was safe from society, the State did not realize that society was not safe from him. Shortly after his release, the killer stabbed a man repeatedly during an argument and left him for dead in a Seattle home. The killer claimed he disagreed with his victim as to how marijuana was supposed to be dried. The killer was 5'11", weighed over 200 pounds and was in top physical condition. His victim was 5'8" and weighed less than 170 pounds.

The killer did not steal any money.

He did not steal any drugs.

Miraculously, the man survived and murder charges could not be filed. But the killer was now locked up again.

At least for a little while.

Killing someone in cold blood, going to prison for it, being released from prison, trying to kill another person after being forgiven for previous transgressions, being given a trade, being given scissors and a straight razor, surely the State of Washington would be justified in remanding the killer to complete his entire original sentence for murder and keep him locked up, away in a concrete jungle, for the full 20 years, until 1994. Certainly they would be justified in adding another ten years for attempted murder.

Yet, despite this history of criminal violence, unstable mental behavior and untreated drug and alcohol addictions, the killer was again released from prison less than seven years later, in 1988 and let loose upon the citizens of the State of Washington.

How was he free to kill again?

In today's society we have decided through our legislators that conviction of certain crimes is cause to remove a person's constitutional right to vote, even to remove a person's constitutional right to possess a firearm, but we are afraid to take away a criminals right to *privacy?*

After his arrest for killing Rich, police and prosecutors questioned the killer on his motives. Given his violent past, police expected Rich may have "looked at him wrong", argued with him about something, and perhaps even appeared threatening to the killer in some fashion?

As the case unfolded, prosecutors discussed whether to seek the death penalty in this case. In response to facing a capital murder offense, the defense began to hint that he was made this way through his experience in Vietnam. For this murder, he did not even offer up a motive. The killer was now at the point that he killed uncontrollably when the urge came over him. It had to have been his experience in Vietnam they claimed.

Psychologists who make a living off of diagnosing and treating such illnesses were shocked that his Post-traumatic Stress Disorder had gone undiagnosed for this long; claiming the cost of this misdiagnosed condition was two lives and nearly a third.

Inquiries into the fashion and manner with which the killer served in Vietnam became muddled with questions. His claims of killing enemy soldiers and dragging them off the trail and into shallow graves could not be substantiated. In fact, the unit to which he was assigned appeared to have been guarding aircraft in Saigon, not killing Viet Cong and dragging them off the trails. Officially, combat operations were over before he even turned 18. Although it is quite clear through conversations with veterans from the 1st of the 7th Airmobile unit that Phil was assigned to, that many skirmishes continued but none of the veterans interviewed ever described missions of the type Phil described. Further, when asked, most felt the description of their role as "setting up ambushes and dragging them off the trail in to shallow graves" was grossly inaccurate.

After interviewing a number of these veterans who served in the 1st of the 7th during March through June of 1972, I was admittedly surprised at their candor, honor and integrity. I had mistakenly assumed that most of these soldiers would 'circle the wagons' around one of their own and simply refuse to answer any of my questions under the pretense that 'I wasn't there' or 'You don't know what we went through.' I grossly underestimated the integrity of these men and after hearing their stories I am grateful for their honesty.

If he were not turned into a cold blooded killer by the U.S. Army, maybe he was this way before enlisting and attempts to see combat in Vietnam were merely an outlet; a legitimatized way to satiate the desire to kill. Prior to his enlistment at 17, he shot himself in the stomach feigning an attempted suicide to get his mother to sign the papers allowing him into the U.S. Army. Friends who knew him as a teen were not the slightest bit surprised when, in 1974, he was arrested, charged and convicted of murder at 20 years old.

It appeared his short enlistment in Vietnam may not be the cause of his violent outbursts, but a carefully calculated and convenient scapegoat for them. Not only had he killed two human beings and nearly killed a third, a defense of this kind can claim thousands of new victims. It can taint the honorable service of thousands of combat veterans who may actually suffer from their combat experiences. It can increase the negative stigma of returning combat servicemen and women.

In today's world, we just finished fighting major foreign wars on two fronts. Post-traumatic Stress Disorder is a real condition and is very often treatable. Prevailing economic conditions should give us great pause as a society. We have had thousands of veterans returning to U.S. soil and unforeseen circumstances will probably require many of these to seek treatment and help as a result of their combat experience. For those who seek treatment with real and legitimate conditions, we must as a society be prepared to provide the funding and means necessary, for if we do not, we will in all likelihood need to be prepared to provide the funding and facilities necessary to imprison some of them. The purpose of this writing is not to lobby treatment over imprisonment or vice versa. That is the work of politicians; and I am not one. But, in either case, we had better be prepared or the costs may become higher than we are willing to suffer.

Washington's Sentencing Reform Act of 1981 (SRA) fundamentally changed the way criminal sentences were handed out. Prior to that, Judges had wide discretion in handing out maximum sentences while the Indeterminate Sentencing Review Board (ISRB) determined when an inmate was eligible to be released earlier than the maximum sentence handed out. The main reason the SRA was enacted was to eliminate disparities in sentencing. In many cases, prior to the SRA, offenders committing the same crimes with similar criminal histories received far different sentences based often on the race of the offender or the victim. The SRA established very clear guidelines as to the standard sentencing range a judge could hand out.

When Phil murdered Newton Thomas and then assaulted James Sylte, both of those sentences were handed out based on the ISRB. Even though the SRA passed in 1981, it was set to go into effect for crimes occurring on or after July 1, 1984. After Phil was sentenced under the SRA in 1990, and his appeals were exhausted his fate was mostly sealed. Short of a commutation of his sentence or a pardon; which both must come from a governor, as the law stands now, there is no way he will be released until March of 2039.

In 1993, Washington took a step in an even tougher direction by enacting the "Three strikes you're out" law; whereby an offender convicted of a third violent felony as described by the law will be given a mandatory life imprisonment without the possibility of parole. Had Phil Hillman been sentenced under this set of laws he would have been give life without parole.

However, as budgets are squeezed tighter and tighter, politicians are always looking for ways to shorten sentences to save money. These same politicians argue that sentence length and structure are meant to be *deterrents* to crime. And if the sentence length does not lower the crime rate or the recidivism rate (the rate at which offenders let out of prison re-offend) then keeping a person in prison is simply not cost effective. Amazingly, a large portion of the voting populous actually believes this logic. Most sentencing reduction movements do however, focus primarily on non-violent offenders.

Opponents to these types of tough sentencing laws fall back on the argument that three strikes laws do not lower crime rates. What these opponents fail to point out is that the *recidivism* rate for someone serving life without parole is 0% with the exception of crimes they may commit in prison or in the event they escape.

Sentencing laws should never be viewed as *deterrents* to crime.

Sentences are the *consequence* of committing a crime.

The best deterrent to violent crime is the ability and right to defend yourself. Very clearly, Rich had very little opportunity to do this. Even if he had been armed with a handgun himself, and assuming Phil and Sharon are telling the truth about how Rich was murdered, the ambush style of attack unleashed on Rich was nearly indefensible.

However, Bob Duggan *was* armed in 1974 and was able to keep Phil from hurting his family. It should be pointed out that Bob held Phil at bay with a six shot revolver and had fired one of them in to the air leaving him with only five shots. He had no idea if Phil had a pistol hidden, or had a rifle somewhere or even if his friend Nick was armed with a rifle, shotgun or pistol.

Five shots.

With all of the criticism about modern semi-automatic weapons such as the AR-15; I know if I were in the same situation that Bob Duggan was in; with his wife, children, parents and siblings with him; I would feel much more comfortable legally defending myself with an AR-15 and a 30 round magazine.

Opposite of this, critics would often ask, "What if Phil Hillman had an AR-15 and a 30 round magazine?" The answer is simple:

No law would or could have prevented him from doing so.

Phil was already in violation of the law by merely possessing a shotgun. He was in violation of his parole by drinking. Phil Hillman showed little concern for the law his entire life. Do you really think he or others like him really care about *gun laws?*

After spending years researching this case I have been left with two very clear and concise revelations:

First, I simply do not believe Phil and Sharon's account of what occurred during the moments immediately after Rich crossed paths with Phil and Sharon. It is implausible that he did not run in to them until 7 PM as claimed on the day of the murder. Nor is it likely that he ever offered to help tow their truck out with his Mustang or hiked a few hundred feet uphill to see if he could help push it out. Only three people know what happened; one of them is dead, one of them is essentially serving life in prison and the third had been granted 'use-immunity' by the Snohomish County Prosecutor's Office.

Myself, my mother and most of those who knew and loved Rich understood why Snohomish County gave her immunity in exchange for the information she provided. Because of this, we were able to get answers that many loved ones of missing persons are never able to get.

Second, despite the lack of response by law enforcement early on, despite the failure of those who knew what Phil Hillman had done, to turn him in sooner; despite the desperation and horror I watched my mother go through during those dark days in May of 1990, by the time anyone even had an inkling that Rich was overdue, *he was already dead.*

No search and rescue by Darrington Police or Snohomish County or Moses Lake Police nor a confession from those aware of Phil Hillman's involvement would have prevented what happened to Rich. The only thing which could have prevented his death at the age of 31, would have been if his killer had *not been released from prison by the State of Washington* back in to society under the conditions which he was.

When my mother spent the entire month of August 1990 stuffing envelopes with Victim Impact Statements, making phone calls encouraging people to fill them out and send them to Judge Kershner; she was not seeking revenge. Her husband was already dead; nothing was going to bring him back. But when she listened to James Sylte tell his story, and when Newton Thomas' nephew called and cried with her on a breezy summer afternoon, she had to do something for them; and for Rich and for any future victim who might not even have been born yet. Without her persistence and determination, this man who had killed two people and nearly killed a third would have been eligible for parole in 2014.

Scholar's claim the best predictor of the future is, the past.

When my mother catches herself, looking out the window of her house into the driveway, and for a fleeting second, remembers, like she did on that very first night Rich didn't come home, she wonders who that person is, and what they are like.

That person, somewhere in the world.

Who is still alive today.

Because the man who killed Newt, and killed Rich, and nearly killed James, is still in prison.

It could be your mother, brother, sister or step-father.

Rich's killer is not eligible to be released until March of 2039. Ironically, he will be 85 years old; two years older than Newton Thomas was when this story began.

When I think of Rich, more than twenty years after his passing. My thoughts are not filled with hatred toward his killer, but the sadness of losing Rich.

Rich never got to get 'onesies' for Joshua with 'Hawthorne Homes' embroidered on them. No more Super Big gulps and Foster's bouncing around his Subaru in the back woods of Duvall or northeastern Oregon. No more thank you cards sent to clients filled with pictures of their homes in different phases of construction. No more grandiose ideas about building a '76 Nova 'sleeper' with a big block in it. He didn't get to be the first one to call me 'Doctor' after I earned my Ph.D. He never got to go home and help Mom move furniture so the carpet could be redone.

He never got to do any of those things and more, simply because he happened to be the one who stopped along the Mountain Loop Highway to aid a couple of stranded people.

No man knows the circumstance or time of his demise. In a strange sort of way, for those who knew Rich, the manner in which he died fit his teddy-bear like demeanor in that he may have died trying to help someone. He was the guy who flew to New York for no other reason than because he wanted to take advantage of the airline miles he would receive. He was the guy who wanted to drive his Subaru 4x4 station wagon to South America only to be able to say he had crossed the Amazon. He traveled, he laughed, he lived and he loved.

But most importantly, to me and to the hundreds who knew him and loved him, he was always a kind and helpful friend.

And we still miss him dearly.

I don't know if ravens hold the spirits of dead loggers like some of the folks in Darrington believe. But when I find myself alone, deep in the forest, or along a slow running river and I hear a raven cry out for its unseen mate, I stop and listen to the wind through the bows of cedars and the gurgling of the deep green water, and I think of Newt and remember Rich, and hope they hear us, too.

And know we have not forgotten.

Murder myself, Murder I am.

Acknowledgments

I would like to thank those whose agreed to be interviewed and those whose support and hard work made this book possible: John Hinds, Lee Trunkhill, Doug Engelbretson, Jerry Hamilton, Jack Beard, John Sundstrom, Bob Duggan, James Sylte, Jill Seidel, Jessica Knoop, John Wolfe, Richard Baranzini, James Kempton, Gerry MacCamy, Brendan Mangan, Bob Paffile, Rey Carson, Ricardo Carson Sr., Amy Keehner, Gina Thornton, Judy Endejan, the crew at Thomas Hammer in Pullman for being so accommodating and especially those who provided valuable information; but wished to remain anonymous.

I also would like to thank the many friends, family and associates who were there for me during and after those dark days in May of 1990: Ray Keehner, Greg Hoggard, Michelle LaPorte, Dave Oberweiser, Tim Long, Jonathan Kagi, Andrew Hartmann, Steve Kagi, Scott Aaenson, Amy Hamilton, Terry Day, Heath Lydic (Bednarski), Steve Wilson, Robert Reid, Dawn LaRoche, Jim Bradbury, Troy Hubler, Marty Klein, Christine Peterson, Dan Harding, Tom Gudmundson, John Gilhang, Jerry Falcone, Erin MacGregor, Pat Davis, Eric Leavitt, Dan Nuber and Rick Hart.

Photos

Please checkout <u>Murder Myself, Murder I am.</u> on Facebook to leave comments and check out a number of photos related to the cases. If you like the book, please 'Like' and share with your friends.

www.facebook.com/duvall1990

Made in the USA
San Bernardino, CA
27 May 2014